The WATERLOO MENNONITES
A Community in Paradox

The
WATERLOO MENNONITES

A Community in Paradox

J. Winfield Fretz

Published by Wilfrid Laurier University Press
for Conrad Grebel College

Canadian Cataloguing in Publication Data
Fretz, J. Winfield (Joseph Winfield), 1910-
  The Waterloo Mennonites

Bibliography: p.
Includes index.
ISBN 0-88920-985 (bound)   ISBN 0-88920-984 (pbk).

1. Mennonites – Ontario – Waterloo (County).
2. Mennonites – Ontario – Waterloo (County) –
Social conditions.   I. Title.

BX8118.6.057F73 1989   289.7'71344   C89-093352-9

Copyright © 1989
Wilfrid Laurier University Press
Waterloo, Ontario, Canada
N2L 3C5

89 90 91 92   4 3 2 1

Cover design by *Vijen Vijendren*

Printed in Canada

The Waterloo Mennonites: A Community in Paradox has been produced from a manuscript supplied in electronic form by the author.

Cover: Photograph of Amish man by David Hunsberger and photograph of teenage girl by James Hertel.

Contents

Appendix

List of Tables

Table

List of Illustrations

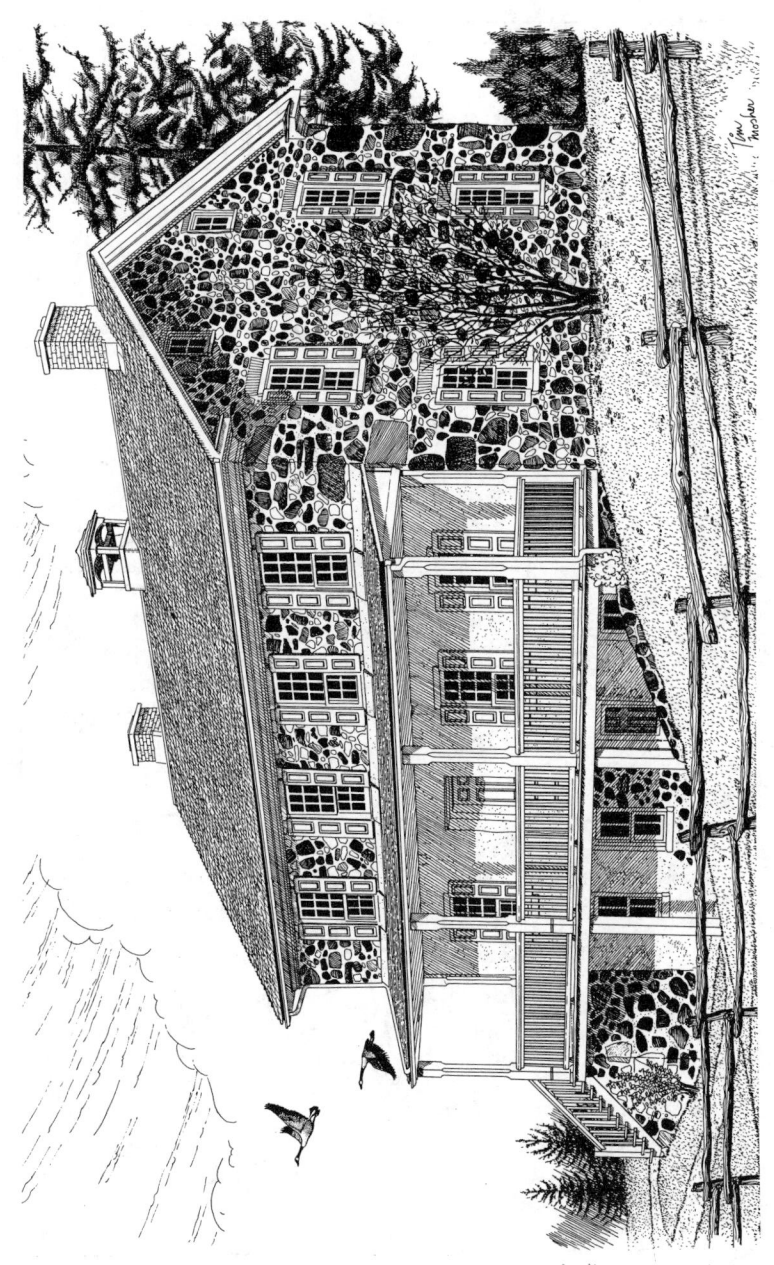

The Brubacher House
(Sketch by Tim Mosher)

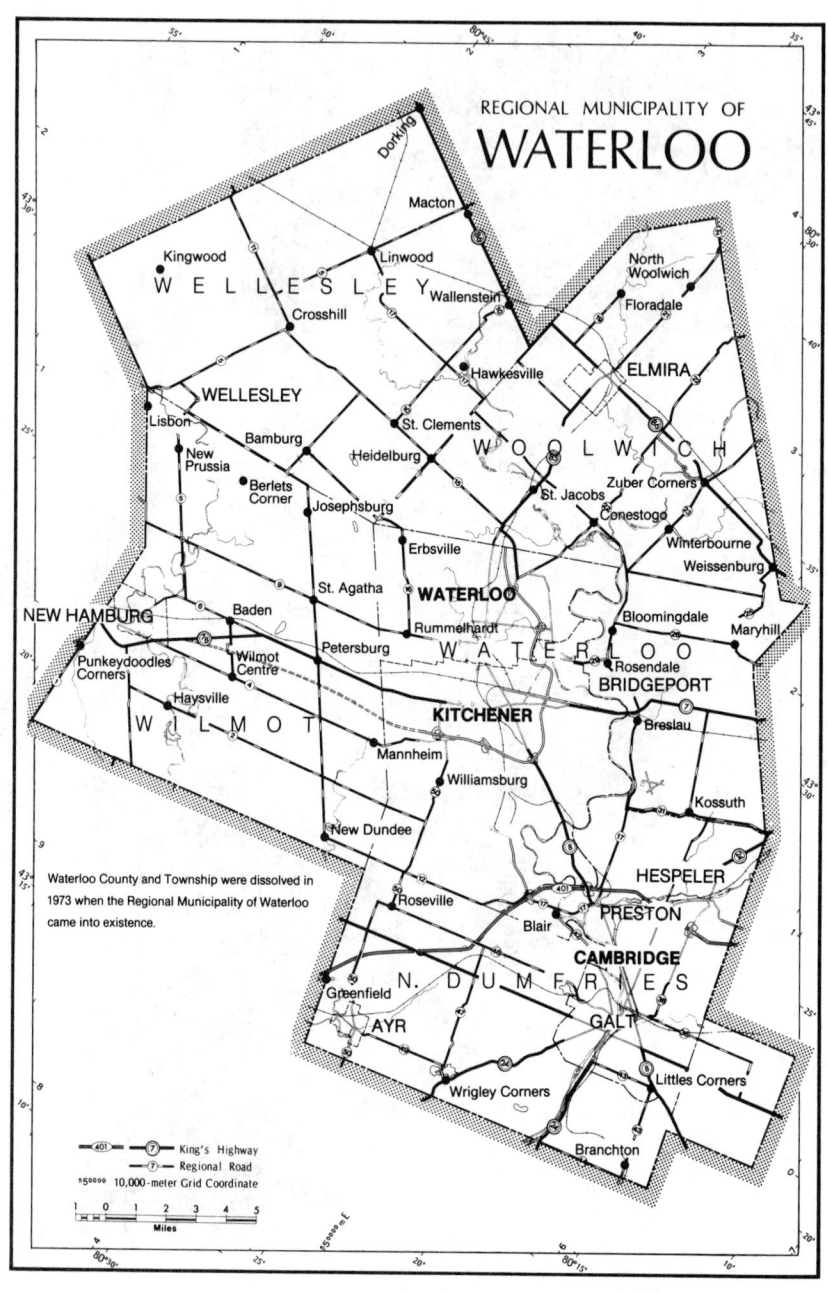

REGIONAL MUNICIPALITY OF

WATERLOO

Dorking

Macton

Kingwood

Linwood

North
Woolwich

Wallenstein

Floradale

W E L L E S L E Y

Crosshill

Hawkesville

ELMIRA

WELLESLEY

Lisbon

St. Clements

W O O L W I C H

Bamburg

Heidelburg

New
Prussia

Berlets
Corner

Josephsburg

St. Jacobs

Zuber Corners

Conestogo

Erbsville

Winterbourne

Weissenburg

St. Agatha

WATERLOO

NEW HAMBURG

Baden

Rummelhardt

W A T E R L O O

Bloomingdale

Maryhill

Petersburg

Punkeydoodles
Corners

Wilmot
Centre

Rosendale

BRIDGEPORT

Haysville

W I L M O T

KITCHENER

Breslau

Mannheim

Williamsburg

Kossuth

New Dundee

Waterloo County and Township were dissolved in
1973 when the Regional Municipality of Waterloo
came into existence.

HESPELER

Roseville

Blair

PRESTON

CAMBRIDGE

N.   D U M F R I E S

Greenfield

AYR

GALT

Wrigley Corners

Littles Corners

Branchton

Foreword

Like Jews and Gypsies, Mennonites can see Canada from an extra vantage point, one defined by centuries of separate, nomadic, persecuted history. Distinct traditions give Mennonites a broader, critical perspective we in the mainstream can acquire only by getting to know minority cultures, working to understand them, and looking at ourselves through their eyes.

Thus did I contact Winfield Fretz in the winter of 1973, asking how I could arrange for some of my students from the University of Western Ontario to visit the Old Order community near Waterloo. Fretz was then president of Conrad Grebel College. As a junior professor who had met him but once, I hesitated to bother him for help, but I knew no one else to call.

Fretz not only set up our visit but took the afternoon to be our guide. He crowded us into the parlor of a minister's farmhouse and let us all sit spellbound by a family's gentleness, simplicity, and intimidating strength. What I remember most was Fretz himself. Information and detail flowed from him, and in their midst not just fascination but reverence for a people whose life is a witness that the best of the twentieth century is not good enough.

Fretz's gift to us that day, refined and enlarged by fifteen further years of research, is now offered in these pages to whoever cares to read. It is a useful gift. No Canadian minority can teach what the Mennonites can. Neither aboriginal nor French nor English, neither Catholic nor exactly Protestant, they have yet been here since the eighteenth century. For that long they have practised here the peacefulness, mutuality and equality to which the rest of us from time to time aspire. Their community has specialized, so Fretz writes, "in producing good common people rather than a few heroes of the faith or one or two persons who by one means or another achieved worldly fame." What a noble specialty!

Sociologists will rank this book with E. C. Hughes's study of Drummondville and Horace Miner's of St-Denis, among the best community studies yet done in Canada. Like Hughes and many other community ethnographers, Fretz comes from the Chicago school of sociology, with its emphasis on fieldwork and a pluralism of techniques for uncovering and portraying life as people live it. But this book copies no previous one. Against the background of the scores of Canadian community studies already published, this work is remarkable not only for its subject matter but for five extraordinary qualities.

First, it rests on two full decades of research, as opposed to the usual two or three years. It is thus more thorough than the typical study, also more sensitive to processes of change.

Second, far from being a new Ph.D., Fretz was already a mature scholar when he began this study, a well-published veteran of community research in the United States and Paraguay. The wisdom of years and comparative experience informs this book.

Third, Fretz defied the still common taboo on choosing one's own culture for ethnographic study. The temptation to "go native" never arose in this case, since he was native from the start—not precisely of Waterloo County, but of the larger Mennonite communion. The compassion in this book is thus no patronizing gesture but affirmation of a common bond.

Fretz does not conceal this fact. The fourth distinguishing quality of this study is its easy, commonsensical mix of rigorous empirical analysis and ethical concern. Fretz's compassion, his sense of solidarity extends beyond the Mennonites to the larger Canadian and North American public. His fascination with facts is not for their own sake, but for their essential place in our common effort to further the human project in our time.

Fifth and finally, this book lacks the arrogance of most social scientific reports. Despite his meticulous research, Fretz refuses to play expert. "These evaluations are a matter of personal judgment," he writes at one point, later urging the reader to "assess the information shared in the light of his or her experience. . . ." Lines like these define this book as an entry into democratic public discourse, not as an effort to dominate readers' minds.

For explaining such little crime as occurs among the Mennonites, Fretz uses the Chicago-school concept of marginality, the
condition of people torn between divergent reference groups. Marginality can indeed breed crime, but it can also generate fresh, creative contributions to the economy, the arts, even to social science.
This book's author—sociologist but yet Christian, academic
administrator and businessman but yet scholar, American-born
but naturalized Canadian with a long Canadian career, fact-finder
but also moralist—is a case in point.

Kenneth Westhues

Preface

On numerous occasions J. Winfield Fretz observed, to anyone who would care to listen, that the Waterloo Mennonites constitute a rather unusual phenomenon. As he would say, "Nowhere else in the Mennonite world do you find such a variety living in one geographical area." From the beginning of settlement in the Waterloo area in 1800, Mennonites were included. They continued to arrive through the Amish immigrations of the 1820s, and the Russian Mennonite migrations of the 1870s, 1920s and 1940s. Many of these latter immigrants intended to settle in Western Canada, but some of each wave stayed in Waterloo County or returned from the West, to add to the mix.

Another significant dimension of Fretz's insight is the complex of divisions within the Mennonite community in Waterloo. Congregational schisms such as the First Mennonite/Stirling Avenue churches; the emergence of groups such as the Mennonite Brethren in Christ; the Old Order Mennonites, the Conservative Mennonites, and ultra-conservative groups such as the David Martin Mennonites, illustrate the variety. The interweaving of the "conserving" and "progressing" tendencies among the various groups creates a rich tapestry, intriguing but almost incomprehensible to outsiders, and a source of embarrassment to insiders.

The most significant sociological differences in the Mennonite community are those between rural and urban practices and lifestyles. There are Mennonites in Waterloo County who work and move in national and international institutions such as the CBC and CIDA, and others, living within a few miles of these first, who have never left the Waterloo region. But interact they do, and seem to sense that there is something binding them together that is more powerful than their different traditions: namely, a belief that Christianity is ultimately the way of peace and community.

In 1963 when Fretz arrived in Waterloo to assume the presidency of Conrad Grebel College, he launched himself on the quest to understand the Mennonites of Waterloo County. And through teaching a course on "The Sociology of the Mennonites," establishing personal friendships with Mennonites of all degrees of conservative-progressive shading, and in myriad other ways, Fretz was able to collect data which would ultimately become *The Waterloo Mennonites*.

Over a sixteen-year period, students from his classes, research assistants funded through sundry research grants, and his own indefatigable energy in gathering information and insights assisted the writing of this book. It had to be written, and he knew it, but there were many distractions and obstacles. Information on such a complex community was never complete, and always changing. And in the light of his other duties—such as helping in the formation of the Mennonite Relief Sale, the Mennonite Credit Union of Ontario, and the Mennonite Historical Society of Ontario—the book was always "almost finished."

In 1979, with Fretz's retirement to North Newton, Kansas, where he and Marguerite had lived and taught for many years before, the time had come to close the research phase and launch the completion, compression, integration and creative phase. At this juncture, lest the many Fretz interests militate against its completion, a committee was appointed to make specific plans for publication and suggest cutoff dates for various steps in the book's preparation. The committee—Rod Sawatsky, Urie Bender, Lorna Bergey, Sam Steiner (executive secretary) and Cal Redekop—represented the Mennonite Historical Society of Ontario, the Mennonite Credit Union of Ontario, and Conrad Grebel College, all of which had committed moral and financial support to the enterprise.

The Waterloo Mennonites is truly a communal book: the substance treats the communal aspect of the Mennonite community in all its complexity, while the book itself came about through communal effort from the students and researchers assisting Fretz, the various organizations and individuals providing support, the larger community including the two universities and Wilfrid Laurier University Press, and public funding agencies. This kind of communal effort is characteristic of the best in the Mennonite tradition, and few persons have contributed more to Mennonite community building than J. Winfield Fretz.

All those who have had some interest or hand in encouraging or supporting the book—and I count myself in this group—consider its publication a fortunate event. Winfield Fretz's life and work, and the content of his book, bring out in bold relief the central theme of Mennonite life—a peculiar interpretation of the nature of Christian community. As Ken Westhues says in his Foreword, this book is a unique community study of a unique religious society.

Calvin Redekop
Conrad Grebel College
31 January 1989

Introduction and Acknowledgments

My primary purpose in writing this book was to derive a clearer understanding of the sociological characteristics of a single Mennonite community. The Waterloo, Ontario Mennonites provided me with an unexpected opportunity to undertake the kind of study I had long wanted to do: one with a basically sociological approach. This meant beginning with the historical and religious background of the Waterloo Mennonites, reviewing their European origins, their ethnic identification and their immigration experience. It meant also examining their basic institutions: religion and the church, marriage and the family, education and the school, economics and earning a living, government and how they relate to it, their use of leisure time and methods of recreation. Finally, it meant looking at the way Mennonites interact with the larger society and how that society responds.

When in 1963 I was invited to the Kitchener-Waterloo area to help establish a Mennonite college on the University of Waterloo campus, writing a book about Mennonites in the community was not an item on my personal agenda. However, after a short time I developed four distinct impressions about the area. One was an awareness of an unusually large number of Mennonite churches with a 20- to 30-mile radius of the Twin Cities. A second was the wide diversity of religious organizations among the many Mennonite groups. A third was the scarcity of research and writing, of a serious nature, about the Mennonites in the area, despite the fact that they were the pioneer settlers, and had helped significantly to shape the wider community's economy and culture.

A fourth indelible impression was the persistent and widespread interest of the larger community, tourists, and many local Mennonites in Mennonite life, customs, and belief systems. Nowhere was this interest expressed more persistently than among university students in my college classes. It was here that I seriously began systematically to gather information for teaching purposes, and gradually to think of writing a book on the subject. In 1968, Canada's centennial year, the Mennonite Historical Society of Ontario invited me to write the small booklet *Mennonites in Ontario*, which has since had its third printing.

With the help of grants from the Government of Ontario and the Government of Canada, I was able to employ students during the summer months and undertake serious data gathering. In 1972 we made a detailed census of church members in every one of the organized Mennonite bodies in Waterloo and adjoining counties. The most valuable component of that census was the data gathered from the Old Order, the Waterloo-Markham and the Beachy Amish groups.

That this book was twenty years in the process of becoming reality has both positive and negative consequences. The twenty years were years of marginal time, not full-time research, necessitating many interruptions and frequent loss of academic momentum. A negative effect of the time span is that the period of study exceeds the statistical data of some tables. This weakness is offset in part by the maturing process that could take place in my evaluation of the overall community life processes.

The Waterloo Mennonite community is unique among Mennonite communities known to me in the countries of the world where Mennonites are located. Its uniqueness lies in its ethnic diversity: Swiss Mennonites, Amish Mennonites—also of original Swiss origin—and Dutch-Russian Mennonites. Each of these groups came at different times, from different geographical areas in Europe, and each had distinctive customs and, to a certain extent, distinctive languages. Further, each of the three ethnic strands had sub-organizations which could be classified as conservative, moderate, or progressive in their religious views and social customs.

Before World War II there was comparatively little interaction between these independently organized groups. Since World War II traditional isolationism has given way to multiple forms of cooperative activity, symbolized by the Mennonite Central Committee and its many subsidiaries: among these are foreign relief, disaster service, self-help stores, and the annual Relief Sale. Other services are prison ministries, the Victim Offender Program and the House of Friendship. The most convincing evidence of the shift among Waterloo Mennonites from isolationism to contemporary cooperation is the 1987 merging of the three largest and most progressive Ontario Mennonite conferences into one new body, the Mennonite Conference of Eastern Canada.

It is impossible for me here to express my deep appreciation to each person who over the years assisted me in this project. I am grateful to the many student assistants, my secretaries and to ministers and laypersons who gave freely of their time for personal interviews. Of all these Pauline Bauman, faculty secretary, assisted in many ways over practically the entire period of the project. Of my research assistants, I owe a special debt of gratitude to Susannah Shantz and Emma Gingerich, two Old Order Mennonite school teachers who spent a good share of one summer assisting me in taking the Mennonite census. Without that data this study would have been considerably impoverished. Much valuable data in that census remains to be sociologically analyzed. John Harder gave valuable assistance in the analysis of statistical data.

This book was made possible by the cooperative effort of the Mennonite Historical Society and the Mennonite Credit Union of Ontario and Conrad Grebel College. I am grateful to each of them for their generous financial support and their constant encouragement. I wish to thank the following persons for critically reading and commenting on all or some portions of the manuscript in early drafts: Lorna Bergey of the Ontario Historical Society; Urie Bender and Nick Driedger of the Credit Union; John Peters of the Wilfrid Laurier University Sociology Department; Leland Harder, former Professor of Sociology of Religion, the Associated Mennonite Biblical Seminaries, Elkhart, Indiana; Kenneth Westhues, University of Waterloo Department of Sociology; and Calvin Redekop, Donovan Smucker, and Samuel Steiner of the Conrad Grebel College faculty.

Sandra Woolfrey and Olive Koyama of Wilfrid Laurier University Press were most helpful at many points in the long process of preparing the manuscript for publication. John and Barbara Thiesen, on the margins of their time, transferred the entire manuscript to computer diskettes. It was pure joy to work with

Maynard Shelly, the general editor, and Griselda Shelly, his assistant, on the numerous tasks of reading the editing and editing the manuscript. I am very grateful to David Hunsberger, James Hertel, D. Michael Hostetler, the Mennonite Credit Union, Zehr's Markets Limited, Conrad Grebel College, the *Mennonite Reporter*, and the Mennonite Archives of Ontario for kind permission to reproduce photographs. Special thanks are due to Sam Steiner for giving his generous time, insight, and assistance in preparing this manuscript for publication.

Finally, I reserve my deepest expression of appreciation to Marguerite, my lifetime companion, for her patience and good spirit over the years I was involved in this project. She never ceased to marvel at the length of my academic pregnancy with this personal labour of love. I alone assume responsibility for the final form and content of this book.

J. Winfield Fretz
North Newton, Kansas
10 April 1989

Chapter 1

Meet the Mennonites of Waterloo

In 1800, the Waterloo County region was indeed a primitive wilderness; a territory of natural forests, unpolluted streams, and an abundance of fish and game. To this land of rich resources, the Pennsylvania Mennonites came to establish their families and religious communities and bring a measure of civilization. They came at a time when the area had no permanent settlers. Those who had immigrated to Upper Canada between the end of the American Revolution and the turn of the century had settled more to the central and eastern parts of Upper Canada, most of them along the shores of rivers and lakes and closer to the United States-Canadian border.

The Mennonites coming to Waterloo found no host population to greet them or to help them with the tasks of establishing new homes and to supply them with the means of survival before the first harvests. Those hearty pioneers knew in advance that they would need to have a large measure of self-reliance. They had only the mutual help they could give each other to make their pioneering efforts successful. Industriousness, determination, and a strong religious faith provided the necessary motivation to accept the challenge.

Mennonites from Pennsylvania came to Upper Canada because they wanted to remain under British government. During the American Revolution, they had lived in the heart of the area where much of the war was fought. In their attempt to remain neutral, they were often accused of being pro-British and unpatriotic. These accusations, plus frightening war-time experiences, left many Mennonites psychologically shaken. Furthermore, the future of the liberated colonies was anything but stable at the close of the war. The three years between the Declaration of Independence in 1776 and the adoption of the United States

Constitution were years of turmoil and uncertainty.

The knowledge that good land in abundance was available free, or to be bought at a low price, was a secondary motive for the migration. The assurance that Mennonites along with Quakers and other peace church members were welcome made Upper Canada all the more attractive.

Early settlements—Indian and white[1]

In the middle of the seventeenth century, the Iroquois Indians invaded the Grand River area. Some thirty years later, in 1784, the area was settled by Six Nations Indians under their controversial leader, Joseph Brant, on land granted to them by the Crown.[2] In 1785, the Indian population of the Grand River area was 1,843. A handful of white settlers had settled on the Six Nations lands by 1790.[3] These families were granted large acreages in the middle and lower Grand River areas. Their settlement had little impact on the environment before 1800 except in the immediate vicinity of their homesteads.[4]

The Six Nations Indian land had been bought from the Mississauga Indians by Governor Haldimand in 1784 as a permanent reserve. The grant was to be a strip of land six miles on either side of the Grand River from the mouth to the source. Because of lack of knowledge of the territory and lack of clarity in the description of the land purchased and granted, the Indians found themselves in possession of land only from Lake Erie to a point a little north of the town of Fergus, some forty miles south of the river's source.[5]

In 1797, the government of Upper Canada, after much delay, decided that the land should be surveyed and some of it sold by the government on behalf of the Indians. In 1798, the Executive Council of Upper Canada signed deeds of conveyance for 352,710 acres, more than half of the entire Indian reservation.[6]

In 1798, Brant therefore sold 352,710 of the original approximately 570,000 acres in six plots. The purchasers, the size of each plot, and the price paid are noted in Table 1-1.[7] There was much confusion and considerable litigation concerning the titles of this Six Nations Indian land. Block 2—the Beasley block—and the Mennonites were not the only purchasers who later encountered defective titles to land purchased.[8]

Table 1-1
Speculators who bought Indian land

Block No.	Purchaser	Acreage	Price (pounds)
1	Philip Stedman	94,305	8,841
2	Richard Beasley	94,012	8,887
	James Wilson		
	Jean Baptiste Rouseaux		
3	William Wallace	86,078	16,364
4	Unknown	28,512	Unknown
5	William Jarvis	30,800	5,775
6	Gift to John Docksteder	1,900	

Definition of the Waterloo Mennonite community

Today the Waterloo Mennonite community includes all those men, women, and children who call themselves Mennonites, or are so identified by the Canadian government and by my personal census records, and who live in Waterloo County and in immediately adjacent counties. About one-third of the Mennonite population in the wider Waterloo area live across county lines in Perth County to the west, Wellington to the north and east, and Oxford to the southwest. However, all of those in these adjacent counties are an integral part of the larger natural Waterloo Mennonite community. It is only the artificial political boundaries that distinguish those outside Waterloo County from those inside.

Telling the Waterloo Mennonite story in a different way

Much attention has been paid to the history of Waterloo County Mennonites but, to date, few have used the discipline of sociology in their studies. I hope that my telling their story from a sociologist's view will help the reader to better understand the many social and cultural factors that go into the making of a religious community.

Sociologists are interested in the social organizations and group behaviour of people. They pay special attention to such universal human institutions as marriage and the family, religion and the church, education and the school, the ways people govern themselves, how they earn a living, and how they use their leisure time. Sociologists, as social scientists, seek to understand the laws of human behaviour. They want to know how organizations or groups control the conduct of individuals and, in turn, how individuals influence the conduct of groups.

Key concepts in the vocabulary of sociologists are terms like culture, custom, conflict, accommodation, adaptation, assimilation, fashion, institution, mores, power, prestige, and status. All of these terms have to do with people's interaction with one another. The sociologist's interest in human interaction is not merely to satisfy personal curiosity but rather for the larger purpose of defining general laws of social behaviour.

Everyone, to some degree, is a sociologist, even though he or she may not be interested in systematically observing behaviour, collecting data, and evaluating findings to the degree that professional sociologists do.

This study of the Waterloo, Ontario Mennonite community is not a scientific sociological analysis. Rather, it is a reader about the Waterloo Mennonite community from the viewpoint and method of a sociologist. It is written, as much as possible, in layman's language and for the general reader. It is an attempt to describe the Waterloo Mennonite community objectively through the eyes of a member of that community.

Chapter 2

Pilgrimage and persecution in Europe

People come first in any community. Therefore, the first questions to be asked of the Waterloo Mennonites deal with their social and cultural background. Where did they come from? When and why did they come? What customs, traditions, and values did they bring with them? What did they contribute to the area in which they live? To answer these questions, we go back to their roots.

Not all Waterloo County Mennonites have the same cultural background. They comprise three separate immigrant groups, each with its distinct origins in Europe, its own time of immigration, and its unique resettlement experience. This accounts, in part, for the many subgroups now found in the Waterloo area.

These three different backgrounds and migrations also account for unique traits such as language, dress, special foods, religious practices, organizations, and distinctive customs.

The first Waterloo Mennonite immigrant group came out of Switzerland in the sixteenth and seventeenth centuries. Because of persecution, most of them were banished or fled from that country across the northern border into the provinces of Alsace and the Palatinate in the Rhine River valley. From there, they migrated in the eighteenth century to Pennsylvania, where they lived for less than a century before moving to Upper Canada in the early nineteenth century.

The second immigrant group to come to Waterloo County were the Amish. They too came from Switzerland, from the very same places as the Mennonites. In fact, for 168 years, they were Mennonites and fled to the Rhine Valley with their co-religionists. But in 1693 one group, under the leadership of a conservative young bishop, Jacob Ammann, left the Mennonites. He found the main body of Swiss Mennonites too worldly. As a result, the Amish formed their own church. They remained in the province of Alsace and in certain scattered areas of Bavaria for a hundred years after the first Mennonites had emigrated to Pennsylvania. During most of that time, the French ruled Alsace. Thus the Amish who came to Upper Canada brought with them a few French traits, one of which was the ability of some to speak French.

The third and most recent group of Mennonites came from scattered settlements in Russia. With few exceptions, they did not settle on farms in Waterloo County as did the Swiss. The Mennonites from Russia came in scattered groups after World War I, in 1923-1930, and after World War II, between 1947 and 1965. At least half of those coming after World War I tried farming in Manitoba, Saskatchewan, or Alberta. When that proved unsuccessful, largely because of the Great Depression, many returned to Waterloo to find jobs in the twin cities. Those coming after World War II came from scattered areas in Russia and were generally sponsored by relatives already in Canada. They came as individuals and small family groups. Some had spent time in refugee camps, and some tried to live in Brazil or Paraguay before coming to Canada.

Anabaptist beginnings

The Mennonites emerged from the social, cultural, and religious conditions of early 16th century Europe. Their origin has a two-pronged root: one in Switzerland and the other in the Netherlands.

At the beginning, in Zurich, Switzerland in 1525, the name Mennonite was not the one by which they were first known. They simply called themselves Brethren, but their enemies labelled them Anabaptists, or in Swiss-German, *Wiedertäufer*, which meant rebaptizer.

At first, Anabaptism was not a church or denomination. It was instead a protest movement that emerged out of the Protestant Reformation. Small Bible study groups sprang up throughout Europe. These groups had one thing in common: although not organized, they all disliked the half-way measures of the Reformers. They claimed that the Protestant state churches were merely substitutes for the state-supported Catholic church, against which they, along with the reformers, had many grievances. And the Protestant Reformers, the Anabaptists said, were not themselves thoroughly biblical.

Many different dissenting groups fell under the general Anabaptist label. Among those so tagged were mystics, self-styled prophets, literal biblicists, anti-trinitarians, revolutionaries, covenantors and nonresistants.[1] As a result of severe persecution, and sometimes because of unstable leadership, these loosely associated groups thinned out and the movement gradually found a measure of discipline and integrity that led to the formation of new churches. Illustrations are the Hutterian and Bohemian Brethren in Moravia, and the Schwenckfelders in Silesia.[2] To distinguish the peaceful and dominant wing of Anabaptists from the more zealously prophetic wing, such as that led by Hans Hut and Melchior Hoffman, proved a long and difficult task for Reformation scholars.

Founding of the first Mennonite church

The founding of what in the course of time came to be called the Mennonite church took place on January 21, 1525, in Zurich, Switzerland. The historic occasion is vividly described in the Cologne letter, quoted here as reported by Leland Harder in his scholarly research on the origins of Swiss Anabaptism.[3]

> Therefore, dear brethren, since you have asked us about the beginning of the brotherhood of the Swiss Brethren, it was about the time when men wrote the year 1522 that Huldrych Zwingli, Conrad Grebel, a nobleman, and Felix Manz—all three very learned men, experienced in the German, Latin, Greek, and Hebrew languages, came to discuss matters of faith, and discovered that infant baptism is unnecessary, also not known as baptism. Thereupon the two, Conrad and Felix, believed and confessed that one must, according to Christian order, be baptized according to the words of Christ: he who believes and is baptized shall be saved. This led to disunity among the three, and Huldrych Zwingli did not wish this and said it would create a disturbance. But the two previously mentioned men held that one could not ignore God's command because of that. Meanwhile it happened that a priest by the name of Jörg, of the house of Jacob, who was called Jörg Blaurock because he wore a blue coat, also came with a particular zeal which he had toward God's will. He was held to be an ordinary and simple priest but with a godly zeal in matters of faith, who through the grace of God which was given him acted in an extraordinary manner. He came to Zwingli and talked to him about the faith, but achieved nothing. Thereupon he was told that there were others who had more zeal than Zwingli. These he sought out and came to them, namely, to Conrad and Felix, and talked with them; and

they became united in these things.

And it happened that they were together. After fear lay greatly upon them, they called upon God in heaven, that he should show mercy to them. Then Jörg arose and asked Conrad for God's sake to baptize him; and this he did. After that, he baptized the others also. After this, more priests and other people were added who soon sealed it with their blood. So also Felix Manz, named above, who was the first; he was drowned at Zurich. Wolfgang Uliman was burned at Waldsee with ten others, including his brother, who was his champion. He was the seventh. After him a cleric named Hans Pretle [Johann Brötli], who was also our servant in the land. And thus it spread through persecution, as with Michael Sattler and many of his relatives. Thus also Melchior Vet, who was Jörg Blaurock's companion, who was burned at Dracha.

Thus you have the facts about what happened at the beginning. Later many things happened, so that many ran disorderly. But the sure foundation of truth remained. The Lord knows his own. Let those who call upon the name of the Lord forsake unrighteousness. And so you have the account of the beginning concerning which you should have no doubt, for we have most surely experienced it.

The first Anabaptist congregation was organized the following week between January 22 and 29, in the village of Zollikon, five miles south of the city of Zurich. Here some thirty-five newly baptized converts met in a private home. They, their wives and their hired help, were from the small-farm class rather than from the wealthier farmers.[4] At this first Anabaptist fellowship meeting at a peasant's house, they practised baptism by the symbolic act of pouring rather than by immersion. They observed the Lord's Supper with common bread and wine in imitation of the New Testament example. Here laymen, not ordained clergy, broke plain bread and distributed wine to all. They did so with clear understanding that taking part in the solemn ceremony meant a commitment from thence to live a pure and godly life.

Sacramentalism and infant baptism rejected

Of the seven sacraments of the medieval church—baptism, communion, confirmation, penance, ordination, marriage, and extreme unction—Anabaptists retained only baptism and communion. And those they considered only as sacred symbolic acts, not as sacraments. They observed both adult baptism and the Lord's Supper in a simple way and with a sense of social equality. This contributed greatly to the feeling of Christian community. Among some of the Anabaptists in Moravia, where many of the Swiss later fled to escape persecution, the feeling of oneness was so strong that it led to the practice of the community of goods as described in the New Testament book of Acts, chapters two and four.

The members of the first Anabaptist congregation did not think of themselves as Anabaptists but simply as Christians or "brethren in Christ." It was their opponents who applied the Anabaptist label to them from the beginning. It had the same pejorative connotations as the label of "communist" in capitalistic countries today, except that Anabaptist referred to a religious heresy whereas communist refers to a political or economic heresy. In both cases, it implies dissent and the holding of a radical opinion that opposes commonly held views or orthodox doctrines. Those who chose to adopt Anabaptism and to preach and practice that faith invited endless harassment, persecution, and discrimination.

A chief cause of Anabaptist persecution was its repudiation of infant baptism. To deny the efficacy of infant baptism was to challenge a thousand-year-old doctrine of the Roman Catholic Church. Ever since the sixth century, the church had considered rebaptism a heresy. The Justinian Code, an ancient civil law, defined rebaptism as a crime to be punished by death. It was seen as one of two serious heresies, the second being anti-trinitarianism. Thus to be named an Anabaptist was to risk being condemned to death. In time, not only Anabaptist believers but also those who sympathized with them or who gave them food and shelter were punished.

The Anabaptists said that the baptism of infants was ineffectual since parents could not make a faith commitment for their babies. Besides, they found no basis in the Bible for this ritual. While this defence may seem reasonable today, it appeared the worst of heresies in the sixteenth and seventeenth centuries. To have granted validity to the argument of the Anabaptists on that point would have undermined, or at least badly shaken, the pillars of the established churches. Anabaptists and their successors, the Mennonites, found their attack on sacred dogmas a dangerous undertaking. In ensuing centuries, it became a heavy cross to bear.

Swiss Anabaptist leadership

During the first few decades of its existence, Swiss Anabaptism drew its leaders from three different sources.[5] According to Paul Peachey, the movement grew out of an academic and theological milieu lasting only a few years. The organizers were former disciples of Ulrich Zwingli, alienated when he opted to retain infant baptism and an established state church. They argued for a scripturally based church, composed of voluntary members baptized as adults upon confession of faith, vowing obedience to a disciplined life. This educated leadership lasted only two years (1525-27), succumbing to early natural death, banishment, or death by execution. The leadership then quickly passed to the middle classes (1527-30), craftsmen who as itinerant workers could move about from community to community in the practice of their trades. But due to the severity of persecution, this group too was shortly decimated, and the Anabaptist movement passed quickly into the hands of the peasantry and became a rural instead of an urban movement. Anabaptism thus, out of necessity, spread primarily among the rural people.

Quite a few of the early converts to Anabaptism, according to Peachey, were former monks set adrift in those countries where Protestant churches had been established and monasteries closed. These ex-clergymen were permitted to marry. Most of these emancipated monks and priests were forced to learn trades because their own class of clergy had been dissolved. Furthermore, quite a few former priests and monks were attracted to the simple gospel and the sincerity of the Anabaptist lay missioners who went about the country preaching and practising their newly discovered form of Christianity.

Peachey found twenty members of the clergy, six monks, and fourteen priests among the Swiss Anabaptists between 1525 and 1540. Half of these were between twenty-five and thirty years of age; nine of the thirty were married. Six had learned secular trades; nine died as martyrs. There were few lay intellectuals because at that time universities were under the control of the established church. Among the twenty early leaders classified as intellectuals was Conrad Grebel, the founder of the first organized Anabaptist congregation. Most of these leaders soon disappeared. Three recanted, some were executed, others were banished.

Among seventy-five craftsmen who were Anabaptists, ten were tailors, seven bakers, others were printers and millers. Peasants numbered about 460, or 60 percent of the total that has been identified by existing court records.[6]

Anabaptism in the Netherlands

Anabaptism spread slowly northward along the Rhine Valley to the Lowlands. It emerged there several years after it was organized in Switzerland. In fact, the severe persecution of the Anabaptists in Switzerland resulted in the banishment of many who then fled to Germany and France and even as far north as the Netherlands. The preachers who introduced this newly organized religion into the lower Rhine region came with a more prophetic character and with a greater eschatological emphasis than was the case in Switzerland. Evangelists like Melchior Hoffman, Jan Matthysz, and Jan van Leyden, radical enthusiasts who preached the new religion, stood in sharp contrast to men like Conrad Grebel, George Blaurock, Felix Manz, Michael Sattler, Pilgram Marpeck and Hans Denk in Switzerland and South Germany.

We mentioned above that Mennonites had two points of origin. One of these places was in the Netherlands. It was the preaching of some of the early Anabaptist evangelists and the persecution of them that attracted a Dutch Roman Catholic priest by the name of Menno Simons to their cause. He was converted and rebaptized in 1536 and became their leader in Holland, northwest Germany, and in East and West Prussia. It was in Holland and in North Germany that Anabaptists were first called Mennonites, a name derived from that of Menno Simons. The name underwent several changes, first *Menist* or *Mennist,* then *Mennonist,* and finally Mennonite.[7]

Menno Simons, like his contemporary Martin Luther, was of peasant origin, having been born in the Frisian village of Witmarsum. Unlike Anabaptists in Switzerland and the Palatinate, those in Holland were permitted to live in cities and carry on the trades of craftsmen, so the converts to Anabaptism were largely middle-class craftsmen, labourers, and farmers. Because of the severity of persecution in the early years of Anabaptism in the Netherlands, even before the conversion of Menno Simons, Anabaptists had moved eastward to the regions of Danzig and Elbing, the coast of the Baltic Sea and into the Vistula River Delta.

Mennonites in West and East Prussia

One attraction of the Danzig and Elbing areas for the Dutch Mennonites was the demand for their skills in building dikes, draining swamps, and rescuing below-sea-level land for farming. For Dutch Mennonites in the sixteenth century the Vistula Delta area was the counterpart of Moravia for the Swiss Anabaptists, a place of refuge, a place where their religious beliefs were tolerated if not necessarily accepted. Scattered Anabaptist groups are said to have lived in the Elbing and Danzig area as early as 1530, but the first organized settlement was not formed until 1539. By 1550, a substantial Mennonite congregation had been formed just outside the walls of the city of Danzig, for Mennonites were forbidden to live or build their church inside the city.

The Mennonites in the Danzig area were largely farmers. In the course of 250 years, large and prosperous settlements were developed. By the end of the eighteenth century, the Mennonite population numbered about 15,000. It was from Danzig, Elbing, and the Vistula River Delta area that nearly 6,000 Mennonites migrated to Russia at the end of the eighteenth century.

Conservative Flemish and progressive Frisians

Since the Mennonites who emigrated to Waterloo from Russia are descendants of Mennonites who in the late eighteenth century migrated from Prussia to Russia, I include here a brief description of church life and customs among the conservative Mennonites in Prussia in the late eighteenth century. Those familiar with the Waterloo Swiss Old Order Mennonite Church organization and worship service will note striking similarities.[8]

Among the Prussian Mennonites were two factions, the conservative Flemish and the progressive Frisian.[9] The Flemish churches were largely in the rural areas. In 1790, an elder by the name of Wiebe reported that the conservatives wore hooks and eyes instead of buttons, and shoe strings instead of buckles; and the men wore beards. Young people were seldom admitted to church membership under the age of twenty, and one or two adults were required to sponsor them. Among the Flemish, sermons were still read from manuscript, and the preacher remained seated while preaching.

At the same time, spontaneous preaching was being introduced by the Frisians. They had no pulpit, but a row of chairs on a raised platform in one corner of the room was reserved for preachers, of whom there were three grades: *Aelteste* (elder), *Prediger* (preacher), and *Armendiener* (deacon). Preachers were elected, and when there were several candidates, one was chosen by lot. They were uneducated and unsalaried, and therefore were generally selected from among the wealthier classes who could afford to take the time to perform the tasks of ministers.

They used no musical instruments in churches. A *Vorsänger* led the congregational singing from a new hymn book which had been printed for the first time in Danzig in 1780, or from the old Dutch psalm book. There was no preaching at funerals. Instead there was a long memorial hymn, composed for the occasion by a close relative of the deceased. On one occasion, at a memorial service for a well-known minister, the hymn had twenty-four verses. For many years, worship services were held in private houses or, when more space was needed, in large barns. But by the end of the eighteenth century, most congregations had meeting houses. Each congregation, as a general rule, also had a schoolhouse and an almshouse to provide for its aged poor who had no families to look after them. Very little literature was found in the homes except the Bible, possibly the *Martyrs' Mirror*, and an occasional confession of faith or other devotional books.

Just as the Swiss and the Palatinate Germans have adhered to the High German for formal purposes and to their dialects for daily conversation for centuries, so, too, have those of Dutch extraction clung to the Low German dialect for family and informal use. For instance, the Mennonites in the Vistula Delta area retained the Dutch language in their church services for well over two hundred years and used the Dutch language in Prussia until shortly before they migrated from Prussia to Russia. Population growth by natural increase accounted for their constant need for additional land.

From the Vistula Delta to the Ukraine[10]

Because of pressure for additional settlement sites for the landless and desire to escape from the frustrations of second-class citizenship, Prussian Mennonites were eager to emigrate to Russia. As early as 1762, Catherine II, empress of Russia, extended an invitation to prospective settlers in Western Europe to immigrate to her newly acquired and unsettled territory, the Ukraine. She offered many inducements in the form of religious freedom, free land, freedom to conduct their educational systems, and temporary financial assistance in the first years of settlement.

Two large Mennonite settlements resulted: Chortitza, founded in 1789, and Molotschna, founded in 1804. Both were named after local rivers. In the course of the following century, the Mennonite population in Russia grew to over 100,000. Between 1789 and 1910, the Mennonites acquired almost two million acres of land, established four mother colonies, 52 daughter colonies, and 346 villages. In addition to being successful farmers raising cattle, sheep, and horses and becoming expert growers of winter wheat, they also built a flourishing flour-milling industry and became large-scale manufacturers of agricultural machinery.

They set up their own teacher-training schools, schools of business, mental hospitals, and a host of community service organizations. In short, within a single century, they achieved a remarkably high state of civilization. They developed a virtual independent religious state within a state. It was the first time European Mennonites were given free rein to develop their own society with almost total political freedom in a land of unbounded economic opportunity. This has been referred to as the golden age of Mennonite history among the Mennonites in Russia. But as so frequently happens, not only did some become inordinately rich, some also became noticeably arrogant and spiritually indifferent.

End of the golden age

After a century's effort, all of the human and material gains by the Mennonites in Russia came to a tragic end as a result of a series of disasters. First came the costly World War I. It was followed closely by the ruthless and bloody Bolshevik Revolution which overthrew the Czar and established the Soviet Union. A frightful famine in the early twenties, and two decades of anarchy, general political and economic chaos were followed by World War II. These demonic and horrible years of anguish and suffering brought down all the Mennonite settlements in the Ukraine and destroyed thousands of Mennonites. Those not killed outright were scattered far and wide throughout Russia. Some thirty to forty thousand were fortunate enough to escape either legally or illegally to western Europe, Brazil, Paraguay, or Canada. The bitter tragedies of the Mennonites in Russia have been compared by them to the destruction of Jerusalem and the carrying of the Jews into captivity in far-away Babylon.

Out of this tragic background, the Mennonites from Russia now living in Waterloo and their parents and grandparents have come. They thus share with the Swiss Mennonites the bitter historical experiences of persecution and the life of uprooted people having to flee for their lives, leaving homes, friends, and families forever. These experiences have reminded Mennonites again and again that this earthly life may be a difficult and sad pilgrimage. For the most part, the suffering which they experienced was not looked upon as a curse or punishment from God but rather as the deeds of sinful mankind and as an opportunity to give a Christian witness.

Positive values of persecution

In reviewing the four and a half centuries of Mennonite history, much of it punctuated with harassment, persecution, and treatment as second-class citizens, we may still discern a number of durable values. Without having gone through the proverbial refiner's fire, a number of religious and ethical principles would not have been retained and venerated today as sacred traditions. In Switzerland, South Germany, Alsace, Holland, Prussia, and Russia, from the sixteenth to the twentieth centuries, Mennonites have repeatedly been reminded that upholding religious principles and Christian discipleship can be dangerous, difficult, and costly. It is not idle talk to be reminded that, ever since the sixteenth century, Anabaptists and Mennonites have taught that a truly Christian church must expect also to be a suffering church. This admonition, repeated in sermons through the centuries, has cultivated a seriousness of purpose among church members.

The conservative churches especially continue to impress upon their members the element of suffering through which the forefathers have gone in order to be faithful to God and to their covenants made at the time of baptism. Persecution helped to shape Anabaptist-Mennonite church organization and the method of selecting leaders. In the first place, the theologically educated men who helped found the church were banished, killed, or died an early natural death. Since the state churches controlled all formal education, it was impossible for Anabaptists to secure any form of higher theological training. Hence, Anabaptist church leadership fell of necessity to laymen.

Leadership pattern for times of distress
All Anabaptist congregations arranged for a three-tiered leadership. At the top was a bishop or elder with supervisory responsibilities; next, a minister whose duty was to preach to and shepherd a congregation. A third person, the deacon, was to oversee the financial matters of the church such as looking after the poor, the widows, and orphans. In times of emigration and flight, the deacon also helped finance transportation for the indigent.

This system of leadership proved useful as an insurance against leaderlessness, since the enemies of the Anabaptists were always on the lookout for leaders to apprehend, imprison, banish, or execute. When leaders were arrested or imprisoned, others in the congregation would be called to fill the vacancies. Thus, like soldiers in battle, as one fell, another would be called to fill the ranks. This system was followed throughout Mennonite history and is still in use among Waterloo conservative and moderate churches. Among the Swiss progressive Mennonite churches, the office of bishop has been abolished only in the mid-twentieth century. In its place is the office of a conference minister. Today none of the progressive Mennonite congregations have the three-tiered leadership while all of the conservatives and some of the moderate groups retain that system.

Persecution strengthened group ideals
While principles such as humility, integrity, self-reliance, mutual aid, and the ethics of love govern interpersonal life and have a solid New Testament basis, the factor of persecution in Mennonite history has also strongly contributed to the development and maintenance of these virtues. Among the conservatives especially, persecution is constantly recalled in hymns and sermons. Since these Mennonites have no radios, telephones, television, and few weekly magazines or daily papers, their church services are still the chief source of information and inspiration. Here biblical knowledge and historical experience are merged and transmitted.

Much historical evidence supports the view that persecution contributed greatly toward shaping the character of the Mennonite congregation as a religious community. It began with the necessity of early converts having to meet in secret. It was further abetted by its members being deprived of normal services, residence in towns and cities, and thus access to earn a living at crafts. They had no other place to turn for help than to fellow church members. Therefore the church fellowship was always more than a worshipping community. Members needed to support each other economically as well as socially and spiritually. The promise to help one another in case of need was in some early congregations a part of the baptismal vow.

Persecuted Mennonites did not at first withdraw into isolated places voluntarily. They were, in fact, quite evangelistic and mission-minded.[11] Persecution forced them into secluded areas as their only means of survival if they wished to remain true to their religious convictions. Had there been less persecution and more toleration for their points of view, it is doubtful if the communal character of Mennonite churches would have evolved. Persecution forced them to substitute evangelism by holy living rather than by verbal teaching and public preaching.

Church-state separation unrecognized advantage for state

It is ironic that European governments with state-supported churches did not see the tremendous economic advantage of the principle of church-state separation long advocated by the Anabaptists. Had they recognized this principle, they would have eliminated, first, the financial burden of supporting the churches, and second, a frequent rival for political power.

Walter Rauschenbusch, a distinguished Baptist seminary teacher and preacher in the early part of the twentieth century, summarized the social characteristics and contributions of the Anabaptists:

> They all tended toward the same type of primitive Christianity. Strong fraternal feeling, simplicity, and democracy of organization, more or less communistic ideas about property, an attitude of passive obedience or conscientious objection toward the coercive and militaristic governments of the time, opposition to the selfish and oppressive church, a genuine faith in the practicability of the ethics of Jesus, and, as the secret power of it all, belief in an inner

experience of regeneration and an inner light which interpret the outer word of God. These radical bodies did not produce as many great individuals as we might have expected because their intellectuals and leaders were always killed off or silenced. But their communities were prophetic. They have been the forerunners of the modern world. They stood against war, against capital punishment, against slavery, and against coercion in matters of religion before others thought of it. It was largely due to their influence that the Puritan Revolution had its prophetic elements of leadership. The Free Churches throughout the world, consciously or unconsciously, clearly or dimly, have passed beyond the official types of orthodox Protestantism and have taken on some of the characteristics of the early radicals. Great church bodies now stand as a matter of course on those principles of freedom and toleration which only the boldest once dared to assert. The power of leadership is with those organizations and movements which have prophetic qualities and trust in the inner light.[12]

This extensive reference to the social background of today's Waterloo Mennonites helps us understand the reluctance of the Old Orders to respond positively to social and cultural change. They seek to perpetuate those values, customs, and traditions which were born out of bitter centuries of experience and handed down to them through oral tradition. Their separation from the world, their aloofness from government, and their adherence to a life principle of nonconformity to worldly goods and social fashions are an attempt to remain true to their Christian heritage.

Chapter 3

The coming of the Mennonites to Waterloo

Of the three Mennonite ethnic groups that immigrated to Waterloo, by far the best known are those of Swiss background who came after living almost a century in Pennsylvania. They were the first and largest group of permanent white settlers in Waterloo County. In fact, until the coming of the Mennonites to the prairie provinces in the 1870s, they were the only Mennonites in Canada.[1]

The Swiss in Waterloo were also popularized by the widely read novel, *The Trail of the Conestoga*, written by Mabel Dunham, a former Kitchener city librarian. The story has been adapted to a three-act drama and is periodically presented to large audiences in the Kitchener area.

To understand why Mennonites chose to come to Waterloo, it will be helpful to look at the situation in which each of the three groups found itself before coming to Ontario. In each instance, "push" and "pull" factors operated in the migration process. The push factors refer to conditions that caused them to want to leave. Such factors were difficult economic conditions, loss of political freedom, religious persecution, and social discrimination. Compulsory military conscription was also an important push factor causing many Mennonites to leave one country for another.

Pull factors, on the other hand, are those which draw people to move from one country or area to another in the hope of improving their economic, political, religious, or social situations. Attractions to other countries have often included guarantees of religious and political freedom, opportunity to own land, to establish businesses of their own, to find gainful employment, and to settle in compact communities.

Coming of the Mennonites from Switzerland

Let's look at the factors that caused the Swiss Mennonites to migrate to Canada. Why would they have wanted to leave Pennsylvania after having lived there for barely a half century? They had eagerly accepted William Penn's invitation to settle in his religious colony because they saw it as a possible end to their always precarious situation in Europe.

They welcomed the guarantee of civil and religious freedom. The opportunity to live unharmed in religious communities of their choice was irresistible. Added to these attractions was the prospect of living under the English form of government. For most of the Mennonites, coming to Pennsylvania was the first time in their history that they truly enjoyed a status of first-class citizens. They were treated as equals, and were as free as any other denomination to express their faith.

Is there any wonder that the political strife and the rumours of war with England should have caused them to question whether this was the beginning of the end of their short enjoyment of peace, prosperity, and equality in this new land?

Three-stage international migrations

Mennonites from Switzerland who eventually settled in Ontario crossed international boundaries three times in their history. The first occurred in the sixteenth and seventeenth centuries when, due to persecution and banishment, they fled across Swiss borders into Alsace, France, southern Germany, and the Low Lands. The second came during the first three quarters of the eighteenth century when large numbers migrated to Pennsylvania from their scattered European locations. The third was the movement from Pennsylvania to Ontario in the early nineteenth century.

The migrations to and settlements in Pennsylvania and Ontario were significant. These migrations guaranteed Mennonites freedom to express and practise their faith without harassment by government officials or antagonistic churches. However, denied such freedoms in Europe, they had never developed the skills nor had the opportunity to take part in any aspects of government.

Waterloo Mennonites distinguished themselves as successful farmers and community builders. Their traditions and social customs also set them apart from the larger society. These distinctions have had external and symbolic reflections in their quaint mode of dress, plain meetinghouses, large and well-kept homesteads, horse-and-buggy transportation, and general separation from mainstream society.

A colonial Mennonite profile
Up to about the middle of the eighteenth century, the Mennonites in Pennsylvania were fortunate to have as their allies the Quakers, along with the Dunkards (Church of the Brethren), the Tunkers (Brethren in Christ), and the Schwenckfelders. The Quakers, as pacifists, were in control of the Pennsylvania legislature until about 1750, and hence waged the political struggle for all peace-church groups in the province. When the Quakers lost control of the legislature to the English, the militant Scots, Irish, and non-pacifist Germans, the question of civil rights for pacifists became more critical. As the confrontation between the colonies and England became more heated and war eventually broke out, Mennonites, along with other peace groups, faced serious choices. Wilbur Bender described the Mennonite pre-revolution situation as follows:

> For the most part the nonresistants had little sympathy with the anti-English agitation which began when the Peace of Paris in 1763 removed the French threat from the North American continent. . . . They had little sympathy with the anti-English agitation, just as they had little sympathy with any political agitation. . . . They were to be a 'separate' people and to let the world of kings and wars and political theory take care of itself. Their religion, their farms and their home communities occupied their time—a people turned in upon themselves and God. Moreover, being farmers, the laws so offensive to merchant and shipowner affected them little. They had done well under British rule and saw no reason to change. They had experienced a longer period of quiet than in any previous period in history. They had become economically and culturally self-sufficient under a government which bothered them not at all. Why should they wish to change? And they distrusted and disliked the radical, poverty-stricken frontier element which was almost a unit in attacking England. The mere fact that this type of person was anti-British would tend to prejudice conservative, peaceful farmers in favor of the Crown. A positive link uniting

them to the royal cause was the Promise of Allegiance they had taken when they became citizens. This solemn promise had great weight among them; to break it was an extremely serious thing. They felt also that they owed their homes in America and their privileges to the British Crown. A successful revolution might take away those privileges. And, above all, their pacifist principles would make them try to avoid any course leading to war.[2]

This summary of Mennonite attitudes toward the general political situation does not necessarily imply that they were actively pro-British. It is merely a description of their traditional attitude toward the existing political situation. As long as the political process was only in a discussion stage, their indifference did not matter. Once war broke out and the colonies had to raise money and manpower, indifference and neutrality were positions difficult to maintain.

Their underlying attitudes were severely tested when their zealously patriotic fellow-countrymen began to accuse them of being cowards, profiteers, and even traitors. Wartime conditions required dealings with government officials on local and provincial levels and later with the Continental Congress on such matters as petitions, appeals, special statutes, military exemptions, and compensations for supplies.

Mennonites and Amish labelled Tories

In 1779 the name of Christian Bowman had the word "Tory" written behind it on the tax list. All of the Amish in that township were similarly identified as Tories.[3] It is not difficult from today's perspective to see the dilemma faced by both government and the peace churches. For instance, in 1777, the Pennsylvania Assembly asked all inhabitants to take the oath of allegiance. Mennonites opposed this act both on principle and on the grounds of having already pledged loyalty to the king of England. They also objected to the payment of a special war tax to the Continental Congress which they considered a government in rebellion. As a defenceless people, they believed they should neither institute nor destroy any government. Already in 1755, thirteen Pennsylvania ministers had stated the case of the Mennonites:

It is our fixed principle rather than take up Arms to defend our King, our Country, or our Selves, to suffer all that is dear to be rent from us, even Life itself, and this we think not out of

Contempt to Authority, but that herein we act agreeable to what
we think is the mind and Will of our Lord Jesus.[4]

Twenty years later, in November of 1775, Benjamin Hershey, a
minister and moderator of the Lancaster Mennonite Conference
during the Revolution, once more set succinctly forth the philosophy of nonresistance as held by the Mennonites:

> We have dedicated ourselves to serve all men in every Thing that
> can be helpful to the preservation of Men's lives, but we find no
> Freedom in giving or doing, or assisting in any Thing by which
> Men's Lives are destroyed or hurt.[5]

His letter was addressed to the Pennsylvania Assembly in the
form of a petition for exemption from military drills by Mennonites. Both of the above statements are clear, simple, and forthright declarations of colonial Mennonite philosophy made by leaders of the Mennonites, some of whom later chose to migrate to
Waterloo County. Respect for the authority of government is
politely noted, but at the same time reference is made to a higher
loyalty to which they have a prior obligation.

After the war broke out, the nonresistant faith of the Mennonites was genuinely tested, as the following brief quotations indicate.

> On the 26th of September, 1777, an army of 10,000 of
> Washington's men encamped in Skippack Township, burned all
> fences, carried away all the fodder, hay, oats and wheat, and took
> their departure on the 8th of October, 1777. Written for those who
> come after me.[6]
>
> Jacob Funk was also a great financial loser by the depreda-
> tions of the British at the time (of the Battle of Germantown,
> October 4, 1777). They took from him all of his livestock, of which
> he had a great quantity, and whatever else they could lay their
> hands on. What they could not take away they destroyed. No
> indemnity was ever paid to Mr. Funk for these depredations, prob-
> ably for the reason that he never asked for it.[7]
>
> It is related that a number of Revolutionary soldiers on a
> foraging expedition came to Bally to the home of Michael Bauer on
> the day of the wedding of his daughter, Fanny, to Christian Moyer.
> Just as the guests were about ready to eat the wedding dinner they
> were interrupted by a group of American soldiers who sat down
> and consumed the whole meal.[8]
>
> Another Mennonite experience during the Revolutionary War
> reflects an uncooperative attitude toward the American Army if
> not an outright sympathy for the British cause. It was reported

that during the war, an American soldier came to the home of John
Fretz, a miller, and asked for Fretz's gun. It was alleged that he
took the gun from its accustomed place and said to the soldier:
"You can have the gun but I'll keep hold of the butt end."[9]

This last incident occurred in the vicinity from where the first
Mennonite families to Upper Canada came. Undoubtedly such
experiences in the tightly knit Mennonite community during a
wartime crisis made a deep impression and would have been long
remembered. John Fretz moved to Vineland, Ontario, in 1800 at
the age of 70 and became the first deacon at the first organized
Mennonite church in Canada. He lived to be 96 years old.

As the war progressed and the situation became more grave,
attitudes toward the pacifists became more strained. Confiscation
of property, pressure to buy substitutes, to supply funds, and,
after the Declaration of Independence, pressure to take the oath of
allegiance caused much additional trouble for the peace churches.

C. Henry Smith summarized the difference between the way
governments and ordinary citizens viewed the pacifist claims for
wartime privileges.

> Governments have usually been more lenient than the people. And
> paradoxical as it may seem, autocracies are more considerate of
> conscientious scruples than democracies. The majority has slight
> regard for the special privileges of the minority. And so, such
> abuses as Mennonites and Quakers have suffered for their faith in
> times of war came not from the governments, but from their neigh-
> bors.[10]

The struggle to draft a constitution for the new government was a
long and difficult one, and so was the drawn-out fight by the thirteen states to have it adopted. When it was finally approved, it
seemed to many a quite radical document. No one was sure that
this democratic "government of the people, by the people, and for
the people," as Lincoln described it eighty years later, would work.
Furthermore, neither the new constitution nor the Bill of Rights in
the form of the first ten amendments made any provision for the
rights of conscience for those opposed to military service.

It is significant that the departure of the first Mennonites
from Pennsylvania for Upper Canada occurred in 1786, between
the end of the Revolutionary War and the adoption of the Federal
Constitution. The evidence is clearer than ever that these families
migrated largely because of their pro-British sympathies and their

doubt that the newly established democratic political system would provide dependable government and guarantee military exemption to conscientious objectors to war.

It must be remembered that the first Mennonite emigrants to Canada originated in the Deep Run community in Bucks County, which at that time was the farthest east of all Pennsylvania Mennonite settlements. These Mennonites were in the heart of the area where crucial phases of the war were carried on. It was also the area closest to the British armies as they moved west and south from New York to Philadelphia.

Mennonite property confiscated

John Ruth has reported significant new research on the background of the first Mennonite group to go to Canada.[11] He refers to "the seventy-six Bucks Countians who were suspected of Loyalist leanings," to "this Loyalist leaning neighborhood on the Tinicum side of the Delaware," and to a certain John Overholt, a miller who "had been among the at least fifteen Bucks Countians accused of treason after the British army had moved out of Pennsylvania." Overholt is said to have fled after the British when his mill was confiscated by Revolutionary officials. It is reported that a cousin, Martin Overholt, had spent time in Canada during the war years with others of his family.[12] It was suggested that the Kulps and the Overholts who farmed on the west side of the Delaware in an area which for a time was under British control were "outraged by the confiscation of the family property by the American military authorities" and that John Overholt's son, Abraham, joined Butler's Rangers—an organization of Loyalist fighting men who made telling raids on American positions. At the end of the war, Butler and his men were given generous land grants in upper Canada.

Abraham Overholt also applied for a grant but it was at first denied on the ground that he had been a horse thief. His defence was that he stole horses only for the British cause.[13] Ruth claimed that Overholt later received a grant. He was encouraged by the fact that his Mennonite cousins and neighbours, the Kulps, had found their requests for claims as United Empire sympathizers if not actual loyalists acknowledged by the British authorities. Four families had received a total of nearly 2,000 acres at the

Twenty-Mile Creek on the Niagara Peninsula where they settled in 1786.[14]

The announcement of free land in Canada for those who had been loyal to the British cause and had suffered for that loyalty resulted in immediate response from Bucks County. One report states that a group of 185 Bucks Countians undertook to migrate to Canada. Among these were four Mennonite families consisting of 28 persons. The families were those of Jacob and Tilman Kulp, Staats Overholt, and John Han (Hahn). A Franklin Albright family came the following year. Three years later, 1789, the Christopher and Francis Kulp families from Lancaster County joined the small Upper Canada Mennonite contingent. They were not brothers of Jacob and Tilman, as had long been the assumption.[15]

The above information came to light at the time of the two hundredth anniversary of the coming of the first Mennonites to Canada. At the time, researchers discovered why this first group had not formed a Mennonite congregation. A Mennonite church in Canada was organized by the second group of families who arrived in 1800, fourteen years after the arrival of the first immigrants. For almost two centuries, the church life of the first Mennonite arrivals has been something of a mystery. Recent research reveals that the Jacob and Tilman Kulp families joined the River Brethren or Tunkers (later the Brethren in Christ). Members of their families later joined the Disciples or Christian denomination. The Christopher Kulp family joined the Methodists and the Staats Overholt family became Baptists.[16]

This report clearly shows that the first Mennonites to settle in Upper Canada were indeed self-acknowledged Loyalists. Hitherto, historians generally admitted that many Mennonites may have had British sympathies but that they were not actual Loyalists.

If the first Bucks County Mennonite families did indeed migrate with other Loyalists to Upper Canada in 1786 as a separate group or in a caravan of immigrants, it is likely that they had at least four things in common. One was their pro-British sympathies; two, their mutual acquaintance, possibly as neighbours; three, their Pennsylvania German dialect; and four, their common religious background. In their early history, the Brethren in Christ had won many Mennonites to their cause as did other evangelical churches on the Pennsylvania frontier. These affinities go a long way to explain why these first families felt little need to organize a Mennonite church.

Motivations of first Mennonite settlers

What is the meaning of this discussion for Mennonites in Waterloo County? It shows that the first emigrants to Canada were moved primarily by a desire for civil and religious liberty rather than only by economic motives such as cheap land. At least some of those who emigrated were well established in Pennsylvania.[17] Unpleasant war experiences were a definite push factor. And the possibility of living under British rule was clearly a pull factor in the migration.

Another attraction for the Mennonites and others with strong religious convictions was Governor Simcoe's announcement that immigrants of good reputation and professing the Christian religion were especially desirable as settlers.[18] No doubt the 200 acres of free land was an added incentive to migrate, but it seems clearly not to have been the primary factor.[19]

At the same time that settlement opportunities opened in Upper Canada, other options appeared in western Pennsylvania, Ohio, and Virginia. If those emigrating to Canada had been interested only in land, they could have found it closer to home. Favourable reports by the first settlers in Upper Canada of their settlement experience undoubtedly created interest in moving there in those who came in 1800 and the following thirty-five years. The Vineland settlement became the stopping place and reference point for the first two Waterloo Mennonite families, Betzner and Sherk, before they moved to Waterloo County, and for many others who were to follow.

What was significant for the later and larger Waterloo settlement is the fact that these Pennsylvania, pro-British Mennonites found the larger possibilities for settlements on farmland in Canada. They could have motivated Governor Simcoe to extend his invitation to Mennonites through the Quakers on the basis of the successful small Vineland and other peace group settlements in the Lincoln County area.

Impact of early immigration to Canada

If the pre-nineteenth century settlements had not been made, it is doubtful whether Mennonites would have been the first to settle along the Grand River in what later became Waterloo County. Hence, they would not have bought land from Richard Beasley and, through that experience, have come upon the crisis which ended in the purchase of first 60,000 and later 45,000 acres of land. Neither would the well-known German Land Company have been formed to fund and systematically distribute the land. These purchases would not likely have been made without the more well-to-do Lancaster Mennonite farmers investing money generously in these large blocks of land. Nor would there have been the large influx of successful farm families from Pennsylvania to Ontario thereby infusing needed capital for the development of family farms, schools, churches, sawmills, and grist mills.

The Pennsylvania emigration to Canada represents the first and only Mennonite mass exodus from the United States in the three-hundred-year history of the North America Mennonites.

Colonial Mennonites strongly German

Another important pull factor in the direction of Waterloo was that of German ethnicity and culture. There is abundant evidence that colonial Pennsylvania looked down upon its German population. At times, their numbers appeared to be a threat to the English. One student of Pennsylvania German culture during those days says they were socially if not politically second-class citizens. They were under attack from prejudiced neighbours and victimized by all sorts of jealousies and misunderstandings. Even such leaders as Benjamin Franklin and the famous Philadelphia physician, Dr. Benjamin Rush, looked down on the German people.[20] One contemporary historian states this point clearly:

> It must not be forgotten that Mennonites were still quite German in their cultural expression. Their religious activity was carried on in the High German of the Luther Bible, and their social communications were in the Pennsylvania "Deutsch" dialect. In the Pennsylvania environment the Mennonites had learned to integrate their religion with British politics, German culture, and colonial land as a total formula for the good life. That good life had now begun to break apart. German culture had felt the fires of the American melting pot before 1756. . . . It was soon apparent that

the British environment in Upper Canada offered not only British privileges, freedom for Mennonite religion, and an abundance of good land, but also the easiest continuance of German culture.[21]

German mercenary troops supported the British during the Revolution, and these troops plus an additional one thousand German loyalist families from New York placed the Germans next in line to the English for land grants. By 1784, German loyalists receiving land grants represented 40 percent of the total.[22] The pioneer Mennonites were totally German in language and in culture. To this original stock were added other European Germans of Catholic and Lutheran religious persuasion. The latter came from some of the same areas in southern Germany, especially the Palatinate. Many spoke the same dialect as the Mennonites.

The Swiss Mennonites from Pennsylvania brought to Waterloo in their well-filled Conestoga wagons much more than household goods and farm tools. This "something more valuable" was the invisible heritage of their religious faith. That commodity, nurtured regularly in their community-centred meetinghouses, provided the necessary spirit to sustain them in times of hardships. Their collective religious life was not expressed in the form of a parish-type congregation covering a wide geographic area with a large and imposing centrally located church structure. For them, the church was the small, close-knit, neighbourhood congregation worshipping in a little frame meetinghouse. This original model of organized religion continued through two centuries and is still the dominant Waterloo rural Mennonite pattern.

The total number of Mennonites who migrated to Ontario and to Waterloo County between 1800 and 1835 is not exactly known. No careful records were kept either of migrating families or congregations, by historians or self-appointed individuals. The closest guesses by church historians is that possibly as many as two thousand came to Ontario; and of those, fifteen hundred settled in Waterloo.[23] Others think the number was lower.[24] Unfortunately, no government census was taken until much later (1841).

Settlement in York County
Indirectly related to the Waterloo settlement history is the Mennonite settlement in York County, generally referred to as the Markham settlement because of its location in the township of that

name. Its first Mennonite settlers were also Pennsylvanians; they
had intended to settle in Waterloo but were deterred by the defective land titles the Waterloo Mennonites were experiencing in
1803. Thus the flow of immigrants from Pennsylvania during
1803, 1804, and 1805 largely turned to Markham Township. Individual families purchased land and settled in neighbourhoods
close to each other, but no large land complexes were purchased as
was the case in Waterloo. Interrelations between congregations
and families have been maintained between the three settlements
throughout their history.

Coming of the Swiss-Alsatian Amish to Waterloo

The reasons for the coming of the Amish to Ontario rather than to
the United States are not clear. Throughout much of the
eighteenth and early nineteenth centuries, Amish from Europe
immigrated to Pennsylvania and later to Ohio, Indiana, and Illinois. Although there were significant Amish settlements in Lancaster County in the early nineteenth century, during the heavy
emigration of Mennonites, there were no simultaneous Amish emi-
grations to Ontario from Lancaster.

The prime mover of Amish immigration to Waterloo County
was Christian Nafziger, a farmer from Bavaria. He must have
been a courageous, adventuresome, and persistent person. From
Bavaria he found his way north to Amsterdam, where he boarded
a freight boat to New Orleans. From this Gulf city he walked
northeast as far as Lancaster County, Pennsylvania, to discuss
with his co-religionists the possibility of finding land for his
people. It may be that he had hoped to find available land in
Pennsylvania near another Amish settlement. This was in the
year 1822 in the midst of the flow of Lancaster Mennonites to
Ontario. It is not surprising, therefore, that Nafziger was advised
to continue his journey still farther north to explore possibilities
where land was much less expensive than in Lancaster County.
One may wonder why exploration of possibilities in western
Pennsylvania, Ohio, or Indiana might not also have been considered since those areas were being opened for settlement at that
time.

At any rate, his friends at Lancaster gave him a horse to ride
on the remainder of his journey north to Waterloo. There he was
directed by Mennonite leaders to unsettled Crown land in what

later came to be Wilmot Township. This evidently appealed to him. He went to York and conferred with Governor Maitland, who agreed to sell him whatever land he might require for his people. Each settler was promised 200 acres at a cost of $2.50 per acre. Fifty acres of that was to be free in exchange for clearing a thirty-three-foot strip along the front of each 200-acre plot, building a cabin, and paying a small surveyor's fee.[25] Nafziger returned to his Bavarian home in 1822, going by way of England and visiting King George to have his land agreement confirmed.

Nafziger did not return to Waterloo until 1826, four years after his original visit. The reason for this gap between his exploratory trip and his immigration is not known. However, it appears that some of his fellow Amish families had immigrated to Pennsylvania and lived there as early as 1823. A Mennonite committee consisting of Abraham, Jacob, and Samuel Erb and Jacob C. Snider had agreed to supervise the prospective settlement for Nafziger. The German Block was surveyed in 1823 and the first settlement established in 1824. By 1829, the surveyor reported that fifty lots had been taken.[26] Assuming an average of six persons per family, it meant that the Amish population was approximately three hundred after the first five years of settlement. Additional immigrants from South Germany and Alsace continued to drift in for the next thirty- five years, marking the end of Amish settlements in Europe.[27] All of the first Amish settlers engaged in farming and a large majority continue in that vocation.

Coming of the Mennonites from Russia[28]

It is a historical coincidence that at the same time as the Mennonites from Pennsylvania were migrating to Ontario (1786-1835), large groups of Mennonites from Prussia were migrating to southwestern Russia and establishing large colonies in the Ukraine (1789-1820). These coincidental migrations were totally unrelated, yet both were motivated by the desire for greater religious freedom and greater economic opportunity. In both cases, those anticipated benefits were realized. But from the time of World War I to the fifties and sixties after World War II, political and social conditions placed the lives of the Mennonites in Russia in a constant state of upheaval.

The first group of Mennonites to come to Ontario from Russia in the 1920s were still able to leave their country legally. Those allowed to leave could take only a few possessions and very little money with them, thus transportation had to be arranged from outside Russia. The Canadian Mennonite Board of Colonization (CMBC) was formed in 1922 and succeeded in bringing about 20,000 Mennonites to Canada in the 1920s.[29] The Board had very little money but was able to work out a contract with the Canadian Pacific Railroad (CPR) whereby the immigrants would be transported to Canada on credit guaranteed by the CMBC. Immigrants were given two years to repay their travel costs. Efforts were also made by the CMBC to raise loan money and material contributions from Canadian and United States Mennonites.[30]

Here, once more, is an example of Christian mutual aid as a priceless resource in time of human crisis. The rescue of 20,000 Mennonites from Russia could not have been achieved without the untiring and sacrificial efforts of their co-religionists in Canada and the United States. They performed heroically in working out seemingly insoluble problems with the Canadian government, the Canadian Pacific Railroad, and their respective Mennonite constituencies.[31]

In July 1924, a trainload of 1,340 immigrants escaping upheaval in Russia arrived in Waterloo and walked from the train station to the Erb Street Church to be parcelled out to their waiting hosts. One or more families from a total of forty different Amish and Mennonite church communities hosted immigrant individuals and families. In addition to opening their homes for weeks and months, many found part- or full-time paying work for their guests. Not all experiences were pleasant, but on the whole, the social experiences were mutually enriching. It was a crash course in intercultural relations. Waterloo area Mennonites were suddenly learning to know brothers and sisters of the faith they had never seen before. Mennonites from Russia and from Waterloo learned in a few months what it would have taken years to learn had there not been this brief but intense interaction as a result of living together in the same house or in houses close to one another. Out of those experiences, many lifelong friendships were formed.

Recollections fifty years later

In 1974, at fiftieth anniversary services celebrating this historic experience, numerous amusing incidents of those first days in Canada were recalled. An Ontario farmer recalled coming to the Erb Street Church to pick up his family in a three-seated carriage. The family consisted of nine members, so he could not take all family members and their possessions at once. The two families eating at one table consisted of sixteen people. The Waterloo Mennonite mother found it difficult to adjust to the extended family and to some of the refugee family's customs during their month-long stay.

An Old Order woman recalled awaking on Christmas Eve late at night and hearing singing. She and her husband investigated in the other end of the house where the Russian guests were quartered and found the entire family singing Christmas carols by candlelight. This was a new and strange custom to the Old Order family.

A large Russian family recalled the bitterness they felt at the Erb Street Church on the day of their arrival when they were not chosen or assigned to a Waterloo family until almost the very last. They said all they could do was keep on praying that someone would still provide a temporary home. Russian women wearing skirts and blouses rather than apron dresses and Russian girls with short hair like boys (to prevent lice) were mildly shocking to conservative Waterloo Mennonites. A Waterloo woman recalled that her Russian family refused to sleep in beds made up with clean white linen sheets, claiming that such were only for high-class people. Differences in cooking and food uses, too, required reconciliation. A Waterloo couple observed the frugality of a Russian woman who put apple peelings in a sandwich. There were also sad experiences like the ten-year-old motherless girl, separated from her brothers and sisters to work in another home, who was so lonely and homesick that she repeatedly wished she could die and be in heaven with her mother.

Three Russian girls who worked in a local factory were saving their money to buy curtains. When they heard of an opera in Toronto, they decided to buy tickets for it and forget the curtains. This unorthodox decision astounded the more practical Swiss Mennonite girls who never forgot this illustration of wasting hard-earned money.

In addition to the Mennonites who came directly to Waterloo from Russia in large numbers after the two world wars, somewhat more than two thousand Mennonites returned from Mexico and settled in southern Ontario along Lake Erie.[32] They or their parents had emigrated there in the mid-twenties from Manitoba and Saskatchewan. About fifteen families scattered in Waterloo County organized a church with headquarters in Kitchener in 1970. It is known as the Old Colony Mennonite church because of its roots in the first Mennonite colony in Russia. This group has been classified with the conservatives, but it has undergone so many changes that it might justifiably have been classed with the moderates.

A second group of Mennonites with a Dutch-Russian ethnic background is the Evangelical Mennonite Mission Church, which had 33 members in 1972 and is composed mostly of converted ex-Old Colony members. This group meets in rented quarters and has grown very little since its founding in 1969. So far, none of these Mennonites have been attracted to the progressive churches in the twin cities that came from Russia.[33]

Each of the three ethnic streams of Mennonites came from a distinct geographical area in Europe. Each came at a distinct time period and had unique cultural experiences. All three groups came to Waterloo in search of religious and political freedom and all were in search of sufficient land in which to make cohesive settlements. Unfortunately, those coming from Russia were unable to realize that goal. Their own economic conditions and that of Canada at the time made farming an impossible option. All three groups also were at least in part trilingual. Each group spoke a dialect, and some spoke the national language of the country from which they came—German, French, or Russian.

In spite of these commonalities, social and religious interaction between the separate groups was minimal. The one exception was the cooperation between the Mennonite Conference of Ontario and the Amish Mennonites who began to work together in the area of foreign missions in the early nineteen twenties.

Chapter 4

Mennonites as community builders

The word *community*, like family, is so familiar that few people stop to reflect on its fuller meaning or on how its meaning has changed and continues changing. The root of the word community is "common" or "commune." It has to do with sharing or having something in common.

Community has come to be used in two distinct ways. One is the traditional sense of an area or place. The other use refers to people having something in common, such as a profession or an interest group without regard to place or location: the religious community, the medical community, the business community.

In this book, I use the word in the traditional sense. Here community is a group of people in a specific place: Waterloo County or, more recently, the Regional Municipality of Waterloo and nearby areas in which Mennonites live. This community has a culture, more or less commonly known and understood, with a distinct social structure. This Mennonite community has selected and fashioned certain aspects of its total culture and rejected others. Individuals and groups make contributions to the preservation of the social system operating in the community. Its members are aware that they have enough in common to set them off from other groups. What they have in common and do not share totally with others is their unique value system and patterns of living: their particular "web of life."[1]

The Waterloo Mennonite community has a common social characteristic known as the great dichotomy. Some live close together in towns and cities, and others live scattered in the open country. The two parts of the great dichotomy are referred to as urban and rural populations.

In the twentieth century, people all over the world have moved from rural to urban areas. This shift is clearly seen in the Waterloo area as well. In Canada and the United States, government census takers have further divided the rural population into two subgroups called farm and rural nonfarm. This distinction identifies the many people who live outside cities in rural areas but who do not earn the major share of their living by farming.

Rural-urban sociological differences

Rural and urban societies have sociological, psychological, economic, and cultural characteristics which affect human behaviour in different ways. The biblical writers alluded to these differences long ago. (See Gen. 13:12-13, 17:4; Num. 35:6-8; Ps. 107:4.)

These differences have been best described by Ferdinand Tonnies, a German sociologist, early in the twentieth century. He called the rural community a *Gemeinschaft*, and the urban community a *Gesellschaft*. Neither of these terms translates easily into English, so both German words have been retained in English usage.

Gemeinschaft (community), according to Tonnies, describes a cohesive society organized on the basis of shared values and norms that command strong allegiance from its members. Members have a kindred feeling for each other and do not easily renounce their membership because it involves deep emotional ties. People tend to be born into this community or grow into it rather than joining voluntarily. Relationships tend to be face-to-face. Members tend to have common ancestors. They know who they are and from whence they came.[2]

Gesellschaft (association or society) is the opposite of Gemeinschaft. It describes a society marked by self-interest, little consensus on norms or values, little commitment to the group, and continued change. Relationships tend to be impersonal and are often based on functional needs of people for each other rather than any emotional commitment. Social control is by formal laws, contracts, and published rules rather than based on informal agreements and local custom. In Gesellschaft, tradition and custom no longer have a binding influence on individual behaviour. Kinship ceases to be the most important basis for social organization. Personal choice rather than birth tends to be the basis of social relations.[3]

Society has steadily moved in the direction of Gesellschaft and away from Gemeinschaft. More and more human activities take the form of a voluntary contractual relationship which is of a secondary rather than primary character. This same trend can be seen among the Mennonites in Waterloo.

Gesellschaft produces what has come to be called the *mass society*. This has weakened the traditional bonds found in the old neighbourhood and local rural community. More and more decisions are based on common sense and reason rather than on tradition or sentiment. Thus labour has become specialized; labour unions, business, and professional associations have been organized. These groups are made up of individuals who are only loosely bound together. Mass society means mass participation. It represents a movement away from the socially responsible and highly integrated communities of a former day.

Mennonites in mass society
The effects of mass production and mass communication have been widely criticized as unwholesome. Yet we silently drift more and more toward that kind of society as though we had no other choice.

Until recent years, Mennonites lived in small, socially responsible communities. Is the Waterloo Mennonite community being swallowed up by the mass culture of modern society? True, the rural culture of a former century cannot be preserved. But cannot some of the qualities of community life of an earlier day be retained or recreated in modern urban society?

"Urban life in contrast to that of the small community has no abiding presentness," says Baker Brownell in describing some of the negative features of today's urban society or Gesellschaft. Cities make the future seem more important than the present. So life exists for "the moment that is not here. It roars on toward endless futures which it never finds. It tips and staggers endlessly into postponed values that never are realized." Confusing as it seems, this way of life "is the secret both of the city's power and its human failure." Brownell concludes that the "city has no present end," but others will argue, he says, that "the rural community has no future."[4]

I do not intend to demean the Gesellschaft and exalt the Gemeinschaft type of community as though the one type of social order was all evil and hopeless and the other all wholesome. I want a type of human community which has not grown to such size and complexity that it exceeds a people's ability to govern for the welfare of the citizens. I assume that communities of moderate size have been able to do this more successfully than have the large urban industrial centres.

Sociologists have used terms other than Gemeinschaft and Gesellschaft to describe the great dichotomy. For instance, Mircea Eliade, a Frenchman, used the words *sacred* and *profane* for the two types of communities.[5] By sacred, he meant highly revered, respected, and, in a sense, religious. By profane, he implied the opposite, namely, secular, not religious, ordinary or common. Robert Redfield chose *folk* community and *contractual* community.[6] By folk, Redfield referred to the common people, those who lived in communities governed largely by tradition and custom, based on mutual acquaintance, and experiencing little change. By contractual, he meant those who live in communities governed by formal laws, written agreements, and fewer face-to-face relationships in the business of living.

Regardless of the words or phrases chosen to describe community, the terms are merely tools used by scholars to describe what they call ideal types. No existing community fits these types perfectly.

Primary, secondary, and reference groups

In primary groups, life-changing human experiences occur. Here, it is said, human nature and personality develop. The family is the best example of a primary group. Here newborn infants first learn the secrets of human interaction. Not only is it the place where humans first learn to walk and talk, but, equally important, here moral and ethical values such as goodwill, compassion, integrity, duty, responsibility, and mutual aid develop. In the primary group, character, both good and bad, is largely determined.

The primary group serves as a link between the individual and society. It is the agency that prepares a person to play his or her expected role in society; the place where a person learns to explore, to play, to work, to exercise self-restraint. It gives the individual emotional support and a place to belong. Finally, the primary group takes account of the whole person.[7]

The counterpart to a primary group is the secondary group.[8] It is marked by interpersonal relationships which are secondary, that is, peripheral, segmental, often impersonal, and even transferable. By transferable is meant that the interpersonal relations are uniform, the same to everyone. Relationships differ little from person to person. In the secondary group, interaction is generally not with the whole person but only with segments of a person and is comparatively superficial. People in secondary groups generally do not know each other well and, from a practical standpoint, circumstances do not allow taking time to become well acquainted.

An example of a secondary-group relationship is one that occurs between a customer and a check-out clerk in a supermarket. The relationship may be polite, the service efficient and pleasant yet extremely superficial and robot-like, since the service provided and the greetings exchanged are identical for all shoppers. A check-out clerk may feel toward the forty-ninth customer what the assembly-line worker feels about a commodity being processed hundreds of times each working day.

This discussion of primary and secondary groups and Gemeinschaft and Gesellschaft communities helps us understand the Waterloo Mennonite community. If such primary groups and communities are central to the development of personality and of moral, ethical, and religious values, then serious attention needs to be paid to developing and maintaining the character and quality of groups and communities. This compels us to examine and assess the character and quality of the families, neighbourhoods, and church communities for which Mennonites are responsible.

Throughout history, Mennonite communities assumed responsibility for the moral character of their members through church discipline. The conservative Amish and Mennonite groups still do. They are not leaving this matter to secular society. Among the progressive segments of the Waterloo Mennonites, especially in urbanized communities, the influence of both family and church over members' behaviour has gradually declined. More and more of the basic functions once carried by church and family are today being performed and heavily influenced by secondary groups. In short, many Waterloo Mennonite communities have become increasingly secularized.

Mennonite reference groups

A third group to consider when studying the Mennonite community is the reference group. This is one to which people and organizations look when making comparative judgments of themselves. Communities, like individuals, judge themselves and their behaviour by other organizations and communities. Those judging themselves may conclude that by comparison they appear favourable or unfavourable; superior or inferior; stronger or weaker. Reference groups are a kind of model, guide, or mirror by which others check themselves to get ideas on making decisions about their own conduct.

For centuries, the favourite and only positive reference group known by Mennonites was the apostolic church as described in the New Testament. Established or state churches were, in fact, negative reference groups: models of what not to be. The apostolic model provided a clear goal and a strong sense of biblical identity. It served well for centuries. However, whenever the Mennonite religion came to be tolerated and members grew wealthy and became socially accepted, their reference group tended to shift from the apostolic church to other contemporary churches and to the secular society. This shift took place in the Dutch Mennonite church of the seventeenth century. It also happened in Prussia and Russia in the nineteenth and early twentieth centuries and it is happening today in Canada and the United States. Coming chapters will test whether this historical experience is repeating itself within the Mennonite community of Waterloo.

Community as a social system

Another window through which to see the nature of community is as a *social system*. This means that every community, including the Waterloo Mennonite community and every larger society, is made up of many interacting parts and, as a whole works as a single system. The parts of the community may be called elements, institutions, or subsystems. Such community subsystems as political systems, welfare systems, economic systems, or educational systems are not totally separate from one another, and yet they have a life and function distinct from every other subsystem. They overlap at times, but play interdependent parts in the whole community.

The Apostle Paul long ago compared the church to the human body (1 Cor. 12). Both, he said, were made up of many interdependent parts all working together for the good of the whole. In today's language, we would say he saw the church as a social system.

Paraphrasing the Apostle's language in describing the community as a social system, we could say: "The community does not consist of one organization but many. If the school system should say: 'Because I am not the economic system, I do not belong to the community,' that would not make it any less a part of the community. If the religious system should say: 'Because I am not the political system, I do not belong to the community,' that would not make it any less a part of the community. If the whole community were the educational system, where would the economic system be? If the whole community were an economic system, where would the political system be? But as it is, God has set the various systems in the community, each one as he chose. If all were a single subsystem, what would the community as a whole be? As it is, there are many parts, yet one community. Business cannot say to the school, 'I have no need of you' nor again the church to the government, 'I have no need of you.'"

Elements of a social system

Some sociologists have described social systems as having at least seven parts, institutions, or elements.[9] They see every social group, every family, and every community with what they call *social* elements, just as the physical scientist sees matter composed of many different chemical elements. The seven social elements, which can be applied to the Waterloo Mennonite community, are the following:

1. *Ends*, *goals*, and *objectives*, or those things which members of the community expect to achieve.

2. *Norms*, *rules*, *laws*, or *standards*, the criteria or guidelines by which a community's objectives are achieved. They define what are the acceptable and unacceptable or the right and wrong ways of doing things. Norms are both written and unwritten. They include moral and ethical ideals such as fair play, goodwill, and decency.

3. *Status-role* is what is expected of persons by way of conduct and performance in a given position. Every person in a community performs a function, however minor it may be, and every person has status at some level even though he may not be aware of it.

4. *Delegation of power* implies authority, influence, or control over others, especially in the area of decision making. Power can be defined as ability to achieve purpose.

5. *Sanctions* are those elements which induce observance of laws, rules, or customs. They may be positive, such as praise, recognition, job promotions or material rewards, or they may be negative such as withdrawal of privileges, censorship, public criticism, ridicule, or even excommunication and shunning (social avoidance).

6. *Facilities*, such as buildings, equipment, machinery, credit, skills, and technology are necessary means to achieve the goals of the system.

7. *Territoriality*, space, or geographical area in or on which a system operates and has recognized rights of occupancy or possession. This may be a new way to see what has hitherto seemed simple and self-evident. To describe a religious community as a social system may seem strange or even unnecessary. Our purpose here is to point out that what has been perceived as simple is much more complex than it appears. A flower, a plant, or a tree may seem simple to the average person, but not to the botanist who understands the internal structure and life of flowers, plants, and trees.

Social systems are composed of human beings who have the power to think, to remember, to plan, and to move, and therefore are far more complex and much more unpredictable in their behaviour than life in nature. To understand the larger society in which we live, we need first to know the smaller intimate social systems such as communities, churches, and families of which we are a direct part. In a democracy, it is important for citizens to understand the political system by which they are governed.

The social elements of a community system are not readily recognized by the average person. Like the various organs of the human body, they and their important work are taken for granted. The persons whose life they make possible are almost totally unconscious of their presence until made aware of them by illness, accident, or the object of special study. So, too, the average person is not aware of the parts of a community until attention is called to them by some event, problem, or unusual experience.

Most people if asked to state the objectives and the norms of their community could give no immediate answer. The same would apply if asked about other elements such as status-role, power, sanctions, facilities, and territory. They would need to stop and think carefully before being able to give coherent answers. Elements of the system are so deeply embedded in custom and tradition that they are seldom examined. This does not mean that they are not important to the life of the community. They are most important.

Communities would work more efficiently and effectively if their citizens better understood the working of each of the interacting elements. Knowledge of the interdependent elements of a social community has the same relation to wholesome group life as does knowledge of the interacting parts of the human body to good personal health.

Mennonite community as a sociological type

In the early part of this chapter, we discussed two general types of communities that are roughly compared to what in North America are referred to as rural and urban communities. Sociologists have introduced us to other concepts with more detailed social characteristics. The concepts briefly discussed were Gemeinschaft and Gesellschaft, sacred and profane, folk and contract.

When we focus our attention on the Waterloo community as a whole, we cannot classify it as being one or the other of these two opposite types. Elements of both Gemeinschaft and Gesellschaft are present in the larger Waterloo Mennonite community. In general, we identify the Old Orders or conservative Mennonites and Amish as having many Gemeinschaft characteristics and the progressive Mennonites as having many Gesellschaft characteristics. Neither conservatives nor progressives are purely one or the other of the theoretical types.

In which direction are the Waterloo Mennonites heading? The overwhelming evidence shows a steady shift away from Gemeinschaft toward Gesellschaft; from the sacred toward the profane; from the folk type of community to the contractual community. Yet longtime trends are sometimes halted and the swing of the pendulum reversed. An eminent authority on the sociology of community has the following insightful comment about the future of the traditional Gemeinschaft community:

> Just as agricultural technology, heralded by some scientists as the greatest revolution of all time, marked the advent of the community, so now modern technology may be marking its demise, heralding a revolution of perhaps equal significance. For modern communication and transportation are changing the significance of locale and space of human relationships as profoundly as agriculture did some ten thousand years ago. As a result, some observers conclude that the settlement or locale concept of the community may soon become archaic or even disappear, or if retained, be restricted to the backwaters of the post city era.[10]

Indeed, modern technology in transportation, communication, and industry has affected the nature of human communities. Geographical location is no longer as important for community as it once was. Nevertheless, the need for some type of intimate primary group, such as the neighbourhood, church, play and peer group, remains essential for the growth of wholesome personalities, as well as for the development of ethical norms and moral standards. These human values are best nurtured in the little communities of society and not in the large impersonal institutions with secondary group characteristics.

Can Mennonite churches retain a genuine communal character in the second, third, and fourth generation in an urban environment or will they in time take on the characteristics of their cultural environment?

The Waterloo Mennonite community
The Waterloo Mennonite community consists of fourteen separately organized bodies. For purposes of simplified discussion, these fourteen groups have been divided into three general categories: conservative, moderate, and progressive, as shown in Table 4-1.

The collection of church bodies in Table 4-1 constitutes the total Waterloo Amish-Mennonite community with the exception of several small independent congregations. While most of the Old Order Amish live in Perth County just northwest of the Waterloo County line, they are historically and biologically related to the large body of Western Ontario Conference members who separated

Table 4-1
Waterloo County area Mennonites
By country of origin, period of immigration,
and three categories of social conformity

Origin & period	Conservative	Moderate	Progressive
Switzerland & South Germany, via Pennsylvania 1800-1830	Old Order Mennonite (OOM) David Martin Old Order Mennonite (DMOO) Elam Martin Old Order Mennonite (EMOO) Reformed Mennonite (RM)	Waterloo-Markham (W-M) Conservative Mennonite Conference (CMC)	Mennonite Conference of Ontario (MC)
France, South Germany, Switzerland, 1824-1860	Old Order Amish (OOA)	Beachy Amish (BA)	Western Ont. Mennonite Conference (WOC)
Holland, Germany, Russia 1923-1930, 1947-1965	Old Colony Mennonite (OCM)	Evangelical Mennonite Mission Church (EMMC)	United Mennonite Conference (UMC) Mennonite Brethren Churches of Ontario (MBC)

from them in the late nineteenth century and the Beachy Amish who separated in the early twentieth century. The Western Ontario Conference carried the Amish name until 1960. Sociologically, the Amish and Mennonites in the Waterloo area are closely bound together. The degree of social interaction between them is directly related to the conservatism in each group. The Old Orders of each group co-operate with all others at two points. One is in making representation to provincial or national governments on such matters as the peace witness, social security, and hospitalization. The second area is in matters of mutual aid in times of disaster from fire, floods, or violent storms.

The elements in the Mennonite community system, described above, are also expressed in and through separate organizations called church conferences. Each of these conferences tends to define its own status-role and what is expected of its members by way of behaviour and performance. Each group decides how authority is exercised and power is distributed. In some groups, power is highly centralized and exercised by older men only. In others, it is widely distributed among lay members including women and young people.

The exercise of group discipline is also expressed in a variety of ways and with wide assortment of consequences. Yet all groups express some form of sanction in order to enforce the rules by which they seek to achieve their objectives. Some groups rely largely on customs and traditions while others enforce desired behaviour by threat of excommunication. Still others appeal to voluntary conformity and individual self-discipline.

In each of the Mennonite denominations, with the exception of the Old Order Amish, the congregations making up a conference have their own meetinghouses for worship. The conservatives use those facilities for religious services only. The progressive groups use their meetinghouses for such additional purposes as religious education programs, men's and women's fellowship groups, youth activities, social and musical events, weekday and evening adult classes, and visiting lecturers or public forums on topics of interest to the congregation. Each of the congregations tends to occupy a given geographical territory which they consider more or less their own. Although it is not required, most Mennonites belong to a church in the area where they live.

In summary, the Waterloo Mennonite community is made up of three tiers. There is, first of all, the community as a whole which includes all Mennonites and Amish in Waterloo and adjacent counties. The second tier is made up of one or more congregations in one locality of the county, usually composed of the same ethnic background. These subcommunities might be illustrated by the Kitchener-Waterloo, the Wellesley, or the Woolwich community. These subgroups have no separate organization. Their primary point of identity is their adjacent location in a specific geographic locality.

A third basis for community in the Waterloo area is the individual congregation. Most Waterloo Mennonite congregations have the characteristics of a small community or a Gemeinschaft. They tend to be composed of a web of interrelated families. The members are well acquainted with each other and provide strong social and spiritual support for one another. Each congregation is a small system with goals, standards, status-role, a power structure, a ranking method, facilities, and a territory of their own.

Are Waterloo Mennonite communities utopian?

Is the Waterloo Mennonite community, in whole or in part, a utopian or visionary community? Students in my sociology classes often raised this question. They saw in conservative Waterloo Mennonite communities similarities to nineteenth-century American utopian communities such as the Harmonists, Shakers, Amana, and the contemporary Society of Brothers. While the Mennonites do not practise communal ownership of property, they strive for the kingdom of God on earth; practise mutual aid, separation from the world, and church discipline; teach morality and integrity, and emphasize simplicity, frugality, and plainness in dress. These are all goals of idealistic Christian communities.[11]

Other similarities are voluntary efforts to establish communities dedicated to the feasibility of living together without the social evils of the larger society; proving that unemployment and wretched poverty can be eliminated and relative equality achieved in religiously oriented communities. In Mennonite communities, as in the utopias, a high regard for the role of leadership has been traditional.[12]

Although the conservative Waterloo Amish and Mennonites would deny being utopian communities, an impartial assessment of their aims, objectives, and social practices finds many similarities to nineteenth-century utopian communities. It is even possible to identify vestiges of utopian ideals among the progressive Waterloo Mennonites such as emphasis on the love ethic, the peace teaching, simplicity, and mutual aid. However, the social characteristics of the progressive Mennonite communities have more similarities to the communities of Waterloo at large than to their conservative spiritual kin.

Among progressive Mennonites in Waterloo, the external symbols of simplicity, frugality, and humility are ever more difficult to find. A high percentage of their members seem happy to be freed from the bondage of the group discipline under which many grew up. Sermons on these subjects are rarely heard in progressive churches. This is in sharp contrast to sermons in conservative churches where these principles are repeatedly stressed. Among progressive Mennonites, each member and family is free to determine the extent of its self-indulgence and materialism. Individualism has replaced group decision-making in matters of personal behaviour and in the acquiring of goods. The churches are silent on the matter of consumerism, no matter how excessive. Accumulating wealth and displaying it no longer embarrasses most progressive Waterloo Mennonites. This is convincing evidence of a shift from a Gemeinschaft to a Gesellschaft type community on the part of the progressives.

A fundamental difference between Waterloo conservative and progressive Mennonite communities is the degree of discipline exercised over members. In the case of the conservative communities, members are held morally responsible for social behaviour and personal lifestyles. In the case of progressive communities, lifestyles and behavioural norms are individually determined, usually in line with those of conventional society. There is every indication that in the foreseeable future, Waterloo Mennonites will continue to nurture two contrasting types of communities, one reflecting Gemeinschaft and the other Gesellschaft.

Chapter 5

Changing population patterns in Waterloo

Two important ways of seeing Mennonite life in Waterloo County are through its demography and ecology. Demography describes certain ways of looking at human populations. It deals with such vital statistics as birth and death rates and the closely related subject of migration. These three ever-changing factors determine population in given areas.

To understand Mennonite demography and ecology, we must compare this data with the population of the county as a whole as well as with other ethnic and religious subgroups with which Mennonites are in competition. Mennonites were the pioneer settlers in Waterloo County and the dominant population for the first few decades of the nineteenth century. But other ethnic and religious immigrants soon outnumbered them.[1]

Between 1802 and 1810, Americans of English, Welsh, Scottish, and Irish descent came from the states of New York, Vermont, Delaware, and Pennsylvania and settled in the vicinity of Preston. From 1811 to 1820, Highland Scots came from New York and located in North Dumfries Township. Between 1820 and 1839, Lowland Scots settled in scattered groups in North Dumfries Township. Beginning in 1830, immigrants direct from England and from Lower Canada migrated to Waterloo County. All of these nationalities, in addition to the German immigrants already mentioned, contributed to the ethnic mix that helped to shape the economic, cultural, social, and political life of Waterloo County.[2]

The Mennonite contribution to the building of Waterloo towns and cities was not primarily that of craftsmen, manufacturers, or business or professional men. Nor were the Mennonites prominent in the field of education or government. Their major contributions were made as producers of food and raw materials, as taxpayers, and as consumers of the goods and services produced in the towns

and cities. Perhaps most important of all, the Mennonites provided a stable economic hinterland and surplus population that
contributed to urban growth.

Historians have estimated that between fifteen hundred and
two thousand Mennonites immigrated from Pennsylvania to
Upper Canada during the first quarter of the nineteenth century.
About twelve hundred to fifteen hundred of those settled in Waterloo County.[3] These numbers include the total Mennonite population, church members, unbaptized children, and cultural Mennonites (i.e., those who claimed to be Mennonites but did not belong
to a Mennonite church). Not nearly all adult colonial Mennonites
were church members.[4] One historian says that even in Puritan
colonies the percentage of church membership was low and that in
Virginia not more than one in twenty (5 percent) was a member of
any church.[5] Since no accurate records of migrations were kept
during the early decades, it is not possible to do more than guess
about early population figures in Waterloo County. Mennonites
were reluctant to keep membership records throughout most of the
nineteenth century. The size of a congregation was generally
assessed in terms of the number of families rather than the number of baptized individuals.

A century of population growth

Statistics Canada is the source of decennial figures for the general
population and for religious denominations.[6] Table 5-1 is an
informative summary of Waterloo County population in general
and of the Mennonite population in particular. The table shows
numerical gains of the county and percentage declines of Mennonites by decades. The table reflects periods of heavy immigration.

From Table 5-1, we learn first that both the Waterloo County
Mennonite population and the population as a whole grew steadily
and rapidly throughout the 120-year interval between 1861 and
1981. Second, the Mennonite percentage of the county population
gradually declined from 11.2 to 4.9. The ratio of Mennonites to
non-Mennonites in a 120-year period declined from nine to one to
twenty to one. The county population during this period increased
almost ten times over its 1861 figure, while the Mennonites population increased about four times. The chief explanation of the dif-
ferential growth rate is the steady flow of immigrants to Waterloo

Table 5-1 Mennonite percentage of the Waterloo County population, 1861-1971[7]		
Year	Waterloo Population	Mennonite Percentage
1861	38,750	11.2
1881	42,740	11.9
1901	50,464	10.5
1921	75,266	9.5
1941	98,720	9.5
1961	176,754	6.6
1971	254,035	5.1
1981	302,700	4.9

County during the twentieth century. Only in the decade of the 1920s was a significant portion of that general stream of immigrants identified as Mennonites.[8]

Mennonite immigration to Ontario had practically ceased by the 1830s. In the nineteenth century only scattered families and individuals immigrated after that period. The coming of the Mennonites from Russia in the 1920s introduced the first of this ethnic strand to Waterloo. These immigrants in the 20th century came from scattered geographical areas of Russia. Some of the new arrivals were hosted by the Amish and Mennonites in Waterloo County for weeks or months. About half of them at first tried to find opportunities for settlement in the provinces of Manitoba, Saskatchewan, or Alberta on farms and in cities with relatives or other Mennonites from Russia. Not finding such opportunities, many returned to Waterloo County to find work in the factories. It is estimated that between three and four hundred Mennonites from Russia settled in the county during the mid 1920s. Several hundred more came after World War II as individuals and families sponsored by relatives who were already Canadian citizens or landed immigrants. Most of these came in the 1950s.

In the decade between 1921 and 1931, the Mennonite population in the county increased by 1,622, a gain of over 22 percent. This was the largest gain of any decade in the entire 120-year period under study. The size of that increase is, however, not reflected in a significantly greater percentage of the population of the county, which also had an increase of 14,586 or 19 percent for the decade.

Loss of Mennonite population

A factor affecting the Mennonite rate of growth is the significant loss of members over the century due to church splits. One such division eventually resulted in the formation of the Missionary Church. A second loss occurred as individuals and families joined other churches. Some reasons were intermarriage, the use of the German language (which young people no longer understood), opposition to rigid church discipline on dress, social behaviour, and unapproved lifestyles.

One need not be confused by what may seem like a statistical inconsistency if sometimes the total Mennonite population in the Waterloo area is shown as 13,000 and at other times 16,000. The 13,000 number is the official 1971 Census of Canada for Waterloo County. The 16,000 figure includes the 3,000 Mennonites in adjacent Wellington, Oxford, and Perth counties. This count included the unbaptized children of members, based on my census of Mennonite church members in Waterloo and adjacent counties.

Between 1871 and 1971, Mennonites in Waterloo County increased at an annual average rate of about 1 percent.[9] (See Table 5-1.) Over one half of this increase occurred in Kitchener-Waterloo in the 1921-1931 decade following World War I with the immigration of Mennonites from Russia. A second factor was the beginning of a heavy flow of rural population to urban areas. Nevertheless, the Mennonite population between 1951 and 1961 did not keep pace with the county population during that decade. The Mennonite increase was only 13.7 percent compared with 40.1 for the county. The combined Kitchener-Waterloo city Mennonite population in 1971 was 3,740 or 2.8 percent of the total county population.

In contrast, the Mennonite percentage of the people in the rural townships of Woolwich and Wellesley was 46.4 and 45.3 percent, respectively. The number of Mennonites in Waterloo Township declined steadily after World War II because of annexations of territory by the city of Waterloo and the consequent displacement of Mennonite farm population. The town of Elmira, although surrounded heavily by Old Order Mennonites, has a relatively small proportion of Mennonites. Normally, retired conservative Mennonites do not move to nearby villages or towns. In most cases, they retire on their own farms in small apartments attached to their large farmhouses. Old Order members living in Elmira are mostly unmarried women or widows who move there to find work.

The data in Table 5-1 raise the question, whether it will not be only a matter of time before Waterloo Mennonites will be swallowed up completely by the expanding urban culture. This could happen, but it is not likely. One reason is that the county population is not likely to keep on growing indefinitely at the rate it has in the past. Immigration is related to local economic opportunity and most communities have limits to the possibilities of growth and economic expansion. With a strong rural base, Mennonites will continue to have a long-time population supply.

Waterloo Mennonite ecology

Ecology is the study of the way living things relate and adjust to their environment. The environment includes both human and natural things. Ecology is really one part of sociology. It is concerned with such matters as co-operation and competition among human groups in their struggle for space. A frequent illustration of ecology is that of densely populated urban areas, where the scarcity of space has resulted in the erection of high-rise apartments and office buildings. The piling up of people in multiple-storey buildings is a social phenomenon with ecological consequences and concerns.

The city of Waterloo's entire northern end is an example of the ecological process at work. Forty years ago, at the end of World War II, most of the area north of Erb Street was open country. It was devoted to family farming. With the coming of the University of Waterloo and its four church colleges, the expansion of Waterloo Lutheran College into a university (Wilfrid Laurier), and the extension of the city limits, competition for land became intense. The farmland next to the city brought so high a price that farmers near the cities could not afford to remain on their farms. It was a clear example of the ecological process at work. The urban community, having the greater economic power, was able to compete successfully for the desired scarce item, namely, land adjacent to the city.

Table 5-2
Rural/urban population distributions, 1971:
Canada, Ontario, Waterloo County, and Mennonite percentages[10]

	% Urban	% Rural	Rural % Nonfarm	% Farm	Totals
Mennonites in Canada	47.2	52.8	43.4	56.6	168,150
Canada	76.2	23.8	72.3	27.7	21,568,310
Mennonites in Ontario	47.2	52.8	41.8	58.2	40,120
Ontario	82.4	17.6	73.1	26.9	7,703,105
Mennonites in Waterloo Co.	39.3	60.7	17.1	82.9	13,015
Waterloo Co.	87.9	12.1	70.3	29.7	254,035

Table 5-2 shows that of the 21.5 million residents recorded in the 1971 federal census of Canada, 76 percent were urban and 24 percent rural. That is a ratio of three urban for every one rural resident. In Ontario, the ratio of urban to rural is almost five to one, while in Waterloo County, the ratio is more than seven to one. When dividing the rural population between nonfarm and farm for Canada, Ontario, and Waterloo County, we see approximately three nonfarm to one farm resident in all three political levels.

The 1971 Canadian Census showed that Waterloo County had a population of 254,000, of which 88 percent was urban and 12 percent rural. Of the 31,000 rural people, 21,600 or 70 percent were nonfarm and 9,100 or 30 percent were farm people. Of the farm population in Waterloo County, 6,500 or 72 percent were Mennonites. This means that approximately three out of four farm people in the county were Mennonites.

The percentage of Mennonites in the cities and towns of Waterloo County is still small despite the steady shift of Mennonites from farms since World Wars I and II. Not only is the percentage of Mennonites low in cities, it is equally low in the towns and villages of the county; this in spite of the heavy Mennonite population surrounding many of the towns and villages. The town of Wellesley is one exception.

The Mennonite percentage of population in the five townships has also experienced interesting shifts. Waterloo Township in 1861 had the highest percentage of any of the five townships in the county. A hundred years later, it had the lowest percentage of the five. Wellesley Township, on the other hand, had a very low percentage of Mennonites in 1861, whereas in 1971, 45 percent of its population was Mennonite.

There are two explanations for this shift in the ratios of Mennonites to total population. In the case of Waterloo Township, an ever larger portion of its land area and population was annexed to the cities of Cambridge, Kitchener, and Waterloo. A significant number of Mennonite families therefore moved not only out of the townships but also out of the county. The establishment of the large new Mennonite settlements in Grey County in the vicinity of Mount Forest, forty miles to the north, supports this point.

A second explanation for the noticeable shift in Mennonite percentages of population in the townships is the major political reorganization that took place in the seventies. In the creation of the Regional Municipality of Waterloo, village, town, and township governments were all combined into a single new governing body. For instance, the town of New Hamburg was merged with Wilmot Township, Elmira with Woolwich, Wellesley with Wellesley Township, Ayr with North Dumfries and Bridgeport with Kitchener. The towns of Hespeler, Preston, and Galt were merged and became Cambridge. Kitchener and Waterloo each retained their identities as separate municipalities.

The information in Table 5-3 expands the data in Table 5-2 by providing the absolute population of the county, townships, cities, towns, and villages in Waterloo County as of the 1971 and 1981 censuses. In addition, it shows the percentages of Mennonites in each of the political subdivisions. This affords us the opportunity to see how and where the Mennonite population is spread throughout the county. Table 5-3 shows that even after almost 200 years, the Mennonite population has not grown in the southern portion of the county; in fact, it has declined. The Mennonite population in North Dumfries Township in 1861 was 5 percent of the total and by 1951 and thereafter was only 1 percent. Galt, the second largest city in the county, had only 90 Mennonites in 1971 or two-tenths of one percent of the total population.

The Waterloo Mennonite population tripled between 1861 and 1981, but in that same period the population of the county increased eightfold. Thus in a 120-year period, the proportion of Mennonites in the county declined from 11 percent to 5 percent.

Table 5-3
Mennonites as percentage of total county population
By county, townships, cities, towns, and villages

Political Subdivisions	1971 Total Pop.	1971 Menn. Pop.	1971 % Menn.	1981 Total Pop.	1981 % Menn.
Waterloo Co.	254,035	13,015	5.1	306,776	4.9
Townships:					
Woolwich	6,354	2,950	46.4	16,369	25.2
Wellesley	5,281	2,390	45.3	6,688	48.4
Wilmot	7,002	1,315	18.8	10,738	12.1
Waterloo	8,733	930	10.8	7,055	3.2
North Dumfries	4,022	45	1.1	4,837	4.4
	31,392	6,700			
Cities:					
Waterloo	36,667	1,195	3.3	54,157	3.2
Kitchener	111,804	2,545	2.3	138,271	2.3
Galt	38,897	90	0.2		
	187,368	3,830			
Towns:					
New Hamburg	3,008	330	11.0	*	
Elmira	4,730	480	10.1	**	
Preston	16,726	265	1.6	***	
Hespeler	6,343	75	1.2	***	
	30,807	1,150			
Cambridge				75,716	1.5
Villages:					
Wellesley	816	325	39.8	+	
Ayr	1,272	40	3.1	++	
Bridgeport	2,375	40	1.7	+++	
	4,463	405			

Notes:
　* Merged with Wilmot Township.
　** Merged with Woolwich Township.
　*** Both towns became part of Cambridge.
　+ Merged with Wellesley Township.
　++ Merged with North Dumfries Township.
　+++ Merged with Kitchener.

It may be that in the coming century, the Mennonite population percentage will again increase in proportion to the population of the Municipality of Waterloo. One basis for this assumption is that immigration from foreign countries and migration from other provinces to the Waterloo area likely will not continue at the rate it did in the twentieth century. A second basis is that out of a total of 9,000 farmers in the Municipality of Waterloo, 6,500 are Mennonites. Farmers, as a rule, are less mobile than nonfarmers. Mennonites may be supplying a higher portion of the future population of the twin cities than they did in the past because Mennonite young people tend to replace their elders on the farms; therefore they will tend to continue to be a seedbed for future urban populations in the area.

Chapter 6

Beyond the ethnic label

Mennonites could be called a religious body, an ethnic group, or a cultural minority. In a sense, they might be any one or all three. An ethnic label generally applies to a large group of people who have a common national background, language, distinctive food, and sometimes unique dress and social customs.

Although Waterloo Mennonites have only two basic national ethnic origins, Swiss and Dutch, the break of the Amish from the Mennonites in 1693 was culturally as well as religiously sharp. The Amish literally developed a Mennonite subculture of their own. In addition, some of them settled in the provinces of Alsace and Lorraine, which were for long periods under French rule, so that in time their subculture became distinct from the Mennonites in spite of their common Swiss origin.

The Mennonites in Waterloo County have a variety of cultural backgrounds. In addition to those nationalities mentioned, there was also the influence of the United States; the largest group of Mennonites coming to Ontario had lived in Pennsylvania for seventy-five to one hundred years before moving to Upper Canada.

Each of these three main ethnic bodies immigrated to Waterloo from different areas in Europe as separate groups and at different times. The Swiss Mennonites settled in Waterloo and Woolwich townships, and the Amish from Alsace and South Germany in Wilmot Township. The Mennonites from Russia settled largely in the twin cities. For more than a century before their arrival in Upper Canada, the Amish and Mennonites in Europe had little social interaction. The same is true of the Mennonites from Russia who came in the first quarter of the twentieth century. This was so, despite the Swiss having helped the Amish establish themselves, and, a century later, helping the Mennonites from Russia by temporarily taking them into their homes and providing temporary work.

Table 6-1
**Ethnic classification of Amish and Mennonite groups in
Waterloo County**

| *Switzerland &
South Germany
(via Pennsylvania)* | *Switzerland, South
Germany, Alsace, &
Lorraine* | *Netherlands (via
Prussia & Russia)* |
|---|---|---|
| Old Order Mennonites | Old Order Amish | United Mennonite |
| David Martin Old Order | Beachy Amish | Conference |
| Elam Martin Old Order | Western Ontario | Mennonite Brethren |
| Waterloo-Markham | Conference | Conference |
| Mennonite Conference | | Evangelical Mennonite |
| of Ontario | | Mission Conference |
| Reformed Mennonites | | Old Colony Mennonite |
| Conservative Mennonite | | |
| Conference | | |

Each of these major Mennonite immigrant groups organized its own churches. Religious and cultural differences kept them from joining the existing churches, even though they all bore the name Mennonite. The Amish at the time of their immigration still worshipped in private homes. They were economically poorer than their Mennonite neighbours. The Mennonites from Russia were not comfortable with the Pennsylvania German dialect and did not know English. Like the Amish, they were relatively poor and preferred fellowship with people of their own cultural background.

Around the middle of the twentieth century, the Amish and the Swiss Mennonites began to co-operate in the area of missions and secondary education. As time went on, the former dropped the name Amish from their formal title. Intermarriages became more common, and the ethnic distinctions between the two groups gradually diminished.

Ethnicity and language

Each of the three groups came to Waterloo with three languages. The Swiss from Pennsylvania spoke the Pennsylvania German dialect and English, but used the High German in formal worship services, primarily for reading Scripture. The Amish, at least those who came from France or the province of Alsace when under

French rule, spoke the Palatinate dialect in their homes and church gatherings, High German in their worship services, and French when dealing with government officials and their French-speaking neighbours.

The Mennonites from Russia spoke the Low German or Plattdeutsch as their mother tongue, used the High German in formal settings, and the Russian language when dealing with government officials and doing business with their Russian neighbours. These Mennonites acquired a fourth language after coming to Canada.

The last language to be learned, English, has now become the dominant one for all three groups. The Swiss conservative and moderate groups, with the exception of the Reformed Mennonite Church and the Old Colony Mennonites, still use Pennsylvania German in their homes and in informal church groups. The Old Colony Church and the Evangelical Mennonite Mission Church both use Low German in family conversations, but are rapidly shifting to English because they are located mostly in towns and cities and are constantly required to speak English. Among the Waterloo-Markham and the Beachy Amish, both in the moderate category, church services are conducted in English. As more of their members find employment off the farm in towns and cities, they find it necessary to speak English. I estimate that up to one-fourth of the words in a typical Old Order sermon are English words, even though the sermons are assumed to be in Pennsylvania German.

Among the progressive and even the moderate Mennonites in the Waterloo area, Pennsylvania German and Low German are rapidly dying out. It is becoming more and more difficult to find members under the age of fifty in the progressive groups who can still speak or even understand more than a few words or phrases of the dialects. The exception to this is found in the post-World War II immigrants who prefer German religious services and the use of the dialect in the immediate family. No general concern has been expressed about the loss of this culture trait. Here and there, older people regret its loss. From time to time, parents enrol children in formal German classes in order to keep them from losing all appreciation for German. These efforts alone, however, will not prevent the eventual loss of the language. "Use it or lose it" applies to a language as well as many other things. But where can it be used regularly if even in the home, church, and friendship groups it is no longer spoken?

Survival of Pennsylvania German

The Pennsylvania German dialect will continue to exist much longer than the Low German, because it is still widely spoken as a mother tongue throughout Waterloo and Perth counties among the Old Order and Beachy Amish, and among the Waterloo-Markham and Old Order Mennonites. Children of these groups will retain it for generations if they continue to live in rural farming communities and separate themselves socially from the rest of society.

The Mennonites from Russia who brought the Low German dialect with them have no comparable rural base. Almost all Mennonites from Russia are town and city dwellers. City cultures tend to discourage the use of dialects by choking out the possibilities of their use. Only in large ethnic population centres can dialects be retained over long periods of time and then only with the greatest of difficulty. Television, movies, newspapers, and magazines, all in English, discourage the use of dialects.

My childhood experience in Pennsylvania illustrates how urban culture quickly quenched the use of dialect in our family. In my parents' Pennsylvania German Mennonite farm family, I was the ninth of eleven children. All of us spoke the dialect at home and had to learn English first in public school. In the middle twenties, my parents moved to a town of about 8,000 people which had few German-speaking people and no Mennonite church. My older brothers and sisters all got jobs in factories or offices. My two younger sisters and I were still in school. At first, we continued to speak the dialect in our new town home as we had on the farm. But slowly we noted that we were the only ones not using English. All our neighbours spoke English. All the places where family members worked spoke English. When we went to church, everyone spoke English. In school, of course, all communications were in English as were all newspapers and weekly magazines in our home.

The radio, then being introduced into American homes, was a further daily reminder that English was the dominant language. Mother, at home alone, had no one to converse with in Pennsylvania German. Of the new friends we as children made, none spoke the dialect. We had been almost completely cut off from an opportunity to speak or even think in our mother tongue. It was inevitable that sooner or later we would switch to English as our family's medium of conversation. Within two or three years, the transition was complete. The dialect was simply no longer useful. The break was even further sealed when eventually seven of my brothers and sisters married non-Pennsylvania German-speaking spouses.

My childhood experience in Pennsylvania was corroborated in Kitchener-Waterloo in 1978 by my research assistants who interviewed 27 former Old Order Mennonite rural residents who had moved to the twin cities after World War II. The mother tongue of all interviewees was Pennsylvania German. All learned English after starting public school. Today, after varying number of years in the cities, the majority of them said they spoke Pennsylvania German only occasionally with each other. Only a few of their children are able to understand the dialect. As parents, they were not concerned about the loss of the dialect.

Pennsylvania German among non-Mennonites

Waterloo County attracted a significant number of non-Mennonites from the Palatinate who spoke the same dialect as the Mennonites. This was especially true among the Catholics and Lutherans who settled at the eastern end of Wilmot township. Interaction between the Roman Catholic Palatinate Germans and the Amish in that area was congenial, and during harvest seasons farmers from those two groups shared work on a barter basis.[1]

Unlike the Amish and the Mennonite experience, however, the use of the dialect among the Catholics and Lutherans disappeared early. For them, the dialect never had the same boundary-keeping function[2] nor the religious meaning that it did for the Amish and the Mennonites. Lutherans and Catholics assimilated more quickly and more willingly with the prevailing culture. Another distinction is that Lutherans and Catholics immigrated more frequently as individuals, single families, or small kinship groups, while Mennonites and Amish tended to immigrate as organized religious and family groups. Furthermore, Catholics and Lutherans did not have a strong religious attachment to the land that the Amish and Mennonites had. Many were labourers

and skilled craftsmen who preferred towns and cities where they
could ply their crafts and establish their own businesses.

	% British	% German	% Other	Total
		Table 6-2		
	Waterloo County's English and German population, 1881-1971			
	By thirty-year intervals[3]			
1881	36.0	57.0	7.0	43,740
1911	38.0	58.0	4.0	62,607
1941	41.0	45.0	14.0	98,720
1971	49.0	29.0	22.0	254,035

Table 6-2 provides evidence of the dominance of the German
population stocks in Waterloo County until after World War II.
The table reflects the century-long contest for dominance between
the German and English nationalities in Waterloo County. It
shows how the Germans were in the majority at the beginning of
the twentieth century but how, at the end of the century, the
English pulled ahead by a 20 percent margin.

Frank Epp in *Mennonites in Canada* points out the attraction
of Canada to the Mennonites. In addition to government under the
British and the abundance of fertile land, they may have been
drawn by the country's strong German cultural element.

> The possible role of German culture in the northward movement
> has, heretofore, been overlooked, but it must not be forgotten that
> Mennonites were still quite German. Their religious activity was
> carried on in the High German of the Luther Bible, and their social
> conversations were in the Pennsylvania German dialect. In
> Pennsylvania, the Mennonites had learned to integrate their reli-
> gion with British politics, German culture, and colonial land as a
> total formula for the good life. That good life had now begun to
> break apart. German culture had felt the fires of the American
> melting pot before 1756. After 1776, the revolution not only ban-
> ished the British Crown but it also hastened the dissolution of the
> German cultural commonwealth.[4]

Other writers have seldom mentioned this point, but it seems
highly significant as an explanation for continuance of the German culture among the Mennonites. It enabled them to set up a
host of small religious communities throughout the county for a
full century before the first serious challenge arose to confront the

dominant Waterloo County Germanic culture. It was no accident
that the county's largest city and industrial centre had proudly
thrived for a century under the name Berlin. The change of the
name to Kitchener also reflects the strong minority population
present in the county and symbolizes the numerical triumph of the
English over the German population fifty years later.

Table 6-3 **Waterloo County ethnic** **composition, 1961 and 1971[5]**			
Ethnic Group	*Rank*	*1961*	*1971*
British Isles	1	71,005	125,390
German	2	69,677	75,395
French	3	6,995	10,770
Polish	4	5,505	6,735
Netherlands	5	3,530	5,195
Ukrainian	6	2,249	3,325
Italian	7	1,950	3,395
Austrian	8	1,776	–
Hungarian	9	1,708	1,708
Scandinavian	10	1,253	1,285
Russian	11	490	848
Czech and Slovak	12	746	–
Native Indian–Eskimo	13	128	–
Finnish	14	126	–
Chinese	15	109	–
Japanese	16	41	–
Asian	17	–	2,605
Other	–	8,753	15,965

The most impressive fact found in Table 6-2 is the 8 percent
increase in the English portion of the Waterloo County population
between 1941 and 1971, while the German population during the
same period decreased by 16 percentof the total. Nationalities
other than English and German also greatly increased in number
after World War II. Table 6-3 reveals the numbers of each nationality represented in the county in 1961 and 1971. In this decade,
only the population from the British Isles had a phenomenal
growth. Ten nationalities had either small or no appreciable
growth during the decade.

Waterloo County in the three decades from 1941 to 1971 reflects a considerable mixture. The social impact this will have on Mennonite life, thought, and behaviour cannot yet be foreseen. However, social interaction in schools, colleges, universities, and workplaces have resulted in intermarriages across ethnic lines and suggest clues to future trends.

Ethnicity and names

Comments frequently heard among Mennonites, such as, "That sounds like a Mennonite name" or "That is not a Mennonite name," clearly reflect consciousness of ethnic identity in Mennonite surnames. The same can be said of other ethnic names such as Scandinavian, Slavic, Italian, French, and Japanese.

An examination of Table 6-4 reflects the persistence with which certain family names are found in each of the three main ethnic streams and in each of the conservative, moderate, and progressive groups. The name "Martin" is especially prolific among the Mennonites of Swiss background. For instance, among the Old Order Mennonites, 633 persons—42.5 percent of the church members in that group—carry the Martin name; 253 or 28.5 percent in the Waterloo-Markham group are Martins, and 332 or 10.7 percent of all members in the Mennonite Conference of Ontario are Martins. Thus a total of 1,218 church members or 22 percent of the total in the three Swiss background groups have the same surname. It should be noted that the Martin name is by no means exclusively a Mennonite possession. The telephone directory for Kitchener lists 309 Martins. Bauman/Bowman, Weber, and Brubacher are also prominent in all three Swiss background groups.

Although all Amish have a Swiss background, none of the predominant family names found in either group appear in both groups. The Mennonites from Russia with a Dutch background likewise have a distinctive set of names not found in either Swiss group. In light of the fact that those coming from Russia to Waterloo came from widely scattered areas in Russia rather than from a single integrated community, it is surprising that there is any concentration of family names. Certain names in each of these groups can be traced back to the seventeenth century.

<table>
<tr><td colspan="6" align="center">Table 6-4
Distribution of most common Mennonite surnames
Percent of church members, Waterloo area, 1971</td></tr>
</table>

Conservative	%	Moderate	%	Progressive	%
		Ethnic Background: Swiss South German			
1,498 members	OOM	887 members	W-M	3,106 members	MCO
Martin	42.5	Martin	28.5	Martin	10.7
Weber	9.2	Bauman	11.4	Snyder	6.2
Bauman	8.8	Weber	10.7	Shantz	5.7
Brubacher	7.8	Brubacher	9.2	Brubacher	4.6
Bowman	5.5	Frey	7.5	Bauman	4.5
Other	26.2	Other	32.7	Other	68.3
		Ethnic Background: Swiss South German Alsace			
		395 members	W-M	1,222 members	MCO
		Jantzi	16.9	Roth	11.3
		Gerber	14.9	Bender	11.3
		Zehr	7.5	Zehr	10.0
		Kuepfer	7.3	Gerber	8.7
		Wagler	6.5	Wagler	8.7
		Other	46.9	Other	50.0
		Ethnic Background: Dutch German Russian			
				866 members	MCO
				Dick, Dyck	6.6
				Reimer	3.6
				Klassen	3.3
				Rempel	2.7
				Neufeld	2.7
				Other	81.1

Nicknames

Many families have the same surnames, and there are also many duplications of given names. This results in practically every male also taking a middle name or initial and sometimes even two for the purpose of distinguishing between those with the same names. In local communities where people come to know each other well, there is a tendency to attach nicknames to people, especially to men. The nicknames may be based on geographical location such as living by a bridge or a creek or in a valley or on a hilltop; they may identify persons by their trade, by certain physical characteristics or distinctive behaviourisms or, in a few instances, they may be titles of honour.

Nicknames which are plainly discourteous are also given, but are seldom used in the presence of the person to whom they apply. They are commonly used by second and third persons obviously with a detracting inference. Table 6-5 presents examples collected by a Waterloo County observer of folkways among the Mennonites. For the benefit of the reader who does not understand the High German or the Pennsylvania German dialect, the nicknames are translated, although in English they lose some of their natural flavour.

The practice of using nicknames to distinguish persons with the same name in close-knit or primary groups is old. The Waterloo Mennonites have at least a two-hundred-year tradition of this practice. A genealogy of the Fretz family compiled by A. J. Fretz,[6] from Bucks County, Pennsylvania, where some Ontario Mennonites originated, reports on four John Fretzes. They were distinguished as Weaver John, Lancaster John, Canada John, and Warwick John. Three Henry Fretzes were distinguished as: Shoemaker Henry, Velvet Henry, and Hurrying Hen. Then there was Big Joe and Fuller Joe Fretz, Lame Anthony, and Tinicum Christian Fretz. The nicknames referred to occupations, geographical locations, and personal characteristics. Velvet Henry acquired his nickname from his custom of wearing velvet pants.

Among Old Order Mennonites, where traditions are strong, it is interesting to note the practice followed in choosing given names. In the Martin congregation, located at the north end of Waterloo, there were 65 male family heads; out of these, there were 43 different given names of which 40 percent were biblical names, the most common of which were Aaron, Amos, James, John, Moses, Noah, Paul, Peter, and Samuel. The other 60 percent were distributed over a variety of names common in any community, such as Alvin, Clayton, Clarence, Henry, Irvin, Milton, and Sydney.

Among the women in this same congregation, as if by design, 40 percent have biblical names such as Esther, Eva, Lydia, Martha, Mary, Rebecca, Salome, and Sara. Among the other 60 percent are Adeline, Ella, Erla, Melinda, Lydiann, Leva, Elmeda, and Susannah.

Table 6-5
Waterloo County Mennonite nicknames

Occupations	Personal Characteristics
Butcher Menno	Bliepencil (Leadpencil) Levi
Dawhglaenah (Day-labourer) Dave	Bludtkopf (Baldhead) Peter
Fertilizer Joe	Cigar Mose
Fieh Kaeffah (Cattle-buyer) Mose	Crazy John
Giles (Horse jockey) Mose	Groszfeesich (Big-footed) John
Hoonich (Honey) Jake	Schtiffel (Boots) Henry
Mangle Soamah (Seed) Menno	Finf (Five) Cent Henry
Hinkle (Chicken) Joe	Fawhssbaennich (Barrel-legged) Dan
Turkey John	Telephone John
Siefeedrah (Pig feeder) Noah	Maeahreddich (Horseradish) Amos
Saegmillah (Sawmiller) Dan	Schwedtzich (Talkative) Noah
Schneida (Tailor) Henry	Chocolate Sam
Schmidtschaap (Blacksmith) John	Gawhksich (Gawky) Mary
Tileyard Amos	Schlaapich (Sloppy) Lizzie
Geographic Locations	Physical Characteristics
Lexington Mose	Grosz (Big) Daniel
Elmira Menno	Glay (Little) Levi
Revvah (River) Dan	Dick (Fat) Mose
Sand Hivvel (Sand Hill) Menno	Dinn (Thin) Jake
Town Line Josiah	Lawhm (Lame) Dave
Schwaamb (Meadow) Sam	Aeh Awrmich (One-arm) John
Yacobschtedel (St. Jacobs) Levi	Lung (Idle) Tom

These names for both males and females seem to be representative throughout the entire Old Order population of 3,000, judging from an examination of the entire list of members and their children. In the Waterloo-Markham group one finds a larger percentage of nontraditional names, especially among younger women. This is in line with the greater latitude of moderates in matters of discipline and in accommodation to change such as dress and the use of English in church services.

Ethnic characteristics of Mennonite congregations
Many churches were officially known by the name of a prominent family or of the family on whose land the meetinghouse was located. In names given to congregations, eleven of the first twelve Mennonite churches still in existence have family names rather than place names. These church family names were or are:

Ben Eby, David Eby, Hagey, Snyder, Shantz, Geiger, Latschar, Cressman, Weber, and Biehn. Churches now extinct with family names were: Bechtel, Clemens, Detweiler, Hallman, Hembling, Reist, and Stauffer.[7]

Even after 150 to 175 years, most of the members in these congregations still have traditional Mennonite family names. This means that after five, six, or seven generations, there have been so few intermarriages with outsiders or so few converts from new families that marriage within the group has consistently taken place. This is true even of newer or "daughter" congregations that have been organized since the middle of the twentieth century.

In the Mennonite Conference of Ontario, ten family names are dominant in 21 congregations. Martin is the most prominent name in five congregations in three different conferences: the Old Order Mennonite, the Waterloo-Markham Mennonite, and the Mennonite Conference of Ontario. The names of Cressman and Shantz are most prominent in four congregations. In eight of the congregations in the Mennonite Conference of Ontario, the leading family name represents at least 20 percent or one out of every five members in those congregations.

Among ten Western Ontario congregations, the names of Bender, Schwartzendruber, Gingerich, and Schultz are most prominent. Practically all congregations listed in this study have a long tradition of endogamous marriages, i.e., marriage within the same conference or ethno-religious group. Growth through the years has been almost entirely by the natural process of excess births over deaths.

The progressive segment of the Mennonite population, which constitutes 65 percent of the total, has lost or is in the process of losing most of its more visible ethnic traces. Another 15 percent, representing the moderates, follow the progressive path. Only the remaining 20 percent of the conservatives are retaining the dialect. Among the Swiss Conservatives, High German is used for Bible reading but is not widely understood. The Mennonites from Russia, who came after World War II, still use High German in church services and understand Low German, but do not use it as a family language, as do the Old Orders of Swiss background. Evidence supporting these two generalizations is seen in the surrender of both High German and much of the Pennsylvania

German and in the adoption of culture traits of Waterloo society in general. The moderate Mennonites still retain the use of the dialect in the homes, but are fluent in the use of English and most of their reading matter is in English. Ethnic foods too are or have gradually given way to food customs in the area. They are mostly produced at times of celebration rather than served as day-to-day fare among the progressive Mennonites. The longer Mennonites are in Canada and the more they move to towns and cities, the more completely they lose their ethnic identities.

It is the conservative 20 percent of Waterloo Swiss Mennonites and Amish who are the chief bearers and the perpetuators of ethnic traditions. It is the conservatives who preserve the Pennsylvania German by using it in their homes, churches, and communities as their chief means of communication. Likewise, the conservative Mennonites restrict marriages to members of their own group and thus maintain another boundary between themselves and secular society. The parochial schools also help to preserve the more distinct customs and culture traits common to the Mennonite tradition. Conservative Mennonites remind progressives of the ethnic traits they gave up long ago.

The Waterloo Pennsylvania German community

At the time I was gathering sociological data about the Mennonites in Waterloo, W. Bausenhart from the Linguistic and Modern Language Centre at the University of Ottawa was doing research on a Linguistic Atlas of the Pennsylvania Germans in Waterloo and adjacent counties.[8] He maintained that the Waterloo County dialect was similar to that spoken in Pennsylvania even after two centuries of separation.

Bausenhart found that the dialect community almost coincided with the Waterloo County boundaries. Only where Mennonites and Amish settled across county lines southwest into Oxford County and west into Perth County did the dialect spread across the Waterloo line. Since his study, the Mennonite population has also spread into Wellington and Grey counties to the east and north. Of 107 farm families surveyed, Bausenhart found a close correlation between religious groups and the use of the dialect. He divided the dialect speakers into three classifications with the results shown in Table 6-6.

Table 6-6 Attitudes of Pennsylvania-German speaking families to future of dialect[9]			
Degree of conservatism	*Most*	*Less*	*Least*	*Total*
Dialect use				
must continue	22	4	7	33
Replace with English	0	1	18	19
Don't care	1	10	39	50
No answer	1	0	4	5
Total	24	15	68	107

Bausenhart found few users of the dialect in the southern part of the county and that in a high percentage of his sample only one spouse spoke Pennsylvania German. This suggests the possibility of mixed marriages. In such instances, there is no likelihood that the dialect will be preserved. The fact that 50 out of 107 families did not care whether the dialect is retained is also a certainty that those families will not retain the dialect.

Finally, there is a strong and constant pressure to switch to the total use of English because it is the dominant language of the country. Both in preaching and social conversation it is difficult, if not impossible, to find German words for mechanical or technological objects like tractor or atom bomb. The same is true for contemporary English verbs, adjectives, and idiomatic expressions. When there is little knowledge of the High German, there is no other recourse for the speaker of Pennsylvania German but to borrow English rather than German words. The progressive groups no longer make any serious attempt to retain the dialect or the High German. The loss of a second and third language is a strong contributor to the loss of a distinctive ethnicity. The shift to nonfarming occupations and to residence in urban communities by moderate group members will contribute to the eventual demise of the dialects among that group as well. Only the Old Orders have any prospect of retaining the Pennsylvania German dialect for future generations. In the light of their present determination and demonstrated capacity to build religious agricultural communities, perpetuate strong family life, and maintain parochial schools to transmit their value systems, there is no reason to assume that they will not retain their ethnic as well as religious character for the foreseeable future.

Ethnic foods

Among Waterloo Amish and Mennonites there are two primary varieties of ethnic foods: the Swiss and the Dutch. Ethnics in the Swiss tradition have been in Canada longest and have few remaining distinctive foods. Their general accommodation to their surrounding culture and customs has included accommodation to food. The widely talked of shoofly pie, composed basically of flour, molasses, or maple syrup baked on a pie shell and decorated with crumbs on top, is no longer the staple ethnic food it once was. Modern dietary considerations have eliminated it as a high priority food item. In many homes, it was a favourite at breakfast with coffee much as sweet rolls are in some homes today. Even at the annual Mennonite relief sale, where ethnic foods are a big attraction, and pies are sold by the thousand, the shoofly pie is not among the most popular. Many of the foods popular among Amish and Mennonites today are equally popular in the population generally. Food items are culture traits easily transmitted from one ethnic group to another.

The Mennonites from Russia who came to Canada more recently than the Swiss have a longer list of ethnic foods still highly popular and regularly used. These include borscht, a type of vegetable soup; zwieback, a type of double bun of kneaded bread dough; vereniky, cottage cheese rolled in dough, boiled, and served with a cream gravy; porzelke, a New Year's doughnut; plume-moos, a plum sauce which can also be made of cherries or other fruit; and pashka, a Russian Easter bread. These distinctive foods will in time be absorbed by the larger society and as cultural inter-marriages take place will tend in time to lose their ethnic distinctiveness.

Distinctive dress

All Mennonites have traditionally emphasized the principle of simplicity as a Christian virtue to be cultivated in all of life. This was to be especially observed in matters of personal attire, for in dress pride and vanity are most frequently and conspicuously displayed. Mennonites through the centuries had not translated the principle of simplicity into specific clothing styles or patterns of dress. The collarless coat, the apron dress, and specific style of head covering like the bonnet for women and black hats for men came to be required dress only in the late nineteenth and early twentieth centuries.[10]

In the area of dress a culture trait of the Amish was already established in the early part of the eighteenth century. When buttons to fasten clothing first came into use in place of hooks and eyes, the followers of Ammann objected to them as symbols of fashion; to this day, Old Order Amish are required to wear clothing fastened only by hooks and eyes.[11] The Old Order Mennonites, the Waterloo-Markham, the Beachy Amish, and the Reformed Mennonites all adhere to regulation dress that is approved as acceptably plain or simple in design and colour. None of the Dutch-Russian ethnic Waterloo Mennonites wear distinctive dress in the sense of a required pattern or colour, nor have they required particular hair styles.

Colourful and distinctive ethnic attire most often reflects distinct nationality rather than religion. The distinctive Amish and Mennonite dress has no national importance. Its significance is strictly religious. Its motivations are based on the attempt to symbolize resistance to vanity and pride. Plain dress is intended to remind members of their commitment to follow Christ and to show that there is a difference in the value systems of the believers and of those in the world.

In summary, food is the least significant of Waterloo Mennonite ethnic traits, and dress and the dialect language the most important. Food is a private matter; dress and language are more publicly noticeable symbols.

Nonconformity and ethnicity

The principles of religious and social nonconformity and separation from the world contributed to the development of Mennonite ethnicity in centuries past. The voluntary surrender of those principles by Mennonites today accounts for the gradual loss of distinctive ethnic characteristics. The very nature of ethnicity implies social and cultural distinctiveness. When there is no longer a distinct language, distinct dress, restrictions on social interaction, and intermarriage, and when there are no longer distinctive food habits, dress, or social control of individual behaviour by the group, it means that all traces of ethnicity have disappeared. It means also that cultural assimilation has taken place. Only the vestige of ethnicity remains. Separate religious identification may also remain, but that in itself does not assure any semblance of ethnicity.

Those classified as moderate are about twenty years behind the progressives in their social accommodation process—the shift toward a total use of English in worship, the adoption of functional technology, and the shift from agriculture to wage earning and business managers and owners. The Old Order Amish and Mennonites are not immune to change, but they will retain ethnic characteristics longest because they are making a conscious effort to retain the tools of ethnicity: daily use of a second language, separation from the larger society, rejection of radio, television, daily papers, automobiles, and, above all, retention of the controlled environment and independent vocation of farming and preservation of traditional family life.

For some, perhaps most, of the progressive Mennonites, the loss of the ethnic label is a goal achieved, a hope fulfilled, not a matter for regret. For them, it is returning Mennonites to a religious denomination without the handicap of an assortment of cultural baggage having to do with hair style, distinctive clothing shades and patterns, a folk dialect which only in-group members can understand, and a lifestyle devoid of many modern conveniences and means of communication. Shedding the ethnic label frees these Mennonites to "let the church be the church."

For what appears to be a small minority, however, the loss of the ethnic label signifies something more than the list of externals mentioned above. For them, these externals are symbols of willingness to subordinate self-will and self-love to God's will and the counsel of the church fellowship. These externals are believed to be paths to humility and sharing. They are believed to be small sacrifices in exchange for group solidarity and spiritual discipline. The end result of the loss of ethnic characteristics among the Waterloo Mennonites has been the development of a Mennonite pluralism characterized by mutual toleration.

Chapter 7

The element of faith in shaping community

Because Mennonites are first and foremost a religious body rather than an ethnic or cultural group, we must devote a chapter to the sociology of Mennonite religion. Sociology makes a distinction between religion and church. Religion is seen as an invisible idea that exists in the minds of people. It is commonly referred to as a spiritual matter.

The church, on the other hand, is visible, a human organization made up of people whose purpose is to teach its members to know and to do the will of God. Sometimes religion and the church are thought of as two separate institutions. It would be more accurate to refer to them as two parts of the same institution. An old definition of an institution is that it is a "concept plus a structure,"[1] a basic idea plus an organization to implement the idea. Thus, religion is the basic idea and the church is the human organization to give expression to it.

Sociologists of religion, like all scientists, see their task as one of accurately observing and describing the structure and function of religion. They do not try to define what is true or false about it. They neither defend nor attack religion. That is left to the theologian, the philosopher, or the teacher of religion. Sociologists are interested in the part that religion plays in the life of individuals, groups, and societies. They want to know how religion affects peoples' lives, how they express their religion, and what people believe religion does for them.

Three elements of all religions
In the early twentieth century, Emil Durkheim, a distinguished French sociologist, identified three elements which he believed were common to all religions: 1) beliefs, 2) rituals, and 3) symbols.[2] He defined beliefs as those shared ideas that explain the

nature of things that a particular religion holds sacred. Rituals are sacred acts through which members of a religion interact with one another in expressing themselves and sharing with others the religious experiences which they think and feel are important. Symbols are objects, images, actions, or words that represent beliefs, reaffirm rituals, and come to have meaning in and of themselves.[3]

The most commonly understood illustrations of beliefs are doctrines, creeds, or confessions of faith. The best known of Christian creeds are the Apostolic and Nicene Creeds. Some religious bodies recite all or portions of one of these creeds in every Sunday worship service; others never recite them.

Common illustrations of rituals are the sacraments or ordinances of Christian churches: baptism, communion, marriage, and ordination. The most prominent symbols of Christianity are the cross, the Bible, the church, whether cathedral or plain meetinghouse, and certain forms of religious attire such as the clerical collar or the prayer veil.

Great is the variety of belief systems, the many forms of ritual, and the great assortment of symbols used by different religious bodies all within the single framework of the religion called Christianity.

Difference of beliefs, rituals, and symbols can be observed among Waterloo Mennonites. In some instances, the differences are distinctly greater between Mennonites than they are between non-Mennonites and other Mennonite groups. Let's consider first the beliefs of Mennonites as reflected in their confessions of faith.

Howard John Loewen in his volume *Mennonite Confessions of Faith in North America*[4] identifies what he calls a common confessional outline in which a number of major accents can be identified within the family of North American Mennonite confessions. The following seven theological categories, he says, follow the lines of the orthodox models of classical theology even though their content differs at a number of points: 1) triune God and creation; 2) word of God and revelation; 3) Jesus Christ and redemption; 4) Holy Spirit and transformation; 5) human nature and salvation; 6) church of Christ and mission; 7) eternal hope and resurrection.

The inner life of the church's mission

Of these seven basic beliefs, says Loewen, the church of Christ and missions receive the strongest accents in the various Mennonite confessions of faith.[5] This area, he says, covers the largest part of their confessions. The emphases concerning the inner nature of the church's life include its goals, membership, offices, mission, ordinances, marriage, and discipline. These seven components of the church are described and identified as to their importance in the Mennonite confessions of faith. The goals of the church are set forth in terms of its biblical basis in the New Testament: its nature, organization, and function; and its general characteristics relating to unity, apostolicity, holiness, universality.[6] Membership in the church is set forth in terms of its nature—its need for regenerate baptized believers to take seriously their responsibilities and duties. The offices of the church are described in terms of the New Testament basis and the institutions of leadership, its qualifications, responsibilities, and ordination: the nature and order of ministry, the service of members, and the servanthood of leaders. The function of the church is described in terms of its internal nurturing and disciplining, and its mission to society.[7]

The ordinances of the Mennonite churches are not called sacraments. They centre around baptism and the Lord's Supper. The mode of baptism and the age of the candidate for baptism is dealt with. In the case of the Lord's Supper or communion, the matter of prior self-examination, right relation with fellow members, and foot-washing as the servanthood example of Christ, is stressed. In some confessions, other articles of faith are noted, among them the role of women, the holy kiss, anointing the sick, marriage, brotherhood, and symbols of separation.[8]

In all confessions marriage as a permanent relationship is stressed and divorce disapproved. But in the latest confessions of the progressive conferences, divorce is no longer cause for excommunication. Emphasis is placed on sacredness of the family and a relationship of love between all members. Loewen observes that singleness is seldom mentioned in any of the confessions. Discipline in the church is described in terms of its New Testament basis. Note that instead of the usual word *biblical*, "New Testament" is deliberately used to distinguish it from the Old Testament. Under discipline, such matters as admonition, separation and withdrawal, excommunication, reinstatement of the offender, and a redemptive attitude of church members are stressed.[9]

The outer life of Christian discipleship

This area of the Mennonite confessions includes nonconformity and discipleship, integrity, oaths, nonresistance and revenge, the Christian and the state, the Lord's day and work. The churches with Swiss background have the strongest emphasis on nonconformity and discipleship, but no uniformity of emphasis. The intent is to maintain a distinction between the kingdom of Christ and the kingdom of the world, sometimes referred to as the kingdom of Satan. The confessions of the Swiss stress holy living and issue warnings against covetousness, worldliness, pride, immodest attire, life insurance, and secret societies. Most of the Mennonite confessions stress the virtue of integrity as reflected in the principle of opposition to the oath. The emphasis again is based on the New Testament (Matt. 5:33-37).

All the confessions give attention to the principle of nonresistance and admonish believers to love their enemies, not seek revenge, and live by the law of love. These admonitions include refusal to take part in war or to take others to court. Believers are not to engage in violence of any kind. Christ is held up as the example. Believers are admonished to respect and pray for their government and be obedient but always to give priority to the higher power of God. Some of the Mennonite confessions also emphasize keeping the Sabbath holy.[10] The Mennonite stress on servanthood is stronger than the emphasis on right belief and correct ritual.

Although Mennonite conferences have confessions of faith, they cannot rightly be classified as creedal churches because their confessions of faith do not carry authority to adjudicate in theological matters. North American and European Mennonite churches' confessional tradition is not a creedal tradition in the classical sense of that term, as in mainline Protestant churches.[11]

Ecumenical implications

The Mennonite confessions of faith cover the majority of the fourteen separate groups included in this study. They speak in a general way to the religion of the Mennonites in the Waterloo area. Howard John Loewen concludes that they have meaning not only for Mennonites but also for all churches.

Loewen says that the Anabaptist vision that has emerged in the twentieth century will need to be considered not only in terms of its Swiss Mennonite origins but also in terms of its continuing Dutch Mennonite developments. It suggests that the twentieth-century vision of Anabaptist origins, which has thus far been considered primarily in theological and historical terms must also be studied in confessional terms.

> Perhaps then the Dutch tradition will do for Anabaptist-Mennonite theology what the Swiss tradition has done for Anabaptist-Mennonite origins. The Dutch Mennonite tradition has given birth to a series of interrelated confessions for each of the Mennonite traditions and has continued to nurture each tradition in a common theology. Hence the Dutch tradition is a basis for affirming the sixteenth-century theology in ongoing, continuous and diverse forms, yet with a remarkably common center.[12]

Loewen says that if the Mennonite confessions, in spite of all their diversity, do reflect a common theological centre, that fact has for too long been overlooked. This has meaning for doing Anabaptist-Mennonite studies within the context of Mennonite denominational pluralism. Mennonites, he says, must turn from maintaining denominational boundaries and begin working from the common theological base of existing denominational confessions. He believes denominational relationships have been too much determined in the past by historical perceptions and misperceptions of one another.[13] Social and cultural differences have frequently been given theological interpretations.

Despite their separate denominations, Waterloo Mennonite confessions of faith have a great deal in common. This is being illustrated at the time this book is being written by the uniting of the three largest Mennonite bodies in Ontario. Each of these bodies brings to this union a distinct religious, cultural, and historical experience: the Swiss Mennonites via Pennsylvania; the Swiss Amish from France and South Germany, and the Dutch from Prussia and Russia. These three streams have now become one. Theological doctrines were no barrier to union.

Mennonite rituals

To a greater or lesser degree, Mennonites in Waterloo all observe rituals. In addition to the two major Christian ordinances, baptism and communion, the Waterloo Amish and Mennonite groups practise other rites: washing of the saints' feet, the holy kiss, and marriage. Some practise anointing of the sick with oil. The moderate and conservative groups of Swiss background observe the *Umfrage* or the inquiry meeting prior to the semiannual communion services.

Rituals vary in the way they are observed. For instance, in communion, some use a common cup, others individual communion cups; some serve communion to the members while seated; others have the people come to the front of the church where they are served by the ordained leaders.

Among the Old Order Mennonites, the bishop serves each participant personally as he moves through the congregation, first with the bread and then the wine. The deacon assists the bishop by providing the elements as needed. The foot-washing ceremony follows the communion service. In this ritual, the women retire to a small anteroom a row at a time while the men observe the rite in the front row of the men's side of the church. The older members begin the ritual and the observances moves through to the youngest members. There are three or four basins and a supply of towels so that two by two the men come forward to wash and dry each other's feet. The rite is completed by the partners rising, shaking hands, and greeting one another with a kiss.

Our purpose here is not to describe Mennonite ritual practices in detail but merely to indicate a few examples of rituals locally practised.

Mennonite symbols

A third universal element of religion found among Waterloo Mennonites is that of symbols. The early Anabaptists opposed the ceremonialism and symbols found in the medieval Roman Catholic Church. Only in recent decades have religious symbols begun appearing in some Mennonite churches. The moderates and Old Orders still prohibit visible symbols in their meetinghouses; this prohibition includes the cross. The Old Orders have many symbols: dress, transportation, separation, education, method of worship; in fact, their lifestyle is full of symbolism.

John Hostetler in the latest edition of *Amish Society* describes the Amish view of the church as the religious community.[14] This characterization could apply to the Old Order Mennonites also.

> The love of God for sinful man requires an appropriate response. This response is "a brotherly community" living in obedience. The model for this "love community"—the life and teachings of the Son of God—emphasizes sacrificial suffering, obedience submission, humility, brotherly love, and nonresistance. Not only is this community made up of surrendered members, but Christ himself is incarnated into the community, or "body." As a corporate offering to God, the brotherly community must be "without spot or blemish" (Eph. 5:27; 1 Pet. 1:19; 2 Pet. 3:14) and must be "a light to the world" (Matt. 5:14). Living in a state of unity and constant struggle to be worthy as "a bride for a groom" (Rev. 21:2), the community must be vigilant, living on the edge of readiness. Within the community the "gift" of God is shared and reciprocated among the members, for since God loves all, "we ought to love each other" (John 3:23). This reciprocation commits members to an indivisible unity according to which each lives in harmony with all the other members.

This brief paragraph summarizes the biblical basis of the most conservative of all branches of the larger Mennonite family of churches. It defines the ideal which the Amish aspire to implement. It serves as a reference group for other churches, Mennonite and non-Mennonite. It is one glimpse into the religion of one branch of the Waterloo Mennonite community.

Hostetler points out that this ideal affects the behaviour of individuals. It has great importance for everyday life because loyalty to God is judged by obedience and conformity to the community's rules of discipline. No other branch of the Amish or Mennonite church makes as great a demand upon its members for holy living in daily life as that of the Old Orders. The justification for this strictness of discipline lies in the principle of nonconformity to the world as expressed in the concept of the "unequal yoke" (2 Cor. 6:14).

Two church types

The religion of Mennonites can best be understood by studying their view of the church. Sociologists have long followed the thinking of Ernst Troeltsch, a German sociologist, who first made a distinction between two types of churches: the church type, and the sect type.

The church type supports the state in times of peace and war, supports the ruling classes, and recognizes the strength and claims of the secular world. It is reluctant to challenge the state for fear of losing its privileged position. It accepts the main elements of the state's rules and defends its decisions as a minimum compromise to maintain harmony with the state. It is said that the church type "dominates the world and is dominated by the world."[15] Because the church type is so tightly interwoven with the state it inevitably becomes an integral part of the existing social order. The emphasis of this type of church is on sacrament and creed and on the inclusive parish rather than on committed believers. It tends to emphasize right belief and correct doctrine. The church type strives to be co-extensive or in tune with society and tends toward ethical compromise. Discipline tends to be moderate and if applied may be more readily used to discipline those who question the faith than those who violate ethical and moral standards.[16]

The sect type of church emphasizes right conduct and ethical behaviour in preference to right theology and proper ritual. Its norms are New Testament-oriented rather than society-oriented. The sect type of church stands in sharp contrast to the church type which is characterized by Troeltsch:

> ... lay Christianity, personal achievement in ethics and religion, the radical fellowship of love, indifference toward the authority of the State and the ruling classes, dislike of technical law and the oath, the separation of religious life from the economic struggle by means of the ideal of poverty and frugality ... the directness of personal religious relationship, criticism of official spiritual guides and theologians, the appeal to the New Testament and the Primitive Church.[17]

These two kinds of churches are to be understood as ideal types, tools with which to analyze the religious situation in society. No such organization exists purely as either one of these types, but all churches tend to have a predominance of one or the other characteristics. It does not mean that one type is good and the other bad. It means that, where given a choice, people have different religious preferences, as they do in other aspects of life such as education, economics, and politics. It means that religion is a by-product of traditions, customs, and culture that help to define the nature of religious beliefs, practices, and organizations in any given society.

On the other hand, religion also has a significant impact in shaping culture and social customs. The evidence of this statement is fairly obvious in communities where there are no churches when compared to those where a large portion of the citizens are active church members. Unchurched communities tend to be disorganized or loosely organized communities; strong churches contribute to the development and maintenance of communities with well-defined social order.

Culture and religion interact

The nature of human social life is so ordered that the two types of churches and their philosophy of religion undergo constant change. These changes are in large part stimulated by the cultural environment in which they operate. The sect type of church is constantly pulled in the direction of the more secular church type. A prime example of this process is the Mennonite church in the Netherlands. Religious toleration came to that country earlier than to the rest of Europe. When persecution ceased and Mennonites enjoyed the same civil liberties as other citizens, many soon rose to wealth and prominence in urban business, industry, and the professions. With that rise in status also came economic and political influence and power.

By the middle of the seventeenth century, Thielman van Braght, a pastor in Dordrecht and the editor of the famous *Martyrs' Mirror*, was alarmed at the speed with which his church in Holland was becoming secular. His concerns are described by Alan Kreider:[18]

> His baptist-minded contemporaries, he was convinced, were "proceeding in [their] pilgrimage in the absence of the Lord" and were being seduced by Satan. Whereas a century earlier Satan had come in undisguised malevolence, as a persecuting "roaring lion," now he was coming as a "kind, pleasant, even divine messenger," as the bearer of safety and luxury. The baptist-minded, whose Anabaptist forebears had been tortured and burned, were living in expensive and ornamented houses. They were "wearing . . . clothes from other countries." They—even "those who are considered sober and temperate"—were selfishly consuming large quantities of expensive food, "of which a portion naturally belongs to the poor." In the light of their now comfortable existence, it is hardly

surprising that their theology and ethics has changed. The Anabaptists had gone to the stake for the sake of fidelity to Jesus' hard
sayings—"the external commandments and ordinances of Christ;"
in contrast, van Braght's contemporaries were comforting themselves that no more was required of the believer than repentance
and faith, coupled with respectability ("a so-called irreproachable
civil life"). By the late 1650s the baptist-minded . . . had made
their peace with the world—from van Braght's view, on unfavor-
able terms.

The two-kingdom theory

Van Braght's views of the nature of the Christian churches is
based on a two-kingdom theology. The two churches for him represented the constant warfare between God and Satan. The one
church, according to van Braght, descended from Cain and was
the persecuting church; the other church descended from Abel
and was the suffering church. The former had been coercive,
inventing and enforcing infant baptism; the latter had been
voluntarist, teaching adult baptism. The former sanctioned war
and claimed that one may spread and defend religion with the
sword; the latter were a nonresistant people.

   Van Braght's view of the two contrasting church types
foreshadowed Troeltsch's typology three hundred years later,
although the seventeenth-century view is phrased in theological
terms while the twentieth-century view is expressed in sociological language. Both writers observed that the Christian religion
was expressed in two distinct forms and both recognized that
changes in religious attitude and practice are shaped by cultural
environment.

Believers' church concept a radical view

Many contemporary Mennonites do not understand the radical
nature of the church to which they belong. Their church is no
longer considered radical by most Mennonites or by non-
Mennonites. In fact, it is regularly classified as a conservative
religion. Radical means proceeding from the root; reaching to the
centre or ultimate source, affecting the vital principle, hence
thoroughgoing or extreme. The radical element is derived from
the attempt of not just a saintly few but an entire congregation to
be governed by the love ethic and exemplary life of Jesus. No

wonder Mennonites were sometimes referred to as Protestant monastics.

Franklin Littell, in *The Anabaptist View of the Church* makes these interesting comments:

> There is something deeper than mere Biblicism in this social program. It is part of an outlook on life which can best be described under the concept of Primitivism. If we inquire as to the goal of these Anabaptist groups we are driven at first not forwards but backwards. Their objective was not to introduce something new but to restore something old. "Restitution" was their slogan, a Restitution grounded in the New Testament. And surrounding their groups was a certain atmosphere whose precipitation point was a certain vision of the Early Church. . . . The single thread running through the Left Wing was this dream of the Early Church.[19]

Emphasis on doing the will of God

These sixteenth-century references to the essential nature of the Anabaptist-Mennonite idea of the church are important for understanding the sociology of Waterloo Mennonite religion. Theological creeds and confessions of faith in Mennonite churches have been somewhat like the written constitutions of political, social, and economic organizations. They are essential explanations of the purpose, function, and guidelines for operation, but once in operation they are seldom referred to except in times of difficulty or the need for a change of course. Mennonite churches do not as a matter of custom or tradition regularly repeat a theological creed as a part of their regular worship service. Church members, therefore, are not constantly reminded of the theological beliefs for which their church stands and to which they at one time made commitment but are constantly admonished to do the will of God in daily life.

In concluding the discussion of religion among Waterloo Mennonite groups, we cannot avoid pointing out the presence of the two universal ideal types of churches. The conservatives have clear earmarks of what sociologists have referred to as sect or Gemeinschaft types of organized religion, and the progressive denominations tend more and more to reflect the characteristics of what are referred to as church or Gesellschaft types of religion. As stated before, no church fits perfectly into either of the so-called ideal types but all tend to fit to a greater or less degree into one or the other type.

Interestingly, each of the fourteen Waterloo Mennonite church bodies claims to be a bona fide Mennonite church. All claim to be New Testament-based, theologically orthodox, in the sense of adhering to the great creeds of Christianity. All acknowledge Menno Simons as the founder of the Mennonite church. The motto: "In essentials unity, in nonessentials liberty" serves all Mennonite groups equally well since each group interprets the terms according to its own understanding. As a result, such practices and principles as foot washing, the holy kiss, the exercise of discipline, simplicity, frugality, separation, nonconformity, the oath, military service, and participation in politics and other aspects pertaining to lifestyles are variously defined and either adhered to or neglected. Religious services are observed and leadership provided in the traditional manner.

In Waterloo, the sect- or Gemeinschaft-type Mennonites tend to be the smaller, rural churches with members largely engaged in farming and related occupations. Church membership tends to be stable and family interrelated with social control exercised through firm church discipline. The church- or Gesellschaft-type tends to be located in towns and cities, to be larger in membership. Members favour education through high school and beyond and are engaged primarily in nonfarming occupations, many in business, the professions, and government service. Social control of members by means of church discipline is largely abandoned. Patterns of church organization and worship have gradually been adapted to those commonly used in mainline Protestant churches. Waterloo Mennonite religion is clearly pluralistic in organization and practice.

Chapter 8

Being the church and doing its work

The Mennonites are the oldest of forty denominations in Waterloo County. They have the largest number of congregations of any denomination; however, this does not mean that they have the largest membership. They stand sixth in rank after Roman Catholics, United Church of Canada, Lutheran, Anglican, and Presbyterian.[1]

Throughout their almost two-hundred-year history in Waterloo County, a dominant characteristic of the Mennonite churches has been their relatively small, intimate, extended family type of congregations. These churches have retained the Gemeinschaft or bonded fellowship type of member relationships which influenced all other aspects of members' lives.

In my census of 1972, I found 16,000 Mennonite men, women, and children in what I describe as the Waterloo area's "natural Mennonite community."[2] Six of 14 Waterloo Mennonite groups came to Canada as separately organized religious groups. The other eight originated in Canada.

Figure 8-1 shows that Waterloo County's Roman Catholic Church membership is more than twice as large as that of the two largest Protestant groups: the Lutherans and the United Church of Canada; and more than six times as large as the total Mennonite membership. The Lutherans and the United Church of Canada each had three times as many members as the Mennonites, and the Anglicans had almost twice as many. The Presbyterians were also more numerous than the Mennonites, although they had only one-third as many congregations. Size of membership is of course only one window through which to look at a religious organization. Throughout much of Mennonite history, large church membership was impossible. Moreover, a small Gemeinschaft

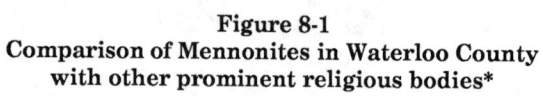

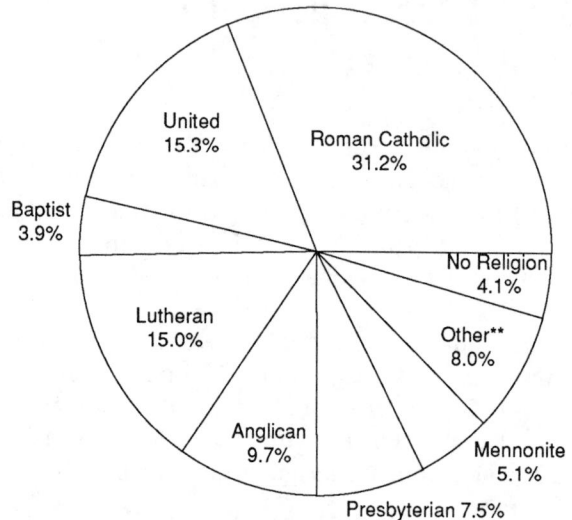

Figure 8-1
Comparison of Mennonites in Waterloo County
with other prominent religious bodies*

Major Organized Religious Bodies in Waterloo County,
Based on 1971 Canadian Government Census Data

*The question asked was "What is your religion?"
**Includes, in order of frequency: Pentecostal, Greek Orthodox, Salvation Army, Jewish, Ukrainian Catholic.

type of a disciplined church was in keeping with the Mennonite ideal of organized religion.

Mennonites as conservative, moderate, or progressive

One criterion for identifying the fourteen Mennonite church groups is their degree of resistance to social and cultural change, or, to state the reason positively, their degree of readiness to accept social and cultural change. For measuring resistance to social change, eight socio-ethical values commonly identified with traditional Mennonite principles of faith and life were used:

1.   Social separation from the world.
2.   Commitment to simplicity and frugality.

Table 8-1
Mennonite groups,
in order of appearance in Waterloo County

Founded	Name (and abbreviation)	1972 Churches in study	Member- ship
1800	Mennonite Conference of Ontario (MCO)	21	2,646
1824	Old Order Amish (OOA)	5	228
1844	Reformed Mennonites (RM)	1	114
1886	Western Ontario Conf. (WOC) (Amish, 1824-86)	10	2,116
1889	Mennoniten-Gemeinde (OOM)	8	1,198
1904	Beachy Amish (BA)	2	304
1917	David Martin Old Order (DM)	1	191
1925	United Mennonite Churches of Ontario (UMCO)	2	746
1925	Ontario Conference of Mennonite Brethren (OCMB)	3	555
1939	Waterloo-Markham (W-M)	5	771
1953	Elam Martin Old Order (EM) (Disbanded 1979)	1	98
1960	Conservative Mennonite Conference (CMC)	3	224
1969	Evangelical Mennonite Mission Church (EMMC)	1	35
1970	Old Colony Mennonites (OCM)	1	50
	Total	64	9,276

See Appendix 1 for notes on each of above Waterloo Mennonite groups.

3. Recognition of the importance of regular meetings for public worship.

4. Nonconformity to changing fashions in dress and hair styles.

5. Limitation of formal education to the elementary level.

6. Resistance to new discoveries and inventions.

7. Adherence to the use of a second language in domestic settings.

8. Voluntary subordination of the individual will to the counsel and welfare of the church fellowship.

Eight of the fourteen Mennonite groups were measured on a scale ranging from 1 to 5 (Table 8-2). Those keeping to the traditional socio-ethical values most closely were rated 1 and those who adhered least closely were rated 5. Total scores were used to determine each Mennonite group's category. There is a strong element of subjectivity involved in this process, but the nature of the situation makes truly objective evaluation difficult.

Table 8-2
Conservative-progressive rating scale of eight
Mennonite groups*

Ethical Values	I	II	III	IV	V	VI	VII	VIII	Score
Conservative									
OOA	1	1	1	1	1	1	1	1	8
OOM	1	1	2	1	1	2	1	1	10
Moderate									
W-M	2	2	2	2	2	5	3	2	20
BA	2	2	2	2	2	5	3	2	22
Progressive									
WOC	3	3	4	3	4	5	4	4	30
MCO	4	4	4	4	4	5	5	5	35
MBO	5	5	5	5	5	5	4	4	38
UMO	5	5	5	5	5	5	4	4	38
Totals	23	23	25	23	24	33	25	21	201

*Old Order Amish, Old Order Mennonite, Waterloo-Markham, Beachy Amish, Western Ontario Conference, Mennonite Conference of Ontario, Mennonite Brethren Churches of Ontario, United Mennonites of Ontario.

These criteria may be used as a basis for the reader's own evaluation of the various Mennonite groups.

The more progressive the group, the more similar are their sociological characteristics. Time also tends to contribute to the gradual diminishing of differences.

Waterloo Mennonite community's unique diversity

I know of no other Mennonite community which has the ethnic and organizational diversity of the Waterloo community. The fourteen groups treated in this study represent three separate ethnic strands and in each of these strands are church organizations which have one or more congregations classified as conservative, moderate, or progressive. Table 8-3 shows the distribution of the fourteen branches according to nationality background and one of three social accommodation classifications.

In Waterloo, divisions occurred in all three ethnic strands largely over differences of rates of accommodation to change in the Ontario culture. There were controversies among the Amish over

Table 8-3 Mennonites by country of origin and by cultural accommodation			
Country of Origin	*Conservative*	*Moderate*	*Progressive*
Switzerland, South Germany	Old Order Menn. David Martin O.O.	Waterloo- Markham	Mennonite Conference of Ontario*
	Elam Martin O.O. Reformed Menn.*	Conservative Menn.	
France, So. Germany	Old Order Amish*	Beachy Amish	Western Ontario Mennonite Conference*
Holland, Prussia	Old Colony Menn.*	Evang. Mennonite Mission Church**	United Mennonite Churches of Ontario* Mennonite Brethren Churches of Ontario*

*Immigrated as an organized church.
**Began as a mission to Old Colony Mennonites.

worshipping in homes versus meeting in houses and over adopting newer technologies such as automobiles, tractors, and telephones. Among the Swiss Mennonites, differences occurred on these issues and the question of adopting the English language in worship services. The latest significant split occurred in the early sixties when the Conservative Mennonite Conference felt that the Conference of Mennonites of Ontario was becoming too worldly, adopting social and cultural changes at so rapid a rate as to threaten existing religious values.

Most of the Mennonites with a Dutch-Prussian-Russian background were culturally progressive when they immigrated to Canada. The small conservative and moderate representative churches among them represent two different origins. They are descendants of the Mennonites who came from Russia to Canada in the 1870s. In the 1920s, after World War I, they migrated to Mexico in protest of Manitoba's and Saskatchewan's provincial government interference in the operation of their own school systems. Since World War II, because of economic hard times, many of these Mennonites in Mexico have returned to Canada. Over

1,000 found opportunities for work in southern Ontario. Some of these drifted into Waterloo County and formed a small church.

Churches as bureaucracies

By contrast, the four conference groups that make up the progressive category of Waterloo Mennonites reflect formal organization. They, like the mainline Protestant denominations, have accepted modified forms of the corporate structures of business and industry. Indeed, the progressive Mennonite church organizations have the same detailed separation of function and stratified layers of administration as do business corporations, and so may be classified as bureaucracies. No insult is intended by so describing this type of church organization. A bureaucracy is "a trained and specialized administrative staff responsible for devising, overseeing, and coordinating the activities of other participants in an organization."[3]

There is nothing necessarily unethical about a bureaucratic church organization as such. It involves a large contingent of mostly volunteer, rather than paid, church members. It is an efficient way of conducting business in an orderly way where there are many individuals and numerous sub-organizations under a central authority.

The progressive Mennonites have moved in the direction of an increasing number of paid staff. Practically all of the congregations in the four progressive conferences have full-time, paid, and seminary-trained ministers. Larger congregations may also have other paid personnel such as associate pastor, youth minister, minister of music, church secretary, and custodian.

Council type of church government

The progressive Mennonite groups operate under a council type of government, based on the democratic principle of authority resting in the hands of the church members. Each member has one vote and all major matters of business are determined by the church members at duly called congregational meetings unless a matter is specifically delegated to the church council. This council is the official governing agency of the congregation between congregational meetings.

The council is generally composed of a chairperson, vice-chairperson, a secretary, and a treasurer, all elected by the congregation. These four officers constitute the executive committee. In addition, the chairperson of each board—such as the board of deacons, the board of education, the board of missions and service, and the board of trustees and finance—serve on the church council. Also, there may be presidents of auxiliary organizations (the women's organization, the youth group, etc.), the chairpersons of standing committees, and the director of music. Members of boards are generally elected by the congregation, and committee members are appointed by the council or by one of the boards.

Progressive minister's role

The total number of persons in these congregations who serve in some official capacity constitute a substantial percentage of the total membership. Ministers in the progressive conferences, in contrast to those in the conservative and moderate groups, perform a relatively minor role in much of the decision-making of the congregations. In most cases, they are ex officio members of boards and committees, but the majority of decisions are made and are carried out by lay members. The ministers tend to be co-ordinators and implementers of what lay members decide rather than determiners of congregational policies.

This does not mean that ministers in progressive churches are not respected or do not participate in decision-making or do not provide innovative leadership. It means that ministers in the progressive churches are hired employees. They come and go after varying lengths of service. They come to a church as outsiders and must spend time becoming acquainted with their members, the congregation's history, its resources, strengths, weaknesses, and numerous unseen items or hidden agendas. Hired ministers can never quite have the identity with a church as can a minister who was chosen out of the congregation. The latter needs no orientation to the congregation nor need fear being voted out by members for taking unpopular positions on controversial issues.

A progressive church organization

An example of the corporate model and bureaucratic character of a progressive church organization in the Kitchener-Waterloo area is presented below.

The church council: consists of twelve members; four of these serve as the executive committee.

Four boards: Deacons (6); Missions and Service (6); Education and Publication (7); Trustees and Finance (6).

Board members are elected by the congregation for three-year terms.

The Council of Boards consists of all Church Council, board members, and chairpersons of standing committees, for a total of 38.

Music Committee (5)

Personnel Committee (6)

Visiting Committee (19)

Positions filled by church council appointments:
Church historian
Chairperson of ushers
Auditors (2)
Social Convener
Mennonite Credit Union representative
Head Greeter
K-W Council of Churches representative
Mennonite Mutual Aid representative
Music director and organist (paid)

Positions filled by the Board of Education:
Youth sponsors (4)
Library committee (5)
Bible School representative
News editor
Children's church director
Church news correspondent
Wayfarers' sponsors (3) (girls' weekday club)
Torchbearers' sponsors (3) (boys' weekday club)

Appointed by the Board of Trustees:
Treasurer and assistant treasurer
Financial secretary
Church secretary
Custodian and janitor (2) (part-time)

Women's Missionary Association (11 offices, 19 persons)
Young People's Society (8 executive committee members)

In this particular church, 114 persons performed one or more official functions. Since most terms of offices are for one- to three-year periods and elected members, in most cases, are not eligible for more than two successive terms, about one-third to one-half of the active members are performing one or more regular functions in the church at any one time. The Inter-Mennonite Conference Yearbook for 1982 describes a relatively similar organization and programs of activity in each of the congregations in the three largest progressive conferences (MCO, WOC, and UMC). The organizational structure and high percentage of member involvement in these churches is especially significant in the smaller congregations. For them it can mean that almost all mentally and physically able members can be expected to perform some active church role in addition to attending services. An examination of the number and variety of interests and activities pursued and the high percentage of members actively involved in carrying out the church programs suggests that the priesthood of believers idea is alive and in practice in progressive Waterloo Mennonite churches.

The extensive organization described above is a direct reflection of the constantly expanding service programs in these churches. The activities embrace all ages and both sexes and cover a wide range of concerns within the Waterloo community, and worldwide relief service and missions.

Several Waterloo Mennonite congregations have women co-pastors and solo pastors. Use of women in church and conference leadership roles has also become a commonly accepted practice in recent decades.

A significant aspect of Mennonite religious organization in the progressive local congregations is the way they are linked to community or conference activities by means of one or more lay representatives. It is the pattern in all the congregations of the three largest progressive conferences. This means that not all communications about church activities flow through the office of the pastor nor are all these duties the responsibility of the pastor. It is an example of assigning responsibility to laymen who have special interests and qualifications to perform such tasks. It is also an effective way of tying a congregation or a support group within a congregation to a community- or conference-wide program. Examples of such a linkage system found in progressive Waterloo

Mennonite congregations with specific causes outside the local congregation are listed below.

Congregational links with conference and community

1. Conference Education Committee
2. Conrad Grebel College Women's Association
3. Family Life Consultants
4. Mennonite Historical Society of Ontario
5. House of Friendship
6. Mennonite Aid Union
7. Mennonite Benefit Association
8. Mennonite Central Committee
9. Mennonite Credit Union
10. Mennonite Disaster Service
11. Mennonite Youth Fellowship
12. Rockway Collegiate
13. Women's Missionary Association
14. Canadian Bible Society
15. Interfaith Pastoral Counselling

These multiple activities are supplemental to, and not substitutes for the Sunday worship service. The auxiliary activities are the outgrowth of concerns about ways in which church members might render service in areas of need in the wider community.

Among the far-reaching implications of this extensive organizational expansion is its provision of opportunity for youth to become actively involved in the work of the church. Young people are not only involved in their own organizations, but today are appointed and elected to official church boards and committees. It is assumed that this stimulates interest on the part of youth in the church. It has resulted in many young people volunteering for two, three, or more years to work in areas of need in welfare agencies, senior citizen centres, and third world countries through mission boards and international service agencies such as the Mennonite Central Committee. For many young people, this has resulted in a deeper commitment to their churches and, in some cases, to entering into full-time service of the church.

The second type of church organization characteristic of the six conservative groups and four in the moderate category is simple and highly informal. This type of organization can be compared to an extended or patriarchal family organization in that it operates more by tradition and unwritten rules than by formal organization. This simple organization tends to work well because the extent of church activity is primarily confined to biweekly Sunday morning worship services and the membership is constant. None of the conservative groups have Sunday schools or any other auxiliary activities. Only the two moderate groups (CMC and EMMC) have Sunday schools, but in both groups the congregations are small and need no more elaborate organization. In all but the one (EMMC) congregation, the ministers are chosen by lot from their respective congregations. This, too, is based on tradition and when it occurs it preserves the organizational status quo rather than introducing new ideas or methods as a result of a change of leadership. Church membership in these small congregations also tends to be stable over a long period of time and, to the extent that separation from the world is practised, there is little chance of outside stimulus to change.

Church leadership

In Waterloo Mennonite churches, there are varying philosophies and forms of church leadership. The conservative groups see leadership as a strongly authoritative role, symbolized and enforced by the method of choosing leaders by lot, thus acquiring a stamp of divine approval on both man and method. The progressives, on the other hand, have adopted the democratic model of electing leaders, including pastors, by popular vote of their members. The person chosen by popular vote is considered a servant of God, and held in high esteem by the membership. The minister in progressive churches is, like the politician, elected to public office in the sense that he or she is constantly subject to criticism. Both politician and preacher are accountable to the people who elect them. This tends to make tenure in both professions somewhat unstable and generates pressure on both politicians and preachers. Church members by virtue of their votes are also automatically partial employers.

In both the conservative and moderate Waterloo church groups, except for the EMMC, the leadership is still chosen by lot. Leadership is defined in these groups by a three-tier system. At the top is a bishop who is chosen from among the ministers. He is in charge of all ritual services such as administering communion, conducting the foot-washing service, performing weddings and baptisms, and leading funerals and congregational meetings. Next to him in rank is the minister who preaches regularly and performs ritual ceremonies when the bishop is unable to preside. Third in line is the deacon. He, like the bishop and minister, is ordained and chosen for life.

Since these churches have Sunday services in their own meetinghouse only every other Sunday and visit a neighbouring congregation on the open Sunday, there are generally two ministers and two deacons at every worship service. They are seated on the preachers' bench behind the pulpit and participate in each service attended. If the bishop is present, he makes the fifth person on the bench and the fifth person to participate in the service, if only to give a verbal testimony following the second sermon. The combined ministers, deacons, and bishop constitute the group's leadership. Their decisions generally are the church's voice of authority and are seldom openly challenged.

This authoritative leadership structure may have contributed to the formation of small splinter groups and new congregations. The conservative churches have no open forum for free discussion of controversial issues, no mechanism for giving or receiving criticism from the congregation as a whole. The existing channels for criticism are through the ordained leaders at the spring and fall inquiry sessions prior to communion. It is ironic that the conservative Mennonites who so highly respect and observe tradition should so largely deny in practice the concept of the priesthood of believers, while the progressives, who treat tradition more lightly, should be devising ways to expand the concept of the priesthood of believers in actual practice.

Church historian Franklin Littell says that Anabaptists firmly rejected the distinction in the established church between clergy and laity and considered every member to be a minister of one kind or another. He says: "In Anabaptism there began ... that ministry of the whole people by virtue of their ordination in Christian baptism."[4]

Nevertheless, it is well known that early in their history, Anabaptists and early Mennonites had ordained members of their churches for the shepherding of local congregations and for preaching the Word to unbelievers. Their distinction at first, says Littell, was not that they had no clergy, but that they had no laity since, at least in theory, every member was his own priest.

Table 8-4
Contrasting characteristics of ministerial roles
Based on four conservative and four progressive groups

Items	Conservatives	Progressives
Recruitment	Chosen by lot from congregation	Normally chosen from candidates in denomination
Support	Self-supported, by farming and other jobs	Paid an agreed-upon salary
Education	Elementary school	College and seminary graduates
Language	High German and Pennsylvania German	English; German for recent immigrants
Sermons	Totally extemporaneous	Prepared topical and biblical expositions
Attire	Prescribed black hats and dark, plain coats	Conventional dress styles
Tenure	Serve for life	Terms fixed by contract
Social	Highly respected by virtue of office	Status depends on person and on performance

---

Table 8-4 once again points to the wide gap between the practice of two groups of churches that live side by side, have a common spiritual heritage, and fly the same denominational banner. Despite these visible and invisible social differences and contrasting organizational patterns, there is general respect for each other and little criticism of differing practices.

In all eight of the leadership factors selected for comparison, the progressives have adopted procedures and patterns of organization similar to those of the mainline Protestant churches.

Contrast in amount of leaders' education

In reflecting on the organizational and sociological contrasts of the Mennonite conservatives and progressives, an old intellectual question comes to mind. How much difference can there be in form before the difference affects substance? In the case of leadership education, for instance, it is not likely that one group of ministers can have only an eighth-grade education while the other group has four years of high school, plus four years of college and three years of seminary without having this affect the kind and quality of church organization. There is a difference of eleven years of education, three of which are focused on acquiring skills of communicating, knowledge of biblical history, theology, interpretation, and pastoral counselling. These differences in leadership education reflect similar differences in the educational level of the respective lay members of the two groups.

Church finances

An integral part of the church organization is that of church financing. Waterloo Mennonite churches reflect aspects of both capital-intensive and labour-intensive methods of financing. At one end of the scale is that of the Old Order Amish, who worship in the homes of members and therefore have no capital expenditures for buildings or maintenance. The Old Order Mennonites have plain, one-storey, rectangular meetinghouses in the open country, usually erected on land of one of their members. Their construction costs are confined to building materials, since the men of the church erect, repair, and maintain their meetinghouses. The capital investment in these church facilities is therefore relatively small. A new brick meetinghouse was erected by Old Order members in 1972 at a total cost for building materials of less than $17,000. The meetinghouses accommodate anywhere from two hundred to five hundred persons.

Small country congregations of moderate and progressive denominations have greater expenditures for their meetinghouses because they generally have finished basements with fully equipped kitchens and Sunday school rooms. Moreover, the sanctuaries on the main floor are furnished with commercially manufactured pews, central heating, lighting, and carpeting. It is generally necessary to employ some skilled craftsmen to provide these additional amenities, which quickly increases the cost of the erection and maintenance of the building. The large congregations in towns and cities require large buildings and more equipment, therefore a larger investment of capital. With the larger facilities come larger maintenance and operating costs. City church members usually are not able to erect their own buildings because they lack the necessary time and the required skills.

The Waterloo conservative and progressive Mennonites also differ in their methods of church financing. The conservatives and two of the moderate groups in the Swiss ethnic tradition do not receive offerings during their Sunday worship services. Their expenses are met by periodic requests for contributions.

Sacrificial sharing

Sometimes unexpected emergencies arise. A specific case came to my attention while attending an Old Order Sunday morning service. At the close of the service, the deacon arose and quietly announced that the congregation's share of a damage suit was $15,000 and that he would be at the meetinghouse on a certain day during the week to receive contributions for this cause. Two young men riding on a tractor in a snowstorm accidentally ran into a car parked on the road. The occupant of the car, although not severely hurt, instituted a lawsuit for a large amount. The suit was eventually settled for less than originally asked for.

These two young men and their father were supported by the entire Old Order fellowship of twelve hundred members. Each of the eight congregations at that time assumed a proportionate share of the liability assessed to the sued party. On the basis of the number of households in that congregation, this meant that the average assessment per family head was just over $200. This is an apt illustration of being one's brother's keeper; members in a church can feel secure when disaster hits a particular family.

Two methods of church financing

All progressive congregations integrate their church giving in the regular Sunday morning worship services. Progressive churches draw up an annual budget. They attempt to anticipate both the amount of contributions and the expenditures for the year ahead and the amount and purposes to be allocated to each of the numerous causes to which a church commits itself.

Progressive and conservative church methods of financing reflect the social and economic background of their members. As the standard and the level of living of individual members rises, so too do the levels of income and spending of the churches. This is more visible among the progressives than among the conservatives. The progressive churches have many more activities than the conservatives and many more of those activities require cash outlay.

An important factor contributing to the low per-member cost of medical care is the established custom of free labour in times of accident or illness which cannot be taken care of by the particular family. It is not uncommon for relatives, neighbours, and/or friends to take turns attending patients around the clock for days and weeks if circumstances require it. This form of mutual aid naturally eliminates extended hospitalization and expensive hired help for home care. The custom requires putting the emergency needs of others before normal demands of personal schedules.

The contrast in the extent of activities and the cash outlay is clearly shown in Table 8-5. The financial figures in the table reflect 1972 dollars. The importance of the information is not in the value of contemporary dollars, but in the difference the programs and the number of activities which those dollars represented in each group. The table clearly shows that the one is capital-intensive and the other labour-intensive, but in this instance, the labour is mostly voluntary. Therefore, in contrast to business and industry, labour is the low rather than the high cost item.

In Table 8-5, the progressive church is one single congregation with less than four hundred members, whereas the conservative church represents the annual financing of eight congregations and twelve hundred members, because the eight congregations are one single organization but have eight meetinghouses. The finances in the illustration represent the total for the Old Order Mennonites in one particular year. The per-member cost of hospitalization among the Old Orders in 1972 was $38, while the cost of that service for the single church's pastor for Ontario Hospital Service (OHS and OHIP) was $295 or almost eight times as high. Note that the per capita giving of the conservatives is slightly higher

Table 8-5
Two contrasting methods of church financing

Progressive Church 1972 Budget		Conservative Church 1972 Expenditures	
Internal expenses			
Property and equipment	$2,800	Minimal, if any	
Utilities and telephone	2,775	None	
Insurance and taxes	900	None	
Office supplies & equip.	1,000	None	
	$7,475		
Paid personnel			
Pastor	–	None	
Church secretary	–	None	
Music staff	–	None	
Custodians	–	None	
Fringe benefits:			
Car allowance & travel	–	None	
Pensions	–	None	
Hospitalization insurance	–	None	
Workers' compensation and unemployment insurance	–	None	
Total personnel cost	$21,880	Paid out of deacons' fund	
Total internal expenses	$29,355		
(Represents 52 % of budget)			
		Benevolence and Mutual Aid	
Benevolences			
Missions abroad and in Canada	–	Aid to own poor	$8,276
Missions and service locally	–	Relief outside church	5,793
Mennonite Central Committee	–	Hospitalization	45,427
Warden Woods and Welcome Inn	–	For new meetinghouse	16,685
Bible Society	–		
Total benevolences	$18,300	Total benevolences	$76,181
(Represents 32 % of budget)		(Represents 42 % of expenditures)	
Education		**Education**	
Conference boards of education	–	Capital expenditures	$57,412
Associated Mennonite Seminaries	–	Teachers' salaries	23,800
Conrad Grebel College	–	Administration	20,355
Rockway Collegiate	–	Interest on loans	3,814
Church periodical	–		
Youth program	–		
Total education budget	$9,100	Total education expenses	$105,383
Total budget	$56,755	Total expenses	$181,564
Giving per member (391 members)	$145.15	Giving per member (1198)	$151.55

than that of the progressives in the year under observation. The difference is that the conservatives contribute to the support of their own medical and hospitalization plan, their own school system, and their own welfare program. The per capita giving for benevolences among the conservatives in 1972 was $63, while the average for the progressives in that same year was $52.

An examination of Table 8-5 reveals surprising information about the financial picture of the two Waterloo Mennonite churches. The overall per capita giving is remarkably similar, but the causes supported in each church are vastly different, or at least financed differently. The progressive church spends half of its money to operate its own plant and support personnel, whereas the conservative church spends practically nothing for that purpose. The progressive per-member giving for benevolence is $46, while the conservative per-member giving for benevolence is $63. The difference in the causes supported, however, indicates that the progressive's dollar is contributed for causes outside the church, while the conservative's dollar is used to support causes within the church, the parochial school program, the care of the church's poor, and the church hospitalization plan.

Who is to judge which of the two methods of church financing is superior? It is merely a reflection of the respective points of view regarding religion, the church, and personal value systems. The one represents the traditional Mennonite church method with few adaptations over the centuries; the other represents many adaptations over the generations. Neither system would be satisfactory to the other group.

Church facilities

Physical facilities in the Waterloo Mennonite churches, such as the church building, styles of architecture, internal furnishings, and the use of space vary characteristically. In the meetinghouses of the conservative groups, few if any changes have been made and no architectural styles modified for over a century, except that the more recently constructed meetinghouses are of brick rather than of wood. The progressive congregations have made many visible changes. It can probably be said without fear of contradiction that every one of the 47 congregations in the progressive category has either erected a new building or significantly remodelled their old one between 1950 and 1980.

The architectural style of the rural churches has tended to follow the simple lines of the traditional plain rectangular meetinghouse. The new and/or modified buildings of the progressives have been enlarged and new pews, chancel furniture, and carpeting installed. Additional space has been provided for religious education purposes. Most churches have installed kitchens and added space for congregational fellowship meals. Horse sheds and hitching posts, with one exception long out of use, have given way to hard-surface parking lots. Within the past few decades, two city congregations have erected large gymnasiums as annexes to their sanctuaries for members' recreation and social activities. Both these congregations are Mennonites from Russia, who have tended to be more innovative than the Swiss.

Some of the moderate groups have adopted the same type of facilities as the progressive groups; carpeted floors, commercially manufactured pews and pulpit furniture, indirect lighting, church basements for social purposes. The character of their church buildings and the furnishings in them reflect the same cultural adaptations as the home furnishings, facilities, and dress of their members. Church buildings, facilities, and furnishings reflect members' values just as surely as do their written creeds.

Church building symbol of values
One segment is saying: "We continue to believe in the principles of frugality, simplicity, and nonconformity, and oppose changes that are unnecessary for serious Christian discipleship." Another group is saying: "Adopting material changes, modern conveniences, new technologies, and secular ideologies can be aids to Christian discipleship." Both segments pursue their respective objectives in line with what they consider proper religious purposes.

The following anecdote illustrates how church buildings may symbolize group values. A Waterloo businessman shared with me his concerns about his adolescent son's disinterest and cynicism about the family's church. The businessman was an active layman in a large Protestant church which had just erected a new sanctuary costing over a million dollars. The son chided his father for the church's spending so much money for a place of worship. Said the son: "What is it that you can do in your million dollar cathedral that the Old Order Mennonites can't do in their twenty thousand dollar white frame meetinghouse a mile north of town?"

Chapter 9

Winning and losing church members

A discussion of church membership in the various Waterloo Mennonite churches is important for understanding the Mennonite religious system. Rather than dealing with individual denominations, membership will be discussed according to general categories: conservative, moderate, and progressive. Greater attention will be paid to the progressive churches than to the moderate and conservative ones because they constitute 65 percent of the total Mennonite population. They also have the greatest variation of practices and the highest rate of change.

Membership sources

Mennonite congregations receive their members from three general sources, two of which lie within the wider Mennonite fellowship. The first is from other congregations within the same conference. When Mennonites move from rural to urban areas, from other provinces or distant places, they are likely to join congregations within the same conference, if possible. The second source of members is from other Mennonite or Amish conferences, either from the Waterloo area or from more distant places. When individuals or families become dissatisfied with what appear to them as burdensome restrictions of church discipline or any of many other possible causes of discontent, they shift to a more progressive group. Table 9-1 provides many illustrations of this inter-Mennonite membership movement.

Waterloo area Mennonites belonging to one of the conservative or moderate congregations, who move to Cambridge or Kitchener-Waterloo and want to join a Mennonite congregation, have no choice but to join one of the progressive congregations because that is the only kind of Mennonite church in these cities. Those not wanting to make that choice have frequently opted for a conservative non-Mennonite church like the Pentecostal, Plymouth Brethren, or Missionary. Findings for this study revealed that a total of 240 Mennonites transferred to these three denominations (1950-1970) in the following respective order: 40, 128, and 74. Interestingly, 75 percent of these came from progressive rural churches. Table 9-1 gives evidence of the number of members and from which sectors of the wider Mennonite fellowship the Waterloo church members came.

Table 9-1
Inter-Mennonite church and conference transfers
1950-1970

From:	To:								
	Progressive				Moderate			Conservative	
	MCO	WOC	UMC	MBC	W-M	CMC	BA	OOM	TOTAL
Menn. Conf. of Ontario (MCO)	504	40	31	8	0	59	7	0	649
Western Ont. Conference (WOC)	23	269	15	2	2	22	0	0	333
United Menn. Conf. of Ont. (UMC)	0	0	13	2	0	0	0	0	15
Menn. Brethren of Ontario (MBC)	1	0	5	494	0	0	0	0	500
Waterloo-Markham (W-M)	198	2	0	0	96	52	0	0	348
Conservative Menn. Conf. (CMC)	3	1	0	0	0	2	0	0	6
Beachy Amish Churches (BA)	1	60	0	0	0	4	11	1	77
Old Order Mennonite (OOM)	12	0	2	0	64	16	0	0	94
Total	742	372	66	506	162	155	18	1	2,022

The dynamics of inter-Mennonite church membership movement are strongly in the direction of the progressive churches. In Table 9-1, it will be noted that no one from any one of the seven Mennonite groups transferred into an Old Order Mennonite Church. One lone transfer from a moderate Amish to an Old Order Amish may be the exception that proves the rule.[1] In contrast, 198 persons transferred from the Waterloo-Markham Conference (moderate) to the Mennonite Conference of Ontario (progressive) and 123 persons from the Western Ontario Conference to the Mennonite Conference of Ontario (both progressive). These two shifts are both within the Swiss ethnic family. The Mennonite Brethren had few gains or losses, while the United Mennonite Conference gained 31 members from the Conference of Ontario. Most of these latter transfers were to the Stirling Avenue Church which in 1924 split from the First Mennonite Church in Kitchener. The Stirling Church, although originally Swiss, has in recent decades attracted numerous Mennonites from a Dutch-Russian background as well as a significant number of members with non-Mennonite background.

The large shift of 198 members from the Waterloo-Markham Conference (moderate) to the Ontario Conference (progressive) follows the well established pattern of a group moving one notch to the left in the direction of a more accommodating church. This may also indirectly reflect the trend away from farming to urban occupations and residence in the Waterloo area.

New conference attracts the dissatisfied

The Conservative Mennonite Conference, organized in 1960, the newest of all the Mennonite bodies in the Waterloo area, drew most of its members from two progressive conferences (MCO and WOC) and one moderate conference (W-M). Those from the progressive conferences left because they thought their parent churches were too worldly, while those from the moderate conference felt their old church was too restraining because it objected to Sunday schools, Bible study, and evangelistic meetings. Why, with thirteen existing Mennonite bodies, could not one satisfy them?

The big numbers in Table 9-1 illustrate heavy movement from church to church within a single conference. In the case of the Mennonite Conference of Ontario, that movement could be from churches in other parts of Ontario as well as in the Waterloo area. The 494-member gain by the Mennonite Brethren is in large part accounted for by the influx of refugees from Europe, and from Paraguay and Brazil where many Mennonites who fled Russia settled temporarily and then immigrated to Canada in the decades following World War II. The smaller groups with as little as two, three, or five congregations, some with memberships of less than two hundred, naturally had limited possibilities of increases from within.

Occupation and education also play a role in determining membership transfers. Increasingly since World War II, rural people left their farms to find work in urban areas. Many pursued academic courses beyond high school and even beyond college to professional schools. Those venturesome enough to seek new vocations were also likely to seek more progressive church connections as they settled in urban areas. These factors no doubt account for the rapid urban Mennonite church growth in the past three decades. As we shall see later, not all Mennonites moving to cities join Mennonite churches.

Members from non-Mennonite denominations

Mennonites traditionally have not been aggressively evangelistic and hence have not won many converts into their fellowship from diverse religious and cultural backgrounds. Even among the most progressive sectors of the denomination where evangelistic efforts recently have been made, success in winning non-ethnic members has been modest. The ethnic reputation, in-group attitudes, and social behaviour may have accounted for the slow progress in attracting non-ethnic adherents. A major source of non-Mennonite converts is through intermarriage. By that same process, many Mennonite churches have lost members.

New members from outside Mennonite denominations were largely won by progressive congregations. The United Church of Canada furnished the largest number (45). Lutherans and Baptists were next in order, both furnishing 26 members. It is to these same churches that Mennonites transfer when leaving their home congregations. At the time of the Mennonite census (1972), eight progressive Mennonite congregations were without a single member of a non-Mennonite background. This was true even of two congregations with memberships of about 300, which illustrates the continuing ethnic solidarity in many of the Waterloo Mennonite congregations.

Non-Mennonite tries to join the Old Order Mennonites

A young non-Mennonite couple asked to join the Old Order Mennonite Church. She was from the Evangelical Church and he from the Roman Catholic Church. They met in a Youth for Christ meeting. Both were strongly attracted to the disciplined lifestyle of the Old Order Mennonite Church. They began regularly attending worship services, took instructions from an Old Order minister, lived on a Mennonite farm in the *Grossdädi Haus,* worked for an Old Order Mennonite farmer, accepted the attire of the group, and adopted horse-and-buggy transportation.

She made the change successfully, learned the Pennsylvania German dialect, and continues to worship and work within the confines of church regulations. He found it too difficult to learn the dialect and to adjust to farm work after living all his life in cities and doing office work. His relations with the Old Order church are congenial, but he joined a Mennonite Church in Waterloo where language, attire, transportation, and occupation are no barrier to him. The couple moved close to town. He has a car and uses it for his purposes. Members of the church take her to and from Sunday services with horse and buggy. Their two adolescent boys followed their father to the Mennonite Church, while the three younger girls stayed with their mother and attend Old Order worship services on Sunday and the Mennonite elementary school during the week.

In the home, mother and daughters live on the main floor of the house, while the sons live in the finished basement where they have their recreational equipment including a television. The family eats meals together as is the general custom. The relations between husband and wife are deeply respectful of each other's religious faith and practices and, contrary as it may seem to outsiders, the family members have a congenial and loving relationship.

This most unusual situation, which has worked for more than a decade, reflects favourably on the patience, tolerance, and goodwill of the ministers and members of the Old Order Mennonite Church. At the same time, it illustrates how difficult it is for even devout Christians to make the social and cultural adjustment from a normal Christian lifestyle to that required of members in the Old Order. It also reflects favourably on the power of love between husband and wife to bridge the many difficulties that would normally arise in such a marriage-family-church relationship.

Table 9-2 provides impressive data showing how few new members have been won from non-Mennonite churches to six Waterloo progressive and moderate churches over a twenty-year period. A total of 44 Mennonite congregations was surveyed. Between 1950 and 1970, these churches had a total of 126 accessions from non-Mennonite church backgrounds. This meant 2.8 members per church or one non-Mennonite acquisition every seven years. A significant percentage of the acquisitions came through marriage. These facts suggest that, lofty as the ideals and religious principles of Mennonites may be, it is not attractive to most of those not born into the church or married to a member of the church.

Table 9-2 Mennonite gains from non-Mennonite denominations 1950-1970							
From	*To* MCO	WOC	UMC	MBC	W-M	CMC	Total
United Church	29	3	8	1	2	2	45
Lutheran	4	4	10	8	0	0	26
Baptist	8	2	2	14	0	0	26
Presbyterian	1	3	4	0	0	0	8
Missionary	5	0	2	0	0	0	7
Pentecostal	3	3	1	0	0	0	7
Anglican	1	2	1	2	0	0	6
Roman Catholic	0	1	0	0	0	0	1
Total	51	18	28	25	2	2	126

The total 126 accessions from non-Mennonite church backgrounds represents only 1.3 percent of the total 10,000 Mennonite membership as of 1972.

Trends over a sixty-year period

An unusual sixty-year comparison of 23 Waterloo County Mennonite congregations is available in a body of church data gathered in 1911. Table 9-3 gives an interesting 60-year comparison of twenty-three Waterloo County Mennonite churches from three conferences in existence in 1911 and 1971.[2] Column three shows the percentage of gain or loss after sixty years.

The sixty-year period saw a total membership gain of 1,369 or a gain of 22 members per church. Eighteen congregations had a gain in membership and five a loss. Note that the greatest membership gains were in town and city congregations. (The St. Agatha Church is a daughter congregation of the Steinman Church.)

Methods of transfer

The three conventional methods by which people join churches are by baptism, by letter of transfer, and by confession of faith. Table 9-4 shows by which of these three methods members came into seven Mennonite Church conferences. For the Old Order Mennonites, baptism is generally the only method employed, while among the moderates, 75 percent of new members joined by baptism and among the progressive 47 percent. One reason for joining another conference or congregation by confession of faith rather than by letter of transfer is that such letters are not granted by some of the conservative groups.

Infant baptism raises problems

Accepting new members from non-Mennonite churches that practise infant baptism presents an interesting theological dilemma to Mennonites who all believe in and practise adult baptism. Should Lutherans, Presbyterians, Catholics, United Church members, and others baptized as infants be rebaptized when joining a Mennonite church? In most cases, such individuals have been lifelong practising Christians. To ask such persons to accept rebaptism is to imply that their type of baptism cannot be accepted without the symbolic rite of baptism as an adult. This, of course, is exactly what sixteenth-century Anabaptists required of new members. Candidates for membership from such churches would in most cases be reluctant to admit thereby that theirs had been less than full-fledged Christian rite to church membership. They might even agree in theory to the validity of adult baptism yet be unwilling to be rebaptized themselves.

Waterloo Mennonite churches, as in many other matters of church practice, answer the dilemma in two ways. The more conservative groups require rebaptism and most of the progressive churches admit such candidates for membership either by letter or by confession of faith. For them, the rite of baptism is seen as a

Table 9-3
Waterloo area church memberships
1911 and 1971

Congregations	Membership 1911	1971	Percent Loss/Gain
Mennonite Conference of Ontario			
Nith Valley (Biehn)	80	92	15.0
Nith Valley (Blenheim)	60	67	11.6
Bloomingdale	50	78	56.0
Breslau	130	122	- 6.1
Erb Street (Waterloo)	180	273	53.3
Floradale	127	190	49.6
First Mennonite (Berlin)	245	551	124.8
Wilmot (Geiger)	90	70	-22.2
Mannheim (Latschar)	100	92	- 8.6
Preston (Hagey)	70	170	142.8
St. Jacobs (Conestoga)	100	393	293.0
Schantz	52	111	113.4
Wanner	90	137	52.2
Pioneer Park (Weber)	55	53	- 3.6
Sub-total	1429	2399	67.8
Western Ontario Conference (formerly Amish Mennonite)			
East Zora	350	314	-10.0
Mapleview	250	295	18.0
St. Agatha		122	—
Steinman	375	335	-10.0
Sub-total	975	1066	9.3
Old Order Mennonites (Wisler)			
Conestoga	110	167	51.8
Martins	170	186	9.4
North Woolwich	90	169	87.7
Peel	50	186	272.0
West Woolwich	160	180	12.5
Sub-total	580	888	53.1
Total membership	2,984	4,353	45.9

symbolic rather than a sacramental rite necessary for salvation. Acceptance of other Christians on confession of faith or by letter of

Table 9-4
Mennonite church methods of accession, 1950-1970

	Baptism	Letter of Transfer	Confession of faith	Total Number
Four progressive conferences	47.3%	40.3%	12.4%	3839
Two moderate conferences	75.7%	20.1%	4.2%	597
One Old Order conference	100.0%			645
Total	57.3%	32.7%	9.2%	5081

transfer thus recognizes the validity of infant baptism in the light of public confession of their faith and their Christian walk in life. The solution to this theological dilemma as worked out by the progressive Mennonites who do not require rebaptism is an example of religious and social accommodation.

Immersion as test of membership
Closely related to the infant-adult baptism question is the issue of the form of baptism, namely immersion versus sprinkling or pouring as proper symbols of baptism. The Mennonite Brethren have maintained, since their inception in Russia in 1860, that immersion is the only acceptable form of baptism for admission to that church. They could accept members of non-Mennonite denominations such as Baptists and Brethren in Christ into their fellowship by letters of transfer or confession of faith because they too were evangelical Christians who baptized by immersion, but could not accept members of any other denomination, including other Mennonite groups, if they do not immerse. Adherence to this practice for a century and a quarter has caused a considerable amount of strain, if not alienation, between Mennonite Brethren and other Mennonite groups. Only in recent decades and in specific cases have Mennonites in good standing been accepted in one or more Mennonite Brethren churches in Kitchener-Waterloo on confession of faith or by letter of transfer.

Results of the above practice are reflected in the low number of transfers into Mennonite Brethren congregations from any of the other seven Mennonite groups. Its own largest number of accessions were from within its own denomination. The Mennonite Brethren have deviated from the other three progressive conferences in the observance of this religious rite.

Baptismal age

Under the subject of church membership comes the important matter of baptismal age. Among Mennonites, what is the definition of adult, as opposed to infant, baptism? The answer to the question has often been: "When a person has reached the age of accountability." That appears to be a very flexible answer if one looks at the ages at which Waterloo Mennonites have baptized children and admitted them to church membership.

In a check of eleven Waterloo area Mennonite congregations in three different conferences between 1950 and 1972, I found that of 1,056 persons baptized, 311 or 29.4 percent were from nine to twelve years of age. All of these baptisms had taken place in progressive congregations. The question must be raised whether a preadolescent child can be said to have reached the age of accountability in matters of religious faith. Even so, these same preadolescent children are not considered capable of holding elected church offices or assuming other normal adult responsibilities for at least another ten years.

The conservative and moderate Mennonite groups never seem to have lowered their age of baptism below seventeen or eighteen. The reason for the lowering of the age of baptism among the progressive congregations seems to have been the result of yielding to outside pressure from other Protestant churches. Evangelistic meetings, both inside and outside the Mennonite churches, were considered tests of genuine Christian spirituality. Records indicate that, since the decade of the seventies, the earliest age of baptism among Waterloo Mennonites has gradually been moving back to fifteen, sixteen, and seventeen.

The percentage of unbaptized children among the progressives is 9 percent below that of the moderates and 18 percent below that of the conservatives. The reasons for these differences are two. The one obvious reason is the larger family size among moderates and conservatives. A second important factor is the later age of baptism (by four to five years) among the moderates and conservatives. Among progressive churches, children even

	Church Members	Unbaptized Children	Total Mennonite Population
		Table 9-5	
		Church membership compared with	
		unbaptized children, 1972	
Progressives	66.7%	33.3%	10,600
Moderates	57.5%	42.5%	2,316
Conservatives	48.8%	51.2%	4,194
Total	61.0%	39.0%	17,111

under twelve years of age would be considered church members whereas adolescents up to the age of eighteen and even twenty-one among the two more conservative groups would still be considered unbaptized children. These factors account in large measure for the wide differences in percentages of ratios of church members to unbaptized children in the Waterloo Mennonite churches.

Mixed marriages correlated with age
Among all Waterloo Mennonites at the time of the Mennonite census (1972), 515 members had non-Mennonite spouses. Of these, 95.5 percent were members of progressive churches. Only the small Reformed Mennonite group among the conservatives permits mixed marriages. Progressive church couples are urged to join the same congregation but the ultimate choice is left to individuals. Common membership of married partners is not a test of membership as it is in the moderate and conservative groups. The incidence of mixed marriages is directly correlated with age. In the progressive churches, 22 percent of the males ages twenty-five to twenty-nine and 21 percent of the females ages twenty to twenty-four have mixed marriages or non-Mennonite spouses. This means more than one out of five young married progressive Mennonites marry partners outside their own church. It is not known how many of these join one or the other spouse's church or how many remain permanently unchurched. The percentages of mixed marriages decline with each increasing five-year age bracket. This practice of exogamy or marriage outside one's group is another evidence of deviating from tradition and from social practices still adhered to among the moderate and conservative Mennonite branches.

Types of church membership

The varying attitudes of church members toward the ideals, purposes, and programs of their churches take the shape of a normal curve. At one end of the curve are the 10 to 15 percent of members who are commonly known as the leaders, those "you can always depend on," those who "carry the load," who "know what's going on," the "workhorses" of the church. At the other end of the curve are the 10 to 15 percent commonly referred to as marginal members. Their relations to the ideals and purposes of the church are nondescript because their participation and support is sporadic, weak, and unpredictable. Between these two extremes lie the majority of members, the faithful followers who are the more-or-less regular attenders and supporters of the church.

Waterloo Mennonites also manifest this normal curve of attitudes toward participation and program. It is more openly recognized in the progressive congregations than among the conservatives. My survey of Waterloo Mennonites as given in Table 9-6 classifies members as either active or inactive.

Table 9-6
Percentage of inactive members in progressive groups, 1972

Conferences	Membership	Inactive Members	Percentage
MCO	3,275	628	19%
WOC	2,368	254	11%
UMO	838	92	11%
MB	591	15	3%

These conferences clearly distinguish between members who are active and those inactive in their local congregations. But the definition of inactive is not uniform. It may mean a variety of things: 1) Those who are absent from the local community so that they cannot attend or participate regularly. Examples would be persons away at school, in church voluntary service, in military service, or temporarily on job assignments. 2) Members who left the local community temporarily and decided not to return, but nevertheless wish to retain membership in their home church. 3) Members living in the local community but no longer attending or supporting the church for various reasons. For all intents and purposes, such members must be disinterested and possibly alienated. 4) Those persons who because of ill health, physical incapacity, or infirmities of old age may no longer be able to attend, support, or benefit from active participation.

Intimacy discourages inactivity

I asked a senior Old Order Mennonite minister how he and his colleagues dealt with the problem of inactive church members. He could not understand how such a situation could exist in a spiritually alert congregation. In their church, all members are expected to attend services regularly unless ill or infirm because of old age or a physical handicap. Chronic inactivity and indifference would be considered a violation of a member's commitment made at the time of baptism to be a faithful follower of Jesus Christ and loyal to his church. Nonattendance would be interpreted by the church as alienation from one's Christian brothers and sisters.

His attitude is understandable in the light of the character of his congregation. Its membership is between one and two hundred, intimately acquainted, and woven together by a web of extended family relationships. Most new members come as the children of members. Few new Mennonites join from other Old Order or any other Mennonite congregations. A majority of all able-bodied family heads are engaged in farming. Absence from such a tightly knit group would be quickly noticed.

In contrast to this situation are the progressively inclined urban Mennonite churches with from two hundred to five hundred members, a high rate of turnover, and occupied in a wide variety of specialized occupations with a minimum of common weekday work experiences. In addition the many agencies and activities compete for time, money, and loyalty with the church.

Thus, we find two contrasting scenarios for members in two Waterloo area Mennonite settings. This discussion is not intended to justify but rather to explain circumstances that may account for the existence of a category of inactive church members. People's attitudes and behaviour are shaped by their cultural environment as well as by their family and church teachings.

The presence of inactive members raises a serious and valid question about a congregation's ability to practise community, share burdens, and provide spiritual ministry for those absentees who are widely scattered or who are totally unresponsive to the church's ministry locally. In the Mennonite Conference of Ontario, one in five members is listed as inactive; in the Western Ontario and in the United Conference churches, the ratio of inactive to active is one in nine. The Mennonite Brethren have an impressively low 3 percent inactive rate.

Some congregations have still another category of memberships variously called associate members or members of the wider fellowship of the congregation. This list is made up of those who were once members and no longer are but wish to be identified to the particular congregation. It may also include partners of mixed marriages who attend a local church with their spouses but continue their church membership in some other community. Whatever else may be said for and against such classification of membership types, it reflects accommodations of churches to requests of individual members rather than conformity of individual members to traditional church customs.

Table 9-7
Absentee-inactive church members, 1972

Conference	Voluntary Service	Mennonite College	University	Total
MCO	11%	1%	31%	43%
WOC	18%	0%	21%	39%
UM	5%	2%	10%	17%
MB	4%	18%	19%	41%
Total	38%	21%	81%	140%
Percentages	27.1	15.0	57.9	

One of the explanations frequently given for the sizable number of members in the inactive category is that members, especially young persons, were away at college, university, or in some form of voluntary service with a church agency. Table 9-7 throws doubt on that explanation. At the time of the 1972 private census, all churches were asked to list the number of their members who were then absent attending a Mennonite college or a university or participating in voluntary service. The question only applied to the four progressive conferences. The findings showed that only 140 persons out of almost 1,000 inactives, or 14 percent, were absent for the above reasons. One must assume that a big share of the remaining 800 are truly inactive, at least so far as relation to the church of which they are a member is concerned.

Membership losses

Mennonite churches have been losing members to non-Mennonite churches in the Waterloo area for much of the twentieth century. Losses became increasingly heavy during and after World War I. Up to that time, most Mennonites were still using the Pennsylvania German dialect in their homes and some churches. Public sentiment against the use of German even in churches and as a subject of study in schools then became strong and often bitter.[3] It was also a period when rural Mennonites began to take jobs and move to the cities. This led to increasing contact with non-Mennonites, the shift to the use of English in the homes and to attendance at churches which had attractive activities for young people. All of this also led to romances and intermarriage between members of different faiths. That fact worked in favour of the non-Mennonite spouses because it was more difficult for the non-Mennonite spouse to adjust to the rigid discipline of the Mennonites than it was for Mennonite spouses to adjust to the limited expectations of mainline Protestants.

Mennonites in First United

The First United Church of Waterloo was the result of a merger that took place in the late twenties between the Congregational, Presbyterian, and Methodist churches throughout Canada. One of the merging congregations locally was referred to as the German Methodist Church. It attracted some Mennonites who had come to Kitchener and Waterloo early in the century and did not wish to attend the two existing Mennonite churches. In this way, some marriages occurred between Mennonites and Methodists and later United Church members.[4]

One such individual was Fred Snider, who married a Methodist woman and became a lifelong member of First United Church. He recounted firsthand experiences with restrictions of the Mennonite Church which frustrated energetic young Mennonites then coming to the cities.

First of all, the church frowned on organized social activities such as church youth fellowships and insisted on dress regulations which made Mennonite young people feel self-conscious and uncomfortable. The church also was opposed to young people entering certain types of business such as life and casualty insurance or any kind of employment with local government agencies. Pursuit of higher education and preparation for the traditional professions were also discouraged because of a fear of diversion from disciplined Christian living. For reasons such as these, numerous young Mennonites joined non-Mennonite churches which permitted them freedom to pursue personal vocational ambitions without restriction.

Our ex-Mennonite, United Church informant became a highly successful farmer and breeder of dairy cattle. He cited others who made significant contributions as business and professional men in the Waterloo community. Among these were a manager of the North Waterloo Farmers' Mutual Fire Insurance Co., the founder of the Mutual Life Assurance Company of Canada, an owner of the *Waterloo Chronicle*, a Kitchener city council member, a druggist and mayor of Waterloo, a director of the County Agricultural Society, and members of the Ontario legislature.

Stigma of pacifism

Two other factors contributed to Mennonites leaving their mother church in their home community. One was the well-known opposition of Mennonites to war and participation in military service. This caused both strong overt and covert feelings of ill will toward Mennonites. This, in addition to the traditional policy of separation from the world, imprinted a powerful stigma on the mostly young people coming to make their living in cities. To join a non-Mennonite church was one way of disassociating themselves from that stigma.

The United Church records indicate that many of the Mennonites joined the Methodist Church prior to the birth of the United Church. Between 1887 and 1914, 68 Mennonites joined one of the churches which later became the United Church. Of these, nine were married couples, 26 were single women, and 15 were single men. At the time of this study, the United Church still had a number of members who had been raised in Mennonite families.

Mennonite losses to Missionary Church

The process of gaining and losing church members is still going on, although the reasons for transfer are constantly changing. An example of Mennonite losses to another denomination occurred within a recent decade in Elmira, a town of about 5,000 eleven miles north of Waterloo. A new Missionary Church was organized in 1968. In spite of the existence of five different Mennonite denominations with congregations in the area, 21 percent of the Missionary Church's 118 new members are drawn from four of the Mennonite churches in the area. The new church had a regular attendance of 214 in the late seventies.

The reasons these Mennonites gave for joining the new church were varied. Those from the Waterloo-Markham and the Conservative Mennonite Church said they were dissatisfied with the rules. Others said friends had taken the step and invited them to do the same. Those transferring from the progressive congregations said they joined because older siblings had joined before them, still others that they disliked their minister. Some said the church was too progressive. Some joined because a spouse was a member. For some there was an interval of years between the time of leaving a Mennonite Church and joining the Missionary Church. Obviously those leaving their home church were dissatisfied but there was no single or overriding reason for leaving nor a single or predominant attraction to the new one.

Table 9-8 Reasons for termination of church memberships, 1950-1970			
Conference	Death %	Transfer %	Dropped %	Dismissed %
Progressive	27.7	58.0	12.9	1.4
Moderate	19.1	33.6	45.0	2.3
Conservative	66.0	26.8	36.0	3.6
Total	29.2	52.0	17.1	1.7

A significant number of church members terminated their membership unofficially and informally without informing anyone in the church of their leaving. Usually these persons were marginal members who were irregular in attendance and support.

The percentages in Table 9-8 are based on a total membership figure of 8,560 members representing the eight largest Mennonite bodies. Note that the largest percentage of members who terminate church memberships do so by means of transferring to another church. Thirty-eight percent transfer to another Mennonite church, either within the same conference or to one of the other conferences in the area. This means that 62 percent of the transfers are to other than Mennonite denominations. The major denominations to which they transfer are shown in Table 9-9.

The transfer rate, as could be expected, is highest among the progressive churches. While the termination rate also is highest there, so too is the accession rate, as shown in Table 9-3. The high percentage of dropped members in the moderate and conservative conferences should be clearly understood not as disciplinary action taken by the churches resulting in the loss of members, but rather because members left of their own accord. In the progressive churches such departures would be recognized by letters of transfer, but that is not the custom among the moderate and conservative groups.

The high percentage of terminations by death among the conservatives and the low loss by outward transfer reflect a high degree of membership stability. The dismissal rate for all three Mennonite groups is low when it is remembered that the data cover a twenty-one-year period. The relative percentages of dismissal reflects also the relative strictness of discipline in each group. The progressives have the lowest termination rate as judged by the "dropped" category.

Where do Mennonites go after leaving the Mennonite church? What non- Mennonite church, if any, do they join? Table 9-9 answers that question in part. Part of the question cannot be answered because there is no information for members who do not receive letters of transfer or who leave no other information.

Of the three general Mennonite categories, the progressive churches lose the largest number of members to non-Mennonite denominations. Of those denominations, the United Church of Canada attracts most Mennonites followed by the Lutheran, Missionary, and Plymouth Brethren. The large number attracted to the Plymouth Brethren and the Missionary churches probably are one-time phenomena. The Plymouth Brethren size of transfer is

Table 9-9
Non-Mennonite denominations to which
Mennonites transferred, 1950-1970

Transferred to	From		
	Progressive	*Moderate*	*Conservative*
	%	%	%
United Church	25.0	6.6	0
Lutheran	19.4	1.9	0
Missionary	10.6	.9	0
Plymouth Brethren	9.5	30.2	0
Baptist	9.3	1.4	0
Presbyterian	6.2	0	0
Pentecostal	5.2	2.4	0
Roman Catholic	3.7	.9	0
Anglican	1.8	0	0
All others	9.3	55.7	0
Total transfers	676	212	17

accounted for by a short but intense evangelistic effort among the Old Order Mennonite and Waterloo-Markham groups during the late fifties and early sixties. By the end of the seventies, this proselytizing had subsided. It is not likely to cause ongoing loss to Mennonite groups.

Mainline Protestant churches readily available
The Missionary Church attraction is also likely a onetime thrust related to the establishing of a new church in Elmira with a special appeal to a variety of dissatisfied members in the conservative and moderate congregations in the Elmira area. In the long run, one or the other of the mainline Protestant denominations will attract the majority of Mennonites leaving their home churches. One of the reasons for joining mainline churches is that one or more of them is likely to be found in the many scattered geographical areas where Mennonites will settle and where there are no existing Mennonite churches. Another reason why United, Lutheran, Baptist, and Presbyterian churches might be expected to appeal to progressive Mennonites is their many similarities in theological outlook, religious organization, physical facilities, and economic and social status. Mennonite Brethren are attracted to Baptist churches because of similar forms of church government

and adult baptism by immersion.

One major reason for terminations of church memberships among the progressive Mennonites is their search for upward mobility. This is reflected in the increasing numbers of progressive-church young people pursuing college and university degrees in preparation for professional and technological jobs. For these objectives, they must frequently move to distant places. A second reason for membership terminations is marriage to a non-Mennonite spouse. An examination of Table 9-8 shows the sharp difference in the number of membership terminations between progressive churches on the one hand and moderate and conservative churches on the other.

Conservatives change churches reluctantly

Out of nine non-Mennonite churches which Waterloo Mennonites joined, only two Old Order Mennonites joined a non-Mennonite church and that was the Missionary Church in Elmira. In contrast, in the twenty-one-year interval between 1950 and 1971, 212 moderates and 676 progressives joined non-Mennonite churches. This is an example of how resistant conservatives are to social change. For them, a switch in church membership introduces severe strains in family and kinship relations, as well as serious economic implications in the form of severing an intensely meaningful and church-centred social security system. The total loss of church members is somewhat misleading in that individual congregations may lose members, but at the same time also be gaining members. As we have seen earlier, a big percentage of gains and losses are really exchanges between congregations of the same conference or from congregations in other Mennonite groups.

The biggest loss to a single non-Mennonite denomination was to the Missionary Church.[5] A significant percentage of ex-Mennonites were the core of newly formed Missionary congregations from the very beginning in the middle of the nineteenth century. In fact, the Missionary Church is a split from the Mennonite Conference of Ontario. It was known for many years as the Mennonite Brethren in Christ. It arose as a protest to the Ontario Conference for not responding promptly enough to the demand for more spirituality, which was then claimed to be evidenced by adopting evangelistic meetings, prayer meetings, Sunday schools, and the use of the English language in preaching.

Comments on church membership

The source of new members is mostly by natural growth from within the existing memberships. This is true of both progressive and conservative congregations. In six of the fourteen progressive and moderate conferences over a twenty-year period, only 126 accessions came from non-Mennonite denominations. Non-Mennonite churches cannot accuse Mennonites of being a proselytizing church. On the other hand, Mennonites have lost at least 903 members to non-Mennonite churches during the twenty-year period from 1950 to 1970. This might be described as unintended ecclesiastical generosity. Membership losses are largely by letters of transfer. This is a reflection of the high degree of mobility characteristic of contemporary Mennonite society.

Fifty-seven percent of the Mennonite accessions are by means of baptism. This ranges from 47 percent among the progressives, 75 percent among the moderates, and 100 percent among the conservatives. This means that the Old Orders have no accessions either by letters of transfer or by confession of faith. The ratio of Mennonite children who are unbaptized is 40 percent, compared to 60 percent of the baptized members. Conservative churches list no inactive members, whereas the range among progressives is from 3 to 19 percent.

Chapter 10

The family's response to change

The Mennonite family in the Waterloo area cannot be discussed meaningfully without recognizing the wider cultural context of which it is a part. A brief summary of the social situation of the Canadian family will therefore be in order.

Evidence of the changing nature of the Canadian family is provided by data in the 1971 Canadian decennial census. In the early seventies Sylvia Wargon, a Statistics Canada demographer, called attention to an unprecedented trend toward age segregation following World War II which raised questions about family-based values of sharing and responsibility.[1]

The census revealed that two major new age groups stood out from all the rest. One was elderly people, especially women, living alone instead of in families. In the second group were young people of both sexes who chose to move away from their families and set up their own housekeeping units.

New family types
More and more Canadians no longer consider the form of the traditional family as permanent, lifelong, and sacrosanct and no longer mainly oriented toward childbearing and rearing. Thus the centuries-old concept of extended and nuclear family forms have given way to a wide diversity of lifestyles and of alternative family arrangements in which individual considerations are given priority over family values.

Examples of these new family types are the single-person households which in 1985, according to Statistics Canada, represented 11.3 percent of all families. Of these, 83 percent were headed by women and 17 percent by men. Single-parent families have been increasing at a more rapid rate than husband-wife families. In 1981, 75.2 percent of Canadian households were family households and 24.8 percent were non-family households (those who live alone or who are unrelated and share a common residence). In the fifteen-year period between 1970 and 1985, non-family households in Canada increased by 62 percent.

The basic changes occurring in the structure and function of the Canadian family are not unique. The 1980 United States Federal Census showed that only 28.5 percent of American households were traditional husband-wife families with children. In 1970, this factor stood at 40 percent. What used to be a typical husband-wife family with two children represents only 11 percent of all husband-wife families today. Couples with no children make up the largest single category of American households representing 30 percent of all households. Single-person households in the United States represent nearly 23 percent of all American households. Twenty percent or one out of every five children in the United States live with only one parent, usually the mother. The number of households consisting of a woman with one or more children doubled between 1970 and 1980, and most of these family units live in poverty.

Single-person households and married couples without children are the fastest growing categories of households in both Canada and the United States. This is especially the case in urban communities where children are economic liabilities and interfere with the now prevailing occupational pattern of both husband and wife working outside the home. The married woman who has not been gainfully employed after marriage is in the minority. Whereas married women, especially those with dependent children, once apologized for working outside the home for fear of being criticized for neglecting husband and children, today they tend to be apologetic for not being a second breadwinner. Today the housewife who does not work outside the home fears gossip and ridicule for not doing what most married women are doing; for not having occupational or professional ambitions of her own; for accepting the status of a dependent rather than earning her own way and thus expressing a measure of social equality. The new family sociological characteristics here described reflect only family patterns of the progressive Mennonites. Conservative and most moderate Mennonite families still adhere to traditional feminine roles, although moderate families are not totally unaffected by basic structural and functional changes.

Summary of changes affecting family life

Most people recognize changes that have taken place if they have been personally influenced by them. However few people note the cumulative effect that such changes have on the family as an institution. Changes in our culture that have had greater or lesser degrees of influence in bringing about permanent changes in family structure, function, philosophy, and lifestyle are listed below. One of these changes alone would not greatly affect family structure, but the sum of these changes results in permanently altering family structure and function.

> Both husband and wife working outside the home.
> The increasing number of working mothers with small children.
> Increasing shift of nurturing, training, and socializing children to day-care centres and baby-sitters.
> An increase in male-female role switches, as where the wife becomes the major breadwinner and the husband the homemaker.
> Increase in the number of childless marriages by choice.
> Widespread practice of birth control and planned families.
> Increase in the number of unmarried members of the opposite sex living openly together.
> Increase in the number of single-parent families who choose to be a parent but not to wed.
> Increase in the number of racially, ethnically, and culturally mixed marriages.
> Decrease in the number of families who observe regular family devotions.
> Increase in the number of families requiring two incomes to maintain their desired standard of living.
> Simplification of securing legal divorces.
> Decline of opportunities for children to make economic contributions in support of self or the family enterprise.
> Decline in the acceptance of marriage as binding for life.
> Decline in home food production and/or preservation in favour of using commercial goods and services.
> Decline in the number of meals eaten together as a family and an increase in the number of meals eaten away from home.
> Decline of family-created recreation in favour of television watching.
> Decline of family businesses where all members can be actively involved in the family enterprise.

Most of the changes listed seemed to focus on the pursuit of individual satisfactions rather than on preserving and strengthening the family as a unit.

Glimpses of the Waterloo Mennonite family

Against the background of the general cultural and environmental changes described above, we come to the characteristics of the Waterloo Mennonite family. Historically, the Mennonite family has been considered strong and stable. It owes its reputed stability, in large measure, to its close ties with the church and the school. In Mennonite communities, family, church, and school have traditionally supported each other. What the church taught, the school and the family believed and tried to practise. All three found natural expression in the vocational institution, the family farm. These four basic areas of Mennonite life have made up the Mennonite community with a traditional Gemeinschaft character. For two hundred years, the Waterloo Mennonite family has nurtured and been nurtured by these intertwined institutions.

Table 10-1 Marital status among Waterloo Mennonites, 1972 No. Family Member Units: 9745				
	Progressives %	*Moderates* %	*Conservatives* %	*Total* %
Married	60.3	72.7	69.5	63.5
Single	26.0	23.0	24.0	25.3
Widowed	6.2	3.8	5.4	5.7
Divorced	.3	.0	.0	.3
Separated	.3	.0	.0	.2
Non-member spouse	7.1	1.0	.5	5.2

The percentage of Mennonites who are married compared to those who are single is highest among the moderates at 73 percent and lowest among the progressives at 60 percent. Reasons for this 12 percent gap can be assumed to be the later marriage age of the progressives, and the larger number of them seeking education beyond the elementary and secondary level. Both conservatives and moderates have no divorced or separated couples. Even among the progressives, the percentage in those categories is very low.

Instead of referring to family size, the census bureau today refers to household size. This is done because of the large number of males and females, or two or more members of the same sex, neither married nor related, who are living together in the same house, and thus do not constitute the traditional definition of a family.

Size of the Mennonite family
My Mennonite census revealed that Mennonites have an average of five members per family, not much larger than the average Waterloo county family. Within the three Mennonite groups, the household size is: progressives, 4.6; moderates, 5.6; and conservatives, 6.7.

I was surprised to discover that among the Old Order Mennonites, the average household size was not as large as generally assumed. Census data showed that only 4.4 percent of the Old Order households had more than nine members per household. Of all Old Order households, about one-third had above the Mennonite average of five members per household. The Old Order family may appear larger by comparison to the smaller progressive families because children remain with their paternal families longer, usually until at least twenty-one, while those in progressive families leave home to attend schools and universities and take jobs away from home three to five years earlier than do conservative young people. The average family size does not mean completed family size.

Conservative Mennonites can be expected to resist adoption of these newer family types as long as they remain solidly rural and engage in farming and related agricultural pursuits. The newer family types are found largely in urban areas. Childless households, single family parents, and temporary unwed live-in arrangements are totally ill-suited and unworkable as farm families.

Mennonite family systems
All of us are so closely identified with the families in which we were raised or of which we are now members that we find it difficult to think about them objectively. The average father and mother would find it slightly puzzling if asked by their children to state the purpose or objective of their family, yet the question

would be a perfectly logical one to ask. Why do people get married? Why do they want children of their own? What kind of family goals do they have? Where do they derive the ideals for their family? By what criteria do they judge their family a success or a failure? These and many other questions are difficult to answer. They are deeply embedded in our unconscious customs, traditions, and cultural value systems. Nevertheless, it is the part of intelligence to attempt to answer such questions. It is the purpose of this study to answer some of these questions pertaining to Waterloo Mennonite families.

Universal family functions

In all parts of the world, the human family performs at least four functions. First, the family is the socially approved way of reproducing the human race and regulating the relations between the sexes for the benefit of society. A second function is that of nurturing the young and protecting and supporting its members.

A third function gives a newborn member an identity: a name, a home, and a social group to which the child has a legal right to belong. A fourth role socializes the new generation: teaches children, interprets the meaning of life, passes on the customs and values of the society of which they are a part. The family is the individual's link with society. It is the primary place in which infants begin to acquire personality. A child without one or more nurturing and caring individuals could not become a normal human being.

The progressives are almost totally nuclear families, which consist of a married couple and their dependent children. Three-generation families among progressive families are increasingly uncommon. Among the Old Order Mennonites and Amish, grandparents live in small houses or apartments attached to the main farmhouse and thus continue to be an adjunct unit to the active young nuclear farm family. Grandparents continue to play vital family roles by doing lighter work tasks, baby-sitting, and providing family counsel and financial assistance. Among the progressives, grandparents today either remain in their own homes or move into a senior citizens' community established by one or the other of the Mennonite church conferences in the Waterloo area.

The patriarchal family

Old Order families are patriarchal in that the father is the unquestioned head of the family and the wife and children are subordinate to him. This, however, does not mean that the father is autocratic. Nor does it mean that the wife and mother or the children have no voice in family decision-making. The fact is that the various family members accept their respective status and roles naturally and generally uncritically. They accept them as biblically based and as the right way for Christian families to be organized. Each family member is taught to love and respect all other members. Ministers in sermons constantly remind children to obey, honour, and respect their parents and, at the same time, they admonish husbands and wives to love and respect each other and not to "provoke their children to wrath." New Testament authorities are constantly cited as the models for interpersonal family relations.

In other words, the patriarchal family works well among moderate and conservative Mennonites. Their entire lifestyle is in tune with this system. Family goals are embedded in the everyday customs and patterns of life. This system works well, in part, because it is supported by the church to which every family belongs and is undergirded by a parochial school system. It works well also because it is appropriate in an agricultural economic system in which the family farm is central. These farms are largely self-sufficient, located in close-knit neighbourhoods, strengthened by consistent mutual support, and socially separated from the secular world.

This centuries-old integrated family system works because its members voluntarily choose to make it work. They prefer it to the options they see all around them. It works also because the people in the Municipality of Waterloo and surrounding counties respect this traditional way of living and the end results which the system produces.

The accommodating progressive family

The progressive Mennonites have chosen to accommodate to the secular cultural changes of the times. Three-fourths of them have given up farming. Many have moved to towns and cities and taken employment in industry, business, and the professions.

This has gradually changed their lifestyle and with it, a noticeable change in philosophy and practice. Some of the rural values and family patterns are no longer appropriate, practical, or even possible in an urban, commercial, and industrial context.

In the typical urban family work is no longer a common activity or focus for the entire family. The father's work takes him away from the family each workday morning. If the mother works, the same is true for her. Whether the children are preschool, in elementary or high school, or old enough to have jobs of their own, they too tend to separate for the day. The preschoolers go to the baby-sitter or the day-care centre, the older children to their respective age-graded schools or places of work. The so-called home, or better, the house is empty and quiet all day long. Home life pretty much ceases from 8:00 a.m. to 5:00 p.m., five days a week in a high percentage of urban Mennonite homes.

One of the most cherished family traditions, that of eating around the family table twenty-one times a week, has given way to at least three major family-fragmenting urban forces. First of all is the all-important demand of the breadwinner's job. A close second priority is the pull of individual family members' interests away from home and family, such as school and community sports, little leagues, hobby groups, club meetings, bowling and curling groups, church and professional committee meetings, and socials of an almost endless variety. These many interests all may be worthy in themselves, nevertheless, they lead to fragmented family life. For the most part, away-from-home activities are individual rather than family pursuits.

A third major force that contributes to individualizing rather than solidifying the urban Mennonite family is the collection of mass media vehicles: the radio, the stereo, the video, and the television. The fare offered through these media technologies is geared to individual interests according to age, sex, education, and occupation. To avoid conflict and to satisfy individual tastes, many families simply purchase radios and TVs for each family member, which reduces conflict but also common family activities.

Whether we recognize it or not, the typical progressive home more and more resembles a motel or boardinghouse where family members come to sleep and spend weekends. It has a kitchen and a well-stocked refrigerator with preprocessed and commercially prepared food from which hungry members may draw when and as they choose. Members of the fragmented family may see each other while coming and going or leave notes to those they don't see. Breakfasts for the contemporary urban family, if members eat breakfasts, tend to be a rushed cup of coffee and toast or a dish of cold cereal taken hurriedly at home or at a coffee shop on the way to work. Lunches are carried or eaten out five days a week at work or at school. Frequent evening meals and Sunday dinners are taken at public restaurants still further reducing the number of family meals at home. It may not be far wrong to say that an increasing number of urban and nonfarm rural families eat only a half dozen meals out of a possible twenty-one in a week as a total family at home. In such a fragmented and individualized family pattern, daily family devotions too have gone by the board in a high percentage of Mennonite homes.

This is not an evil plot to destroy the family. It is the result of our membership in a society that is highly committed to constant social and technological change; to the pursuit of material advancement and the satisfaction of individual goals of physical comfort and pleasure. Given this kind of cultural environment, when and where and how do Mennonite families teach moral, ethical, and spiritual values? More importantly, when and where and how does the modern Mennonite family demonstrate the sharing, caring, servant-role virtues so essential to character development and the disciplined Christian life? How can significant family solidarity be developed when family members have so limited a number and so superficial a quality of common experiences?

This emerging individualized family system is the product of contemporary industrialized culture. It is the family's response to an economic system that has exalted individual freedom above values of family, church, and community. Unbridled individualism has come to be accepted as normative both socially and ethically.

Progressive families
In contrast to the patriarchal rural Waterloo Mennonite family among the conservatives, the progressive Mennonite families have been described as equalitarian. The fact is that the great majority of Waterloo Mennonite families are not purely one or the other of

these ideal types, but variations of both. By equalitarian is meant that power or authority in decision-making is not vested totally and finally with the father, but is shared by parents and children. This sharing of power is in part the result of necessity.

In many instances, parents no longer have superior knowledge or a fund of experience on which former authority rested. Children in school may have learned more than their parents, not only in geography, history, politics, and science, but also about nutrition, technology, computers, and outer space. And since children are no longer only interested in following their parents' occupations, their elders are limited in what they can teach by way of preparing their children for adult vocations.

The moderate Mennonite family

The moderate Waterloo Mennonite families stand midway between the conservative and progressive groups. They have modernized and mechanized their lifestyles. They have adopted electricity, telephones, tractors, trucks, and cars, and with these all the accompanying laboursaving devices in house, on the farm, and in business. Therefore, like the progressives, a large portion of their income dollars must be spent for capital equipment purchases and maintenance. With mechanized equipment in house and barn, the need for the labour of a large family has declined. A significant number of both men and women have taken employment off the farm, mostly in agriculture-related businesses and industries. As a result, they have become wage earners rather than enterprising farm operators. This is the first step toward urbanization and the need for additional education, especially vocational training.

The moderate Mennonites have sought to preserve traditional religious and family values and lifestyles. These aims are reflected in their adherence to plain dress, worshipping in plain meetinghouses, and maintaining the Pennsylvania German dialect in their homes. They maintain the principles of nonconformity and separation from the world and emphasize simplicity, frugality, nonresistance, integrity, and industriousness in all aspects of life. Nevertheless, some of these values may gradually give way to social accommodation demanded by nonfarm occupations and increased education. Today's moderates are where today's progressives were thirty years ago.

Courtship patterns and weddings

Among the Old Orders, both Amish and Mennonites, the practice of casual dating is frowned on. Dating, if any, focuses on marriage. However, among the Old Order young people, the well-established custom of the Sunday evening singings in the homes of members provides much opportunity for young people to become well acquainted. These singings usually take place on the same Sunday that church services are held in the host member's meetinghouse. The songs sung at the singings are not the slow tunes used at the worship services, but are mostly English gospel hymn tunes and folk songs.

The host family may join in the singing until about ten o'clock, when they retire and the young people, who range in ages from about 15 to 22, play folk games, enjoy refreshments, and socialize informally. At the close of the singings young people pair off, and young men may take their preferred partners home. A great deal of secrecy surrounds the seriousness of a particular couple's relationship and plans for marriage. Couples normally do not talk about their prospective marriage, and serious dating partners will try not to be seen together in public. Only after the banns have been published, usually three weeks before the wedding, are bride and groom openly seen together. One minister, his wife, and daughter advised me that the customs of secrecy about dating and marriage are no longer strictly adhered to.

The young people in the moderate groups observe much the same courting patterns as do the conservatives, except that the young men in this group have cars instead of spirited horses and buggies. In this instance, slow transportation may be advantageous to the conservative young couples. Many teenage young people in the conservative and moderate groups work for several years before marriage as hired help for families in other Mennonite communities. In this way, they come to know and be known by prospective marriage partners outside their immediate church and community.

A dominant characteristic of the conservative and moderate Mennonite courtship pattern is its group setting, in contrast to the exclusive pairing and spending time alone that is the custom in almost all contemporary dating practices in secular society. Young people interested in forming friendships that eventually lead to marriage have a better opportunity to get to know the one they are attracted to in a group setting than do two people who spend time exclusively with each other. In the group, they see each other through the eyes of third parties and observe how the special friend functions socially. These two Mennonite groups do not permit divorces, but the careful mate selection process also prevents the need for divorces in most marriages. Marriage partners must be chosen from within their own or a more conservative group, but not necessarily from their own local congregation. Pre-marital sex is forbidden and, if the code is violated, is cause for confession before the church or dismissal by the congregation.

Following the reading of the banns on three successive Sunday mornings, the wedding date is announced. Weddings tend to be concentrated during the spring and the fall when outside work is least demanding and unfavourable weather is less of a problem for home weddings. Weddings in the middle of the week are preferred to those at the beginning and the end of a week, because of the time needed to prepare and again restore the house to normalcy after the celebration. Weddings are usually held in the home of the bride. Preparation for this occasion begins well in advance of the wedding day and involves friends and relatives who assist in looking after such details as preparing food, moving furniture, providing seating, and arranging accommodations for 100 to 130 or more guests, as well as arranging parking for fifty to sixty horses and buggies.

The bride customarily wears a new navy blue dress that she has made. If the bride cannot sew her own dress, it is said, she is not ready to be married. The groom usually wears a new, dark suit and a new black hat. The wedding, which is a two-hour service, may begin either at nine in the morning or one-thirty in the afternoon. It is a service much like any Sunday morning service, except that the Scripture reading, the hymns, and the sermons focus specifically on the meaning of marriage and the importance of establishing a Christian home. The congregation is admonished to undergird the new couple with love, prayer, and a good example (Mark 10:1-12). The wedding ceremony is a bonding experience between congregation and couple. It symbolizes the solidarity of a primary group behind a prospective new family.

The bride in the moderate group wears a dress of light blue, as if to symbolize a shade more freedom of choice than her more conservative sisters. Wedding gifts of a practical nature are given the bridal couple, which in all probability will be starting house-keeping in their own farm home following the wedding.

Courtship and marriage among the progressives

Today the courtship process among the progressives closely follows the general mate selection pattern of the larger society. Marriage within one's own group is no longer required. Casual dating, in contrast to dating only one person with the serious intention of marrying, is now the accepted custom. Although all congregations urge young people to choose Christian friends as life-mates, the ultimate choice is up to the individual. Young people in the pro-gressive churches mix freely with a crossection of other young people in the wider community. Opportunities for this occur in public high schools and colleges, places of work, community recre-ation centres, sporting events, and social gatherings of many kinds. Casual dating is followed by steady dating of one person, then engagement, and finally marriage. In our 1971 study of fam-ily life among Waterloo Mennonites, 95 percent of the progressive church members who married did so within the Mennonite denom-ination and most of them within their own congregation or confer-ence. This indicates that a high percentage of the marriage part-ners had common religious backgrounds.

Among the progressive churches, dating is of course not secre-tive as it is in the more conservative churches. Young people in open communities do not have the same opportunity to know well their many acquaintances. Random or casual dating provides an opportunity for wider relationships and for building deeper friend-ships. Among progressives, socialization does not take place exclusively within the local church or neighbourhood group and within the home of church members.

In the interviewing done in connection with the Mennonite census for this study, no inquiry was made about premarital sex-ual practices among young people in progressive groups. This was one of many aspects of the community study which could not be considered in detail because of limited time and space. However, there is no reason to think that Mennonite young people in

Waterloo have attitudes and practices on matters of premarital sex that vary from the youth population generally, except for those in the conservative and moderate groups.

It is quite common, but not universal, for the man to symbolize the engagement by giving his intended bride a diamond ring or perhaps a watch. This is a sharp departure from tradition, because as late as the 1920s and 1930s, wearing jewelry of any kind was condemned as unbiblical and unbecoming of Christians. Among other customs adopted by the progressives are the sending of commercially printed formal wedding announcements and placing photos in the local newspapers. Brides usually are given bridal showers, and wedding rehearsals are held on the day before the wedding, commonly followed by rehearsal dinners for all those in the wedding party. Almost all wedding ceremonies today are observed in churches with more or less elaborate rituals. The bride may wear an ordinary length dress or a fancy bridal gown. There may be anywhere from one to four attendants for the bride. Special vocal or instrumental music is usually a part of the formal service. A wedding ring is used to symbolize the uniting of the couple. Sometimes both exchange rings. An interesting innovation introduced at progressive Mennonite weddings is the custom of the bride and groom writing their own vows and reciting them at the ceremony.

The final stage of the contemporary Mennonite wedding in the progressive churches is a reception either in the fellowship room of the church or in a rented hall or meeting room in a local hotel or restaurant. At this occasion, there is food, speeches, toasts, singing, and, in a few cases, dancing. If the reception is in the church fellowship room, the viewing of gifts is common. There is little essential difference in either the courtship pattern or the wedding ceremony of the majority of progressive Mennonite churches from that of mainline Protestant churches.

Separation and divorce

Our study of Mennonite family life in Waterloo revealed a surprisingly low number of divorced and separated families. Out of 7,034 church members, there were 33 cases of family breakdown of which nine were divorces and 24 were separations. These findings are misleading. There are indeed more divorced families than reported to census takers. There are several reasons for this unintentional inaccuracy. Until well into the 1950s, incompatible marriages were kept secret and painfully endured, separations were regretfully tolerated, and divorces were forbidden on pain of dismissal from church membership. Therefore, married couples who decided to separate or seek a divorce tended to leave the church before being excommunicated. Thus the church could truthfully claim that there were no divorced members among them.

Another explanation for the low rate of broken marriages among Waterloo Mennonites is that churches considered divorced people who remarried as no longer divorced and thus could be reported as members in good standing. This was especially true of couples who joined the church after one or both had been divorced. Congregations in the sixties began to accept divorced people for membership if they qualified otherwise.

In 1977, the Mennonite Conference of Ontario, which has 21 congregations in the Waterloo area, approved a new set of guidelines for dealing with divorce and remarriage. It encouraged its congregations to form counselling groups to help families confronted with acute marriage problems. A paper on the subject read at an annual conference stated: "We are all creatures of conflict. We cannot control all the forces that make or break relationships with other people, whether they be spouse, child, neighbour or parishioner." *The Kitchener-Waterloo Record* (March 15, 1977) carried an editorial commenting on the conference's action:

> To those outside the Mennonite church, the move has a somewhat different significance. It means that these admirable people, who have sought for centuries to try to keep the lures of affluence and personal ambition at bay, are finding that they cannot cope in the way they formerly did.
> So the Mennonite Conference of Ontario is going to do what it can to understand the forces making for this kind of conflict, and try to help its people to circumvent and eventually rise above them. They deserve every encouragement in their attempt.

Church attitude redemptive

Even with an additional number of divorced Mennonite couples in recent years, it is estimated that the percentage of divorced Mennonites in the Waterloo area is still between one and two percent of all marriages. But one may also assume the divorce rate is rising as an increasing number of urban Mennonites become second- and third-generation city dwellers and gradually adopt the norms in their environment. Most of the progressive churches have adopted a redemptive and reconciliatory attitude, rather than a punitive one, toward those inside and outside their congregations who face the sadness of broken interpersonal family relationships.

Family survival crucial

In concluding this brief discussion on the sociology of the Waterloo Mennonite family, it is important to be reminded once again that the family is the ultimate bearer of a people's religious faith and ethical values. The church may proclaim the Word, but the laymen and laywomen in daily family life must, in the final analysis, be the bearers of that Word. Without the survival of the Mennonite family, there will be no meaningful survival of a Mennonite church. The Christian family's greatest contemporary failure is its seeming inability to educate for moral behaviour.

I am aware that many subjects pertaining to the Mennonite family in Waterloo such as the quality of communication and decision-making, sex roles, compatibility of marriage partners, readiness for marriage and parenting, external roles and marriage, coping with stress, and adjusting to changes in marriage could not be explored. Since this study focuses on the total community rather than on any single institution, discussion of each part of the community had to be limited.

Chapter 11

As the school so goes the church

Three closely intertwined institutions—the church, the family, and the school—have carried the Mennonite spiritual and cultural heritage through the centuries.

In preparing children for elementary school, Mennonites have been much more concerned with such fundamental virtues as obedience and respect for authority, integrity, dependability, courtesy, sharing, and a sense of fair play than with cultivating a big vocabulary, knowing how to read and spell before they enter first grade or how to be the smartest child in school. Moral values are considered the foundation on which all later factual knowledge will need to be deposited and integrated.

The Waterloo Mennonite philosophy and theory of education was well expressed and demonstrated by Benjamin Eby, the early nineteenth-century bishop and community leader in Berlin. He built the first school in Kitchener and taught in it for most of the first twenty-five years of the school's life. The school was in his church annex. Besides teaching, he wrote his own spelling, reading, and history books, edited a hymnbook, and drew up a confession of faith for the Ontario Mennonites. This school served as a model for other church communities and continued to be used until public school education was adopted. It remained the conventional school system in Waterloo County for well over a century.

Conservatives reject centralized public schools
In the 1960s, the Ontario Department of Education moved to centralize its rural one- and two-room schools. At the same time, it extended compulsory education from age fourteen to sixteen.

Most Waterloo citizens accepted this change. For them, the advantages outweighed the disadvantages. Among these were: 1) opportunities for vocational training not available in country schools; 2) graded classrooms by ages instead of one room for eight grades; 3) a larger variety of subjects; 4) specialized teachers in such subjects as art, music, and physical education; and 5) expanded social contacts with children from the wider community. A major disadvantage of the new system was the need for the daily bus transport of children, which required an extra hour or more per day of the children's time.

All of these proclaimed advantages, however, did not outweigh the advantages of the old system for the county's many conservative rural Mennonites. They were satisfied with their one- and two-room rural schools, over which they had effective control, even though they were public schools. The system was doing for them what they thought a school should do: prepare children to live as responsible adult church and community members.

Ideals held by Martin's School

A record book of the Union School, better known as Martin's School, reflects the form and content of their educational continuity. Changes during an 85-year period (1862-1947) were few and gradual. The average length of time that each of the 38 teachers taught during that period was 2.2 years. Sixty percent of the teachers during the first twenty years were men. During the latter part of that period, practically all teachers were women. Possible explanations for the high teacher turnover were low pay and low esteem for the role of teacher, one of few job openings for single women.

As stated in Chapter 6, 42 percent of Waterloo County Swiss Mennonite family surnames are Martin. Of the 38 school teachers, sixteen or 42 percent were also Martins. Teachers were paid from $350 to $500 per school term between 1862 and 1906. This meant a 44-year period without a change in basic pay rates; from 1907 to 1914, the rate was from $500 to $800 and from 1915 to 1920 it was raised to $1,000.

In view of this long tradition, it is quite natural that the proposed Ontario educational changes of the 1960s were greeted with alarm and resistance. The changes came at a time when public school systems in the United States and Canada were under severe criticism. They were faulted for poor lesson materials, for lack of discipline, and for ineffective teaching, as well as an inadequate philosophy of education.

Conservative Mennonites were opposed to the surrender of control of their children's education. They objected to having them bused to school, while they were still using horses and buggies. Their children would need to leave for school an hour earlier each morning and return an hour later in the evening, depriving parents of help with the daily chores. In a centralized school system their children would be pressured to conform to dress codes or be ostracized by their peers. They feared educating their children in a school with vocational courses which would attract them to non-farming occupations. They saw nothing that would help them preserve their way of life but much that would destroy it.

Mennonites confront the Ontario government
The hard part of their choice was how to refuse the provincial school closing law. It meant petitioning the government of Ontario to release them from the mandate and to permit them to set up their own parochial schools. They offered to co-operate with the Ontario Department of Education in using the recommended curricular materials, and adhere to the required annual number of school days.

Four groups: the Old Order Amish, the Old Order Mennonites, the Beachy Amish, and the Waterloo-Markham church, created a committee to present their case to the Educational Committee of the Ontario Government. This inter-Mennonite committee asked Mennonite Central Committee executives to help them present their case.

Members in the Ontario Legislature raised serious objections to granting the Waterloo delegation their request.[1] Typical comments by committee members were: "These kids are being squelched by the very persons (their teachers) who are supposed to be fostering an interest in them" (New Democratic Party, Sudbury). "The Mennonite schools are not up to the same standards as ours" (Progressive Conservative, Hamilton). "In this day and age, children need a real education and these children do not have the freedom of choice" (PC, Ontario South). An NDP Roman Catholic from Lakeshore noted that the parent rather than the state should have the last word about a child's future.

Douglas Snyder, director of the Ontario Mennonite Central Committee, served as spokesman for the delegation. He pointed out that the real education of Mennonite children began when they got down to working on the farm with their parents. "We believe," he said, "that the early teen years are a valuable time for teaching religion, apprenticeship in agriculture, and responsibility to the brotherhood and family. We believe that the Lord has blessed us with our children and that it is our duty and responsibility to teach them the ways of honesty, integrity, simple living, and the fear of God."

Several factors helped the Mennonites obtain a favourable decision. One was the outcome of several court trials between individual Amish and school administrators in the United States. These aroused a great deal of publicity in the news media and attracted moral support for their cause in Canada. Help also came from Edward Good, a man with Mennonite background and a member of the Ontario Parliament from Waterloo. His interpretation of the Mennonite cause to his colleagues and his counsel to the Mennonite delegation were invaluable in winning approval for the compromise solution.

The Old Order Mennonites in Waterloo and the Amish in Perth counties had strong support both in the press and among the general public. In one instance, a member of the Waterloo County Superintendent's office was quoted in the local newspaper as saying, "What this all boils down to is this: does the child belong to the state or to the parents? Most of us, I think, believe the child belongs to the parents to raise as they see fit."[2]

The editor of the *Milverton Sun*, published in Perth County in the heart of Amish country, strongly criticized the new Ontario school laws for shortchanging farmers in their vocational training program. Thus, he justified the Mennonites for withholding their children from school an additional two years.

> One can hardly blame them for taking matters into their own hands. The educational system as we know it offers very little to the farmer. . . . The Department of Education has more recently realized this wasn't enough and have now incorporated trade courses at the high school level. These offer graduates diplomas in motor mechanics, electronics, photography, business and finance, you name it—they teach it—everything but agriculture. They

learn arithmetic, reading and spelling, all essential for life, but when they graduate or quit they have learned absolutely nothing about their chosen field—farming.[3]

New church schools in old public schoolhouses

The lengthy confrontation resulted in a satisfactory solution for the Waterloo school administrators, the conservative Mennonites, and the general public. A major reason for the success of the new program was the surprisingly high level of elementary education carried on in the parochial schools. It is a historic anomaly that after more than a century of supporting the public school system, the conservative sector of Waterloo Mennonites returned to the church-owned parochial school system with which they began under Bishop Benjamin Eby 150 years earlier.

They took over a school system which the government abandoned. They bought many of the old schoolhouses for a song and found them useful for their purposes. The new school system fell within the Private Schools Act of Ontario, the same law under which other private schools in the province had long been operating.

The Mennonites made a wise decision by hiring James Bauman, a qualified superintendent, to administer their schools. He is a local person of conservative Mennonite background in sympathy with their philosophy of education. At the same time, he is respected by the Waterloo Board of Education. All administrative matters pertaining to the operation of the school can be handled through his office. This school administrator visits each school, counsels each teacher during the year, and conducts two summer teachers' institutes: one devoted to orientation for new teachers and another for the experienced teachers.

Where there's a will, there's a way

The organization of the present parochial school differs little from the public school system of a former day, except that the church instead of the government owns and controls it. School districts are formed throughout the Mennonite area. Each district elects three school directors. These may be elected by either the Old Order Amish, the Old Order Mennonites, or the Waterloo-Markham Mennonites, according to their respective numerical strength. These directors serve without pay and assume responsibility for maintaining the building, hiring the teacher, and seeing that teachers have supplies for operating the school.

Table 11-1 shows the Mennonite and Amish parochial school picture in the wider Waterloo area. There are 33 schools with 44 classrooms. They were all established between 1966 and 1978. Three of the Old Order schools are located in Wellington County; five schools are Old Order Amish located in Perth County; and five are owned by the newly-formed Conservative Conference. In 1978, there were only three male teachers; the others, with one exception, were single women.

The two-year extension of compulsory school attendance from fourteen to sixteen was met by accepting farm work by boys as meeting requirements for vocational agriculture. Work in the house and garden under parental supervision and with periodic reporting on educational progress passed as domestic science for girls. This solution reflected common sense on the part of the provincial educators and found favour with the Mennonites. It gave academic credit for what these teen-age boys and girls would have been doing had they dropped out of school at age fourteen.

Table 11-1 provides a clear picture of the size of the conservative Waterloo Mennonite parochial school program which sprang up within a decade. The total enrolment at the end of the system's second decade had increased to 1200 with a few more schools added. Of the 33 schools in operation, five are owned by two moderate conferences, five by Old Order Amish, and the other 23 by the Old Order Mennonites. A two-room school at Beachburg, Ontario, a new Waterloo-Markham settlement in the Ottawa Valley, is not listed above. Eleven families, 75 persons, from the Waterloo area established the settlement in the early 1980s.

Teachers recognized although uncertified

One of the objections to Mennonites operating their own schools was that they lacked trained and certified teachers. But the Mennonites, who up to that time had been having provincially certified teachers in the public schools, nevertheless proposed using as teachers their own members even though they had only an elementary school education. They claimed that properly selected persons with aptitudes for teaching and a liking for children could do the job satisfactorily. Public school officials and the general

Table 11-1
Waterloo area Amish and Mennonite elementary schools
Source: *Blackboard Bulletin*, 1978

School Name	Founding Date	No. of Pupils	No. of Rooms
Balsam Grove	1966	38	2
Beechville	1966	41	2
Red Hill	1966	26	1
South Woolwich	1966	32	1
Winfield	1966	17	1
Winterbourne	1966	34	1
East Heidelberg	1967	27	1
New Jerusalem	1967	26	1
North Woolwich	1967	37	2
Yatton	1967	51	2
Macton	1968	30	2
Maple Grove	1968	54	2
Smithside	1968	13	1
S. Heidelberg	1968	28	1
Fourth Peel	1970	28	2
West Montrose	1971	42	2
Bricker	1973	21	1
Floradale	1973	25	1
Clear View	1973	24	1
East Dorking	1973	27	1
Farewell	1974	36	2
Lindale	1974	30	1
Riverdale	1978	16	1
*Goldstone	1986	46	2
*Maple Drive		29	1
*West Hesson	1977	24	1
**Cedar Grove #1		22	1
**Cedar Grove #2		25	1
Amish #1	1966	35	1
Amish #2	1967	36	1
Amish #3	1968	34	1
Amish #4	1968	48	2
Amish #5	1977	18	1
Totals (33 Schools)		1020	44

*Schools owned by W-M Conference
**Schools owned by Conservative Mennonite Conference

public were skeptical. But opposition was minimized by the fact that the Mennonites were, after all, undertaking to teach only their own children. Furthermore, the Amish school model in the

States showed that the plan could work.

The conservative Mennonites believed that successful teaching at the elementary level was more the result of natural gifts and personal motivation than a skill acquired through higher education. They assumed that the basics of communication and calculation could be taught by anyone who had mastered them and enjoyed teaching them to others. This put the elementary teacher on a par with parents who transmit skills and knowledge as well as moral values to their offspring without regard to formal settings.

After twenty years of experience, the Waterloo Mennonites are generally satisfied with the results of their educational program. They believe that their schools are adequately training their children to take their place as future farm parents. Over a ten-year period, I visited one- and two-room schools with university classes of which experienced Waterloo County schoolteachers, some with administrative experience, were members. We met with teachers and school board members in their own schoolrooms. Lesson materials, student work, subject outlines, and daily class schedules were examined. Our general consensus was that the educational level of the parochial school was commendable. It might be enlightening to compare learning achievements of pupils in the two school systems.

The parochial teachers are strongly motivated and are highly regarded in their communities. Teaching is almost the only vocational alternative other than work as housemaids open to conservative Mennonite young women before marriage. The teachers in the parochial schools come to know their students well. If they continue teaching in the same school, they may be the only teacher that some students ever have. In many ways, they are like an older sister or brother to their students. One problem not found in these schools is that of discipline. Children are taught at home to respect their teachers as they do their parents.

For many of the teachers, the day begins at six o'clock. Some board with one of the families in the school district. For some, it means a walk of a half mile or a mile or possibly a horse-and-buggy ride of several miles. Most of them try to be in school by 7:30 in order to be ready to open the school at 9:00. After students and teacher greet each other, a portion of Scripture is read without comment, followed by prayer. A typical day's schedule includes: health, current events, arithmetic, and history for grades three to eight. Desk work is followed by an hour's lunch period. After lunch, a 15-minute reading period, then science, geography, music, literature, and writing. Every Friday, time is given to art and Bible study. The textbooks used are those approved for Ontario public schools at the time parochial schools were organized. Teachers use their own discretion and the counsel of James Bauman, Inspector, as to what is taught and what is omitted.

After the close of school each afternoon, the teacher marks student papers and prepares for the next day. She usually has from twenty to thirty students in her room in grades one to eight. At six o'clock, she walks to the nearby farm where she keeps her horse and buggy, then rides to her boarding home where she arrives in time to join the farm family for supper.

Moral and ethical values stressed

The Mennonite schools strongly emphasize moral training. They want to be assured that all subjects will be acceptably taught so as to accord with home and church values. This concern is reflected in the epigrams on the walls of the schoolrooms where children frequently see, read, and memorize them. Following is a typical list:

> Good habits are like muscles; the more you use them the stronger they get.

> Intelligence is like a river; the deeper it flows the less noise it makes.

> Seven prayerless days make one weak.

The Pupil's Creed

1. I will try to do my best work in all my lessons, not only to please my teacher, but because I know I will gain more by doing so.
2. When I do not understand my work, I will wait until my teacher has time, then I'll kindly ask her for help.
3. I will do my work quietly, so as not to disturb my classmates and teacher.

4. I will join in games without showing partiality to my favourite playmates.

5. I will not complain to my parents or teacher about others, when I know I am wrong.

6. When the teacher punishes me, I will take it to heart and try to improve myself.

7. I will not use bad language at any place.

8. When a classmate reaches a certain goal before I do, I will rejoice rather than be jealous.

9. I will be honest with my lessons. I know that by cheating, I am cheating no one more than myself.

10. I will remember that I am a member of this school family. I must keep in mind that I don't want to disappoint my parents and teacher.

Special public schools for one group of Old Order Mennonites

The small David Martin Old Order ultraconservative group worked out a unique arrangement with the Waterloo County Board of Education in what is known as the Three Bridges Public School and the town of Linwood Public School. The Three Bridges school students are 100 percent Mennonite and most of them belong to the David Martin group. This school was never closed as a public school. The D.M. group was unwilling to join the other Mennonite churches in a parochial program. They are not opposed to public school per se but restrict their children's participation in some school activities. For instance, children may not take part in physical education classes or in family life classes or join other students who go to Elmira once a week for home economics or shop classes.

Linwood, a town school, accommodates the Mennonites in a unique way by providing special classes for Mennonites only. These are not to discriminate against Mennonites, but rather to work with their language handicaps. Most of them must begin learning English in the first grade, hence are at a disadvantage with other students who use English exclusively.

In this school, 132 out of 330 students (40 percent) are Mennonites; most of them belong to the David Martin group of Old Orders. Although there are six or seven parochial schools in the area, none of their children attend any of them. The special classes for Mennonites began with grades one and two. Two grades of six and seven students each are all Mennonites. Most of them are extremely shy and find it difficult to express themselves in English, hence the advantage of having special classes. It is less embarrassing for these Mennonite children to be with their own than to be left behind when regular students attend classes from which Mennonite children are forbidden by their church. The school principal and the specially appointed teacher have been sensitive to what is permitted and what is prohibited by the D.M. Church. Almost without exception, these children withdraw from school the very day they become fourteen years of age.

Ontario Mennonite Bible School

So far, we have focused on Mennonites with a conservative philosophy of education. Until about the middle of the twentieth century, the overwhelming majority of Mennonites both in Ontario and in Waterloo were conservative—educationally and theologically. The most progressive element of the Swiss Mennonites bestirred itself in 1907 when the Mennonite Conference of Ontario organized the Ontario Mennonite Bible School. It was first called a Bible study class and lasted four weeks. In 1908, the day and evening class enrolment stood at 65. By 1927, enrolment had grown to 102 and the term was extended to eight weeks, plus a Ministers' Week. In 1929, the term was extended to twelve weeks.

This Bible school provided learning opportunities beyond the elementary school level where most of Mennonite young peoples' formal education ended at that time. It was a welcome winter activity for rural teen-agers and older farm youth. It afforded social opportunities beyond the local congregation, and contributed to the development of lay leadership in the conference and to a continued interest of young people in the church.[4] The school was discontinued in the 1960s largely due to greater attendance at public high schools, the establishment of Rockway High School, the increase of rural young people taking full-time jobs in the city, and the shift from lay to college- and seminary-trained ministry.

Rockway Mennonite High School (Collegiate)

Up to World War II, Waterloo Mennonite views on education differed little. At that time, Mennonites were still mostly rural and engaged in farming. Waterloo County in 1941 had a population of 99,000 and only one high school. Even those Mennonites living in or near towns, as a rule, did not have their children finish high school. During and following World War II, Mennonites joined the wave of rural people moving to towns and cities. Special skills and additional training in offices and factories as well as in the service professions demanded more formal education.

Compulsory military cadet training program in a local public high school raised serious questions in the minds of Mennonites. Administrators of the high schools were sensitive to Mennonite opposition to military training and exempted Mennonite students from wearing military uniforms or marching in drills. They were permitted instead to train for service in first-aid units. Instead of wearing military uniforms, they were permitted to wear white shirts with a Red Cross armband. Yet the agitation for a Mennonite high school continued.

From 1943 to 1945, the issue was discussed at sessions of the Mennonite Conference of Ontario. In 1944, a study committee recommended that a high school be established in 1945. Steps were taken to raise $50,000 and efforts were set in motion to find a suitable location and qualified and willing faculty members. The school opened in September of 1945 in a farmhouse on Doon Road, the site of the present school. This was the first venture into secondary education by the Swiss Mennonites in Ontario. Its stated purposes were to train future church leaders and provide an alternative to public high school education. The newly arrived Mennonites from Russia had opened the United Mennonite Educational Institute in Leamington, in Essex County, in 1944. A Bible school, which later became a high school, was opened in Virgil in 1942 by the Mennonite Brethren.

Rockway High School experienced severe difficulties in the late sixties and early seventies. During those stressful years, the school was taken over by a private group of Mennonite supporters. In the late seventies and early eighties, Rockway was able to regain support from its original constituency plus that of the Western Ontario Conference and some from the United Mennonite and the local Dutch Reformed Church. At the time of this writing, the school announced that it was expanding its program to include seventh and eighth grade offerings. This is the first instance of a progressive Mennonite group offering parochial school elementary education in the twin cities.

Conrad Grebel College

It is ironic that Waterloo Mennonites in the decade of the 1960s were going in opposite educational directions. At the time that conservatives and moderates were rejecting the newly revised Ontario elementary school system in favour of their own private system, the progressive Mennonites were entering into a relationship with a provincial university. Conrad Grebel College was not only a new venture for the Ontario Mennonites, but for all Mennonites in North America. One Mennonite sector in Waterloo found the government's educational program threatening to its own survival; the other sector found the government's program inviting and potentially capable of fulfilling a Mennonite need. Both Mennonite groups were concerned with preserving and transmitting their heritage. The conservatives decided that owning and controlling their own educational system was the way to preserve that heritage. The progressives decided that they needed the help of the government and accepted a co-operative arrangement to preserve and transmit their heritage.

The University of Waterloo was founded in 1957. It had its beginning in Waterloo College, now Wilfrid Laurier University. Plans to expand the Lutheran college into a university at that time aborted. As a result, the college continued to operate as a private institution and those favouring the university moved to a new area a half mile away and established the University of Waterloo as a completely separate educational entity. From the beginning, the newly established university invited a number of Ontario religious denominations to establish church colleges on the university campus. Four denominations responded favourably to the invitation. St. Jerome's, a Roman Catholic college, already in operation since 1864, was the first to take positive action. It worked out a federated relationship which was different from the other three colleges, since it already had almost a century of history, tradition, and reputation as an independent denominational liberal arts college and an administration and faculty in place. It moved to the university campus from its location on the eastern end of Kitchener in 1962. Although it had worked out its agreement with the university in 1960, it functioned from its old campus for the first two years.

Renison College was established in 1959 by the Anglican Church. It operated out of a family dwelling until 1962 when it erected its first college buildings on the university campus. The United Church of Canada followed by organizing St. Paul's College and erecting its buildings in 1963.

Conrad Grebel, the last of the church colleges to affiliate with the university, began its building program in 1963 and opened its doors to students for the first time in September 1964. It is one of the many ironies of history that the family farms of the pioneer Mennonite settlers, who had consistently rejected higher education as unnecessary, should subsequently become the campus of one of Canada's youngest, yet most distinguished universities. The chief remaining evidence of that fact is the blue-gray limestone farmhouse on the north campus which was preserved by the combined efforts and financial support of the Waterloo Heritage Foundation, the University of Waterloo, Conrad Grebel College, and the Mennonite Historical Society of Ontario.

University made college possible
Without the University of Waterloo's invitation of affiliation, it is doubtful that there would have been a Mennonite college in Ontario. And without effective leadership by a congenial group of progressive young ministers, two university professors, and a handful of forward-looking businessmen, it is unlikely that the progressive Ontario Mennonites would have responded positively to the university's invitation. It was fortunate that these people and the university's bid came together when they did. The ministers were positive forces in interpreting to their congregations the meaning of a college for the future of Ontario Mennonites. They minimized resistance that easily could have developed among a people traditionally suspicious of universities and university-educated students.

By the 1960s, it was also evident to all branches of the progressive Mennonites that education beyond high school was essential. Waterloo area students were enrolling in many different colleges, universities, technical schools, teachers' colleges, and nurses' training programs in Ontario and the United States. The founding of Conrad Grebel College was an appropriate response to a demonstrated need. The founding of a Mennonite college marked the end of an old Mennonite pattern of refraining from discussion of intellectual questions or debating controversial public issues. It was a bold step for a small, generally conservative religious group that had traditionally opposed all forms of higher education to establish a liberal arts college on a university campus. Instead of embarking on a course of traditional separation from the world, the Mennonite segment that supported the college chose to locate its residence on the university campus and have its students and faculty members interact with all phases of the university community. By its geographical proximity and academic participation, it faced up fully to the challenge of attempting to be a Christian presence in the university community. By virtue of their setting, Conrad Grebel students and faculty are forced to give a witness, either strong or weak, good or bad, positive or negative, for the spiritual, ethical, and intellectual values they profess.

The three Mennonite conferences (MCO, WOC, UMO) and the Stirling Avenue congregation, the supporting bodies of the college, demonstrated courage in getting it organized and into operation. They have provided the needed financial and moral support during its first twenty-five years of existence. These four separate entities, in 1987, formed a single church conference.

Opportunity in co-operative relationships
Conrad Grebel is owned and operated by the three Ontario conferences of Mennonites and Stirling Avenue congregation which was formerly independent but has since joined two of the conferences. These three bodies govern the college through elected representatives, one representative at large from the faculty, alumni, and student body, plus representatives at large. Conrad Grebel and the three other church colleges on the campus are all integrally identified with the University either as federated or affiliated bodies. Each college has its own constitution and separate contract with the University that sets forth the legal limits and responsibilities of the respective parties. Each college president

and an additional college faculty member have full voting rights as members of the University Senate, the highest governing body. All college faculty members have full standing in the University and its various academic departments. College faculty members serve on faculty departmental committees and on university-wide committees. All college students may enrol in any department of the university where qualified, and university students may enrol in any college courses where academically qualified.

This co-operative arrangement is advantageous to church college students because they have the privilege of living in a residence community with a religious orientation. They have access to religious instruction, religious services, a common dining room, study facilities, and recreation which results in the possibility of an intimate social life. At the same time, the setting gives opportunity for a university wide choice of vocational courses. Of great importance economically is the financial advantage of affiliation of the church colleges with the University. Since students are all enrolled or registered in the University, college faculty members get paid for the instruction at the same rate as university faculty members. This is why a small constituency of under 15,000 can afford to maintain its own church college.

The college has not only met a need for young people wanting to pursue higher education programs for vocational purposes, but also has been a significant resource for the entire Ontario Mennonite constituency and especially those in the Waterloo area. As a result, a faculty of fifteen to twenty full- and part-time professors are employed, plus a support staff of about the same size. This has meant participation and contributions in various churches, the giving of lectures, the writing of books, the creating and performing of music of high quality, and a general lifting of religious, cultural socio-ethical interests in the community. The presence of the college has also been responsible for bringing to the community many distinguished guests as speakers and performing artists who would not have been brought there otherwise.

A major contribution of Conrad Grebel is to the university academic community through its courses in Bible, theology, history, social studies, music, and peace and conflict resolution. Two academic programs offered by Conrad Grebel are unique to the university, in that no other college or the university itself offers any course for credit in the field of music or in peace and conflict resolution. Both of these areas provide opportunities in which to earn degrees. No other Mennonite college anywhere offers such an extensive peace studies program. The course offerings reflect the most advanced thinking in contemporary peace studies. It is the most aggressive academic peace thrust carried on by present-day Mennonites anywhere. Note the following course titles: Roots of Conflict and Violence, Conflict Resolution, the Nuclear Crisis, the Politics of Nonviolence, and Introduction to Peace Research. In addition, students can choose from over one hundred related courses in the departments of history, political science, psychology, philosophy, sociology, and religious studies.

Educational changes over twenty-five years
Among conservative Mennonites, the adage, "As the school, so goes the church," is often repeated. It is interesting to reflect on this folk wisdom and apply it to the Waterloo Mennonite situation. This brief description of education among Waterloo Mennonites provides a test of the adage. The conservatives believe it and seek to assure that objectives and practices of school and church remain integrated and mutually supporting. If the church owns and controls the school, then it is inevitably true. If it is applied to the progressive Mennonite choice of educational courses, the conclusion is not so self-evident.

Will the progressive churches follow their schools, Rockway Collegiate and Conrad Grebel College? Or will the two pull apart in the course of time? Will the philosophy of the schools eventually become the philosophy of the churches? These questions can only be answered after a generation or two have passed. After remaining educationally static for 150 years, Waterloo Mennonites made a giant leap forward educationally in just twenty-five years. It reflects the same kind of quantitative leap which has taken place in other aspects of progressive Waterloo Mennonite life. Mennonites cannot stop the flow of change. They can select the most beneficial changes and train people to make intelligent decisions under the new conditions.

An Old Order Amish man transporting a gasoline engine. There is no rubber on the wheels of this nod toward mechanization.

(From the collection of David Hunsberger)

Mutual aid in traditional form—a barnraising.
(From the collection of David Hunsberger)

Mutual aid in contemporary form. All members of the Credit Union are Mennonite or Brethren in Christ.
(Mennonite Credit Union)

The first of the Zehr's Market chain opened by a progressive Amish Mennonite on Highland Road in Kitchener in 1950.
(Zehr's Markets Ltd.)

An Old Order Mennonite farm that illustrates the many additions to the family home—perhaps to care for aged relatives.

(From the collection of David Hunsberger)

Old Order Mennonite school with children playing.
(Photo: James Hertel)

A symbol of progressive Mennonite education: Conrad Grebel College, which is affiliated with the University of Waterloo.
(Conrad Grebel College)

A traditional Mennonite art form — the quilt — being presented to Ontario Lieutenant Governor Lincoln Alexander at the time of the 1986 Mennonite Bicentennial celebrations.

(Photo: *Mennonite Reporter*)

Sixtieth anniversary commemorating the arrival of Russian Mennonites and their walk up Erb Street West in Waterloo to the Erb Street Mennonite Church to meet their "Swiss Mennonite" hosts. This young man is dressed as his grandfather was when he arrived in 1924.

(Photo: *Mennonite Reporter*)

Interior of an Old Order Mennonite meetinghouse. This traditional design was originally used by all the Mennonites who immigrated from Pennsylvania.

(From the collection of David Hunsberger)

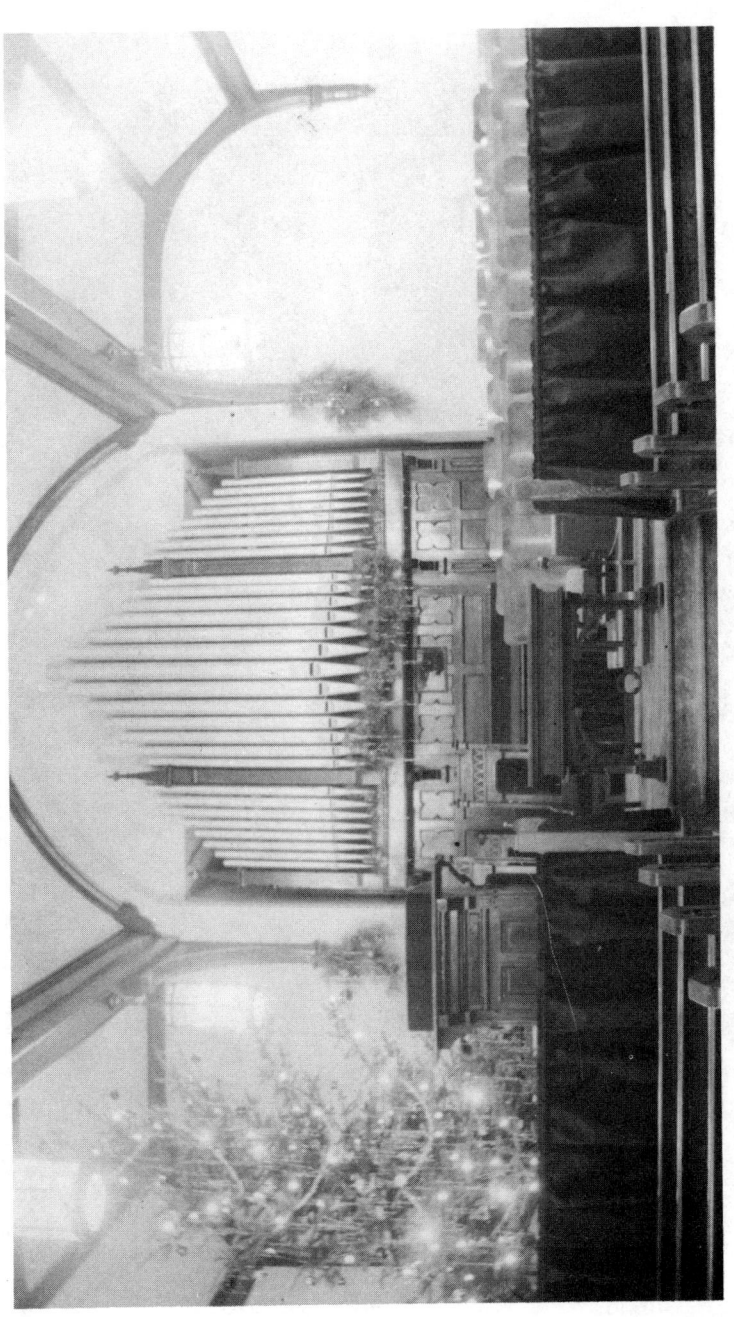

The Waterloo United Mennonite Church in 1953. This was the first pipe organ in a Mennonite church in the Waterloo region.
(Mennonite Archives of Ontario)

Wedding photograph of a progressive Mennonite couple of the 1890s. Even for these Mennonites, clothing styles became more conservative in the decades that followed.
(Mennonite Archives of Ontario)

Old Order Amish boy. He uses hooks and eyes instead of buttons on his coat.
(From the collection of David Hunsberger)

Recycling instead of waste. Mennonite Central Committee initiated a vigorous
recycling program in the Region Municipality of Waterloo
before it was generally popular.
(Photo: *Mennonite Reporter*)

Old Order Mennonite boys returning to the barn with a full load of hay.
(From the collection of David Hunsberger)

"Progressive" Mennonites at a youth convention. Painted faces or not, society would be hard pressed to distinguish them from their Lutheran, United or Catholic friends.
(Photo: D. Michael Hostetler)

Chapter 12

Farming—the sacred vocation

Throughout their entire history, farming has been the predominant way Mennonites earned their living. In early centuries, farming was often a necessity, but during the past two centuries, it has been the occupation of their choice. It came to be a preferred, almost sacred, vocation because it afforded them more than a livelihood.

Farming above all other occupations or professions provided an ideal environment in which to carry out the church and family ideals. Closeness to nature, in a setting for raising and nurturing a family where all members could take part in the work and enjoy the fruits of their labour, has always been attractive to Mennonites. Farming was also historically favourable to the concept of the believers church and its adherence to a policy of separation from the world.

Farming for Mennonites has not been only a family enterprise. It has been a church-centred community activity, a neighbourhood of families in which friendly competition and habitual co-operation were part of the annual harvest cycles. Farming in communities made it possible for the strong and the fortunate to assist the weak and the unfortunate. Without such mutual support, sharing, and spiritual encouragement, many individuals and families could not have succeeded or even survived. Nothing is more characteristic of Waterloo Mennonites today than their role as productive farm families. The family farm is for young and old, male and female, grandparents and grandchildren. All contribute and all benefit.

Mennonites brought a long list of distinctive farming practices and culture traits from Europe. They brought the huge two- and three-storey barn style and the familiar earthen banks that lead to the second-level driving floor, the method of intensive farming,

highly developed animal husbandry, summer and winter stable
feeding, fodder cultivation, clover hay sowing, the use of natural
and commercial fertilizer, the rotation of crops, and the industrial
use of by-products. These innovative and successful methods were
the result of generations of trial and error and from intensive
sharing of experiences with one another. Ernst Correll, a historian, even attributed Mennonite farming practices to religious
roots.[1]

> Mutual aid, practiced to conform to a religious norm, leads to
> brotherhood credit, which in turn makes of the congregation a
> credit corporation. Having thus perfected the system of personal
> credit long before any system of rural credits became known else-
> where, the Mennonites benefited greatly from credit integration
> and credit distribution.

Swiss farmers succeeded because of the invisible factors of social
organization and religious motivation. We all know the importance of credit in the capitalistic system. The word credit comes
from the Latin *credere* which means to trust or believe in. This
lies at the basis of all credit systems. Anyone who belongs to a
group which believes in or trusts him or her has an advantage
over others who lack such an asset. Trust is an integral component of mutual aid.

The eminent authority on the Amish people, John Hostetler,
identifies closeness to nature as one of the fundamental principles
of the Old Order Amish.[2] This same claim could be made of the
Old Order Mennonites. Love of the soil has become an acquired
value through a long heritage of dependence upon the soil for survival. To them, the soil is like an old friend that responds to nurture, faithfulness, and care. Hard work is rewarded with harvest
year in and year out. Farming and religious principles such as
separation from the world, frugal and simple living, the ethics of
love and nonviolence all go well together.

Farming is one of the few remaining occupations that lends
itself to a non-specialized family enterprise. Even so, it is moving
more and more in the direction of greater and greater specialization. But it still lends itself to participation by men and women,
boys and girls, grandparents and grandchildren. It is one contemporary industry which can be more labour-intensive than capital-
intensive and still be economically viable. This is being

demonstrated by conservative Amish and Mennonite farmers.

These farmers have a comparatively low capital investment because of their generally smaller acreages and their use of older and more limited kind and amount of machinery. Since the labour used is almost all supplied by the family or by the exchange of labour with relatives or neighbours, labour costs are low. Even where farmers must hire help, they do so by hiring young teen-age boys from other church members' families who work for modest wages.

Credit union—a farmers' resource

Several factors determine whether Mennonite children remain on the farm. Among these are the pursuit of education (among the progressives), personal preferences and aptitudes, the degree of satisfaction on the farm, the number of opportunities open to them, the attitudes of parents and their capacity to help them purchase farms of their own.

Farm purchase has become difficult in the seventies and eighties. A study by Hugh Laurence of the progressive Amish in Wellesley Township found that up to 1940, most Amish Mennonites were still farmers because the price of land had not yet inflated to the levels of the sixties and seventies.[3] The custom had been for a previous owner of a farm to leave about 60 percent of the purchase price as a first mortgage to the buyer. Second and third mortgages, if necessary, generally came from parents, relatives, or church members. By 1955, this began to change; farmers were forced to seek commercial loans since sufficient private resources from individuals were no longer available. Because commercial loan rates and land prices were high, many left the farm and sought their livelihood in towns and cities.

This difficulty is reflected in the use which farmers from both the Old Order Amish in Perth County and the Old Order Mennonites in Waterloo County are making of the Mennonite Credit Union of Ontario. The credit union has established branches in Elmira and Milverton, towns easily accessible to conservative and moderate Mennonites and Amish who had previously been largely able to satisfy their credit needs among their own members.

Methods of farming

In Waterloo County, Mennonite farmers have been considered successful. That success has been measured not only by economic criteria, but also on such additional bases as stability, industriousness, integrity, good stewardship of property, and reverence for the soil. They have been praised as law-abiding citizens and as builders of religious communities.

Financial gain for Mennonites has been important but not an end in itself. It is important as it enables them to continue engaging in what they believe is a God-approved vocation for themselves and their children. One valid test of this is that most Waterloo Mennonites or Amish will not sell their family farms voluntarily merely for a higher dollar. They cherish their own homesteads and endeavour to make it possible for children and grandchildren to occupy them in the future.

Mennonites have been successful farmers because of their love of farming and the confidence, persistence, and single-mindedness with which they undertake their work. Although individual families buy and own their own farms, they do so with the interest and awareness of the extended family and the local church community. Tremendous psychological and social support stands behind a young couple's financial venture when they first rent or purchase a farm. This moral, spiritual, and financial support by the larger community stabilizes individual families and in turn builds stable agricultural communities.

Rehabilitating old farms

In 1965, an Old Order minister told me that he had helped his son, one of eight children, purchase a 150-acre farm along Highway 86 near the hamlet of Dorking, in the northwest corner of Waterloo County. It was at the time on the fringe of the Mennonite expansion toward the northwest. The purchase price was $16,000 or $107 per acre. The farm was bought from a retired farmer whose son had acquired it for $8,000, but gave up farming after a short time. Both house and barn were in poor condition and the land had been neglected. The first thing the new owners did was to cut down trees on the farm and have them sawn into lumber to repair the barn and later to remodel and repair the house. This work was done by the minister, his son, and other members of the family.

The next item of improvement was to tile the land with 55,000 tiles to assure good drainage. The cost of the improvement was probably as much or more than the purchase price of the land. After twenty years, the family is successfully continuing to farm this land. Since then, enough other Mennonites have moved into the area to warrant establishing a new congregation and building a new meetinghouse. The minister's son in the meantime has been chosen by lot to be a minister in the Weaverland congregation. Later he was chosen by lot as a second bishop to assist in the work of the growing conference.

Rebuilding an old community

Because of the scarcity and high cost of land in the immediate area of Waterloo, in large measure due to urban expansion, Old Order Mennonites began buying farms in the vicinity of Mount Forest, forty miles north of Waterloo. At first, they farmed the land and remodelled buildings while still living in the Waterloo area.

Over the last two decades, about seventy-five families have moved from Waterloo to Mount Forest, and are scattered over an area within a 17-mile radius from that town. Many farms there were for sale, often with neglected land and buildings. "Big Ed" Martin was one who bought one of these neglected farms. His story shows the determination of an Old Order young man to get a farm of his own when his immediate family was unable to provide the necessary help.

Ed had no living father, so he worked as a hired man and saved what money he could and borrowed the rest to buy a run-down farm which had been owned by two bachelors. The house was both flimsy and filthy, and the barn had scarcely any place for stabling animals. He cleaned and enlarged the house. Putting a new roof on it, he assured himself that the house was dry and would not collapse.

He next provided adequate stabling for his livestock, erected a straw shed, implement shed, and milk house. He cemented the barn yard and put new siding on his barn. Then having taken care of the buildings, he cleared off five acres of willow bush and tiled the swampy land it covered, plus eleven other acres. He put all sixteen acres into production and with the income from that once unproductive acreage realized enough income to repay a big share of his debt to a Mennonite brother who had loaned him the money.

Big Ed Martin showed how the Mennonite ladder from hired man to farm ownership works. It includes commitment to a goal, hard work, careful planning, a spirit of enterprise, good steward-ship of resources, and mutual financial aid from a brother at a low rate of interest. Note that there is no mention of any paid labour. Both families did all their own building, thus keeping capital costs at a minimum. Their one major cash outlay was for building materials. Building skills are learned from each other and by trial and error.

In addition to the move of Old Order families from Waterloo County to Mount Forest in Grey County, a dozen Waterloo-Markham Mennonite families have gone to the Ottawa Valley, some three hundred miles northeast of the twin cities. Their use of cars and trucks makes a move of that distance feasible. The set-tlement effort is still relatively new but appears to have growth possibilities. Waterloo farmers are able to buy good quality improved farms for much less per acre than they got for their Waterloo area farms.

Muriel Maybee, a University of Waterloo geography depart-ment student, made a study of Mennonite farming methods in Waterloo County.[4] "These traditional Mennonite families," she said, "do not just take care of their own; they have a sense of com-munity matched by none. If a neighbour needs extra hands for a busy season or after a tragedy, free labour is offered. Such cash-less exchange of labour is common among Mennonites, as is exchange of machinery and custom work." No doubt Big Ed Mar-tin received such free help at crucial points in his farm rebuilding and land-clearing work.

Of the 1,974 farms in the county, 1,205 or 61 percent are Men-nonite farms. As expected, Old Order Mennonite farmers own the largest number and percentage of the farms. The distribution of farmers by Mennonite religious body is reflected in Table 12-2.

Table 12-1
Farms and farm population by townships, 1971

Townships	Farm Population	Number of Farms	Percentage of all farms
Wellesley	2,912	557	28.2
Woolwich	2,472	448	22.7
Wilmot	1,916	434	22.0
Waterloo	1,392	357	18.1
North Dumfries	795	178	9.0
	9,487	1,974	100.0

Township population shift

Of the five townships in Waterloo County, only one was not originally occupied by Mennonites. Wellesley Township was first settled by Scots, English, and some of German background. North Dumfries, to which the first Waterloo Mennonite pioneers came, also attracted English and Scottish settlers in large numbers. Mennonites gradually moved northward into Waterloo, Wilmot, and Woolwich townships. In 1861, the Mennonite population in Wellesley Township represented only one-half of one percent, compared with 21.5 percent in Waterloo Township.[5]

By 1971, Mennonite population in Wellesley had increased to 45.3 percent while in Waterloo Township, the Mennonite population had declined to 10.8 percent, a decline due to the expansion of the twin cities. Woolwich Township, in that same period, had its Mennonite population increase from 14.1 percent to 46.4 percent.[6] The significance of this Mennonite population shift had direct consequences for Mennonite agriculture in the county. Whereas Waterloo Township was for many decades the most densely settled by Mennonites, today it is the most sparsely settled of the five townships in the county.

Table 12-2 includes only eight of the fourteen groups in this study. Four of the groups with a Dutch-Russian background have only one known farmer among them and he is highly specialized. The number of Old Order Amish farmers in Waterloo County is twenty-five. Of the 1,205 Mennonite farmers in the county, 42 percent are progressives; 37 percent conservatives, and 21 percent moderates.

Table 12-2			
Percentage of Mennonite farm ownership by conferences			
OOM	36.3	BA	5.2
WOC	24.3	CMC	2.3
MCO	17.2	RM	.7
WM	13.3	UMO	.7

Types of farming

Maybee's paper examined the agricultural systems of three different Mennonite groups: MCO, W-M, and OOM, representing progressive, moderate, and conservative Mennonites.[7] All three of these groups of farmers live in the same area, upper Waterloo township. The variations are found in the mean acreage per farm, the amount of machinery per farm, the amount and kind of livestock, the feeding practices, the kinds of crops grown, the amount of labour hired and the degree of specialization. The Ontario Conference was found to have the greatest diversity. It had no limitations set by the church on modernization or choice of occupations. Each farmer pursues his own goals, basing his decisions more on the marketplace than on religion and tradition.

Varieties in types of farming are usually related to factors of climate and soils. In Waterloo County, experts agree that the northern and western portions of the county are the most promising for farming.[8] These areas consist almost entirely of Class I soils. Their rolling topography and friable, rich soils contrast with the hilly terrain, gravel, and sand of central Wilmot, southern Waterloo, and most of North Dumfries townships.[9]

The agricultural economy of Waterloo County has been based on mixed farming throughout its entire history. The climate has been favourable to mixed farming, and the Mennonites have historically been strongly committed to it. Mixed farming is deeply embedded in their philosophy of economic self-reliance. It is a way of freeing themselves from total dependence on the marketplace, of not "putting all one's eggs in a single basket." Mixed farming distributes the risk of uncertain weather, pestilence, and the commodity market in a systematic way. It assures at least elemental survival by providing food, feed, and shelter for humans and animals. Finally, it is a way of using the labour of all family members, male and female, young and old, the year round.

Mixed farming may have a lower cash flow than does specialized farming. It may even result in a lower standard of living, since it tends to be labour-intensive rather than highly mechanized with labour- saving devices. Wellesley and Woolwich townships, which have the highest percentage of Mennonites according to the 1971 Canadian census, have not only the highest percentage of farm ownership but also the highest percentage of houses without indoor toilets and running water. This reflects the order of priorities: economic security over personal comfort. These two townships have the highest concentration of mixed farming.

Additional insights regarding Mennonite mixed farming practices are reflected in the production of such supplemental cash items as maple syrup, apples and berries, eggs and garden vegetables. I was told of three Old Order young women who regularly produce garden vegetables for sale at local markets as a major source of income in preference to doing housework or teaching school. Those doing mixed farming often have small orchards for supplemental cash income as well as for domestic purposes.

Woodlots are found on a high percentage of Mennonite farms. Only on the larger specialized farms have they given way to crop farming. The size of these lots ranges from ten to thirteen acres. They provide a source of firewood which many of the conservative Mennonites use in their stoves, and they provide various kinds of lumber for building purposes. These woodlots also fit into the self-sufficiency philosophy by providing maple trees to be tapped for maple syrup which is used in baking and for table use, the surplus being sold for cash.

Part-time farming

Mage, in 1969, found that 72 percent of all hog farms and 93 percent of all beef farms in the county were operated by part-time farmers (Table 12-3).[10] Part-time farmers tend to avoid the type of farming that requires constant labour input. Only three percent of all mixed farming was done by part-time farmers. Cash-cropping was another type of common agricultural involvement by part-time farmers.

Table 12-3
Distribution of types of farming, 1969*
Sample of 149 Waterloo County farms[11]

Farming Type	No. of Farms	% of Total	Part-Time Operators	% Part-Time, Each Type	Full-Time	% Full-Time, Each Type
Dairy	30	20	1	3	29	97
Hogs	18	12	13	72	5	28
Beef	14	9	13	93	1	7
Hogs & beef	17	11	6	35	11	65
Mixed	38	26	1	3	37	97
Cash crops	11	8	7	64	4	36
Specialty	5	3	4	80	1	20
Poultry	3	2	3	100	0	0
Combination	4	3	2	50	2	50
Corporate	9	6	–	–	–	–
Total	149	100	50	33**	90	60***

*Total number of farms includes 90 full-time, 50 part-time and 9 corporate.
**Part-time farms as a percentage of total farms.
***Full-time farms as a percentage of total farms.

In his study of Waterloo County types of farming, Mage selected thirty farms, embracing about 3,500 acres in a mixed farming area where 85 percent of the farms are owned and operated on a full-time basis by Mennonites.[12] The average acreage of these farms ranged from 110 to 133; the average for the sample was 121 acres. About eighty acres were devoted to cropland; woodlands ranged from six to thirty-one acres per farm. The dominant crops were hay and mixed grain, nearly twenty-five acres of each and one field of six to eight acres devoted to corn. About eleven acres were devoted to pasture. The corn acreage was normally sufficient to fill one twelve-by-forty-foot silo.

Rotation of crops is practised with some variation, but the common practice is to grow grass for two years, then corn, oats, and some wheat the third year and finish with two years of mixed grains. During the cycle, the land is heavily manured at least three times. Mennonite farmers take pride in using as much of their land as possible every year so that very little land lies fallow at any time. Some farmers use commercial fertilizer but less is required when the farm produces much of its own.

Life on an Old Order farm

A Mennonite Old Order 114-acre family farm illustrates high-lights of farming methods still carried on in Waterloo.[13] On this particular farm, ninety acres is in cropland. Of this, thirty acres is in hay, forty acres in mixed grains, and eight acres in silage corn. Eight acres is in rotation pasture and four acres in wheat. Four acres is bottom pastureland along a creek. An eighteen-acre wood-lot yields firewood and maple syrup. Livestock consists of fifteen milk cows, seventeen calves and steers, twenty-seven breeding sows, 1,100 hens, and four horses. In 1968, when the data were gathered, the farmer had gross sales of $23,000; gross expenses of $17,000, and a net income of $6,000.

The farmer was 42 years old. He, his nine children, and his wife were their chief source of labour. This farmer devoted about eighty hours per week to farming. Even the youngest children had regular light chores. Teen-age sons, already skilled farm workers, aided their father with heavy tasks of cultivating, har-vesting, and looking after livestock. Teen-age daughters played equally important roles in helping their mother with work in the house, garden, and often with milking and harvesting.

Equipment on the farm tends to be old but functional and ade-quate. Larger items such as threshers, balers, and binders used only seasonally are often shared with neighbours and relatives. By using inexpensive older machinery and not hiring labour, this farmer keeps capital and operating costs at a minimum. The land value of the above farm in 1968 would have been about $500 per acre or a total of $57,000; machinery about $5,000; livestock about $9,000 for a total capital investment of $71,000. This case is rep-resentative only of Old Order farms in the area. It does not typify the more highly mechanized moderate and progressive farms with newer, larger, and more expensive machinery and, in the case of progressives, larger acreages.

Farm financing

The method of farming chosen determines the amount of capital required. Maybee interviewed 23 farmers (seven Old Orders, and eight each in the Waterloo-Markham and the Mennonite Confer-ence of Ontario) about their farming methods and financing.[14]

She also noted the amount of work and machinery that were exchanged in each of the three groups studied. The W-M and the MCO farmers owned and rented similar amounts of machinery; both used almost twice as much machinery as the Old Order farmers.

While the Old Orders almost all own one tractor for their heavy farm work, they use horses for much of the lighter work. Their gasoline or diesel fuel bills therefore are lower. That saving is offset in part by the feed that must be raised. The progressive Mennonite farmers own three tractors per farm compared to one for the Old Orders.[15] The average acreage of Waterloo County farms is 126 acres compared to just over 100 acres for the conservatives. The Waterloo-Markham and Old Order farmers take advantage of their communities for sharing machinery much more than do the Ontario Conference farmers. This means savings on capital investments.

Another measure contributing to the self-sufficiency of the Old Orders is that they buy only about one-third of the amount of ready mixed feed used by the Waterloo-Markham and Ontario Conference farmers. They tend to buy more supplemental concentrates and mix their own feeds, while the others buy the ready-made feed entirely. The Old Orders also use pasture for summer feeding, while the others tend to give their livestock year-round storage feed and use what would be pastureland for crop production, thus generating greater cash income but also greater tilling, seeding, and harvesting costs, and greater cash outlay for purchased feed.

In contrast to the older and smaller farm implements commonly used by the Old Order farmers, a Waterloo progressive dairy farmer, a member of the Ontario Conference whom I interviewed, owned all of the relatively new, large, and sophisticated machinery listed in Table 12-4.

At the time (1976), his estimated capital machinery investment was $125,000. In 1988, the cost of a similar line of equipment would no doubt be double or triple that amount. To arrive at the total capital investment of this particular farm, one would need to add the cost of the livestock, the market value of the land, and such other items as trucks, cars, and household furnishings, which at the time could have been an additional $50,000 to

```
Table 12-4
Machinery inventory
of progressive Mennonite farmer

100 HP tractor                Two self-unloading
60 HP tractor                   forage wagons
35 HP tractor                 Forage harvester
Five-bottom plow              Forage blower
One 18-foot disc              Manure spreader
  harrow                      Hay rake
Four-row 14-foot              Two 200-gallon
  corn planter                  sprayer tanks
Two-row 14-foot               Milk pipelines
  corn cultivator             Milk cooler
Two-row corn picker           Generator
One 10-foot, 17-spout         Backup generator
  grain drill                 Pressure pumps
Self-propelled combine        Septic tank
Rotary mower                  Hot water heater
Haybind conditioner
```

$75,000. This should not be thought of as a typical or representative progressive Waterloo Mennonite farm inventory. Table 12-5 shows that this total farm value was considerably higher than the average for the county of Waterloo as a whole or for any of its townships in 1971.

Waterloo and Dumfries townships have the largest urban populations of the five townships in Waterloo County. They also have the smallest number of farms, the largest per farm acreage, the highest average value of land and buildings and of machinery and equipment. This illustrates how proximity to urban areas influences scarcity of land, land values, and land usage.

Old Order access to low interest money

The conservatives and moderates said they seldom or never borrow money for farm operations. The progressives said they borrowed occasionally or regularly.[16] Borrowing by the conservative farmers is most often for the purpose of purchasing land either for themselves or for their children. Whenever possible, funds are borrowed first from members of the immediate family, then from near relatives, and thirdly from fellow church members. These sources not only provide much of the Old Orders' needed capital,

Table 12-5
Agricultural census data, 1971
(Statistics Canada)

	Ontario	Waterloo County	Welles-ley	Wool-wich	Wilmot	North Waterloo	North Dumfries
					Townships:		
Number of farms	94,722	1976	558	449	435	335	179
Average acreage	169	126	115	116	123	141	164
Average value land and buildings	$54,722	72,895	45,931	60,612	69,994	120,287	100,823
Average value machinery and equipment	$9,396	9,654	6,898	8,834	11,044	11,744	12,775
Average value of live-stock	$8,696	14,000	14,797	17,282	20,811	15,467	22,606

but it is money borrowed at far below prevailing commercial interest rates. Since the late 1970s, conservative Mennonites have increasingly used outside funds (see chapter 17).

A member in one of the Old Order congregations sold his farm at a good price, because the city of Waterloo demanded the land for expansion. He told me he was offered high interest rates by investors in the twin cities, but he refused to consider all such offers. Instead, he made loans to young men in his church to help them buy farms, and he made the loans at five percent interest when the market rate was two and three times that rate. He said he did not need a big return on his money and was happy to make it possible for young couples to have a start at farming.

Few farm failures among Old Orders
This constant sharing of goods, services, and money helps keep costs of farm ownership at a manageable level and helps avoid financial failures. Two senior ministers were asked what was the rate of farm failures among Old Order farmers. After consulting, they were unable to recall any outright failures, but remembered a few farmers whose financial difficulties were solved by fellow

church members who helped the distressed farmers reorganize and better manage their affairs. Even during the much discussed farm crisis of the 80s, I was told that while the cost of land and interest rates were high, few Old Order farmers had large outstanding debts for machinery or livestock.

Some farmers from the progressive and moderate groups who expanded their farming operations by acquiring more acreage and additional mechanical equipment on borrowed money are in greater financial difficulty. The progressive Mennonite farmers have no comparable mutual aid credit system among themselves and do not generally practise sharing machinery or exchanging labour as do the conservatives and to some extent the moderates. Hence, they must secure their financial needs through commercial financial institutions and pay going market rates. The Mennonite Credit Union organized by the progressives is today meeting many of their credit needs.

The role of Mennonite farm women

Mennonite farm women are still full-time partners with their husbands in operating their farms. This is at least true of families engaged in full-time farming. It may be less true of those farmers highly specialized, such as the scientific production and care of large flocks of poultry, hogs, or cash cropping. In such cases, it is possible that the farmer's wife is not directly needed in the business and may be working outside the home. The large majority of Waterloo County Mennonite farm women work the same long hours as do their husbands.

There are no Old Order and moderate farm women and few rural nonfarm progressive women who don't do some growing and preserving of their own food. There seems to be a close correlation between the amount of producing and preserving of food and the degree of conservatism among Waterloo Mennonites. The conservatives are more concerned than the moderates with economic self-sufficiency, and the moderates are more concerned than the progressives. This is again related to family size, to philosophy of education, the attitude toward labour-saving devices and to the source and amount of family income. The contrast between the consumer habits, practices, and philosophy of the Old Order farm women and those of the progressive and many moderate Mennonite farm women is quite distinct. The rural farm homes of the progressive and many moderate Mennonites are generally as well furnished as are the homes of urban Mennonites, but not so the homes of the conservative Mennonites.

Conservative farm women do not worry about such household items as matched dining room sets, or upholstered chesterfields with matching easy chairs. No wall-to-wall carpeting, no expensive drapes, no china dishes, sterling silverware, king-sized beds, dishwashers, or microwave ovens are found in Old Order homes. Nor do these women need to spend time studying the mail order catalogues or go shopping for the latest styles of attire. Their grocery and clothing bills, for the most part, are minimal, compared to the less self-sufficient and fashion-conscious Mennonites. Their commitment to simplicity and frugality sharply curtails wants and needs. The woman's big economic contribution to the family enterprise, in addition to the daily care of children and household duties, is her role in food production and preservation.

Katie and Melvin Bearinger are a young married couple who had moved from Waterloo to Mount Forest. Katie outlined clearly her role as a conservative Mennonite farmer's wife. "I got seven quilts and five mats," she said. "The quilts were made by my five sisters, who during the winter before our marriage came to my parents' home for a few weeks, while not needed at home, to work on the quilts and floor mats. Our kitchen chairs and all the dishes and cookware were bought for us by my mother at auction sales. Melvin and I refinished the chairs." Before marriage, Katie worked out for four years doing housework for other Mennonites—two years for one family, one year for another, and a fourth year as housekeeper for a schoolteacher. After staying at home with his father till he was sixteen, Melvin worked "out" five years— on a farm, in a factory, and in a lumber mill.

"Our people always serve fruit and pie for dessert. That is one reason why we always do a lot of fruit canning," said Katie when showing me her well-stocked cellar. "We always like to preserve enough food for a full year and a little more in case of poor crops some years."

This was in October after the fruit and vegetable canning season had ended. Her inventory included 30 quarts of pears, 27 quarts of strawberries, 12 quarts of plums, 10 quarts of cherries, 25 quarts of peaches, 48 quarts of rhubarb (flavoured with orange peelings), 9 pints of blueberries, 12 quarts of golden pickled string beans, 16 quarts of mustard sauce beans, 14 jars of pickles, carrots and cucumber relish, 22 jars of mixed vegetable relish (tomato and corn), 30 quarts of corn, 65 bottles of ketchup, plus a dozen quarts of ketchup which is used in the preparation of meats. In the family deep freeze were uncounted packages of peas and green beans, twelve chickens, and baked goods such as rolls, pies, and bread.[17] Also in large jars were sliced roast beef and sausage, easily prepared on short notice and frequently served for Sunday noon dinners. The Bearingers grow their own potatoes, using from fifteen to eighteen bushels and selling the rest of the two-acre crop.

The Bearinger food supply is not uncommon. Another home visited by Lynn McKinda maintains the reputation of Waterloo Mennonite farm women as diligent providers of food for their families.

> In a dark pantry off the kitchen, there were crocks of cheese, elderberries, apple butter, bags full of schnitz (dried sliced apples), dried corn and beans, pails of maple syrup and sacks of sugar and flour. Her cellar looks like a store. A room twelve feet square has shelves all around it from floor to ceiling filled with quart and half-gallon jars of canned beef and chicken, and pork sausages hang from the beams above. There are great bins of potatoes and turnips. Other vegetables are stored in boxes and there are barrels full of apples.[18]

These two illustrations are evidence of the important roles Mennonite farm women play in their family enterprises. They see no need to struggle for women's rights and social equality. By virtue of the way they perform their roles, they enjoy the respect of husbands and children. Generally husbands and wives consult each other before making major decisions. They know their respective roles, accept them willingly, and generally enjoy performing them to the best of their abilities.

Industries on Waterloo Mennonite farms

Although farming is still the main occupation of Waterloo Mennonites, and although the Old Order Mennonites and Old Order Amish still strongly prefer farming above every other occupation, the percentage engaged in farming has been steadily declining over the past fifty years. The pressures of urbanization and industrialization are evident even among conservatives.

Incontrovertible evidence is the more than fifty rural manufacturing and service businesses and industries found on Mennonite farmsteads as of 1979, and the significant number of conservative men who find nonfarm work as craftsmen and labourers.

Table 12-6
Types and numbers of Mennonite farm industries

Harness and shoe shops	6	Lumber dealer	1
Farm wagon builders	5	Hydraulic sprayer factory	1
Buggy builders and repair	4	Tractor cultivator factory	1
Stable equipment factory	4	Scraper blade factory	1
Blacksmiths	4	Contractor, builder	1
Furniture and woodworking	4	Sawmill	1
Metal fabricators	3	Manure bucket factory	1
Foundries	3	Wood shaft and wheel factory	1
Welding services	2	Metal products factory	1
Machine shops	2	Tinsmith	1
Sheet metal shop	1	Cider press	1
Tractor repair shop	1	Total	50

One reason for the growth of farm industries is the growing demand for farm equipment repair services. Some of these businesses grew out of the mechanical gifts and interests of farmers who began repairing their own and neighbours' equipment and gradually grew into full-time businesses. Most of the fifty businesses are located on farms which the owners continue to farm on the side. A high percentage of the employees in these industries also live on farms and do part-time farming. Practically all of these businesses are family-owned.

All three groups are literally and figuratively losing ground to urban expansion and all are losing an ever larger share of their members to nonfarming occupations. They are all modifying their farming methods in response to contemporary economic conditions. The use of tractors probably illustrates this response to technological change as well as any single culture trait.

When the tractor was first introduced in the 1920s, all Mennonites were slow to accept it. Gradually, the more adventuresome and bold farmers bought tractors and discovered their superiority over horse power. Still, it was not until after World War II that the tractor replaced horses on most progressive farms and was slowly adopted by the moderate and conservative Mennonites. Today none of the progressive and very few moderate farmers do any work with horses. At least 88 percent of Old Order farmers own and use a cleat-wheel tractor. Only the small David Martin group still uses only horse power.

Farming and freedom of choice

Waterloo Mennonites all live and work under the same economic and political systems and are subject to the same laws and economic forces. However, farming still represents the occupation with perhaps the greatest freedom of choice in day-to-day living. It has its routine and yet its tasks vary almost from day to day and certainly from week to week and from season to season. The weather dictates many day-to-day choices. There is outdoor and indoor work, there is work with machinery and with animals, there is plowing, sowing and reaping, there is buying of supplies and selling of products, there is the sad experience of livestock dying and crops failing and the joyful satisfaction of a good harvest. Farmers have the constant challenge of being good stewards or skillful managers of time, materials, labour, and money.

Among the nonfarming Mennonites, there is great diversity of occupations, but within each occupation there is great specialization so that the specific job of each person tends to require narrower decision-making demands. There is also less variation in the type of work from day to day and week to week, and for most nonfarming jobs the weather has no direct effect. A major difference between the occupation of farming and nonfarming Mennonites is the farmer's uncertainty of income in return for labour expended. Assuming the nonfarming worker has employment, his pay and social security benefits come at stated periods of time and in fixed amounts. He is thus able to plan expenditures more exactly. In that respect he may enjoy greater freedom of choices than the farmer. The farm family has greater freedom in the use and size of buildings and space. He is less restricted by zoning ordinances, utility lines, sidewalks, garbage and sewage disposal, and water supply. Finally, farm families are still able to produce a large percentage of their own food whereas nonfarming families are primarily consumers of food and other necessities.

Chapter 13

Occupations shape the church

Research for this book showed that the progressive Mennonites in the Waterloo area engaged in no less than 223 separate occupations. This contrasts sharply with the fewer work choices open to Old Order members who are limited by church restrictions.

Work as a means and an end
A distinction should be drawn between work as an occupation and work as a vocation. An occupation occupies or engages one's time as a person's principal work or business. Often, we set it apart from a profession, a calling for which persons have gained special knowledge, by training or by experience, so that they may guide and advise others. We assume that a profession has a service motive as distinct from moneymaking. But many new occupations are now called professions so that the line between a highly skilled job and a profession is somewhat blurred. Today, the moneymaking motive appears as prominent a drive in those who pursue professions as among those who engage in other lines of work.

Those who view their work as a calling, whether that call is considered from God or from a strong personal will, see it as something important that needs to be done to benefit society. It may be something as common as motherhood or as unique as a specialized science. A calling has a strong sense of *ought* as a motive. A person with a strong sense of vocation sees the work as a challenging task that may merit an entire lifetime of commitment. The task for that person has intrinsic worth. It is an end in itself rather than a means to wealth or fame.

The concept of calling is often used by those who enter religious work. They chose their work, such people say, because they feel they have the gift for it or they may feel they have a divine call. But the same reasoning can lead a person to many other kinds of work not strictly religious. The term vocation should not be applied only to those occupations which in the past were identified as professions, such as medicine, law, education, and ministry. A vocation may be any kind of work that is socially useful and that a person has a gift for doing and/or a sense of ought about doing. It provides satisfaction for self and for others.

These two general views of work—as occupation or as calling—provide a basis for testing the vast array of jobs open to Mennonites in the Waterloo area. Are these jobs a means to an end or ends in themselves? Do Mennonites view the work they do as mere jobs at which to earn a living, or as vocations or callings? Only those doing the work can answer. Much work in present-day industrial society lacks the satisfying characteristics of a vocation.

Many, if not most, mass production jobs lack the elements of a calling. They tend to be a means to an end, the end being the money reward. A high percentage of modern industrial jobs have no element of craftsmanship. They are repetitive and fragmented parts of a larger whole. Many employees never see and do not share in completing the finished product. They do not know the customers or ultimate consumers they serve. They merely do one or two repetitive jobs all day long, day after day. Result: boredom.

I recall vividly my own experience one summer, fifty years ago, when working for the Ford Motor Company at Dearborn, Michigan. One of my jobs was putting four-inch bolts into motor blocks day after eight-hour day. That job held not one iota of challenge. The same was true of dozens of similar jobs from one end of the long assembly lines to the other. The thought of doing this work for life was numbing. The job had no redeeming aspects. The only reason for doing this work was the $96 per month. Work such as this dehumanizes. It does not provide workers a sense of fulfilment or achievement. Rather, it breeds alienation, resentment, and anger. Still, millions of people endure this way of earning a living because for them it means survival. They may have no favourable alternatives. An auto plant worker probably spoke for many when he said, "I have worked twenty-five years in this factory as an assembly line foreman and hated every day of it."

The industrial worker's lack of control over tools, skills, and working conditions has created a feeling of powerlessness and alienation from employers. A familiar cliche describes the current industrial scene: "Labourers do not own and owners do not labour." The most common response of workers to their feeling of powerlessness is to form labour unions. This is a means of collective rather than individual bargaining for a greater share in decision-making because individual bargaining is ineffective.

In such occupations, one's worth in one's own eyes, as well as in the eyes of others, gradually declines. High wages may keep workers at such jobs but produce a low degree of self-respect. The increased income is often used up in the search for satisfaction in leisure-time activities after working hours and on weekends.

Unlike the Old Order Mennonite farmer and his family, the urban assembly line worker has little if any chance for decision-making on his job. He is at the mercy of technology and decisions made by others often unknown to and unseen by him. The psychological and spiritual effect on employees is deadening. The factory worker has a 40-hour work week and high per-hour wages, the Old Order Mennonite an 80-hour work week and uncertain income. Between these extremes, most Waterloo Mennonites must earn their livelihood. Which of the 223 occupations held by Mennonites are callings and which are unsatisfying jobs?

When Kitchener-Waterloo turned urban

Waterloo Mennonites did not leave the farm in large numbers until after World War II, although the growth of towns and small industries began a hundred years earlier. European artisans arriving in a steady stream after 1835, spurred the growth of Preston, Galt, Hespeler, and Berlin. Ivan Groh says that many of these early artisans first found work among Mennonite farmers who had become well established and could afford to hire labour.[1]

Ananias Martin, a well-informed, retired farmer, recalled his father telling him of having hired one of these artisans, a Lutheran who was treated as one of the family. He was so considered years after he had moved to Kitchener and set himself up in a trade. A major reason for the good relations between Mennonite farm families and these immigrant artisans was the fact that many of them were also Palatinate Germans who spoke the same dialect and had a common culture except for religion.

Few Mennonite businessmen in the nineteenth century

In his history of Kitchener, W. V. (Ben) Uttley lists 82 Berlin businessmen and craftsmen to whom he refers as "citizens of the sixties."[2] Forty-seven different occupations are identified with those names. Galt, at the time, was the largest town in the county with a population of about 3,000. Berlin had just under 2,700, of which 128 (4.2 percent) were identified in the 1871 Canada Census as Mennonites. However, not one of the 82 businessmen could be identified as Mennonites by their names.

In a second list, nine years later, Uttley gave 72 Berlin names with their businesses. In this list are three men with names that could well have been Mennonite—David Eby, a pumpmaker; Henry Eby, a wagoner; and Peter Erb, a harnessmaker.[3] Sixty-five years passed before Mennonite businessmen were to be found in Kitchener in substantial numbers. As late as the 1920s, the Mennonite Conference of Ontario warned its members to be cautious about entering business without approval from the church brotherhood.[4]

In 1855, the town of Preston had a population of about 1,600, while Berlin had a little over 1,000 and Waterloo 500. The early Mennonite settlers first located in the southern end of the county and gradually moved north. Preston's location on the Speed River made it attractive as a source of water power for sawmills, grist mills, and textile mills. The coming of the railroad through Berlin and the naming of Berlin (now Kitchener) as the county seat at mid-century gave it and Waterloo the edge in becoming the larger commercial and industrial centre. With the coming of steam power and the railroad by the second half of the century, a location along the river was no longer an advantage for industry. Already in 1835, Waterloo Township had distilleries, two woollen mills and one oil mill.[5]

Niagara hydro promotes industry

During the latter half of the nineteenth century, important changes came with the improvement of farm-to-market roads, the development of steam engines, and perhaps best of all, the introduction of hydroelectric power from Niagara Falls. The early introduction of new technology explains, at least in part, the present industrial specialization existing in the county.

Among these highly developed industries still in existence are heavy machinery and equipment in Cambridge, rubber products, furniture, electronics, clothing, brewing and distilling, meat packing and insurance in Kitchener and Waterloo.[6] Large industrial and commercial centres depend on a prosperous hinterland for an ample food and labour supply. The rural area in Waterloo County helped to provide these. Beginning with the second quarter of the twentieth century, rural Mennonites began to flock to the twin cities for work and permanent residence.

The two world wars led many young Mennonite men and women to leave the farms to take employment or be drafted for military or alternative service. After the war ended, many of them did not return to the farm. Most of them had only an elementary education or at most a year or two of high school and were not prepared to go on to university. Thus they learned a skill or took unskilled or white-collar jobs in industry and business.

In 1978, I undertook a study of Old Order and Waterloo-Markham ex-Mennonites who had left the farm and moved to towns and cities over the past fifty years.[7] It showed the kinds of jobs taken by these early Mennonite migrants to towns and cities. Table 13-1 illustrates jobs taken in three stages: the first jobs, next jobs, and jobs held until retirement. Notice that none of the first jobs taken were factory or assembly-line jobs. The job listings include both men and women and cover a time span of about fifty years.

The total interviewed in 1978 was twenty-seven persons. A number became owners or managers of businesses. This is a mere glimpse into the early shift of some Mennonite farmers to towns and cities and the jobs they found to support themselves. It is safe to assume that the nine persons whose first jobs were as domestics were women who had few other skills. But then, as now, Mennonite women are highly sought after by those who hire domestic help because they have a reputation as diligent and competent cooks and housekeepers. In the final job lists, none of the twenty-seven persons interviewed were employed as domestics. For the nine women so employed in their first jobs, it was a means to an end. As soon as more desirable occupations became available, these women accepted them, likely because the alternative jobs paid a higher wage, but also because they provided a step or two

---

Table 13-1
Jobs taken by former Old Order and
Waterloo-Markham Mennonites
when leaving the farm for the city

First jobs	*Second jobs*	*Final jobs*
Director, Bible School	Gravel business	Feed mill
MCC work	Feed mill	Oil business
Office work (5)	Chemical and dye	supervisor
Machinery factory	work	Computer programmer
Domestic (9)	Missionary	Minister
Feed mill	Store clerk	Nurse
Cider mill	Domestic	Implement shop
Machine shop (3)	Fireman	Fertilizer company
Saw mill	Restaurant	Watkins Products
Warehouse	Foundry	Store
Carpenter	Dairy	Housewife (7)
Steel mill	Security guard	
Machine shop	Cook	
Factory (7)	Stationary engineer	
Delivery	Machinist	
	Shipper	
	Furniture factory	
	Fabric factory	
	Carpenter	
	Truck driver	

upward in terms of social status.

This study also revealed interesting data about the jobs of the children of the first-generation conservative and moderate Mennonites who left the farm. These occupations reflect upward mobility. They included owners of service station, implement, and lumber businesses, computer operator, dental hygienist, hairdresser, and telephone employee. Not all of the second-generation children were in the above list of occupations. An estimated three-fourths of them followed the occupations of their parents.

After almost two hundred years in Canada, the majority of Mennonites are no longer engaged in agriculture. In Waterloo, for the first time, those engaged in farming are in a minority occupation. This means a marked difference in the way of earning a living, hence a lifestyle that affects the organization and function of four basic institutions: the family, the school, the church, and the community. The changes come about slowly and almost unnoticed. They become apparent only over decades and generations.

The shift of Waterloo Mennonite culture from one mostly agricultural to one steadily becoming mostly urban means a surrender of the way of life known as the self-sufficient family farm. The majority of Mennonite families have already made this transition. And for a substantial number of Mennonite farm families in the Waterloo area, the trend away from the family farm shows no sign of abating.

In place of the family farm is the urban and rural nonfarm occupational pattern of specialization, or what French sociologist Emil Durkheim called "the division of labour."[8] He points out that societies with little division of labour have a solidarity which comes with common sets of values and patterns of behaviour. In other words, people whose ways of earning a living or whose lifestyles are similar develop a common bond and mutual trust. Specialized labour splits up social tasks. In such a society, people are held together not so much by shared values as by mutual interdependence.

This exchange of shared values and common life experiences for division of labour results in religious communities being slowly and subtly affected by the individualized goals of urban society. Thus the family is fragmented and the spiritual community atomized. The believers' church,[9] once a disciplined community, becomes only a specialized interest group.

Never before have so many drastic occupational changes taken place in a single generation. Never before have Waterloo Mennonites had so many occupations from which to choose ways of earning their living. Table 13-2 provides an overview of eleven categories for the 223 occupations in which Waterloo Mennonites are gainfully employed. It also shows how these occupations are distributed according to conservatives, moderates, and progressives by numbers and percentages.

Table 13-2 shows a concentration of occupations among conservatives and a scattering among the progressives. Two out of every three conservatives are engaged in farming, compared to fewer than one in six among progressives. Those conservatives not engaged in farming are employed in closely related occupations. The high percentage (11.5%) of conservatives and

Table 13-2
Waterloo Mennonites by major occupational categories

	Progressive %	Moderate %	Conservative %	Total
Farming (owners, workers, managers, tenants)	17.8	48.6	65.6	1547
Machinists (metal workers, fabricators assemblers)	8.4	5.1	5.8	372
Education (elementary, secondary, vocational, college)	7.2	1.3	1.7	277
Nursing (registered nurses, nurses' aides, orderlies)	5.1	3.6	.56	207
Secretary, stenographer, typist	4.0	.0	.11	142
Truck driver	3.6	4.1	.0	154
Food processing (millers, bakers, milk processors, canners, packers)	3.5	1.6	.9	143
Agribusiness (animal husbandry, dairy tester, egg grader)	3.5	.7	.22	129
Mechanics, repairmen	2.9	3.4	.0	127
Carpenters	2.9	3.7	1.3	141
Personal services (housekeepers, homemakers, hired girls)	2.4	11.6	11.5	349
All other occupations	38.7	16.7	6.3	972
Total	2983	672	905	4560

moderates engaged in personal services is explained by the large numbers of single women, especially teen-age girls, who do housework among their own people in the years between leaving elementary school at about fourteen years of age and getting married at about twenty.

Almost six percent of conservatives are occupied as machinists and metal workers in the many farm industries described in the previous chapter.

Unusual Mennonite occupations

Among the progressive churches, no occupations are excluded by church discipline. One or more progressive members are engaged in the following unusual (for Mennonites) occupations: artist, chemical engineer, civil engineer, detective, engine assembler, electric power lineman, filer, food inspector, forester, funeral director, geologist, government administrator, glazier, hide processor, motel owner, milliner, power station operator, paper products fabricator, radio and TV announcer, securities salesman, statistical clerk, salesman, sound recording equipment operator, taxi driver, typesetter, upholsterer.

One Waterloo County urban Mennonite church reported 47 distinct occupations out of a total of 124 gainfully employed. Table 13-3 lists the occupations, and the numbers in parentheses indicate how many members in each of the occupations.

The occupational spread in Table 13-3 above is probably more or less representative of the Waterloo County town and city Mennonite congregations. The spread would presumably not be as varied in the open country churches, yet even there a surprisingly large number of members, if not living on farms, have second jobs.

Several observations can be made on the basis of the information found in Table 13-3. Only eight of the 47 occupations are family-owned businesses. The persons in the other 38 occupations, which represent 83 percent of the total, are wage earners and as such have little, if any, share in significant decision-making concerning their work and workplace. This shift from ownership and independence about one's work has a major impact on Mennonite life styles. It is an important illustration of social accommodation that has taken place unconsciously over the years and tends to cultural assimilation. In terms of religion, it contributes to a transformation of a Mennonite church from a community to an association.

Table 13-3
Members of one Waterloo area urban church, 1980
(The 47 occupations of 124 members.
Number in parentheses indicates number in same occupation;
* indicates family-owned business.)

1. Auto agency (2)*	19. Minister	35. Secretary (9)
2. Accountant	20. Missionary	36. Social work
3. Administrator	21. Musician	37. Service
4. Baker	22. Nurse's aide	station owner*
5. Bank clerk	23. Personnel	38. Supermarket
6. Dietitian	24. Press	manager
7. Estimator	operator	39. Supermarket
8. Excavator*	25. Printer*	owner*
9. Editor	26. Packing	40. Technician
10. Engineer (2)	house (6)	(IBM)
11. Farmer (6)*	27. Meat cutter	41. Truck driver
12. Fuel, building	28. Real estate	42. Retired (18)
supplies*	29. Restaura-	43. Unemployed
13. Insurance (3)	teur (4)*	44. University
14. Hostess	30. Railroad	professor (2)
(restaurant)	31. Rubber	45. Teacher
15. Hardware	factory (2)	(elementary)
(wholesale)	32. Salesman	46. Teacher (high
16. Homemaker (32)	33. Sales clerk	school) (2)
17. Librarian	34. Stone	47. School
18. Maintenance	memorials*	administrator

Indifference to a job's impact on religion
Progressive urban Mennonites have paid little attention to how their members earn their living. Nor have their churches thought about how their members' occupation affect church participation. It seems to be assumed that occupation per se is neutral and has no impact on ethical values and Christian life styles. In contrast, the conservative Mennonites see a close relationship between what their members do for a living and the impact that many occupations have on religious convictions and social behaviour. They see urban living as a threat to religious community life and as a surrender of the doctrine of separation from the world.

Calvin Redekop, professor of sociology at Conrad Grebel College, began a serious discussion of the sociology of occupation in his 1983 Benjamin Eby Lecture, "The Promise of Work."[10] He pointed out how work has been separated from family, kinship, and community; that jobs have become means to status and security; that work has become merely a commodity with a price tag that is bought by the employer and sold by the employee without primary regard to social and spiritual consequences or meaning.

Redekop raises basic questions about the absence of Christian biblical standards of work and the role of work in a plan of salvation. He appeals to today's Christians to recover a biblical view of occupations as a calling. He suggests that doing so may require major changes in the way we choose jobs, the way we prepare for the work we choose, the places we choose to work, and the motives that lie behind those choices. Were Waterloo Mennonites to follow Redekop's suggestions, it would alter their occupational profile and their religious behaviour as well.

Mennonite work preferences in Waterloo County

Douglas Snyder, a graduate student in 1972, studied the work ethic among 304 Mennonite Conference of Ontario families.[11] The numbers of men and of women were about equal. Only three persons out of the total were engaged in factory work. This may have accounted, in a large measure, for the low interest in labour unions. The Snyder study showed a number of significant facts about Mennonite work attitudes and preferences. Fifty-six percent of the women worked full or part-time outside the home. None of the 304 were unemployed. A high percentage were self-employed as truck drivers, salesmen, electricians, building contractors or auto mechanics. Others were farmers, teachers, social workers, nurses, and administrators.

Ninety-seven percent expressed job satisfaction. This finding was supported by the length of tenure on a particular job, or by the few jobs held in a lifetime. Only three men and three women expressed dissatisfaction with their jobs; only 6.4 percent of the males and 16.8 percent of the females said they planned to change jobs in the year ahead. Thirteen percent of the women and 39 percent of the men expressed a desire to remain at their present job until retirement. Eighty-four percent of the respondents were home owners. This is significant in view of the fact that the 304 persons included those nineteen years of age and older. Only eight persons thought their jobs were insecure. Fifty-one individuals or 16.7 percent of the total held a second job. The reasons given were: to fill up their spare time, to raise their standard of living, to pay debts, to educate their children, and to avoid the necessity of the spouse working outside the home.

Few Mennonites join labour unions

Only a small percentage of Mennonite workers belong to unions. It is not accidental that the percentage is low. Snyder found that the question about membership in labour unions was carefully answered, showing that these persons wanted to make it known that they were either not members of a union or, if members, were only token members. If they were unwilling members, they availed themselves of the opportunity to designate their checkoff dues for charity. Likely their opposition to labour union membership reflects the kind of jobs they seek in the first place. Few if any of those who belong to unions participated in picket lines during strikes. Opposition to unions is in line with the Mennonite tradition of refraining from joining service or fraternal clubs other than their local church. Until the middle twentieth century, Ontario Conference Mennonites were discouraged or forbidden by their church from joining labour unions.

At the conclusion of his investigation, Snyder made the following comments: "The study portrays a people secure, well entrenched in home ownership, above-average income, unemployment almost unknown and expectations for present employment to continue until retirement. Many expect to retire early."[12]

We have no evidence that these many jobholders have selected their jobs from the view of a Christian calling. Their work appears to have been chosen on such pragmatic bases as availability, convenience, remuneration, friendship, or prestige. Christian motives such as service, mission, or a sense of direction from God are not evident.

The Waterloo economic system strongly influences the lives of Mennonites and shapes their institutions: the family, church, and schools. It is my opinion that progressive Mennonite religious philosophy and beliefs may flavour but do not totally shape their institutions. It appears that the more progressive the group, the greater the amount of economic domination; the more conservative the group, the less the economic domination of its institutions.

Jobs determine social status

The way people earn their living or secure their income generally determines their social standing or prestige. In rating occupations, we find a difference in status between the filling station attendant and the filling station owner, the nurse and the doctor, the hired man and the farm owner, the bank teller and the bank president.

Whether these many and varied urban industrial jobs are socially productive or whether the products and services produced are beneficial to society seems not to have been seriously debated and evaluated, at least in recent decades. In today's society, a prevailing attitude toward occupation is that it makes little difference what one does, so long as the salary is satisfactory.

Mennonite conferences and congregations seem to have approved any occupation that members chose so long as it was considered legitimate in the wider community. This is in marked contrast to the Mennonite Conference of Ontario's official concern, fifty years earlier, about its members pursuing occupations that were thought to jeopardize their spiritual welfare.

The church fails to note that the environment in which one works throughout his or her lifetime has important bearing on the spiritual, moral, and ethical life of the individual church member, and for his or her family.

Separation from the world need not necessarily mean geographical or physical separation. It could mean an expression of concern for work that is in line with values taught by the church. It is interesting that the Amish and conservative Mennonites are more sensitive about the ways their members earn their living than are the progressives. This is especially surprising in view of this group's recognition of the importance of counselling in schools, churches, hospitals, and industries.

Chapter 14

Leisure shapes a way of life

Leisure has come to have a special place in today's society. The combination of leisure and recreation is one of the six basic human institutions along with economics, education, government, religion, and the family. Today, leisure and recreation are among our major industries. They play an important role in a society's economy. Modern technology has increased leisure and leisure, in turn, has helped to shape the nature of our culture.

Waterloo, Ontario is as much affected by this new and growing industry as any other Canadian community. This chapter will consider leisure and recreation in this community and how it affects Mennonite life. Attention will be paid to the community's response to tourism.

The University of Waterloo is one of few universities in North America with a department devoted entirely to the study of leisure. It does research on all aspects of leisure that affect society. And it trains students to become teachers and community leaders in the field of leisure as well as providing information and counsel on recreation and leisure theories and philosophy.

Leisure is changing our way of life
Leisure is an old word with a new and larger meaning. Throughout much of history, leisure belonged to the rich, the powerful, and the privileged. Today, throughout Western society, leisure belongs as much to the common people as to the elite, to the poor as well as the rich. Many older Mennonites still identify leisure with idleness or laziness and, as such, tend to suspect the abundance of it as unworthy of a self-respecting person. These conclusions seem to be based on the ancient adage: "Idleness is the devil's workshop." There is a grain of truth in the proverb, but it does not help us understand the place of leisure in society today.

Leisure refers to attitude as well as to activity. It includes more than just pleasure or play. Leisure can be defined as activity used at an individual's or a group's discretion. It is a break in a work commitment for the purpose of renewing energy—what is generally called *re-creation*. One scholar defines leisure as "time oriented toward self-fulfilment as an ultimate end."[1]

An increase in the amount of available leisure time is the result of technological improvements in commerce, transportation, communication, and many other industries. New technology has reduced the amount of time required to do society's work, yet at the same time has increased total production and services. The result of all these changes has been a vast increase in the amount of time most people now have to spend on what they like to do.

As required work diminishes, leisure time increases; and as work increases, leisure time diminishes. The effect of one on the other is relative to such factors as personal interests, the amount of work available, the age and strength of individuals, and the customs and culture of people in any given place. An illustration of this point is the common practice of many people to moonlight—to take second jobs. Thus so-called leisure time is devoted to additional work rather than rest, relaxation, or play. Some argue that such voluntary part-time jobs are a form of recreation. A high percentage of rural nonfarm and urban women whose children are grown and whose homes are equipped with modern conveniences now use the time saved by working outside the home. This doubling of their work time suggests that these moonlighters prefer to earn extra money rather than to rest, relax, and play.

Leisure as index to living standard

The amount of leisure a society enjoys is an index to that society's standard of living. The longer the working day or week, the lower the standard of living. The shorter the working time, the higher the standard of living—and the greater the amount of leisure time.

The fourth of the Ten Commandments recognized the need for leisure and established a ratio of six workdays to one for leisure. Jesus invited his disciples to "come and rest awhile." Practically all religions provide for a regular way of alternating work and leisure. In the Western Hemisphere, Christianity has consistently honoured, usually with support from secular governments, one rest day out of seven, even though that day is no longer considered sacred or observed for a particularly religious purpose. Saturday has become for all practical purposes a day of leisure and the eight-hour working day has provided more leisure hours to the week. The long weekend, late Friday afternoon to Monday morning, has also come to be accepted as a fixed part of our leisure-oriented culture.

Leisure in our culture

Leisure also has a special bearing on a society's total economy. It affects and is affected by business and industry. In fact, commercial recreation is one of the newest and largest of the world's industries. Amateur, professional, university, and collegiate sports are leisure-time activities but also have great economic importance.

A high percentage of society's people are actively taking part in or passively watching sports and often paying to do so. Even those not involved in sports support the recreation industries which supply us with everything from Ping-Pong balls to recreational vehicles, from outdoor tennis courts and shuffleboards to massive recreation buildings and luxurious bowling alleys.

Organized labour must be given part of the credit for shortening the workday, creating legal requirements for vacations with pay, improving working conditions in industry, and, in some industries, gaining a voice in management. All of these gains have deeply entrenched leisure and recreation consciousness into the fabric of our culture.

The school more than any other institution gives a high place to leisure. Annual school schedules provide for two to three months of summer holidays for students and teachers as well as about one holiday a month throughout the school year. The study of leisure in contemporary academic curriculums is highly appropriate.

Professional sport preferred to religion

Organized religion too is directly and indirectly affected by the place and prominence of leisure in today's world. Whether in local churches or in denominational offices, the patterns of leisure-time activities are taken into consideration when scheduling religious events so as not to conflict or overlap. Churches regularly defer to a community's or a society's secular events in what the mass media have come to call prime time. So prominent are professional sports such as the annual Stanley Cup, Grey Cup, World Series baseball or the Pro-Bowl football games that church administrators are careful not to schedule church events at the same time. Should they be scheduled at the same time, attendance at church services would be greatly diminished. Even the so-called good church people would in many instances choose the secular sports events.

This point is illustrated in the following newspaper account about a special religious event planned next door to a special sporting event. The headline stated: "Empty seats steal the show at Canadian Christian Festival in Calgary." The news article went on to say:

> It is going to be remembered as the festival that inadvertently exposed religious apathy when the major worship events coincided with the hockey play-offs. There were over 16,000 fans to cheer the Flames next door in the Saddledome, and only 2,500 to worship in the Corral.[2]

Conservatives still work from sunup to sundown

Against this background, it will be helpful to observe the Mennonite response to leisure in Waterloo County. The progressive and conservative Mennonites react in contrasting ways to more leisure. The conservatives have a hard time appreciating the concept and use of leisure. For them, the work week has not been reduced from seventy to forty hours. Nor has this century given them two- or three-day weekends, a dozen holidays, and two to four weeks of annual vacation with pay. Their way of earning a living and their work schedules in the house and on the farm remain much the the same as always: determined by the weather, the seasons, and the unlimited amount of work to be done. Leisure for them is still identified with idleness and loafing, rather than as a time for rest, relaxation, and recreation.

For the Old Order and moderate Mennonite farm families, the rule is still to work six days a week, a twelve-hour day from sunup to sundown, and even longer during sowing and harvesting seasons. For them, leisure time is still primarily confined to Sundays, religious holidays, weddings, funerals, auctions, quiltings, and occasional barn raisings. All of these, except Sundays, are considered a kind of holiday that converts otherwise serious workdays into relaxed times of social pleasure.

The conservative rural Mennonites integrate work and leisure. The two are not easily separated. Much of their work is not boring, irritating, or alienating. Rather, it is enjoyable, challenging, and fulfilling. It may be physically exhausting, yet mentally and spiritually exhilarating. One never hears conservative farmers or their wives talking about needing to "get away from it all" by going to a lakeside cottage to fish, swim, boat, play golf, or sunbathe. On the whole, Mennonite families, parents and children, seem generally happy and contented with what they are doing.

A mature student in one of my classes was the guest in an Old Order Mennonite home for Sunday dinner. She reported the following conversation:

> Following a meal I shared with a Mennonite family, I approached the woman responsible for its preparation saying, "Let me take care of the dishes, while you sit down and relax, after all the work you have put into preparing the dinner." To my surprise her response was: "What I have been doing isn't work; it's what I do every day." Similarly, in asking her what she did in her spare time, she responded with a rather perplexed look as if to say, "What is spare time?"
> From these two brief comments I have come to the conclusion that for this Mennonite woman, and indeed possibly for Mennonites in general, there is no emphatic difference between work and play or what has more recently been termed leisure. All activity appears to be a united whole.[3]

Outsiders often express concern about the effect of the long working days, of children withdrawn from public school at the end of the eighth grade, and the few opportunities they have for enjoying the wide range of recreational facilities available to children in the wider society. A student in a class visiting at the home of an Old Order minister asked the minister's twenty-year-old son how young people can get along without television and the radio in the home. The young man replied that they didn't miss them at all because they had never become dependent upon them. He might have added that farm young people have other, fulfilling types of leisure time activities such as hunting, trapping, skating, swimming, climbing, hiking, playing with pets and farm animals.

An adult member of one of my sociology classes once taught in a one-room country school in a Mennonite community. She shared her recollection and evaluation of one type of recreation and its setting in the Mennonite scheme of things as she experienced it.

> What is work for some is leisure for others and what is leisure for some is work for others. To many, leisure time and entertainment must be spent outside the home, or it must be something that costs money. It must be organized and planned. Not so with the Mennonites. Many of their work bees and ways of making a self-sustaining living are actually very enjoyable get-togethers with friends, family and relatives. I lived among the Mennonites as a young girl and later taught in a one-room school in a Mennonite community.
>
> Recreational facilities and leisure time activities are more numerous and varied than outsiders realize: checkers, crokinole, jigsaw puzzles, quiltings, apple schnitzing (paring and slicing to dry), Sunday evening singings followed by folk games, farm sales, wood carving, knitting, skating, and swimming in season at local creeks, repair work around house and barn, barn raisings and reunions, weddings and funerals must all be considered as meaningful and pleasant leisure-time activities for old and young.
>
> I envy these people as I look back at the time spent in their midst. There was so much fellowship, free entertainment, and busy times that were fruitful. Family visiting was such a great event. We don't seem to have the art of home visiting like the Mennonites. We are so afraid to have people in our homes for fear of ruining our finery. Family visiting is good for the soul—problems are shared, solutions found, and all go back home ready for another week of work.[4]

This same student described a social event she enjoyed in the company of a group of Old Order young people which may show why the absence of radio and television does not result in a sense of deprivation or social impoverishment. It will be noted also that the activity described is an event that is seasonal, spontaneous, attractive, participatory, healthy, and without monetary considerations.

A memorable occasion was attendance at a Sunday evening singing. Two large farm sleighs full of young people thirteen years and
older set off for a farm near St. Jacobs. The sleighs were pulled by
a team of heavy work-horses. There was so much snow that year
that the farmers drove through the fields and over fences. County
roads had one lane. In some places the snow reached the hydro
lines.

The young people, led by a song leader with a tuning fork,
sang hymns in parts for hours. Then it was time for folk games.
This was shocking to me. Saturday nights one could not have folk
games but Sunday night it was quite acceptable. They could not go
to public dances but could swing their partners until they were
dizzy. After a lunch of donuts and cider we again sleighed back
home. It was a delightful evening and didn't cost a cent. How fortunate these young people are to be able to have so much fellowship and they need no money to do it.[5]

Sunday evenings for relaxation

This observer would have been less surprised that the young
people would be permitted to have folk games on Sunday evening
but not on Saturday evening had she realized that the restraint on
Saturday nights is because that is the time to prepare for worship
on the following day, while Sunday evening is a time for relaxation before beginning another workweek. The observer also
failed to understand that the young people could engage in folk
games among themselves but not in public recreation centres
because of the meaning they give to separation from the world.
The objection is not to folk dances per se but to indiscriminate
socialization with people of differing moral and religious standards and in social environments considered spiritually and morally unwholesome.

Waterloo's response to the culture of leisure

The Kitchener-Waterloo area lacks natural water resort facilities
so community leaders have developed other tourist attractions.
Among four prominent ones, the first and oldest is the Kitchener
Farmers' Market for which a spacious new building was erected in
the middle seventies in the heart of the city. Two other farmers'
markets have sprung up in the last decade in the open country
between Waterloo and St. Jacobs and are highly successful.

A second tourist attraction is Pioneer Village at the south end of Kitchener which in 1969 attracted 60,000 visitors. It is a museum of pioneer artifacts and a collection of pioneer buildings of historical significance. Two more recent tourist attractions are the one-day Maple Syrup Festival sponsored by the town of Elmira, eleven miles north of Waterloo. One of the day's attractions during the festival's early years was the special train, called the Sugar Bush Express, which ran between Kitchener and Elmira. Each year between 20,000 and 30,000 people attend the festival.

The latest and largest of the manufactured tourist attractions is the annual Oktoberfest sponsored by a Kitchener-Waterloo Oktoberfest Committee. This occasion attracts an estimated 75,000 people from outside the city each year. It has some of the atmosphere of the original Munich, Germany, beer festival. The event is not looked upon with approval by all citizens as the most constructive use of leisure nor the best way to develop a particularly distinguished community reputation. The Stratford Shakespearean Festival Theatre at Stratford, Ontario, thirty miles to the west of the twin cities, brings many visitors to the Waterloo County area each year.[6]

Mennonites as a tourist attraction

In the Waterloo area one of the major tourist attractions is the Conservative Mennonite lifestyle. The Chambers of Commerce and other promoters of tourism have been discreet in their promotional literature. They have sought to respect and protect the privacy of the conservative Mennonites who are the objects of tourist curiosity. Much of the publicity is by word of mouth and is the result of normal newspaper stories and photographs covering items of general interest throughout the years.

There are about three thousand Old Order Mennonites in the Waterloo area. This does not include about one thousand Old Order Amish scattered in seven southern Ontario communities, the largest group in Perth County. The Old Orders, both Amish and Mennonite, are identified by their horse-and-buggy transportation and their plain regulation dress. Amish men all wear beards, Mennonites do not. In addition to these external identifiers are their large houses, and barns, the well-kept vegetable gardens and flower beds surrounding their homes, plus their usual clusters of fruit trees and woodlots. These people and their attractive farmsteads are a natural attraction to tourists as well as to a large portion of the Waterloo urban population. One reason is that they represent a living demonstration of a way of life in past centuries.

A spirited driving horse hitched to a buggy, a matched pair of heavy draft horses, or possibly a four-horse team pulling a two- or three-bottom plow or harrow in a field near a huge barn, a dozen small and large service buildings, and a herd of contented cattle are enough to slow down most motorists, much more the curious tourist for whom this is an unfamiliar sight.

Progressive Mennonites confront tourism

In the northern end of Waterloo County where most of the conservative Mennonites are located, progressive Mennonites early took steps to prevent the exploitation of their Old Order co-religionists. They set up what they considered appropriate ways of meeting tourist interests. The Elmira Mennonite Church (progressive), many of whose older members and their parents were originally Old Order members, have organized an information service, bus tours, and dinners in the church fellowship room for tourist bus groups. As a part of the service, the pastor or a designated assistant gives a brief historical and sociological explanation of the Mennonites. A tour guide then accompanies the group on a trip through the countryside and answers questions about religious beliefs, customs, and traditions of the Mennonite people.

Another major innovation in the Waterloo tourist industry was that of Milo and Laura Shantz, a progressive Mennonite couple. They envisioned giving the village of St. Jacobs, located in the centre of the Old Order Mennonite settlement, a major face-lift. They began by remodelling an old business building, formerly used as a grocery store, into a first-class restaurant with authentic Pennsylvania German decor and ethnic food. They called it the Stone Crock. This successful business venture stimulated a host of other new business and artistic ventures of likely interest to tourists. The combined effect of all the new enterprises has had a major economic, social, and psychological impact on the formerly quiet village of St. Jacobs.

The old landmark gristmill, on the banks of the Conestoga Creek on the north edge of St. Jacobs, became a craft centre for about twenty craftsmen and women each operating a business of their own. The old grain silos were converted into shops for a weaver and a potter. The mill sheds provide space for a glass studio, a jeweler, Cedar Designs, and a quilt shop. On the main floor of the old mill are a country gift shop, a sweet shop, an antique centre, a Doll Studio, an art gallery, and a folk art studio.

The old shoe and felt factory building shelters seven shops which include Heritage Leather, the Farm Pantry, Heritage Yarn, the Plane and Chisel, Iris Arts and Crafts, Les Chandelles, and the Maple and the Butterfly. The twelve-room home of the former mill owner, E. W. B. Snider, has been turned into a bed-and-breakfast guest house with furnishings reflecting the turn of the century era. There is also Maple Syrup Museum, Family Kandy Korner, a village bakery that bakes all it sells, a Mini Market, and a Schnitzelbank Gifts and Tea House.

Most significant and informative of all is the St. Jacobs' Meeting Place, a comprehensive information centre, providing authentic historical information about the various Mennonite ethnic groups. The centre features automated lectures, visual aids, and documentary films of contemporary Mennonite life and culture.

The various St. Jacobs private ventures have been successful in their objective to control the quality of service available to tourists. They have attracted additional businesses and services to the village and have provided authentic information to visitors. They have been a model of co-operation between civic, business, and religious interests in the community. Tourists visiting the village of St. Jacobs with an interest in learning something about Mennonites can be certain when they leave that they have been exposed to accurate sources of information.

The Shantzes demonstrated the courage of their convictions by their willingness to risk finance capital to undertake the restoration of old buildings and the replacement of new businesses for the old. Their courage and persistence in pursuit of their goal was rewarded by the present reinvigorated economy and morale of the entire St. Jacobs community. The old, quiet village has been given a face-lift and is happy with its local place in the sun.

No desire for monopoly ownership

The family who initiated the change in St. Jacobs did not seek to own and control everything that money could buy. They tried rather to interest and encourage others to invest their skills and money in enterprises of their own. A primary consideration, however, was to assure that all new businesses would serve a useful purpose and would carry quality merchandise, preferably making or processing the products to be sold rather than importing commercial goods.

To make this possible the Shantzes encouraged their employees wherever possible to acquire at least half of the ownership of the businesses in which they were working, thus assuring ongoing interest in their respective enterprises. Likewise, in the twenty or so craft shops in the Old Mill building, most of which were undertaken by individuals or families with modest capital resources, the Shantzes introduced an unusual and a fair way of charging the tenants rent. It was based, not on what would guarantee the owner a good return on his investment, but on a percentage of the tenant's income. Thus if a shop operator had a small income his rent was small. If his business was flourishing, his rent was correspondingly high. In each case, it was based on ability to pay. Thus far, this innovative and imaginative system of enterprise has worked well. It is an unusual demonstration of venture capitalism.

This idea of establishing new businesses in St. Jacobs is the result of a vision motivated by altruism and a desire to serve tourists without exploiting either them or the local community, and discouraging others from coming into the community and doing so.

With all the positive things that have been said about the infusion of new economic life built around the culture of leisure, a note must be added about a clash of values that the tourist industry has brought to the town of St. Jacobs. The bus loads of tourists that invade this once quiet little village in the Conestoga Valley over weekends result in booming business for the workers in the mill and in other shops, but since some of them are open on Sunday, it means that instead of Sunday being a day of rest, it tends to be business as usual.

Mennonite attitudes toward leisure

Anthony Bender, in his research, listed what he considered to be twelve traditional Mennonite leisure-time activities and twelve which he considered nontraditional. His first assumption was that rural Mennonites participated more in traditional than in nontraditional activities, but his research findings did not support his assumption. He discovered no significant difference in the frequency of participation between rural and urban Mennonites so far as traditional leisure-time activities were concerned. A second Bender assumption was that Mennonites living in urban areas were participating more frequently in nontraditional recreational leisure activities than Mennonites living in rural areas. This assumption was sustained by his findings when ten out of the twelve nontraditional activities supported the hypothesis.

The selection of leisure activities for the traditional and nontraditional categories is obviously arbitrary. The new culture of leisure has freed both rural and urban progressive Mennonites to engage in activities of their choice. Available transportation today makes it possible for rural residents to respond to typically urban recreational facilities as readily as do urban residents. Nevertheless, there are noticeable rural-urban differences. Waterloo progressive urban Mennonites go to concerts, theatres, movies, art galleries, camping and hiking significantly more often than do ruralites, according to Bender's findings. About six percent also frequent pubs and go dancing more frequently than rural Mennonites, and eating out is more frequent among urbanites. It is surprising to discover that as of 1977 rural participation in home entertainment was less than urban participation. The same is true in worship and Bible study, in visiting friends, knitting, reading, and swimming. Quilting, sewing, baseball, and skating, however, were more popular among rural residents than among urban residents.

The results of this study may or may not be a reliable basis for generalizations. But they are indicators of trends in rural-urban Mennonite participation in a selected number of leisure-time activities. If a study were made of leisure-time participation by the moderate and conservative Mennonites in Waterloo, the comparative participation tables above would have been heavily favoured on the rural side and the nontraditional list would have

Table 14-1			
Types of leisure-time activity and percentage of rural-urban participation[7]			

	Rural	Urban	Difference
Traditional Activities	(%)	(%)	
1. Worship & Bible study	84.0	86.5	- 2.5
2. Visiting friends	87.1	90.0	- 3.8
3. Entertain at home	66.1	78.0	- 9.8
4. Singing	54.3	56.1	- 1.8
5. Quilting	27.3	23.3	+ 4.5
6. Knitting	10.6	27.0	-16.5
7. Sewing	32.4	32.2	+ 0.2
8. Reading	80.1	83.0	- 2.9
9. Fishing	29.0	24.5	+ 4.5
10. Skating	38.4	32.2	+ 6.2
11. Baseball	47.6	40.0	+ 7.6
12. Swimming	15.8	16.1	- 0.3
Nontraditional			
1. Going to pubs	7.8	14.1	+ 6.3
2. Dancing	13.8	19.3	+ 5.5
3. Going to movies	33.1	49.0	+15.9
4. Going to theatre	22.4	33.5	+11.1
5. Going to concerts	23.1	44.5	+21.4
6. Playing musical instruments	24.4	23.8	- 0.6
7. Hiking	41.7	45.1	+ 3.4
8. Hunting	6.6	5.8	- 0.8
9. Camping	43.5	53.5	+10.0
10. Going to art galleries	7.9	16.1	+ 8.2
11. Travelling outside North America	15.8	20.6	+ 4.8
12. Dining out	61.1	80.6	+19.5
+ indicates more rural than urban participation - indicates less rural than urban participation			

been lightly marked if at all. The moderates and conservatives were not included in the several special surveys of leisure questions because it was known in advance that participation would have been unwelcome. Moreover their leisure attitudes and patterns are already well known.

Church leaders talk about leisure

Another source of information about Waterloo Mennonite attitudes toward leisure were interviews with 115 progressive church members in 34 congregations with an average of 3.4 leaders per congregation. An attempt was made to conduct interviews with the minister, the deacon, the president of the women's society, and the leader of the youth group in each congregation. This was not always possible nor were all questions answered in every interview. The views of those interviewed were not necessarily typical of the total congregation.

Replies to the question of how leisure time was spent indicated similarities to those in society in general, namely pursuing hobbies, watching TV, bike riding, sports, sewing, games, reading, and knitting. However many held reservations about certain forms of recreation and leisure-time use. Movie goers frequently criticized movies as having too much sex, crime, and violence. Sports were generally approved if they were not overindulged in. Some persons opposed expensive leisure-time use as questionable stewardship. There were those who opposed movies on principle.

Asked how increased leisure affected their church, 39 percent said that church attendance and participation were affected negatively because of extended vacations, weekends at cottages, extended travel, camping, and other special events such as family gatherings and conventions. Some did not express a personal opinion on the merits or demerits of leisure. Young people said that they were having more non-Mennonite friends as a result of wider participation in leisure activities. Old people said they continued to have most of their friends within their own church.

Value of leisure depends on use

A significant number of respondents expressed doubt about the benefits of leisure and how wisely Mennonites were using this extra free time. Some of the older respondents had difficulty separating leisure from idleness and laziness. But most interviewees expressed pragmatic views, indicating that the value of leisure depended entirely on the ways in which it was used.

A minister of a 300-member congregation in a small Waterloo area town summarized the effect of leisure on his congregation in the following words:

The members of this church have a wide range of interests both in work and what they do with their leisure time. This congregation has moved rapidly over the past decade from a farm congregation to a semiurban one. There is still a small percentage of persons who make their living from agriculture and still think rurally and follow a rural lifestyle, however most members make their living from nonfarming occupations.

Since more and more of our people are moving or have moved into the urban community, leisure time takes on a whole new dimension within the church community. Many new forms of leisure activity are now commonplace with the older meaningful forms such as entertaining in the home becoming less common. The church program now has competition with hockey, camping, bowling, and other recreational activities. I was surprised at the few times our families entertain in their homes. This, in our tradition, was the primary way of using our leisure time.

Our leisure-time interests and activities change with our occupations. Some members talk of bowling with groups from their work. Diversity of occupations brings diversity of interest and programs. Mennonite families are no longer isolated. In the past congregations discouraged members from participating in dances. Now nonagricultural persons mostly under forty-five indicated that they danced at least once a year with others indicating they danced several times a month.

Leisure time has become much more costly because many of the activities are outside the home where one needs to pay in order to participate. Church members have a rather substantial investment in leisure items such as color television, stereos, snowmobiles, summer cottages, and golf club fees.

The challenge I face as pastor is to help create and coordinate programs that challenge the members of this community so that they can continue to be faithful to their calling and live up to their ideals.[8]

This pastor's assessment of leisure reflects neither enthusiasm nor dismay. He recognizes the fundamental nature of change that has taken place in his members' occupational situations and in their residential shift from rural to urban areas. He properly saw his task as a challenge to continue working under the new conditions.

Chapter 15

Health and welfare in forms old and new

During the 1960s, the Province of Ontario enacted the Ontario Health Insurance Program, commonly referred to as OHIP. The plan was generally well received despite critics labelling it socialized medicine. During the discussions leading up to enactment and adoption of the plan, conservative Mennonites were among its strongest opponents. They did not object because of a fear of socialized medicine nor because of the mandatory payment plan. They were opposed because OHIP threatened to eliminate their own mutual aid system in which they were already sharing their unusually heavy medical and hospital expenses. Their own aid plan was simple, easily understood, and without complicated forms to fill out or red tape to become entangled in.

The individual or family incurring medical expense pays it, then submits the bill to the deacon who reimburses the member for 80 percent of the costs. The deacon's fund is replenished by semiannual freewill offerings. To have joined OHIP would have either duplicated or eliminated this traditional method of burden bearing. Their method of sharing is a deeply meaningful bonding experience between members. It has long been a substitute for commercial insurance and paid nursing service.

At first, the Ontario Government opposed any exemption to the new plan. However, because of persistence, a considerable amount of public sympathy with Mennonite reasons for opposition, the fact that they already had a practical plan of their own, plus the good offices of Edward Good, Waterloo, member of the Ontario Legislature, to interpret the Mennonite position to other legislators, exemption was eventually granted. The compromise appears to be working to the satisfaction of all parties concerned. To be exempt from OHIP, church members must have letters of endorsement from the church bishop indicating that the person is a member in good standing.

The largest of the moderate groups, the Waterloo-Markham Church, also had a hospitalization plan somewhat similar to the Old Order mutual aid plan. About one-third of the members are in the church plan and about two-thirds in OHIP. A large percentage opted for OHIP because they are employed in nonfarm jobs, many by non-Mennonite employers. They are obliged to enrol in OHIP and have all or a portion of their assessment paid by their employers. The split in the church membership between OHIP and the church aid plan is an example of the way moderates have one foot in the conservative camp and the other in the progressive camp. The progressive Mennonites have totally accepted OHIP and seem generally satisfied.

Some people not familiar with Mennonites in Waterloo assume that because communities are relatively closed there must be considerable inbreeding and, as a result, a high rate of mental retardation. In testing this assumption with local medical doctors and nurses and by making inquiries throughout the community over a sixteen-year period, I found no basis in fact for it. The rate of mental illness and mental retardation is apparently no larger than in the population generally. The largest body of Old Order Mennonites is aware of the dangers of too close marriage and disapproves of it. There is no reason to assume that the health condition of Old Order Waterloo Mennonites is not average for the community as a whole.

Waterloo Mennonites and welfare

Welfare, unfortunately, has come to have a demeaning sound. The word really means "to do well," and refers to the well-being of a community, a people, or a society. Various programs of the Mennonites in the Waterloo area provide for their own welfare and the welfare of needy people outside their own communities. As with other subjects, welfare is viewed and treated differently by conservative and by progressive Mennonites, while moderates reflect mixed ideas and practices.

In general, the conservatives have a two-tier philosophy of welfare. The first tier is that of the individual and the family, who are expected to be as self-sufficient as possible. Self-reliance is looked upon as a basic virtue. From childhood on, family members are taught not to seek or accept help from others if it is possible for them to provide for themselves. If that is not possible, then the church is expected to render the needed aid. This is what is meant by the second tier. That assistance, however, is not easily and generously given unless it is clear that all efforts of individual, family, and close relatives have been exhausted. In other words, it is not easy to be a freeloader in Old Order Amish and Mennonite communities. Public assistance is rejected without question as a matter of principle. This philosophy has been well stated by an Amish bishop who said:

> We do not want to get rich. If we are able to live from what we are able to get from the land, then we are satisfied. We try to live so that when it is time for us to retire, we can have a little to take care of ourselves. We feel it is the duty of the father to help his children get on their own farms. Then when we get older, we look for the children to return again and take care of us as we need it. So far as Social Security is concerned we just don't need that. We do not want it. We do not intend to accept it.[1]

Old Order opposition to social security

The conservative Amish and Mennonites of Ontario strongly opposed the federal government's compulsory social security program not because it was wrong or in any way evil. Their opposition was not on philosophical, moral, or even economic grounds. They opposed the program because it threatened to replace their own centuries-old brotherhood system of bearing one another's burdens. It would have destroyed what they believed was a clear scriptural instruction: "Bear one another's burdens, and so fulfil the law of Christ" (Gal. 6:2). The state was proposing to do for them what they wanted to do for themselves. If other citizens wanted the government to look after matters of retirement in old age, they had no objection. To prove that their opposition was not based on financial grounds, they offered to pay the equivalent of the anticipated assessments into a charitable fund. They pointed out that their opposition to the program was not in any way to deprive other citizens of the benefits of the proposed service.

A considerable amount of approval was expressed in the press for the Mennonite position. Some chided the government for trying to prosecute citizens wishing to save the government money.

In an effort to force Mennonite compliance to the new law, the government actually began to seize the milk cheques of some Mennonite farmers in Woolwich Township. The local papers gave this confrontation front-page publicity. In this instance, public opinion was more strongly behind the Mennonites for defying the law than for the government for attempting to enforce it.

Efforts by the Old Order Amish and Mennonites seeking exemption from the program were at first unsuccessful. The Mennonite Central Committee negotiated the issue with the Federal Government at the Cabinet level. The struggle for exemption went on until in the early seventies it was finally settled in favour of the Mennonites. Despite earlier statements by the Ministers of Health and Finance that no exceptions to the compulsory insurance plan could be made, a plan was finally worked out to satisfy the Mennonites, Amish, Hutterites, and the Government.

Max Saltsman, the Member of Parliament from the Waterloo South Riding, introduced a private member's bill which provided for exempting the Mennonites. He argued that such exemption would not be setting a dangerous precedent and that there would not be others asking for the same privilege, and willing to assume the full financial responsibilities for their own members' social security. The *Kitchener-Waterloo Record* ran a four-column headline "Mennonites Hopeful of Pension Victory."[2] The article carried comments by the MP in defence of his bill:

> Although it doesn't sound as if it means much when the cabinet says it is 'considering' exemptions, it really means a great deal. It means my private bill is not dying. Mr. Munro [Minister of Health] says he has consulted, too, with the minister of internal revenue which indicates some action may be taken. . . . We should recognize the right of people to dissent as long as they are not hurting the rest of society. There is a distinction to be made between those who dissent and step all over other people in the process and those who dissent and just want to be left alone to live their lives in peace. And that's all the Old Order Mennonites want: to be left alone.

This is a good example of how a powerful democratic government through its chosen leaders takes the time and shows patience over a period of years in considering a serious grievance of a religious minority. After much debate and repeated hearings, this political body, through one of its own members of Parliament, is convinced that it can change its mind and can honour the pleas of a small group and do so without being unjust to the rest of the country's citizens. Few governments in the world can match this degree of political and social sensitivity to its minorities. The decision of the Government of Canada in this instance is at the same time a compliment to the reputation for integrity and responsible citizenship of the Old Order Mennonites and Amish.

The struggle for exemption lasted more than two years. In their quiet effort to maintain their beliefs, the Old Order people made several representations to appropriate cabinet ministers. The central point in the Mennonite defence was their opposition to commercial insurance of all kinds. They quoted Paul's admonition to Timothy: "If any one does not provide for his relatives, and especially for his own family, he has disowned the faith and is worse than an unbeliever" (1 Tim. 5:8). Because of their strong belief in this matter they refused old age pension cheques, family allowance cheques, and some subsidy cheques for farm products. The government refused the offer of the Mennonites' willingness to contribute the amount of their pension deductions to a worthy charity.

Divine law above human law

The passive resistance of the Mennonites to the Canadian Social Security Act and their ultimate victory testify to the triumph of nonviolent direct action over the almost unlimited power of government to coerce conformity. This was a case where the Mennonites interpreted a Canadian law as a human law in conflict with a higher law of God. They were clear which law they wished to obey. When the penalties for violating the Canadian law were levied and milk cheques seized in payment of fines, the Mennonites did not resist. A press headline reported the Mennonite reaction to the cheque seizures: "Some Mennonites Shun Milk Subsidy." The newspaper article described the event:

> An example of the sincerity of the Old Order Mennonites in their methods of fighting social welfare benefits was revealed today by Harry Edenborough, manager of the Silverwood Dairies Ltd., in Elmira.
> Mr. Edenborough said there are approximately 200 Old Order shipping to the plant. At least 10 percent of them consistently refuse to accept the government subsidy for milk. . . . At this time

of the year, a subsidy payment is more than $120 a month. This
means he is refusing up to $1,200 a year. He felt it was a handout
from the government which he had not earned. We have 20 to 25
of these people who refuse the payments.[3]

The exemptions from Social Security taxes and other subsidies
applied also to the Hutterite Brethren in the western provinces of
Manitoba, Saskatchewan, and Alberta.

To qualify for exemption each applicant had to be verified as a
church member by the church head. The bishop of the Old Order
Mennonites in Waterloo stated that where members are working
for employers who are required to deduct social security payments
church members are forbidden to accept such benefits. While
refusing to take part in the Canada Pension Plan, some Old Order
farmers accept cream subsidies or deficiency payments for hogs
and beef cattle. The Old Order Church does not favour these
plans and discourages members from accepting these subsidies,
but no church discipline is applied for accepting them.

Two ways of caring for the elderly

An example of caring for the aged poor among the Old Orders
when no immediate family or close relatives can provide is the 94-
year-old man who had exhausted his personal savings. The deacon of the church arranged with one of the church families to take
the elderly member into its home. The church paid the family for
this service. The arrangement was less expensive than placing
him in a registered nursing home and was personally more satisfying to the aged member.

While most Old Order families still provide for their elderly in
a farm family dwelling attached to the main farmhouse, this is not
possible in all circumstances. There are those who for one reason
or another cannot be cared for in that traditional and most common way. For those who need other care, the conservative Mennonites have established at least two multiple-unit homes in the village of St. Jacobs.

For the Waterloo-Markham Mennonites in the moderate category, the Canada Pension Plan and agricultural subsidies are
matters of individual choice. A senior minister estimated that
about 50 percent of the members take part in the Canada Pension
Plan. The other 50 percent are in the church mutual aid plan. He
said that older church members felt they should not accept

benefits to which they had not contributed, such as the allowance payments to all families with children under eighteen years of age, and the old age pension which the Canadian Government pays to all Canadian citizens and qualified landed immigrants.

Younger church members are more and more finding employment off the farm and are thus compelled to contribute to the Canada Pension Plan. The senior minister expressed concern with this trend as an example of the danger of the "unequal yoke." He observed also that members were no longer making as many loans to each other as formerly, because high interest rates and excessively high land prices require large amounts of capital for those needing to buy farms.

The progressive Mennonites have adopted the philosophy and benefits of the social security system. There have been few expressions of concern that it is threatening their religious values. Many, on the other hand, express great appreciation for the program. Their ways of earning a living and their respective lifestyles have accommodated to the government social security program. The self-sufficient methods of earning a living on the farm cannot be transferred to most rural nonfarm and urban living conditions. Abundant food production and preservation, large amounts of space and large houses, and ample work for everyone from children to octogenarians are conditions not found in highly industrialized and urbanized communities. Hence, new methods of social security need to be provided by and for citizens in nontraditional farming situations.

Urban life needs different ways of caring

Urban Mennonites are likely to seek protection for themselves or be required by law to accept insurance of various kinds for a surprising number of insurable risks. In Canada, as in most modern industrialized countries, laws require certain types of insurance. In Canada, these include hospital or health and accident insurance, worker's compensation insurance, unemployment insurance, automobile liability insurance, and old age pension insurance. Many citizens, including progressive Mennonites, voluntarily carry other coverages: supplemental health and accident policies, property insurance against fire, storm, floods, and theft. In the professions and in management circles, it is common for salaried persons to carry salary continuance insurance and business interruption insurance. Many property owners carry liability insurance to protect themselves against lawsuits for personal negligence. To protect themselves against losses caused by their own negligence, a high percentage of automobile owners carry collision insurance in addition to the legally required liability insurance.

The Old Order Mennonites face many of the same uncertainties but solve most of them with their own system of mutual aid. This method works for risks and losses due to sickness and accidents, natural disasters, unemployment, old age dependencies, or occasional liabilities from lawsuits. Their social security system works because they live in highly organized and integrated communities and because their members believe in it and trust one another.

Each family is an independent entrepreneur. If men and women are not working for themselves, they are most likely working for each other rather than for outside employers. Although they have many of the same risks as those in society generally, their members seem to have fewer anxieties. They seem too busy with their work to spend time worrying about future misfortunes. Living in stable families in the midst of extended families and communities of faith provides a sense of security that no amount of commercial insurance can provide.

In 1971, there were 1,141 Mennonites sixty-five years old and over in the four progressive conferences. representing the progressive group. At that time the Canadian Government was paying $150 per month or $1,800 per year in old age pensions to those Mennonites for a total of $2,053,800. During that same year, 351 conservative and moderate Mennonites were over sixty-five years of age. Assuming that this group of Mennonites refused to accept the $1,800 in old age pensions, they saved the Canadian Government a total of $632,000. This represents about 30 percent of the amount paid out to the progressive Mennonites in Waterloo County.

How different are the philosophies and logic of these two Mennonite groups! The conservative 30 percent rejected the pension money because they believed they had not done anything to earn it and they did not want to be beholden to their government by accepting it. The progressive 70 percent accepted the money with few qualms. This is one more illustration of a socio-ethical accommodation to the larger society by the progressive Mennonites and of resistance to change by the conservatives.

Retirement

Conservative Mennonites care for their older people by providing an apartment in the farmhouse or a small separate dwelling near to it. In this way, one or both grandparents can continue living in a familiar environment, assist with light work in the home and on the farm, and, when necessary, be looked after by the children and grandchildren. This system works in the context of the Old Order farm family although it is not without intergenerational conflicts. It is not workable for urban families or for an increasing percentage of families who no longer live on farms or whose lifestyle and family housing no longer provide for extended family living.

Progressive Mennonites have adopted the usual method of providing living centres for their senior citizens who no longer wish to or are not able to live in their own homes. They have built multiple-unit facilities referred to as retirement communities. In Waterloo County proper are four such communities: Fairview in Cambridge, begun in 1956, operated by the Mennonite Conference of Ontario; Nithview, located in New Hamburg, established in 1972, and sponsored by the Western Ontario Conference; Waterloo Mennonite Homes, in Waterloo, opened in 1981 and sponsored by the George Street Mennonite Church of the United Mennonite Conference; and the Eastwood Mennonite Community located in Kitchener, and sponsored by a group of privately interested Mennonites. The latter, the most recent of the four, is a 103-unit multiple-storey community of condominiums owned by the occupants. This residence is open to applicants from the public at large.

The Canadian Government through the Central Mortgage and Housing Corporation makes it possible for properly accredited local communities and religious groups to organize and operate such retirement facilities by guaranteeing the loans made by local private financial agencies. Not only does the government guarantee the loans to these nonprofit organizations but it provides generous subsidies which in fact reduce the effective interest rates and permit the operators to adjust the rental rates to incomes.

This means that senior citizens with limited savings and smaller pensions can, nevertheless, be accommodated in the retirement communities. This adaptation to urban retirement seems generally satisfactory.

Deviant behaviour among Waterloo Mennonites

Deviant behaviour, another aspect of Mennonite welfare, refers to church members either disobeying church rules or violating the laws of society. In most instances, violations of public laws are also considered violations of church rules.

I made an effort to ascertain the nature and extent of deviant or illegal behaviour among Waterloo Mennonites from 1950 to 1975. The research revealed a total of 28 legal offences that were recorded in the Regional Municipality of Waterloo Police department. All 28 cases were persons with characteristic Waterloo County Mennonite names and 26 of the 28 had some link with one or another Mennonite church. Only two of the deviants were considered active church members. Ten attended church occasionally, 14 were inactive, and three had no known church identity at the time of arrest.

For 23 of those arrested it was the first offence and for all 28 deviants there was no record of a subsequent offence. Seven of the offences were liquor-related, five were acts of vandalism, three were assaults, and three were traffic violations. There were two drug offences, two were charged with murder, and one each of fraud, robbery, incest, public disturbance, injuring cattle, and one indecent act. Of the 28 cases, the dispositions were as follows: probation (13, 46%), jail (8, 29%), reformatory (1, 3.6%), mental hospital (1), fine (1), out of court settlement (1), loss of driver's licence (1), loss of professional licence (1), suicide (1).

Thirteen (46 percent) of the offenders were under twenty years of age. Worthy of note is the fact that 20 of the 28 offences were committed from 1970 to 1975 while only eight were committed in the twenty-year period from 1950 to 1970. This would mean one offence by a Mennonite every two and a half years between 1950 and 1970 but a higher rate of four offences per year between 1970 and 1975. When I first asked the chief of police about Mennonite deviance, he laughed and said any time a Mennonite was arrested it was headline news because it happened so seldom.

Mark Yantzi, a Mennonite probation officer and member of the Kitchener City Commission, observed that Mennonite young men who had committed legal offences such as vandalism, burglary, theft, and assault were often adopted sons who seemed to be expressing rebellion and hostility against foster parents for their lack of self-identity and self-respect.[4] The bishop of the Old Order Mennonite Church could not recall a case of legal violation among his members but stated that when there were infractions of civil law it was generally among unbaptized and unmarried young men who in social gatherings sought attention among peers by excessive bravado.

As in society at large, so among the Waterloo Mennonites, the deviants are for the most part marginal people. A marginal person is one who relates to two groups but is not a full member of either. He rejects the norms of both, yet somehow tries to survive in the twilight zone of both. Among the 28 Mennonite offenders, 23 (81 percent) had not completed either elementary or high school. Fifteen were still in school and had no skills and seven were unemployed.

Ex-Old Orders not among disorderly

Popular wisdom has it that members of the Old Orders who leave their churches and home communities become marginal persons and thus candidates for personal disorganization. Our research found no evidence to support this assumption. Interviews with 46 former Old Order Mennonites provided opportunity to test and correct that assumption.

Why don't Old Order members become marginal? In the first place, those leaving their church, community, and family are not necessarily hostile or rebellious against their heritage. Their leaving is more likely due to such personal and practical reasons as dislike of farming, failure to find a farm, poor health, an opportunity to take a nonfarm job, or a desire to pursue further education. Another reason is that they are hard workers and are successful in finding and holding jobs. Thus idleness and unemployment that contributes to deviancy is not present.

Whatever Old Order children lack by way of formal education, they are taught from early childhood to respect the authority of parents, older people, teachers, ministers, and public officials.

Our research showed that most conservative and moderate Mennonites leaving their churches and farms tend to find work on the outskirts of their old communities rather than going directly to the larger towns and cities. The social adjustments, therefore, are not too difficult. Furthermore, one of the more progressive Mennonite churches in the vicinity is likely to attract them and thus new social ties are readily made.[5]

If young people are not married when they leave their home church it is highly probable that a marriage partner will be found in their newly adopted church and hence a new religious and social arrangement is likely to take place without serious maladjustment. Our research revealed that typical jobs found by those leaving the farm and the conservative church were at the local egg grading plant, a local feed mill, construction crews, tile factory, implement dealer, wholesale hardware distributor, and the K-W Hospital maintenance staff. The low incidence of deviance among Waterloo Mennonites of all branches must be attributed, in large measure, to effective functioning of the Mennonite family, church, and community as nurturing and guiding institutions.

Unfortunately, space does not permit discussion of deviant behaviour that occurs among Waterloo Mennonites at large. Deviance is any violation of a social group's expectations, any failure to do or be what the values of society or the group in question thinks is right. The term covers a broad spectrum of behaviour ranging from the most trivial to the most serious. Among Mennonites it ranges from hair styles, cut and colour of clothing, type of recreation, theological belief, and form of worship. Among Waterloo Mennonites, what is deviant in one group is not necessarily deviant in another.

The House of Friendship

In 1938, a group of three Mennonite ministers and thirteen laymen organized the House of Friendship. A rescue mission located in the centre of Kitchener, its purpose was interdenominational evangelization, particularly trying to reach transient new Canadians in the twin cities. It aimed also to assist, feed, clothe, and rehabilitate the needy. Over the years, the House of Friendship came to be recognized as one of the chief sources of help for transients and other poor who, for one of many reasons, could not qualify for emergency food, clothing, shelter, medical care, and temporary funds from public welfare agencies.

In its fifty-year history, the House of Friendship has undergone a gradual change in method, structure, and function. During the first decade, its emphasis was almost exclusively on making Christian converts. During its second and third decades, the emphasis shifted to providing basic social, personal, and economic needs. In its fourth and fifth decades, the House of Friendship moved toward developmental and self-help programs while still providing services to transients and those experiencing crises whose needs cannot be met by public welfare agencies. The program throughout its history has been operated by an inter-Mennonite board of directors. One-third of the nearly $1.6 million annual operating budget is derived from donations of which 25 percent comes from Mennonite churches. Local businesses, service clubs, individuals, and the United Way also support the program with annual donations. Government agencies who pay the House for particular services provide about 50 percent of the income. Guests of the facilities, who have income with which to defray expenses for services received, contribute about 17 percent.

The House of Friendship has a two-fold program: residential and community service. The *residential program* consists of seven phases. One of these is a crisis housing service. The other six are all treatment/developmental programs.

Eby Village is an apartment building for socially disadvantage single women and men and is intended as permanent housing. Support service workers will help the tenants learn to live independently with success. It will be mostly one-bedroom self-contained apartments. Construction was scheduled to begin in 1988 and to be completed by mid-1989. The capital budget for this innovative service was around $3.5 million.

Community services include client participation, advocacy, permanent housing, community development, and chaplaincy. The House of Friendship is a courageous and needed venture into constructive human rehabilitation. Its motivation is intelligently Christian, in that it is using the best known and most promising methods of dealing with the disadvantaged members of the Kitchener-Waterloo community. It is an example of co-operation between church and state. Churches and individuals provide the personnel, ideals, and part of the money with supplemental financial support from public sources. (See Appendix 5 for more details.)

Leadership staff members of the House of Friendship are professionally trained social workers. Presently, there are 40 full-time and 35 part-time staff. Modern facilities include a hostel for homeless men; a drop-in centre for unemployed single men; a home for five permanently unemployable men with health-related problems and low income. In the city of Waterloo, the House of Friendship has two additional services. The first is a halfway house with fifteen beds which is a treatment centre for recovering alcoholics. It is a live-in program with a full-time director, a cook, and a counselling staff. A second unit is a nine-bed centre for graduates of the halfway house who are not yet ready to function entirely on their own.

The aims of the House of Friendship are to supplement the services of Waterloo area public agencies. It seeks to minister to the total person. One client described the House of Friendship as standing with the poor. "You are doing the kind of social work which the profession was originally intended to do." A question is being raised about the effectiveness of the program which treats alcohol abuse rather than attacking the social, cultural, and economic causes of alcoholism. For example, the more alcohol available, the greater the rate of alcoholism; the younger the legal age of drinking, the greater the rate of alcoholism. The director of the House himself raises these questions and wonders if he and his directors are afraid to tackle the root causes because of their dependence upon Government for financial support for a large measure of the present treatment program.

The House of Friendship symbolizes the progressive Mennonite collective concern for the poor and needy in the local community. It is the most permanent Mennonite welfare service to the non-Mennonite poor in the area. In this respect, it performs an important function along with agencies like Catholic Charities and the Salvation Army. The quality of service to its clientele has risen above the traditional skid-row, revolving-door, rescue-mission level of a former day. Clients are treated with respect and encouraged to recover a measure of self-respect.

The Mennonite Central Committee (MCC)

The Mennonite Central Committee is an international relief and service agency with five provincial offices in Canada. The Ontario MCC office is located in Kitchener. As a result, many Mennonites in the Waterloo area do voluntary service for it. The MCC carries on various types of benevolent service in fifty needy areas of the world with a personnel corps of about 1,000 volunteers. Waterloo area Mennonites normally supply about thirty of the volunteer force which calls for initial periods of two to three years of committed service. Adult volunteers in Waterloo and from other parts of Ontario donate from several hours to several days a week to one of the many services sponsored either by the Ontario or international MCC.

The gamut of MCC services include material aid relief, agricultural, medical, educational, home economic, construction and technological assistance such as simple irrigation systems, digging wells, and supplying pumps and other machinery.

The separate organizations under MCC Ontario's supervision include a variety of ministries.

1. *Community Justice Initiatives* develops alternatives to weaknesses in the present justice system by settling minor criminal cases out of court.

2. *Immigrant Advisory Committee* helps Old Colony Mennonites from Mexico settle in communities in southern Ontario.

3. *Peace and Social Concerns Committee*, in addition to promoting peace education, gives assistance to Central American and Southeast Asian refugees who come to Ontario.

4. *Material Aid Program* gathers new and used clothing, bedding, bandages, layettes, soap, yard goods, and school, health and sewing kits to distribute to the needy overseas.

5. *Community Services Committee* is responsible for voluntary service personnel and projects in Ontario and helps to process volunteers for foreign service, Native (Indian) Service projects, Victim-Offender programs, aid to handicapped, Hispanic ministries.

6. *Mennonite Disaster Service* (MDS), a volunteer group, responds to calls for emergency assistance in areas hit by natural disasters such as tornadoes, floods, hurricanes, or fires. Their donated service may consist of days, weeks, or months of free

labor. In such instances, MDS people work in co-operation with the Emergency Measures Organization and Red Cross units.

7. *Selfhelp Advisory Committee* is the local tie with the international Selfhelp Program. It serves as a marketing outlet for the products of skilled craftsmen and women in developing countries. The warehouse for Selfhelp products for all of Canada is located in New Hamburg. More than a hundred Selfhelp gift shops are scattered throughout Canada and the United States. In many of these stores, recycled clothing is received and sold. These shops are staffed largely by volunteer workers, many of them retired persons.

8. *Native Concerns Committee* sponsors a summer gardening project.

9. *Choice Books* sells about 60,000 paperback books a year through book racks in supermarkets and corner stores.

10. *Shalom Counselling Service* is staffed by professional counsellors on a voluntary or minimum cost basis.

11. *Handicapped Ministries Committee* helps psychiatrically handicapped persons released from institutions but living in the community without appropriate support of family or friends. It also supervises an *Independent Living Centre* for physically handicapped persons and a central office for consultation, peer counselling, advocacy, and vacation relief.

The heart and soul of the MCC program in Waterloo and elsewhere rests on a vast army of volunteers who staff the hundreds of service posts wherever work is carried on.

The annual Mennonite relief sale

A southern Ontario regional annual event of importance is the annual Mennonite Relief Sale at New Hamburg, a town eleven miles west of the twin cities. The sale is sponsored by an independently-organized body of Mennonite laypeople for the benefit of the Mennonite Central Committee of Ontario. The purpose is to raise funds for humanitarian causes in stricken areas throughout the world.

The sale is a kind of annual folk festival of special appeal to families. The central attractions are two large auctions, one a quilt auction at which upwards of three hundred quilts of various sizes, shapes, and qualities are sold. A second auction sells a great variety of donated but useful items. In a large tent, hand-crafted items and fancy needlework are offered for sale. Ethnic foods in large quantities and varieties are perennial attractions. One of the most popular items is the 3,000 home-baked pies which are regularly sold out by ten or eleven o'clock in the morning. The annual attendance is between 30,000 and 40,000 people. The several thousand individuals who prepare for and take part in the sale all donate their time and materials. No one gets paid. This includes the board of directors, the sale chairperson, the auctioneers, the workers who put up and remove tents, and those who clean up the grounds following the event which is held each year on the last Saturday of May. The sale proceeds have ranged from $39,000 in its first year to over $300,000 in its twentieth year.

Refugee sponsorship

In co-operation with MCC Ontario, Mennonite churches in the province sponsored up to 100 Southeast Asian families numbering about 500 persons between 1979 and 1984, according to Ray Schlegel, executive director of MCC Ontario. He estimated that from twenty to thirty families in one church could be involved in settling one family. Among services and things required were housing, furnishings, utensils, beds and bedding, food, finding work, assisting in language training, enrolling children in school, driver education, orienting new families to facilities and procedures for getting utilities, licences, paying taxes, and finding social and religious groups with whom to identify.

A successful recycling program

In the late 1970s, a temporary committee formed by MCC's Community Service Committee undertook an area-wide program to collect and recycle paper, tin cans, glass, scrap metal, cardboard, and used motor oil. A previous effort by a group of interested K-W citizens had failed for lack of support. A renewed effort began by and for the Mennonites in the twin cities. Each church was asked to appoint one or two persons to be responsible for collecting and delivering waste materials from members of a particular congregation and see that it was delivered on a designated Saturday morning to the Kitchener city auditorium parking lot between eight and twelve o'clock two or three times a year.

Semitrailer trucks owned by Mennonites were secured on a donated basis to convey the waste to recycling centres. Between 1976 and 1980, 980 tons of materials were collected for recycling and sold for $23,000. In 1981, the cities of Kitchener and Waterloo accepted the responsibility for this program by collecting waste on a door-to-door basis for all twin cities residents.

Two approaches to welfare and health care

As in other topics discussed in this book, so in health and welfare, we find among Waterloo Mennonites two distinct philosophies and methods of implementing them. The conservatives have their own systems of covering hospital expenses and providing for their dependent aged. Their dollar expenses are low. Only in exceptional cases is it necessary for the churches, through the deacon's fund, to provide modest support.

The progressives, on the other hand, have totally accepted the government medical and hospitalization plans and the national old age pensions, child support and Canada Pension Plan system of benefits. However, while accepting the public assistance plans for taking care of their dependent sick and aged, they carry on an extensive service program for the poor, dependent, and powerless outside their own members in the Waterloo area and throughout Canada and the world in response to human need. An impressive percentage of members in the progressive churches donate generously of their time and money in the many ways described in this chapter, volunteering in ministries of service to others.

Chapter 16

Finding in politics a way to serve

During their first twenty-five years in Waterloo, the settlers had little need for government of any kind. Everyone was a member of a farm family; church discipline was strict, and codes of behaviour were well understood and obeyed. However, by the beginning of the second quarter of the century, villages began to appear and elementary government became necessary. The first town meeting of Berlin was held in 1822. At that meeting, George Clemens was elected the first clerk, Samuel Erb and Daniel Snider the first assessors, and Abraham Erb the first tax collector.[1]

This first set of officers, judging by the names, were all Mennonites. John Erb, founder of the town of Preston, erected the first saw and grist mills and served as the first magistrate. As the population continued to grow and as non-Mennonites began to settle in the county, especially in the towns and villages, Mennonites withdrew from holding public office. They deferred to their German and English non-Mennonite neighbours.

In Waterloo towns and cities, streets bearing Mennonite family names reflect the prominence of the Mennonites in earlier decades. In Kitchener and Waterloo, streets are named after Betzner, Bingeman, Brubacher, Burgetz, Clemens, Eby, Erb, Martin, Schneider, Shantz, and Weber. Weber Street is the second longest business street in the twin cities, running from the east end of Kitchener to the northern end of Waterloo, while Erb Street is the main east-west street in Waterloo.

The town of Preston has streets named after the Bauman, Clemens, Eby, Erb, and Wismer families. In Hespeler there are Bergey and Groh streets. Mennonites seem to have had no interest in naming towns after European places from which they came or after family names. Conestoga Creek and village are named after places in Lancaster, Pennsylvania.

British law before confederation in 1867 forbade service by pacifist church members such as Brethren in Christ and Mennonites on juries or in any office in government. This ban was really not needed since they were forbidden by their church to do jury service or hold public office. Ironically, in the 1970s, Old Order Mennonites in Waterloo County were called for jury duty. By an act of legislation, the province of Ontario changed the voting act and made jury service a civic duty. This was a 180-degree legal turn. Intercession of the director of Mennonite Central Committee Ontario and the local representative in the Ontario Legislature secured in 1981 exemption from jury duty for those with religious objections to such government service.

A second example of legal discrimination against so-called free churches in Upper Canada in the first third of the nineteenth century was that clergy in those churches could not perform marriage rites for their own members. Up to 1831, the Church of England claimed that only its clergy and those of the Roman Catholic and Lutheran churches had the right to perform marriages. Methodists, Presbyterians, Mennonites, and other free church ministers could not officiate. If no Anglican priest was within eighteen miles, a justice of the peace was permitted to serve. Ivan Groh, a St. Catharines schoolteacher, reported that in 1911 his great-grandparents were married by John Erb, a justice of the peace and a Mennonite, but not a minister. The nonconformist Methodists carried the battle to the English Parliament, and recognition of all clergy in Upper Canada to perform marriages for their own members came about in 1831.[2]

Groh says that, prior to 1834, all Mennonite churches in Upper Canada were held in trust by a deed that contained the clause "for the use of all denominations without distinction."[3] This meant they were not strictly owned as Mennonite churches. This may have contributed to Mennonite churches at first meeting in homes rather than building meetinghouses.

It may be historically significant that in some of the documents pertaining to early land purchases for church building plots, organized Mennonites are referred to as "Mennist" societies rather than as Mennonite churches.

Two views of government

Waterloo Mennonites hold two views of government. The old view is that the state or government belongs to the kingdom of this world. It is ordained of God to provide order in society and punish the evildoer. As an instrument of God, it is worthy of church members' taxes and prayers but not their participation in government because its power and authority finally rest on the use of force and violence. Also, the motives, methods, and objectives of the political state are secular and pragmatic while those of the church are spiritual and ideal. There must be a clear line of separation between the methods and objectives of the church and the state or government.

Critics of the old view of the state remind us that the governments in Canada and the United States are no longer autocratic or tyrannical, but democratic, made up of representatives elected by citizens. These elected officials are accountable to those who elect them and can be removed from office if the citizens wish to do so. A dramatic example of this was the removal of Richard Nixon from the office of President of the United States in 1974 by means of a democratic process.

The structure and function of government in Canada is quite unlike governments in Bible times or in the sixteenth century in early Anabaptist-Mennonite times. Besides the changing nature of government, great changes have appeared also in the functions of government. Maintaining order and punishing wrongdoers are only minor items today compared to the many services democratic governments provide for their citizens. These expanding functions are the result of demands by citizens; they are not services forced on citizens by government.

A few of the hundreds of vital services governments at the local, provincial, and national levels provide for their citizens are roads, city streets, and national highways; schools from the elementary to the university level; parks and recreation; water, sanitation, and sewer; fire protection, health, medical services, and hospital facilities; flood control; social security for aged, handicapped, and dependent women and children; provisions for the unemployed; and planning and zoning for orderly development of rural and urban communities. A century ago, few of the above services were known or required. Those needed were generally met

privately. Truly democratic governments today are what their citizens want them to be.

Old and new views of the church

Religion, expressed mostly through organized churches, like government was once more simple in structure and more limited in
function than it is today. This is true of almost all churches
regardless of denomination, with the exception of small groups
like the Amish and Mennonite Old Orders. Until the latter part of
the nineteenth century, all Mennonite churches in the Waterloo
area were a simple social structure of loosely organized conferences governed by bishops, ministers, and deacons. Changes over
a century were few, and functions were confined largely to Sunday
morning worship services, annual baptism classes, and routine rituals of baptisms, weddings, and burials. Sunday schools were
few. No concern was given to missions or evangelism. There were
no Bible schools or Christian academies. The total focus of the
Mennonite church was turned inward. It was more tradition-
oriented than innovation-directed.

The more progressive branches of the Mennonite church in
the Waterloo community began to change in the first half of the
twentieth century by beginning to support foreign missions. The
churches began Sunday schools, opened a Bible school in Kitchener, began Bible study meetings and protracted evangelistic
meetings, and undertook large-scale shipments of grain and flour
to India and Russia in response to famines. In 1920, the Mennonite Central Committee (MCC) was organized on an inter-
Mennonite basis across the Canadian-United States border. Thus
began noticeable changes in philosophy and outreach in the progressive Mennonite churches.

Overlapping church and state interests

In recent decades the expanding service programs and welfare
goals of both church and state have often brought them into a
close working relationship. Both church and state express concern
about social problems rising from poverty, discrimination, social
injustice, and suffering among the homeless and powerless. The
churches claim religious motives for this service as the MCC
motto, "In the Name of Christ," implies. While the state's motives
may be secular, its humanitarian concerns and extensive social

services benefiting all is clearly influenced by the religious influences of its mostly Judeo-Christian citizens.

Today's churches, like their members, depend on the state for aid. In Canada and the United States, church property is exempt from taxation. Churches in every community receive police and fire protection and comply with local building codes and safety regulations. Most city and county governments as well as state and national governments are kindly disposed to the aims and programs of churches. Both institutions are based on democratic principles of rule by the people. In light of this mutual respect, and often co-operative effort toward common goals, it is natural to question the traditional meaning of church and state separation.

Why is politics more worldly than business?
Why have Mennonites defined politics as spiritually dangerous while accepting participation in business as an honourable vocation? Menno Simons and other Anabaptist contemporaries warned strongly against the spiritual risks of engaging in the business of buying and selling for profit and the charging of interest. One Anabaptist said:

> We allow none of our members to do the work of trader or merchant, since this is sinful business; as a wise man saith, "it is almost impossible for a merchant and trader to keep himself from sin. And as a nail sticketh fast between door and hinge; so doth sin stick close between buying and selling."[4]

Both conservative and progressive Mennonites have long ago approved of their members engaging in buying and selling. At the same time, most Mennonites still feel that taking part in politics and government service is somehow spiritually more dangerous.

Over the past forty years the four progressive groups of Mennonites have held a number of national meetings questioning the church's consistency in church-state relations.[5] In recent decades, younger church leaders have called the traditional philosophy and church separation a "strategy of withdrawal."

Both of these vocational areas require dealing with the public, and both present possibilities of spiritual and ethical dangers as well as genuine opportunities for useful and ethical service.

Also, service experiences in foreign relief, teaching abroad, doing agricultural and medical services in third-world countries by working with government agencies have cast doubt on the high wall of separation between a service-minded church and a democratic state. One purpose of church voluntary service is to give a Christian witness to government. The lines between church and state, or church and government, have become blurred as employees of both agencies have worked toward common goals. Nonresistant Mennonites have also become more and more involved in civic affairs, in litigation, and in using government loan funds to build schools, hospitals, and senior citizens' homes.[6]

In 1959, at a Canadian study conference on the church and its witness to society, attention was paid to the church's solution for social and economic problems. This concern was bound to overlap with those of government. At a 1961 conference in Chicago sponsored by the General Conference Mennonite Church, Edgar Metzler, then pastor of the First Mennonite Church in Kitchener, spoke about Mennonites and separation of church and state.

> The Schleitheim articles claimed the sword was "outside the perfection of Christ." The state was the bearer of the sword. Therefore the state was not the proper sphere for Christian participation. Persecution confirmed that theory and cultural isolation perpetuated it. But now we are confronted with a massive state that still bears that sword but on the other hand wants to help us do the work of the church. The increased state planning and controls designed to cope with the technological revolutions has meant that we are involved with the state at many levels and the simple formula of separation seems inadequate to guide the church in these complex relationships.[7]

When we discuss the relation of the church to the state, we are at the same time considering the relation of the church to the world. Just as today's progressive Mennonite churches are deeply involved with the agencies of government, so too are they deeply involved in affairs of the world.

Reassessing the traditional Mennonite concept of church-state relations does not imply discarding it. It does suggest that past views and practices can be modified. In recent Mennonite history, basic changes in attitude and practice have taken place even without formal conference action. As a church, Mennonites have traditionally forbidden their young people to do military service, secure divorces, and engage in certain social practices such as dancing and drinking, often on pain of censure or exclusion. Today, progressive churches still teach against such practices but they tolerate members who, for various reasons, engage in such activities.

An increasing number of Mennonites are finding their way into service at various levels of government, especially in civil service rather than in elective offices. It is of interest to note that many Mennonites who served one or more terms of voluntary service under agencies like MCC or CUSO, upon completing their terms accept assignments with a government agency such as Canadian International Development Association (CIDA). The MCC experience provided excellent training for later career employment in some form of governmental technical service.

Research for this study discovered a surprisingly large number of Mennonites or persons with typical Mennonite names in Ontario and the four western provinces who have run for provincial and federal offices. The earliest recorded Ontario Mennonite running for a seat in Parliament was Dilman K. Erb from the riding of Perth South. He was a school teacher running as a Liberal candidate.[8] Also running was J. S. Hendricks as an Independent. Erb ran a second time in 1900 and won. Also running in the 1900 election was Peter F. Shantz from the Waterloo South riding; he came in second. The name Erb could have been either Mennonite or Amish but in 1900, it would most likely have been Amish. However, at that date he could not have been a member in good standing in either church so we must conclude that he chose to seek and hold a political office rather than remain in good standing with the church of his heritage. Hendricks is not a common Mennonite name today but there were Hondriches among the early Amish in Wilmot Township. What was said about Dilman Erb could also be said about Peter Shantz. He could not have been in good church standing and at the same time seek an elective political office.

Between 1949 and 1980, no less than seven Waterloo County Mennonites sought office in a federal election. Only one, John Reimer, Progressive Conservative, was a winner. The names and ridings of the others are Harvey Graber, Waterloo North, P.C. (1949); Elizabeth Janzen, Waterloo North, P.C. (1952, 1953); Peter Fast, Waterloo South, Social Credit (1962); Herbert Epp, Waterloo,

Liberal (1968); Frank H. Epp, Waterloo, Liberal (1980). Whether Graber, Fast, and Janzen were Mennonite members at the time is not certain. Herbert Epp's parents were Mennonites. Don Weber entered the race for a seat in Parliament in 1963 as a Liberal but was defeated. He comes from a Lutheran background. Many other candidates in Ontario with typical Mennonite names but were not necessarily Mennonites ran unsuccessfully in federal elections. Following are a few: Honsburger, Snider, Dick, Brubacher, Good, Heppner, Lepp, Fehr, Martin, Penner, Funk, Peters, Cornelsen, Krause, Unger. Most of these persons represented ridings where there are no Mennonite churches or nearby Mennonite communities.

The Mennonite Central Committee's Ottawa office provided me with 110 names of persons in five of Canada's western provinces who ran for offices in a federal election, and 184 names of people seeking provincial seats in legislatures, all assumed to be Mennonites. Of the 110 seeking seats in the federal parliament, only eleven (10 percent) over about fifty years were successful. Of the 184 seeking seats in provincial legislatures, only 32 (17 percent) were successful. What this tells us is that many more Mennonites or former Mennonites were taking part in politics than was generally assumed. As some of those who are presently holding public office have testified, their co-religionists were skeptical and sometimes critical of their deliberate entrance into the political arena. It has been the Dutch-Russian Mennonites throughout Canada, especially those immigrating after World War I, who have most freely and openly entered the ranks of politics and consequent involvement in controversial issues.

Mennonite participation in Waterloo County
In 1965, Waterloo County had no Mennonite filling the offices of mayor, alderman, or member of the provincial or national parliament, and only two city councillors and three town clerks. By 1986, there were three Mennonite aldermen, two in Kitchener and one in Waterloo, two mayors, one each in Wellesley and in Wilmot, and one councillor in Elmira, all six of the above having a Swiss-Amish ethnic-religious background. In addition, one Mennonite with a Russian background was a member of parliament in Ottawa. Two with direct Mennonite backgrounds were members

of the Ontario legislature.

An article in the *Mennonite Reporter* in 1976 carried the attention-getting headline: "Forsake 400-year tradition; Mennonites enter politics by the dozen."[9] "A radically dissident departure from the faith of the fathers," said the writer, "has caught up with the quiet and traditional Mennonites."

> The present departure from a lifelong tradition, another in a line of many abandoned previously, is political involvement in all lines of government, beginning from school boards and local councils and up to federal administration in Ottawa.
>
> Appropriate to Mennonite custom, political involvement entered the scene hesitatingly, was treated with opposition, and is now gradually being accepted. . . . Mennonites today are holding public office by the dozen. They are entering public life and politics in unprecedented numbers. . . . Involvement in Canadian politics by Mennonite church members and persons of Mennonite descent began about thirty years ago.

On March 6, 1980, the *Mennonite Weekly Review* reported that 16 Mennonites campaigned for election to the national parliament, five as Progressive Conservatives, four as Liberals, three as independents, two as New Democratic Party members, one as a Marxist-Leninist, and one as a Libertarian.[10] Out of the 16 candidates, three were elected. This was one less than had held office in the previous session. For some unexplained reason, more Mennonites have served in the national government than in provincial legislatures.

An example of the intensity with which Mennonites in Canada have entered the political arena on a local level is in the Regional Municipality of Niagara. In 1976, Mennonites held the following offices: Federal Member of Parliament, William Andres; Lord Mayor of the town of Niagara-on-the-Lake, Jake Froese; representative for the Regional Municipality of Niagara, Wilbert Dick; administrator-treasurer for the town, George Voth; works superintendent, Ben Redekop; road department foreman, Henry Nickel.[11]

Mennonite members of Parliament were asked if they faced criticism from fellow church members for seeking public office and for participating in the political process. Almost without exception, they replied that at first a few church members expressed concern that once in office they would lose their Christian convictions and thus would no longer make an effective witness. However, once in office and seeing what good could be done, practically all criticism based on religious grounds of separation of church and state disappeared.

Mennonites in politics not apologetic

The four Mennonites or sons of Mennonites who were in Parliament in 1976 all strongly defended the importance of Christian input in politics. Benno Friesen, 46, of White Rock, British Columbia, said that, after twelve years of teaching Bible in Trinity Western College,

> I became involved in the political scene because Christ's mission is devoted to all the world and that includes the political arena as well. Involvement in our world, while not participating in the life-style and philosophy of it, is an essential part of Christian growth and character.

Dean Whiteway, 30, was first elected to Parliament from Selkirk, Manitoba, in 1974. Without a long-standing Mennonite background, he entered politics without any scruples or reservations after a successful high school teaching career. He believes any work men are called by God to do is honourable and worthy of effort. "I believe God leads men into politics and government offices as he leads them into other ministries. My special mandate from God is to serve as an MP."

Jake Epp, member of Parliament from Steinbach, Manitoba, a former high school teacher and municipal councillor is presently (1986) a member of Prime Minister Mulroney's Cabinet. On the matter of religion, he said, "As Christians we have the admonition that we are in the world but not of the world and that all men are our brothers. It is our responsibility to serve them."

William Andres, 50, MP for the riding of Lincoln in the Niagara Peninsula, was involved in municipal politics for fifteen years before becoming an MP. His occupation is farming. He said,

> I had no scruples because of Mennonite tradition when entering politics. Government is ordained of God and traditions are instituted by man. I believe we as Christians have a duty and an obligation to serve our fellowmen in a political capacity. . . . I believe firmly that it is the Lord's will that I serve in the capacity as a politician. It gives the Mennonite community a sense of belonging and

participation in the affairs of the government by having one of
their own members representing them.

It is interesting to note that all of the Mennonites who have
been candidates for Parliament, whether elected or not, have a
Dutch-Russian ethnic background. This includes the only Mennonite from Waterloo County to have served as a national MP, John
Reimer of Kitchener.

Ontario Mennonites with a Swiss background even today
have not entered politics beyond the local city, township, or county
level. There is, however, evidence that the progressive Mennonites with a Swiss background are shifting attitudes away from
their traditional views of opposition to political participation.
North and South Waterloo Mennonites gave strong support to
Frank Epp and John Reimer in their 1979 respective Liberal and
Conservative bids for seats in the national parliament.

As of 1986, six Mennonites of Swiss background were holding
political offices: Mark Yantzi and Carl Zehr as aldermen, Kitchener City Council; James Erb, formerly campaign manager for
Frank Epp, as alderman on the Waterloo City Council; David Leis,
a young man of twenty, as a member of the Elmira City Council;
Ralph Shantz, as mayor of Wilmot Township, and Albert Erb, as
mayor of Wellesley Township. These cases illustrate the likely
trend of the future with regard to Waterloo Mennonite participation in political activities. Those who seek office on the provincial
and national level frequently do so on the basis of satisfactory
experience on the municipal or county level.

Mennonites and litigation

Litigation—the legal procedure for settling disputes in court—
usually means that the plaintiff (the one who sues) and the defendant (the one being sued) engage lawyers to assist them in argu-
ing their cases in the light of the laws that apply. If the case cannot be settled between the parties outside of the court, it proceeds
to a hearing before a judge and/or a jury. A high percentage of
lawsuits are settled out of court by negotiation between the oppos-
ing lawyers and their clients.

Mennonites have usually shied away from the use of lawyers
or the courts. If difficulties cannot be settled between the parties
in conflict, Mennonites have been encouraged to accept losses

rather than go into litigation.

Just as Mennonites have been taking more part in politics and taking government jobs more often, they have also been resorting to the courts for settling legal problems. *They*, in this case, means Mennonites in Waterloo County. Conservative and moderate Mennonites still stick to the rules of their churches not to begin a lawsuit. They are unable to prevent being a defendant when someone sues them.

Progressive Mennonites are aware of the New Testament teaching about Christians settling disputes among themselves rather than going to law. Nevertheless, in the business and professional world of science, technology, and highly complex industrial organizations governed by special laws, it is often necessary to engage legal experts to find out what is or is not permissible or ethical. Many business and professional conflicts are so complicated legally that two adversaries in conflict cannot come to agreement themselves. They literally do not know what is in their own or the other person's interest. Thus a third party with expert opinion and relevant information may be needed and welcomed by both parties in a dispute.

MCC maintains Ottawa office

An interesting new proof of Canadian Mennonites' interest in the political process and the workings of government is the appointment by MCC Canada of a professionally educated observer in Ottawa. This office was created in 1975 on a three-year trial basis. The experiment proved so valuable that it has been continued on a permanent basis. Many times, the Ottawa office has saved members in the provinces from making trips to Ottawa. The Mennonite Central Committee with its worldwide relief programs, the Selfhelp program of marketing third-world products, the foreign travel of Mennonites as well as the need for business and professional information and advice from government agencies have demonstrated the usefulness of a permanent Ottawa office. It is another commentary on the ongoing involvement and interdependence of Mennonites and government.

Reassessing church-state relations

At least two-thirds of Waterloo Mennonites have experienced a major shift of attitude and practice in church-state relations. This change has taken place at three levels: in the local town, township, and county; on the provincial level; and on the national level.

While it is important that the church remain the church and the state remain the state, it is not necessary that contacts between the two be marked by alienation, confrontation, and hostility or even by competition. Both have important yet distinct things to do that can be helpful to each other. Just because the state is a secular agency, that does not make it wicked. Many of the ends or goals of church and state are the same even if not all are identical and even if methods of reaching these goals are not similar.

Nowhere else in the world have Mennonites, over a two-century period, had such good relations with government and with the public as in Canada. It is not because problems have not arisen. There have been many. What has been impressive is that the confrontations have been forthright, above board, and the issues at stake have been argued by both sides with mutual respect for one another. In all instances, acceptable solutions have been worked out by the state, the church, and the public to the benefit of all parties concerned.

The early denial of the right of free church ministers to marry their own members, wartime difficulties for both church and state, the more recent parochial school issue, the opposition to Medicare and to national social security programs: all these were settled not by the government silencing or crushing the religious minority but rather by listening to that minority and earnestly seeking for a solution satisfactory to all. Canada has found a way of recognizing conscience as having a rightful claim to legal protection in a way few other governments in the world have.

Politics as legitimate Christian vocation

In the light of this two-hundred-year record by the Canadian government and the positive experience of the Mennonites over two centuries, it is appropriate for Mennonites to redefine their relation to the state. Perhaps no other Mennonite gave as much thought or wrote more persuasively on this issue than the late

Frank Epp. He clearly perceived the arena of politics and government service as a proper place in which to express Christian vocation for himself. He wrote:

> The civil servant, also known as a public servant, is a servant of the state. But his relationship to the state is not one likely to compromise his Christian independence to any degree greater than will the relationship of any other employee to his employer. In fact, in many instances, he has far less opportunity for wrongdoing.[12]

For Epp, uninvolvement and neutrality in politics concerned him. "Urban Mennonitism," he said, "faces the challenge of finding both a new involvement and a new separateness, of discovering itself in the world but identifying as not of the world." Epp was clearly speaking for a new generation and defining church-state relations for the twenty-first century. Had he been elected to Parliament, he would undoubtedly have helped to define, clarify, and exemplify the new separateness. After being defeated in his quest for a seat in Parliament, he was asked by a reporter if the opportunity presented itself whether he would run again for a political office. His reply reflects how deeply he felt about the possibilities of making a creative contribution through participation in the political process both inside and outside a particular office.

> For me, the bid for public office was only part of a process. If you are deeply concerned about the relationship of resources and people and the Creator in this world, you don't have to sit in parliament or have an office in Ottawa to be involved in that process. Whenever you generate good ideas and communicate them you're involved. I won't make any speeches in Parliament, but as I have time, I will certainly feed ideas. I will certainly reinforce the idea of an ambassador for disarmament, which was suggested in the throne speech and things like that.[13]

Waterloo Mennonites are not fully aware of the depth and Christian quality of Frank Epp's political philosophy. It is sad that he was denied the opportunity of serving the North Waterloo Riding and of making the creative contribution of which he was capable. Perhaps some of what he was unable to accomplish in person can be carried on by the Institute of Peace and Conflict Studies at Conrad Grebel College which he was instrumental in establishing. This research and teaching centre in co-operation with MCC and the academic departments of the University of Waterloo will be a natural source of ideas and motivation for further studies and serious discussions in Canadian churches and in government in the twenty-first century. As a result of the political processes now in ferment, Waterloo progressive Mennonites may exchange their present ambivalent political attitudes for greater and more direct involvement in government than has been their practice up to now.

Chapter 17

Credit, money, and mutual aid

Capitalism, socialism, and communism are the three prevailing economic systems of our time. The basic difference among them is the role of government ownership and control over the production, distribution, and consumption of a society's material resources and services. Capitalism, the system with least government ownership and control, is the oldest and still the most popular of the three systems. Socialism and communism have become prominent only in the twentieth century along with the rise of urban, industrial, and technological revolutions.

Mennonites have favoured the free enterprise system of capitalism, although always modified by New Testament ethics. In the sixteenth and seventeenth centuries in Europe, when Mennonites lived as small persecuted religious communities, they were sometimes accused of being communists because of their sharing and mutual burden bearing in daily life.[1]

The economic system which Mennonites adopted most consistently was a modified capitalism marked by a blend of self-reliance on the one hand and mutual aid on the other.[2] Mennonite mutual aid, however, never took the form of a compulsory community-wide co-operative body. If organized, it was for the purpose of doing certain things together to benefit the members of a community. The Mennonites in Russia had a wide variety of mutual aid organizations for fire protection, livestock breeding, cattle shipping, and collective land purchasing. Later, in western Canada, co-operative grain elevators, creameries, gasoline filling stations, and general stores were begun as mutual endeavours. These enterprises always operated as voluntary organizations by church and community members. They were never compulsory church- or community-owned and operated.

Mutual aid for Mennonites has as much of a religious basis as do such ethical and theological principles as nonresistance, simplicity, frugality, integrity, discipleship, and the ethics of love. Two of many New Testament passages that serve as a basis for mutual aid are: "Bear one another's burdens, and so fulfil the law of Christ" (Gal. 6:2) and "If any one does not provide for his relatives, and especially for his own family, he has disowned the faith and is worse than an unbeliever" (1 Tim. 5:8).

The Waterloo area Old Order Mennonites and Amish still demonstrate this informal mutual aid practice in their community life, particularly in the almost unlimited liability that is assumed by the church for need beyond the immediate family's ability to provide. However, they have never equalled Mennonites from Russia in extending this informal mutual aid into the realm of economics and business.

The Mennonite Credit Union Ontario in a very real sense reflects a merging of the Russian and Swiss Mennonite brands of informal and formal mutual aid. It is also a blending of Old Order welfare types of needs with progressive Mennonite economic and business types of needs. A summary of the economic status of the progressive Mennonites in the Waterloo area will provide a good background for understanding the organization, growth, and extended service now provided by the Mennonite Credit Union (MCU).

Economic status of Waterloo Mennonites

In 1976, Douglas Snyder, then a graduate student under my supervision, made a study of the work and leisure patterns of Waterloo area Mennonites.[3] The sample was taken from every tenth member of congregations in five conferences. (The Old Orders were not included in the study.) A total of 590 members received questionnaires. Of these, 304 usable ones were returned and tabulated. This was considered a valid sample. In the list of questions were those concerning home ownership, family income, employment, and job satisfaction.

Snyder found that 83.3 percent were homeowners, compared with 58.3 percent for all of Canada and 63.3 percent for Ontario. None of the 304 were unemployed. In fact, 51 persons (17 percent) said they had second jobs. More than half of the second jobholders took them to use up extra leisure time. One-fourth said they worked on the second job to raise or maintain their standard of living. Their values of domestic security and family stability are reflected in the high rate of home ownership and work as a measure of self-worth so far as full employment is concerned. Of the women who responded, 56 percent were working outside the home. Over 97 percent of both sexes indicated satisfaction with their jobs.

Table 17-1 compares incomes between the general public in Waterloo County and the Mennonites in the Waterloo area.

Table 17-1 Income categories by households, 1976[4]		
Income Categories	*Waterloo County (%)*	*Mennonites (%)*
Under $4,000	7	4
$4,600 - $9,359	23	23
$9,360 - $15,599	26	21
$15,600 - $23,399	28	24
$23,400 +	16	28
	100%	100%

The data in the table show that compared to all Waterloo County households 3 percent fewer Mennonites are in the lowest income brackets. Twelve percent more Mennonite households had incomes of over $23,400 than did all Waterloo County households. The decade-old absolute income figures are insignificant compared to the percentages. It is assumed that the percentages have not changed much in the last dozen years.

Table 17-2 shows the distribution by ten-year age categories by household according to eight categories. The table lends itself to comparison with incomes in Table 17-1 if the income categories are approximately matched. The income amounts and percentages will, of course, be only approximate. It will be noted that household incomes do not automatically increase with age. Those with under $5,000 income vary little with age. There are as many under forty earning over $50,000 annually as there are over forty. The findings of the Snyder study and Statistics Canada clearly reflect the generally high average level of Mennonite income. In

Table 17-1 (1971), 52 percent of the Mennonites had incomes of
over $15,600 and in Table 17-2 (1976), 31.7 percent had incomes of
over $20,000. While the dollar amounts will have increased in the
past decade, the percentage distribution may not have changed
significantly.

Table 17-2
Mennonite household incomes by age groups, 1976[5]

1976 Income	0-19	20-29	30-39	40-49	50-64	65+	Total	%
$0 - 3,000	1	2	1	0	1	2	7	2.8
3,000 - 4,999	0	1	1	0	4	2	8	3.2
5,000 - 9,999	3	11	7	8	17	13	59	23.7
10,000-14,999	1	15	13	6	14	4	53	21.3
15,000-19,999	2	13	11	10	7	0	43	17.3
20,000-24,999	2	9	13	14	5	0	43	17.3
25,000-49,999	4	3	10	4	4	0	25	10.1
50,000 +	0	2	4	2	3	0	11	4.3
Totals	13	56	60	44	55	21	249	100.0
Percentage	5.2	22.4	24.9	17.9	22.9	8.4		

These findings placed about 75 percent of Mennonites in
middle income brackets or above: in other words, in a favoured
economic position where they enjoy discretionary income. This
means having money to spend for items over and above necessities
such as food, clothing, housing, taxes, transportation, and utilities.
It also means having money to save and deposit in a bank or credit
union.

Evidence from the above annual income tables shows that a
significant percentage of Mennonites have annual incomes that,
by proper investment, could have resulted in affluence or wealth.
There is a difference between these two terms. Economic affluence
has reference to the flow of money or material goods and services
from one person, family or organization to another; it passes
through the person's or agency's hands but does not remain there.
Such persons or agencies handle much money but spend all or
most of it for consumer goods, thus accumulating little by way of
savings and investments.

Wealth, on the other hand, has reference to more or less permanent ownership and/or control of accumulated amounts of money and physical resources. The difference is in the amount people save, not in the amount they earn. Given the combined incentives of hard work, simple lifestyles, and frugal habits on the one hand, and regular employment and relatively high incomes on the other, a high percentage of Waterloo Mennonites are bound to be financially well off and enjoying a high standard of living. With financial independence comes a measure of self-confidence, prestige, and power. Power is a term which has been defined as ability to achieve purpose. This brief glimpse into Waterloo progressive Mennonite economic status may help to explain the steady growth, the membership support, and the financial strength of the Mennonite Credit Union.

Waterloo Mennonites, in the last quarter of the twentieth century, find themselves in a highly prosperous and rapidly expanding industrial-commercial community. Standards of living as well as actual levels of living have risen markedly within a single generation. This resulting affluence has become confusing for many. Progressive Mennonites, in contrast to conservatives, have provided few guidelines by which members may struggle through the ethically confusing situations facing them. The vices of excessive materialism and unbridled individualism can be readily identified among Waterloo Mennonites.

Enter the Mennonite Credit Union

The Mennonite Credit Union was born in Kitchener in 1964. The Credit Union, like so many other contemporary Mennonite service agencies, found the community ready to accept the added services it offered.

As rural Mennonites moved to the towns and cities in the Waterloo area after World War II, they unknowingly left behind some of their neighbourhood traditions, among which were their many informal mutual aid activities. In urban areas, they found fewer natural ways to practise such things as exchanging labour, borrowing and loaning tools and machinery, sharing each others' losses, and caring for the ill and the aged. One of the few organized mutual aid services available to them in their urban settings were two established casualty groups. One, the Amish Mennonite Storm and Fire Aid Union, organized about 1858, was the oldest such aid organization in Canada and the United States; the other, the Mennonite Aid Union, was organized in 1864. These two aid societies cover property damages due to natural causes for members in rural or urban areas.

The newly-arrived rural Mennonites soon found that urban society is dominated by money. Their free exchange of labour, a form of barter, required no cash. Urban life goes on without much of the do-it-yourself strategy and money-free work sharing practices of the country. Many services in the cities and towns are publicly provided, are compulsory, and must be paid for in cash.

Land use is restricted and zoned. Buildings must be erected according to specifications as to materials and location on lot. Improvements must be provided and maintained for water, sewer, lighting, and fire protection. Providing necessary food from one's own garden becomes ever more difficult except for a few vegetables. Furthermore, when husband and wife both work outside the home, time and energy for gardening are limited. Maintaining children in school, providing transportation for parents to get to and from work often requires the purchase and maintenance of two or more cars. These and many other modern customs illustrate the need for money as the medium of exchange for needed goods and services off the farm. The transition from rural to urban environments created a readiness for a Mennonite credit union in Waterloo County.

Credit union offers mutual aid

Many of the older Waterloo urban Mennonites grew up on the farm, but a majority of today's urban Mennonites are second and third generation urbanites who have never lived on a farm. These newer generations are the backbone of the Mennonite Credit Union. Young farmers, too, experience many of the same demands for money as do their co-religionists in the cities and towns. Their financial services are being provided throughout the wider Waterloo community by the Mennonite Credit Union. In fact, a change in the charter has altered what was once the Waterloo Credit Union into the province-wide Mennonite Credit Union Ontario.

This denominational credit union is a literal extension of the older mutual aid idea. It is a vehicle for meeting a central economic need for all Mennonites who wish to avail themselves of its services. The early promoters of the credit union were aware that a new generation of Mennonites was growing up unaware of the mutual aid aspect in their tradition. The existing banks, trust companies, and loan companies had gradually come to be seen as the only agencies through which to process personal financial business. Furthermore, this generation was growing up in an affluent society where money was plentiful and easy to come by, so that many had little appreciation for money as a scarce commodity. The new and younger generation was not being taught traditional frugality and good stewardship or careful money management. Banks, merchants, and unwise parents commonly encouraged borrowing and credit buying that led to reckless consumerism, self-indulgence, and unmanageable debts.

Awareness of these circumstances moved a few of the early promoters of MCU to take steps to organize a credit union. They saw it as a useful vehicle for church members to share their funds for mutual benefits and as an educational device for teaching good stewardship.

As a result of these germinal interests, early in 1964 a meeting was called and interested parties in Kitchener-Waterloo Mennonite churches were invited to attend. The response, although modest, encouraged further meetings, a charter, and a formal organization. Since the several organizational meetings were held at the Mennonite Central Committee headquarters in Kitchener, it was decided to ask MCC for the services of its secretary, Alice Snyder, to receive deposits and keep records of the credit union's activities. This arrangement, with the assistance of Irmgard Miller, an MCC accountant, continued for the first five years under the supervision of the president, Howard Snyder, who was at the time manager of the Bell Telephone Employees Credit Union in Toronto, and the treasurer, Fred Pfisterer, a certified public accountant.

Pfisterer demonstrated old-fashioned mutual aid in making available to the credit union Robert Tjart, one of his accounting firm employees, on a part-time basis. By 1976, twelve years after its founding, the credit union elected Tjart to the board of directors and engaged him as full-time manager.

In its first decade the credit union grew relatively slowly. This may mean that its merits were slow to be recognized, or that its advocates failed to promote it aggressively. Waterloo Mennonites generally were unfamiliar with credit unions. One cannot attribute the slow growth to opposition either within the various Mennonite churches or in the wider Waterloo community.

The MCU Twentieth Anniversary booklet described the organization's beginnings: "The fledgling WCMCU could have been called a shoe-box operation, at the outset. It had no employees of its own. Its office was a shared desk, a telephone, and a filing cabinet in MCC space. All the accounting was done manually. Interest rates were computed or drawn from a book of interest tables."[6] The early years reflected an uphill effort. By the end of the first year, membership numbered 92; assets were $13,192. At the end of the first five years, the membership had about doubled to 197 and assets were $34,624. After ten years, membership stood at 525 and assets at $404,760.

In its second decade, MCU membership took off almost as if it had suddenly been infused with a high charge of electricity. By 1978, at the end of the fifteenth year of operation, membership had spurted up to 2,041. It was in this period that Tjart, the enterprising young manager, with the support of a strong staff and board of directors, began to attract new members at an amazing rate. Between 1979 and 1980 almost 1,100 members joined MCU, bringing the total to almost 4,000. By 1984, the membership had climbed to over 5,000 and by the end of the 1987 fiscal year to over 6,000.

The MCU opened new ways for today's Mennonites to systematically help each other in money matters such as savings, investments, and loans. A credit union is a pure mutual aid society. It is a convenient and inexpensive way for church members to share and bear burdens. One member's prosperity and plenty today can supply another's needs. In the future, the roles may be reversed. Both parties benefited from such services. Genuine mutual aid, in the long run, must always be reciprocal.

A lay organization

The credit union is both a service and a business organization. It was not started by an official church conference or congregation, but by a group of inter-Mennonite church laymen. None of the Mennonite conferences or congregations ever officially opposed or approved the organization. This is because the church bodies were never asked for permission to form such a body. MCU is similar in organization and in relationship to the churches as is the Mennonite Central Committee and all of its many auxiliaries. Founded by lay men and women for the purpose of serving a needy world, the lay organizations have the blessings of all branches of the church in spite of the fact that the church exercises no direct control over any of them.

The formation and functioning of MCU is evidence that Waterloo Mennonites have an abundance of lay leaders interested and committed to their church and voluntarily undertaking to give concrete expression to the ideals their churches teach. It also reflects the degree of freedom to initiate new organizations by which lay member benefit.

Interestingly, MCU in its constitution and statement of philosophy prescribes no theological doctrines as a condition for membership. It accepts members from any of the fourteen separately organized Waterloo-area Mennonite and Brethren in Christ churches. At least ten of these groups have some members who participate in MCU activities and services. In other words, MCU is one more instance where church members from different branches work harmoniously together to achieve useful objectives, even though they maintain separate religious organizations and worship services.

The MCU has come to play an important role in the life of more and more Mennonites in the Waterloo region. The evidence of its importance is best illustrated by the size of the membership and the variety of services performed (Table 17-3). The swift growth of the credit union in the past decade may be ascribed, in part, to the sense of ownership that members have begun to feel in it. Likewise, the opening of five branch offices in Elmira, New Hamburg, and Milverton, as well as in Kitchener and Waterloo must have added interest as well as easy access to its services.

| | | | | | | Loan |
Fiscal Year	Member- ship	Assets	Loans Granted	Net Income	Dividend Paid	Interest Rebate
1965	93	$13,192	$13,061	$118	3.0	5.0
1970	281	$53,347	$49,052	$2,258	6.5	4.0
1975	650	$648,944	$390,684	$17,272	8.0	2.4
1980	3,996	$20,034,658	$5,751,523	$59,560	8.0	0.0
1985	5,280	$41,920,271	$16,039,994	$385,103	12.0	0.0
1986	5,608	$49,669,888	$22,068,383	$331,159	10.0	0.0

Table 17-3
MCU summary data by five-year intervals
Annual Reports, 1965-1985

The most impressive fact shown in Table 17-3 is the growth rate of the union and the extensive use of its services by members. In 1986, the MCU's average assets per member were $8,857. One year later, assets had jumped to over $62,000,000 and membership to over 6,000 making an average asset of $10,333 per member.

Fulfilling its purposes

One of the primary purposes of organizing the credit union was to carry on the long-standing practice of mutual aid in the context of an urban industrial-commercial environment. In a real sense, the Waterloo Mennonite community owes its existence to a now famous example of mutual aid. The 10,000 or $20,000 cash advance of the 23 Mennonite farmers from Lancaster, Pennsylvania in 1805 saved the first Waterloo settlement from possible extinction. What is equally important is the by-product of that dramatic act of mutual burden bearing. In addition to bringing money to Upper Canada, it brought a significant number of prosperous settlers to Waterloo. As in all genuine mutual aid, it resulted in a blessing to the donors as well as to the recipients.

The more specific purposes of founding MCU were to establish a mutual saving and loaning vehicle that would be owned and operated by those who could most benefit by it, namely, its members. To implement these goals required employing skilled and knowledgeable administrators and counsellors who were committed to the credit union's ideals. Leadership for the union was drawn from its members rather than hiring outside professional managers.

How the credit union works

The credit union, as one form of a co-operative, is perhaps the best example of democracy in business that can be cited. It is an example of modified capitalism. In contrast to the conventional corporate structure where members have votes in management in proportion to the shares owned, in the credit union each member has just one vote, no matter how many shares owned. In this sense, it is like a church organization where members have only one vote regardless of the amount they contribute. This type of organization places power in people rather than in the money they own or control. Since members in a credit union are both depositors of savings and borrowers of funds, it is possible that members are alternately creditors and debtors to each other. For this reason, all members, at least in theory, should have common interests in the welfare of the organization. The management team and the board of directors normally set interest and rebate rates, but these are open for discussion and review at annual membership meetings at which time members may accept, modify, or reject management recommendations.

The board of directors is divided into committees. Six of the seven are normal for governing boards: executive, audit, communications, facilities, personnel, and services. The seventh, a committee on church relatedness, is somewhat unusual for a business.

The organization calls for two standing committees. One is the credit committee which is standard for all credit unions. The other is a church-relatedness committee discussed later in this chapter. The credit committee is elected at the annual membership meeting. It is a loan approval body and has final authority in distress situations which cannot be solved by normal procedures. This committee plays an extremely important role in the total program of the credit union. If it does not do its work wisely, it can endanger the welfare of the entire organization.

Services performed for members

The credit union performs a full line of banking, loaning, and investment services. Included are interest bearing and non-interest bearing checking accounts, term deposits, registered savings plans, lines of credit, and first and second mortgages. In addition, there is a lengthy list of auxiliary services such as night depository, safety-deposit boxes, money orders, travel insurance, mortgage and loan insurance, and automated teller machines.

Besides these more or less common banking services, MCU provides a number of unusual member services. One of these is the somewhat elaborate effort made to solve personal difficulties members may encounter in repaying interest and/or principal on loans. When a loan manager identifies an account in default, several possible steps may be taken: 1) extension of the time period; 2) forgiveness of part or all of the accrued interest; 3) renegotiation of the interest rate; 4) possible reduction of the loan principal. Should these efforts not succeed in solving the particular problem, one of the following options is possible: a) negotiations through mediation; b) arbitration; c) cancellation of debt; or, d) as a last resort in extremely unusual cases, litigation. The justification for these numerous settlement options is that every available effort is to be made to achieve mutual agreement in the solution of each member's problems.

The Fellowship Fund

A most unusual facility of the credit union is known as the Fellowship Fund. It is an administrative instrument specifically designed to make it possible for members in financial distress to get help. Money for the Fellowship Fund comes from two sources: freewill contributions and low-interest or no-interest deposits on loans to the union. The latter may be repaid or the depositors may decide to cancel a part or all of the loan. The purpose is not designed as a long-term loan commitment, but rather as a short-term or temporary source of funds to assist where normal collateral may be inadequate.

Those who place low-interest or no-interest money in the fund may designate the individual or the purpose for which the money is to be used or they may leave the matter to the credit union staff. The Fellowship Fund is a way whereby generously motivated members may help someone in need without being personally identified. This unusual facility spells reality to the union's stated purpose of helping its members work out personal financial problems to the satisfaction of member and credit union.

Loan services

Of equal importance to receiving member deposits is the provision of loans at a reasonable rate and on a viable repayment schedule. Table 17-3 shows the growth in membership, the amount of annual assets, and net incomes. It should be noted that congregations, church conferences, and Mennonite institutions as well as individual members may become patrons of the credit union. Table 17-4 gives a picture of the size and extent of the credit union's loan operations for the years 1985 and 1986.

Table 17-4 lists twenty-one purposes for which loans were made. The largest single category of loans was for the purchase of automobiles. The second largest was to consolidate personal obligations, and, surprisingly, the third was for investment. Normally, borrowing money for investment is considered a risky venture unless the borrower has ample collateral as security for the loan. This may be the case of the credit union members who made loans for that purpose. Investment may mean different things for different people, so that not every investment is a high-risk venture. Items that increase in value with time such as rare stamps, coins, antiques, or even rare books would illustrate such investments. However, investments generally refer to purchase of stocks, bonds, or real estate.

In view of the widely heralded farm crisis in the 1980s, it is significant to note the number of loans made for three categories of farm purposes: 1) farm purchases, 2) farm equipment, and 3) farm operating expenses. In 1985, the credit union made a total of 158 loans for these three purposes for a total of $3,212,000 and, in 1986, a total of 159 loans for the sum of $4,539,000. This represents 15 percent of all loans in 1985 and 12 percent of all loans in 1986. If Waterloo area farmers are among the hard-pressed element of the population, this means that the union is helping to bear at least a portion of that financial burden by making credit available.

	1986		1987	
MCU membership	5608		5280	
	No.		No.	
Types of Loans	*of Loans*	*Amount*	*of Loans*	*Amount*
Automobile purchase	287	$ 1,923,948	232	$ 1,437,800
Automobile repair	12	17,740	12	25,960
Investment	101	1,343,092	70	911,835
Education	62	163,733	64	168,587
Consolidation	200	1,280,741	131	997,578
Vacation	30	71,260	26	106,075
Home improvements	78	665,780	76	574,523
Refinanced mortgages	32	1,401,927	49	2,213,073
Property purchases				
New	70	2,595,277	35	947,163
Used	100	3,926,484	86	3,375,167
Farm	32	2,709,664	21	1,550,540
Commercial	8	372,598	4	401,000
Church	5	322,000	7	358,750
Equipment purchase				
Household	14	56,800	9	48,900
Farm	47	715,370	74	756,483
Commercial	38	986,114	43	610,125
Church	0	0	3	48,000
Operating expenses				
Household	67	449,750	15	71,349
Farm	80	1,104,125	63	915,286
Commercial	86	1,937,480	37	514,800
Church	5	24,500	1	7,000
	1,354	$22,068,383	1,058	$16,039,994

Table 17-4
Mennonite Credit Union loan statistics, 1985-1986

Assuming that the loans represent one loan per member per year, the union assisted 20 percent of its members with loans in 1985 and 24 percent in 1986. This means one in four or one in five in these two years. The large number of loans made for consolidation purposes suggests that this may be the result of the credit committee's counselling of applicants to consolidate their obligations. This simplifies repayment of accounts outstanding and at the same time avoids having to pay high interest charges. Another significant purpose for which members made loans in 1985 and 1986 is for refinancing of mortgages. Over the two-year period, 81 borrowers used over three and a half million dollars for that purpose. The average amount borrowed was $44,640. New and used property purchases accounted for 170 loans and a total of over $6,600,000. Table 17-4 gives ample evidence that the credit union is doing a good work for its members.

A credit union weakness

One of the uncomplimentary aspects of MCU is the small amount of money invested as share capital. Any person who qualifies for membership may join by purchasing a minimum of five shares at five dollars each. In the subsequent ten years, members must purchase a minimum of an additional twenty-five dollars per year until they own fifty shares or have invested $250. In the meantime, they have the full privileges of membership, and are entitled to vote, borrow money, and hold office with as little at stake as a twenty-five dollar investment. With so small a share of money invested in ownership shares, the demand for loan capital is sometimes greater than the amount available to loan. The result is that the union must then borrow money from outside sources in order to satisfy member demands, or temporarily refuse member requests for loans, which is an undesirable alternative. Were all members to assume what might be called their "fair share" of ownership, it would demonstrate realistic responsibility of mutual burden bearing in a democratically owned and operated business.

Mutual concerns of the church and credit union

The Mennonite churches in Waterloo County did not seek or create the Mennonite Credit Union. It was organized independently of the churches, but for the purpose of rendering a collective voluntary service to the churches. The MCU has a provision in its organization for a standing committee which it identifies as the Church Relatedness Committee. In its 75-page anniversary booklet *Working Together*, two and a half pages are devoted to the purpose and work of this committee.[7] It says that MCU works as an autonomous organization and is directly accountable to its members and controlled by them through an elected board of directors and a credit committee. The MCU, nevertheless, considers itself a partner with the congregations and church conferences with whom it has common biblical grounds and common objectives.

These bonds translate into an effort to help church members apply Christian stewardship and mutual aid principles to their financial affairs. The credit union provides a ministry to the church in contrast to being a ministry of the church.

The MCU concludes its statement on church relatedness thus:

> It is clear that the commitment to church relatedness is firmly established and that other initiatives will also be nurtured in order to insure that Mennonite Credit Union continues its motif of service to members throughout the bond of association.[8]

To assure that this objective is carried out, six regional co-ordinators are appointed to see that there is some ongoing personal contact between MCU and every conference, non-conference group, congregation, and individual in Ontario Mennonite and Brethren in Christ districts. There are presently 46 such voluntary MCU representatives appointed and plans are under way to increase the number to 80.

Potential impact on the future of Waterloo Mennonites

The Waterloo Mennonite Credit Union is a young and dynamic independent organization with over 6,000 members concentrated within a radius of thirty-five miles of the twin cities. It is indeed in a position to play a decisive role in helping to shape the character of the Waterloo Mennonite church in the twenty-first century. To the extent that it will succeed in achieving its goals, it will demonstrate a better way and a higher motive for being in business than for profit alone.

The MCU has begun an interesting experiment in culture grafting by taking the young twig of the credit union and grafting it to a branch of an old mutual-aid tree. If it succeeds, as it now appears it can, it will add vigour to both old and new forms of Mennonite stewardship.

Chapter 18

Standing in the way of change

Change is a universal human experience. To the adage that nothing is more certain than death and taxes can be added a third certainty: change. Weather is never the same two days in a row; neither is human behaviour. If change is too slow, people complain that life is boring. If change is too rapid, people become frightened and begin to resist it.

Social change modifies social behaviour. Changes in hairstyles and in styles of dress are examples of social change. Cultural change happens when the way people make a living shifts from doing work by hand to working with machines. Another illustration of cultural change is to exchange a new idea for an old one, such as accepting as fact that an illness may be caused by a virus rather than by evil spirits.

All human groups have differing opinions as to the proper rate of change. One part of the group favours change at one rate and another part at a different rate. Thus, struggle goes on all the time as to whether, and at what rate, proposed changes should be adopted. Those who favour change most readily are called progressive; those who resist change most vigorously are called conservative. Whether progressive or conservative, each group believes its point of view is best for the welfare of the group as a whole.

Students of social behaviour note that change is more quickly adopted in the case of material inventions or social customs such as a labour-saving machine or a style of clothing than a new idea which is not visible. A farmer will accept and even buy a diesel engine or a tractor long before he will accept the idea of higher education as a method of learning the principle by which those machines operate. Likewise, he will accept medicine for himself, his family, and his cattle before he will be willing to permit

himself or his children to pursue the necessary study to understand the science of producing that medicine and uses for it.

Change occurs at different rates
Waterloo Mennonites furnish many examples of attitudes and
practices regarding the acceptance or rejection of change. In fact,
the differences in attitudes toward these changes account, in large
part, for the many separate Waterloo Mennonite churches. Among
human institutions such as education, economics, politics, leisure,
family, and religion, it is religion that is most conservative, most
slow to change. No other modern institution adheres to ancient
creeds and centuries-old practices as does religion. Changeless-
ness may contribute to institutional stability but it may also lead
to social, economic, and educational irrelevance.

An important word to sociologists is *culture*. Culture does not
mean refinement or polished social behaviour. It is all those
things which are human-made in contrast to that which is biologically inherited or God-given. Culture is both material and nonma-
terial. It is the sum total of human inventions and discoveries,
beliefs and social organizations, past and present. It refers to all
the shared products of human society, both material and nonma-
terial.[1] Culture and people are closely related and cannot exist
apart from each other. Cultures vary widely from one place to
another and even within a given local area, as Waterloo County
itself shows.

All cultures change, although they do so at different rates.
Changes in one area of a culture are often followed, sooner or
later, by changes elsewhere in the culture. When one part of a
group refuses to adopt important changes adopted by others, that
is a cultural lag. Job activity is so important to human life that all
other cultural elements have to adapt to it. Culture tends to be
conservative. People are slow to give up old values, customs, and
beliefs in favour of new ones. If this is true, why then is change a
constant mark of culture?

Three processes leading to change
Three distinct events are involved in cultural change: discovery,
invention, and diffusion.[2] *Discovery* is the awareness of something that already exists. An illustration of this is the discovery

that the smoking of tobacco causes lung cancer and other diseases. That was a fact long before the medical profession discovered the link between the two. A large part of the public was slow to believe this discovery and kept on smoking. Only after overwhelming evidence from public and private health, medical, and educational groups, has this discovery been generally accepted and legal steps taken to curb the use of tobacco.

Invention is the combination or new use of knowledge to produce something that did not exist before.[3] The gasoline engine, the automobile, and the airplane, as well as a university or the United Nations, are examples of inventions that are new but based on something invented before.

Diffusion is the spread of elements or traits from one culture to another. It is probably the source of most cultural change. Cultural diffusion, like gossip, spreads by word of mouth. New discoveries and new inventions create curiosity and sometimes excitement by the nature of their newness and the ability to do old things in a new way. If these inventions and discoveries appear to have practical uses, others begin to imitate the inventions or improve upon them, and thus spread these cultural traits.

Some cultural elements which appear new are in fact many hundreds and even thousands of years old. The Chinese, for instance, claim to have invented the iron plow (sixth century B.C.), paper (second century B.C.), the wheelbarrow (first century B.C.), use of thyroid hormones (seventh century A.D.).[4] These illustrations, if accepted as true, make the point that inventions and discoveries of a culture can be lost or totally destroyed with the culture and the society which nurtured them. Archaeology, the study of past human and material remains, bears witness to the fact that the gains of a culture can be lost.

Causes of change identified

Still other factors besides discovery and invention give rise to change. Sociologists identify the following:[5]

1. *Physical environment.* In Waterloo environment had a strong influence on the economic development and hence social change of the area. Its forest coverage, fertile soil, abundant rainfall, and natural drainage all contributed to a myriad of changes that resulted in the conversion of a totally virgin area into the

present urban industrial civilization.

2. *Ideas*. An often debated question is whether ideas shape social conditions or whether social conditions shape ideas. If social conditions are really unpleasant, they may spur change. It may be that poor climate or unhealthy physical conditions may stimulate change even if social conditions are satisfactory. The civil rights movement in the sixties and seventies was inspired by the ideas so well expressed by Martin Luther King, Jr. His followers furthered them by popularizing them with songs like "We shall overcome" and "Blowing in the wind."

3. *Technology* is both a cause and a result of change. The more advanced a society's technology, the more rapid social change tends to be. It is also true that one invention tends to bring on another or possibly a host of others. Note the evolution of grain harvesting tools from the scythe, to the reaper, to the binder, to the combine. That sequence inspired inventions for other crops: corn binder and harvester, the mechanical tomato, potato, cotton, cherry, and grape pickers.

4. *Events*. Random, unpredictable happenings—natural disasters like tornadoes, fires, floods, and hurricanes or socially caused riots and war—may be the cause of radical and permanent changes. Such causes of social change are hard to explain in terms of social theories because they are generally unpredictable and, when man-made, cannot be linked to single causes. Natural catastrophes, in most cases not predictable and not immediately preventable, nevertheless, may be important causes of social and cultural change.

5. *Human action*, individual or collective, whether intentional or not, may be a cause of important change.

The influence of persons on social change is hard to measure, yet dynamic leaders do influence the societies in which they live. This poses an ancient riddle. "Do times make the man or does the man make the times?" One can apply the question to Moses, David, the Apostle Paul, Abraham Lincoln, Martin Luther King, Jr., or to Bishop Benjamin Eby. In every case, the person's life and actions brought about important change.

One reason these leaders were able to bring about change is that the times in which they lived were ready to accept them. Many times the introduction of new ideas or new inventions failed because their societies were unwilling to accept them. Most of the great inventors experienced difficulty in getting their inventions, discoveries, or new ideas accepted. New laws are often only reluctantly accepted and are unwillingly obeyed.

What has been said about change in general applies to the Waterloo area and to its Mennonite communities as well. One way to understand differences among the Mennonites is in the way they accept or reject social and cultural change. The more conservative the group, the more it resists change of any kind. The reason behind this reluctance is the fear that new ideas and new ways will threaten the desired unity and harmony within their fellowship.

Progressive and moderate Mennonites tend to accept new ideas and new ways of doing things with little thought about possible disharmony. In these groups, individual choice is the expected norm. All Waterloo Mennonites, to some degree, resist change, but the conservatives have developed more defences against change than have the progressives.

Religion tends to resist change

Religion provides the most impressive examples of keeping the old ways. The Amish Sunday morning worship services held in the homes of members, rather than in even the simplest meetinghouse, follows the apostolic model of the New Testament. The order of worship has barely changed for centuries. The use of the four-hundred-year-old hymnbook, the *Ausbund*, without notes, symbolizes commitment to the religion of the fathers.[6] More than fifty of the hymns were written by sixteenth-century Anabaptists held in prison. The *Ausbund* has been printed more than thirty times. The martyr hymns sung often in the course of a lifetime remind the Amish that they belong to a suffering church and that they are to be a separated people. Sunday worship, the most sacred period of the Amish Old Order week for the entire family from the youngest child to the oldest members, is a powerful reinforcer of the entire Amish belief system and fuels the Amish resistance to change.

The Old Order Mennonites are a shade more progressive than the Old Order Amish in that they meet in plain rural meetinghouses rather than in homes. Their meetinghouses are symbols of their faith as well as places for worship and renewal of their commitment to follow in the footsteps of Christ and their forefathers. Sunday morning worship is a regular two-hour experience for the entire family. The order of worship has not changed noticeably for centuries. This example of historical continuity in resisting change sets the pattern and the reason for resistance in other aspects of life, in family and in the lifestyle generally. The hymnbook used is the almost two-hundred-year-old *Unpartheyisches Gesangbuch*. Like the *Ausbund*, it is without notes and each hymn has many verses. Both Old Orders use the German languages, High German for the reading of Scripture and the Pennsylvania German dialect for the sermon. Without this regular religious reinforcement of their commitment to lives of discipleship, their resistance to change through the week could not be sustained. Even so it is difficult.

Moderate Mennonites selective of change
The Waterloo-Markham and Beachy Amish churches, representing the moderate Waterloo churches, reflect less resistance to change than the Old Orders. For instance, the use of German language in worship has given way to English both in singing and preaching. This means their hymnbooks too have changed. Dress regulations are less rigid and reflect variation especially for children. One Beachy meetinghouse has indirect lighting, shaped pews, carpeted aisles, and a fellowship room in the basement. These slight changes symbolize the degree to which change has been adopted as a lifestyle.

The four progressive groups all worship in conventional type Protestant churches. Their orders of service are much like those of Protestant evangelical mainline churches. One subculture trait still retained by those of Swiss ethnic background is congregational singing without instrumental accompaniment. Almost all progressive congregations have organs and/or pianos which are used in some parts of the service. The church buildings of the progressives, especially in the urban areas, can no longer be described as plain meetinghouses. In terms of architecture, they cannot be distinguished from Protestant church buildings in general.

A middle-aged Old Order Amish farmer observed how his people were almost forced to accept modern technology. The example he cited was an air-tight (Harvestore) silo which requires an electric powered auger to remove the silage. Not to use the required auger is to choose not to use the silo. This option presents the Amish farmer with the dilemma of abandoning one of the most expensive facilities on his farm. If he has dairy cows, the silo is vital to his enterprise. The same dilemma confronts him if he buys a farm with an electric stable cleaner and/or an installed milk cooling tank. The newly-acquired farmhouse too may be supplied with electricity which among other items would provide current for a deep freeze for preserving vegetables, fruits, and meat.

It is becoming difficult to buy farms today that do not have electricity already installed. In addition to being expensive to remove, it means that dairying is almost out of the question because farmers without electric- or diesel-powered cooling systems can no longer sell milk to local processors except for cheese making. I believe Old Order Mennonite and Amish farmers will eventually adopt electricity and telephones on strictly practical economic grounds. They will conclude that the merits outweigh the demerits and that the uses will not destroy their religious customs even if they modify some of their labour practices.

An Old Order farmer's wife explained to me why her family had hired the services of a farmer with a mechanical potato picker. As long as most of their eight children were at home, they could harvest ten acres with their own family's help. Now only a few of the younger children were still at home; with twenty-five acres of potatoes, it was impossible to harvest their crop alone.

Church splits over acquiring modern technology

The pressure to adopt modern farm machines is not new. It began after World War I and grew until 1939 when it expressed itself in a split in the Old Order Church, and in the formation of the Waterloo-Markham Church. Some Old Order members bought cars, which was against church rules in Waterloo County but not among the Old Order Mennonites in York County. As a result of the tolerance in York County, a number of Waterloo County Old Order members bought cars and drove to York County to take communion twice a year, thus remaining in good standing.

This situation could not be tolerated for long, so those who favoured adopting cars, electricity, and telephones withdrew from the Old Church and formed their own congregations. The new group chose to retain the social customs of plain dress, the order of service in worship, and even to continue worshipping in the same meetinghouses on alternate Sundays. In other words, they were not dissatisfied with the social customs but only with the restriction on the use of technology.

This church separation illustrates the conflict theory of social change. It contends that some conflicts benefit both parties. In this instance both groups, after the first discomfort of the separation, seem happier and more harmonious because both have been able to pursue their objectives and still be true to their social and religious convictions. They prefer two separate and peaceful groups rather than one contentious congregation. This church split illustrates how conservative groups that are rigid in their opposition to change may eventually bring about a separation, as is the case in the Waterloo-Markham Church. The Beachy Amish congregations separated a generation earlier from the Old Order Amish in protest by the Old Order Church's opposition to worshipping in meetinghouses.

The Mennonite Conference of Ontario and social change

The Mennonite Conference of Ontario at its annual meeting in 1926 passed a most unusual resolution for a church body: Since there are resolutions on our Conference records that seem to be no longer needed, and others that seem more or less difficult of putting into practice, Be it resolved that this Conference appoint a committee of three brethren to tabulate past resolutions under the following heads: Obsolete, Doubtful, and Practical and report to the next Annual Conference.[7] This action is a sensible and practical one but most unusually honest. Usually outworn resolutions or rules are not removed from the records but are merely ignored and forgotten. It is an appropriate admission by an official church body of the need for change, a need for updating its rules of conduct. A partial list of this conference's resolutions of almost a century will indicate the accuracy of referring to some of them as obsolete, doubtful, or impractical. It is not known what recommendations the appointed committee made to Conference or what was done with the recommendations. What is known is that social practices once forbidden became, in time, acceptable.

Arguments against the adoption of new ideas and new inventions, such as labour-saving inventions for house and farm, are numerous. Often the reasons lack convincing logic. Among the conservatives, a common reason for opposition is that such inventions are unnecessary. The critics point out that previous generations did without such things, therefore they too should live without them. Others argue that the old is better than the new, therefore trying the new is pointless.

An ultraconservative Mennonite argued that modern machinery is contrary to the teachings of the Bible which admonishes people to earn their bread by the sweat of their brows, and machinery makes sweat less likely. Others argue that modern machines lessen work for family members, especially children who learn adult roles by working. Others resist changes because of fear that the new gadgets and machines would harm their sacred lifestyle.

No matter how intense the resistance to change, it continues to occur in every realm of Waterloo Mennonite society. Only the rates and kinds of change have varied. This has resulted in the transition to a dynamic from a static society. The conservative Waterloo Mennonites have seen these changes and responded to them slowly.

Only the majority of Old Order Amish and the David Martin Old Order Mennonites have refused to adopt the tractor. Nevertheless, the David Martin group has become heavily involved in starting small farm industries where power machinery is essential. The fact that they use diesel power rather than electricity weakens their opposition to technology in principle. They recently approved the use of telephones because phones are important for their new farm businesses. It will be only a matter of time until other mechanical equipment and requirements for industrial work will persuade them that electricity is economically necessary and will therefore be approved.

The Mennonite Conference of Ontario was the main body of Mennonites in Ontario, in fact in all of Canada, until the coming of the Mennonites from Russia in the first quarter of the twentieth century. Its main competitor during that time was what is now the Missionary Church. It is against this background that the following resolutions between 1847 and 1957 must be seen. The resolutions are divided into two groups. In one, the Conference acted to give permission to congregations to make changes. A second list of resolutions warned members not to make changes on pain of church discipline. Some resolutions merely asked for conformity to certain practices without reference to penalties.

Resolutions permitting change[8]

1847: Permission granted to hold prayer meetings.
1894: Ministers given permission to do evangelistic work.
1896: Marriage ceremonies permitted to be performed in churches.
1897: Bishops permitted to perform marriages of nonchurch members.
1898: All who can conscientiously vote for prohibition should.
1898: Congregations to hold collections on Thanksgiving for Home Missions.
1899: Conference favours holding a Bible conference in district.
1900: Appoint a committee to receive volunteers for mission work.
1904: Ministers to preach a mission and evangelistic sermon yearly.
1904: Congregations to hold one or more collections a year for missions.
1920: Conference favours some system for complete Bible instruction, Christian training, and more advanced education to prepare young people for Christian service.
1927: Appoint a committee of five brethren to investigate the question of auto liabilities through mutual aid union.

Resolutions forbidding change[9]

1864: Witness against pride and fashion in the world.
1873: As some try to set aside the office of bishop, it was unanimously decided by Conference that there should be bishops as heretofore.
1877: Advise executors of estates not to go to law to collect accounts.
1880: When outsiders bury their dead in our burying ground they should have the charity toward us not to have processions nor . . . rituals of secret orders.
1882: Advise our members not to have hearses at funerals.
1883: Advise our members to clothe their dead for burial in a white shroud, as was the custom of our forefathers.
1883: When brethren accept the office of counsellor, such brethren are not considered as members of the church.
1892: No church members shall have permission to join any secret order or society.
1893: Advise brethren and sisters not to have their photographs taken.
1895: No monuments or costly tombstones be erected over the departed.
1898: Brethren should not wear badges at funerals when acting as pallbearers.
1899: Fully put our trust in God, and advise our members not to get lightning rods.
1899: Greater simplicity at funerals be observed and flowers not be advised.
1901: We deem it unscriptural for Christians to belong to labour unions.
1904: Flower girls at weddings are discouraged, and modest apparel advocated.
1905: Disapprove the entertainment features of literary societies and discourage attendance of young people at such meetings.
1907: We consider it contrary to the Word of God for our members to have their lives insured, or belong to a secret order, and that we cannot retain anyone as member who is connected with either.
1918: Because of the trend of worldliness evident among the people, and because the power of God grants his followers who are manifestly separated from the world, we, as members of the Ontario Mennonite Conference, declare that we favour the wearing of the bonnet by our sisters, and the regulation coat by the brethren.
1922: That we, as a conference, recognize the need of a proper regulation of the apparel of the church members. We regret the liberties assumed by some who have exceeded the advice and counsel of the church. Therefore, be it resolved that we earnestly appeal to all of our members to maintain the standards and practices repeatedly confirmed by our annual Conference, expecting that there

shall be a reasonable and faithful compliance with this request, or expect the proper discipline by the officers of the church.

1923: The Conference reaffirms its position on the use of tobacco.

1957: Christians who live in a fashion-conscious world need to guard against ultra-sheer clothing, sleeveless dresses, flashy ties, ornamental watches, brooches, clasps, and the wearing of other forms of worldly adornment. We exhort our members to secure serviceable clothing, dress neatly and modestly, and in every way be in harmony with our profession of godliness. We lament the practice of cut hair in our Conference among our sisters. We believe that according to God's Word, Christian women should wear their hair long, by which we mean uncut.

This lengthy list of one century's resolutions from the Mennonite Conference of Ontario is a priceless document for the study of social change. It provides insight into the efforts of a believers' church to exercise discipline over the social behaviour of its members as a witness to its separation from the world. As one statement expresses the objective: to "in every way be in harmony with our profession of godliness."

To this generation of progressive Mennonites and to non-Mennonites unfamiliar with church discipline in matters of personal behaviour, the detailed concern of a church conference for the style of clothing, hair style, kind of jewelry and use of leisure time may seem quaint and even humorous. It was not so considered by Ontario Mennonites during their first century and a quarter in Ontario. Nor do the moderate and conservative Mennonites in Waterloo County so regard it today. Such resolutions gave meaning to church discipline. It was and still is considered the duty of church leaders, as spokespersons for the group, to encourage self-restraint, and discourage self-indulgence and display of pride.

Appeal to voluntary conformity

The overall tone of the resolutions is generally in the form of a gentle reminder or as an appeal to conform to what is assumed as group standards or norms. For instance, the 1901 admonition stated that: "We deem it unscriptural for Christians to belong to labour unions." There is no sharp statement forbidding membership or a threat of punishment. In 1904, flower girls at weddings were discouraged. In 1907, the admonition was "We consider it contrary to the Word of God for our members to have their lives insured." In 1922, a resolution said frankly that "we, as a conference, recognize the need of a proper regulation of the apparel of the church members."

This last statement is significant in the light of the wide-spread discontent that existed in the Conference over the matter of dress and hairstyles in the nineteen twenties. It was only two years later, in 1924, that about half of the members of the First Mennonite Church withdrew and formed the Stirling Avenue Church, largely as a protest against the attempt of a bishop to exercise discipline over a minister who declined to deny communion to women who refused to conform to the prescribed dress code. This church division had strong repercussions throughout the Mennonite Conference of Ontario. Some ministers softened their emphasis on conformity in dress; others took an even stronger stand in defence of the traditional position. The 1957 Conference statement reflects the latter position.

At any rate, the Ontario conference continued on its journey in a progressive direction. Within a decade after the last resolution quoted above, matters of clothing and hairstyle disappeared from the records. Even more, it seems to have disappeared from the consciousness of most church members in that clothing styles no longer identified them as Mennonites nor set them apart. Social change had brought members of that conference from the ranks of nonconforming Mennonites to the ranks of Waterloo citizens generally. It is an illustration of social accommodation, the process by which individuals or groups adjust their underlying differences in attitude and behaviours in order to work together.[10]

Resolutions reflect fear of change
The list of varied resolutions cited above reflects an overall concern to preserve traditional ethical principles such as simplicity, humility, separation, and brotherhood. Even more, it reflects a fear of losing these cherished traits. Interestingly, no mention is made of concern for the loss of nonresistance. Was it considered safe even during World War I? Had they not feared a loss, the resolutions would not have been enacted. Behaviour patterns being adopted by some members were considered contrary to group customs. These undoubtedly reflected the pressure for change felt by Mennonites who had come to the cities before and during World War I and were adopting fashions and customs contrary to earlier rural regulations. The regulations covered a wide range of behaviour concerning the dead as well as the living. The

appropriate cemetery ritual, proper clothing of the dead, forbidding the use of flowers at weddings, funerals, and in cemeteries, adherence to uniform dress for men and women, refraining from joining secret societies and labour unions, buying life insurance, or using tobacco—these rules intended to insure behaviour showing godliness and separation from the world.

An interesting anecdote was told to me by a Mennonite who had come from Russia in 1924. These Mennonites at first worshipped with the Swiss Mennonites. His mother died and the memorial service and burial took place at the First Mennonite Church. Since flowers were not permitted at the church service, the Russian placed some flowers and a small cross on his mother's grave. Later, when he visited the grave, he found both flowers and cross gone. He asked the caretaker where he had put them and why they had been removed. He was told they were thrown into the horse sheds at the edge of the cemetery because "they were too Catholic." The Russian asked: "Don't you think there will be Catholics in heaven?" The caretaker replied, "Not unless they change."

Noticeable changes are reflected in the decline of family size, in the roles of husband-father, wife-mother and in the roles of children. The role changes are reflected in the shift in residence from farm to non-farm and from rural to urban areas.

Basic changes in the family
The weakened stability of the family is reflected in higher rates of separation and divorce. Birth control methods have been generally accepted because children in urban areas are an economic liability. Among progressive Mennonite families in Waterloo County, as in Canadian families generally, the socializing role of the family has been steadily on the decline. The process of teaching and modelling acceptable and unacceptable ways of behaving are today being performed more and more by the school, leisure-time groups, the radio, movies, and television.

The wider Mennonite church in Waterloo County, like the Mennonite family, has been affected by change in different ways. Swiss-background congregations especially reflected the pressure for change from outside. Beginning with World War I, the Mennonite Conference of Ontario and the Western Ontario Conference gradually dropped many of the regulations listed above.

The progressive Mennonites with a Dutch-Russian background never practised similar church discipline. We have already discussed changes such as the shift to representative government by elected church councils rather than by ministerial leadership (Chapter 8). Other changes were the switch from unpaid lay pastors to seminary-trained and paid, full-time pastors. We noted also the growth of church-centred activities both within and outside local congregations, in contrast to the single weekly Sunday morning service of an earlier day. These changes were going on in old-line Protestant churches generally.

No change in Old Order churches

By contrast, the Old Order Amish and Mennonite churches were almost untouched by such changes. One reason was that their members were not moving to towns and cities. All their meetinghouses too remained in the country. With the exception of one Old Order Amish district, they continued to use horse-and-buggy transportation; the automobile and the hard-surface roads did not greatly affect their lifestyle.

They rejected electricity and the host of labour-saving devices coming with it. Their church leadership continued to be drawn by lot from their own members and remained financially self-supporting. In short, they successfully resisted adoption of practically all of the social and technological changes which the progressive Mennonites adopted. Even late in the twentieth century when conservative farmers have widely accepted the use of tractors and a few have adopted the use of electricity or diesel power and the telephone for business purposes, these innovations have not altered the structure or function of the church or family.

In the four decades since World War II, education among Waterloo Mennonites has clearly felt the winds of change. Among the progressives, the Ontario Mennonite Bible Institute, established in 1907, was closed; Rockway Mennonite High School and Conrad Grebel College were founded. These changes reflected the massive waves of demand for additional opportunities in the province of Ontario in the fifties and the sixties, a period in which five new provincial universities were simultaneously established.

The progressives opted for educational accommodation of a sort, while the conservatives opted for a separate course. Although moving in different directions, both conservative and progressive groups followed courses of action thought best to effectively serve their churches.

In finding jobs, too, the post-World War II decades saw big shifts in response to general trends in society. The progressives in large numbers abandoned farming for nonfarming occupations in villages, towns, or cities. They generally looked for more education. The conservatives tended to remain on the farms and instead of leaving the farms in search of other jobs, tended to find secondary sources of income by establishing small industries on their farms or by working in nearby towns in allied agricultural businesses. Conservatives showed a greater discrimination in the kinds of work and the locations of work they pursued than did the progressives. Conservatives taught that certain kinds and places of work had a negative influence over their members' lives, something they wished to prevent. The progressives seem to have had few such concerns. One group reflected a strong commitment to the doctrine of social separation, the other did not.

Outreach aimed at serving the needs of others

Two other areas of life reflect noticeable changes among Waterloo Mennonites after World War II. One was the rapid expansion of service agencies organized by lay church members with the approval, but not the official sponsorship, of a church body. The Mennonite Central Committee (MCC) is a good example of such a lay organization. It serves as an umbrella for a host of related organizations which need only be mentioned to be recognized; yet neither MCC Ontario nor any of its auxiliaries existed before 1940.

The role played by the Mennonites in MCC's various outreach programs is indeed a dramatic change in collective social behaviour from that played prior to World War II. It reflects a marked shift from a passive to an active role in the Waterloo community. While the outreach organizations are Mennonite owned and sponsored, those they assist are almost without exception non-Mennonites. They are designed to help those in society who are in need.

In agencies such as the Justice Ministries and the Peace and Social Concerns Committee, serious efforts are made to provide models for improvements and changes in the justice system. Attempts are being made to influence the public to find better ways of handling chronic human relations problems than society's "revolving door" treatment of criminals, alcoholics, handicapped, and those involved in interpersonal conflicts—repeated arrest and imprisonment without changing the person or removing the cause of the problem.

During the past half century, the new culture of leisure has stood in sharp contrast to Waterloo Mennonites' traditional work-oriented ethic and frugal lifestyles. Progressive Mennonites, especially those under fifty years of age, have generally adopted the conventional leisure-oriented lifestyles of the times. This social change has caused only minimum concern in the progressive churches. One sees no signs of religious displeasure or alienation between church and society. Material blessings are gratefully accepted as a divine blessing to be shared with the poor after their own comforts are provided for.

The large proportion of conservatives who have remained on the farms and rural nonfarm areas have no comparable flourish of new outreach service organizations. Likewise, they have not shifted noticeably in the direction of adopting the pattern of today's leisure-oriented society.

Conservative Waterloo Mennonites do not seem to feel the need to conform to every wind of change. They have a strong commitment to their own lifestyle and prefer continuing to conform to it rather than to the many new ideas, fashions, and inventions that constantly present themselves. This for them spells a significant measure of stability and avoids the constant need to adjust to the new, the unknown, the uncomfortable, and often the impractical. The disparity in the rates of change between the two Waterloo Mennonite groups means that the conservatives reflect culture lag when compared to the progressives.

Chapter 19

Mennonites as seen by their neighbours

Most of what has been written in this book up to this point is what I have seen and reflected upon. I have attempted to describe the nature and character of the religious and cultural group of which I am a member. An account by one Mennonite about other Mennonites is bound to reflect some bias and some lack of objectivity. In this chapter, non-Mennonites assess Mennonites in Waterloo as they have seen and known them.

These opinions and attitudes have been chosen at random from my files. They include a variety of perspectives. Among them are those of eminent scholars familiar with Mennonite history and theology, representatives of students and teachers from elementary to university levels. Information was also gleaned from national and provincial government agencies, chambers of commerce, and a wide range of press reports in local and metropolitan newspapers. The assessments sometimes refer to Mennonites as a whole and at other times to certain segments, like the rural Old Order or the urban progressive groups.

Non-Mennonites evaluations of Mennonites are, on the whole, quite positive. This has not always been so. For centuries Mennonites, if not despised, were only tolerated. What accounts for this reversal of attitudes? Especially toward the conservative groups, with their strong and consistent commitment to separation from the world and their willingness to confront governments whenever legislation threatened to destroy their religious values?

Over the centuries, the shift in public attitudes toward Mennonites moved by stages from alienation to toleration to total acceptance. Until recent decades, many members left their church ashamed of their Amish or Mennonite identity. Today, however, many of those individuals or their descendants proudly claim or even boast of their sectarian heritage. Mennonite farmers who a few decades ago were characterized as self-conscious, rustic, and culturally backward are today pointed to as staunch pioneers and sturdy citizens contributing to the welfare of the community. Who has changed? Have Mennonites conformed to society's standards, or has society become more tolerant of minority differences?

Two scholars assess Mennonites

In 1975, Conrad Grebel College invited two distinguished scholars to speak at the 450th anniversary of the founding of the Mennonite church. Each one in the course of his address commented on the contributions the Anabaptists-Mennonites have made to society. Gregory Baum, professor of theology at St. Michael's College, University of Toronto, and the author of many books and scholarly writings including a theological reader in sociology,[1] credited the Mennonite forerunners, the Anabaptists, with six contributions:[2]

1. They influenced such major documents as the statement on religious freedom at the Second Vatican Council led by Pope John XXIII. Baum credited the change in Roman Catholic and European Protestant attitudes toward Mennonites to two recent developments. First, the image of the radical reformers as "caricatures" in most history books has been changed by Mennonite scholars. Second, the mainline churches now recognize that the day of Christianity as a state religion is over.

2. Baum credited the early Anabaptist reformers with separating church and state. They anticipated, in their attitudes and teachings, events that happened over the following four centuries. The church, he said, can no longer inspire conformity and obedience to the state; conversely, the state cannot protect church authority.

3. Theologians are returning to the free church ideal of the creative minority, said Baum. The radical reformers created a new sense of community. Modern Christianity has taken up the ideal of small renewal groups within the larger structures, such as prayer groups, house churches, and cells of 20 or less.

4. The Toronto Catholic theologian credited the Anabaptists for being pioneers with their doctrine of believers' baptism and their ban of infant baptism and its implications of sin and evil. This doctrine, said Baum, was both a critique of culture and a separation of religion from the prevailing culture.

5. To reject infant baptism was to repudiate original sin, said Baum. The Anabaptists did not think sin came through newborn children but rather through human institutions and a sinful environment. They stressed the sins of the world. Sin was seen by them not only as a private affair but also in social and cultural terms.

6. The sixteenth century Anabaptist-Mennonites called for a basic reshaping of society. Their efforts produced a genuine renewal movement. Their willingness to listen to others was later seen as religious toleration. This was unique in that they were most willing to listen to those lower on the social scale. Baum concluded by saying, "We need to ask for this type of impatience with a world that hurts and pushes people."

The second scholar to comment on Mennonite contributions was Jarold K. Zeman, an eminent Canadian historian, author, and Baptist churchman, who is professor of church history at Acadia University in Wolfville, Nova Scotia. He warned Mennonites that continued emphasis on cultural traditions at the expense of religious identity could make the Mennonite church a museum piece, a curiosity, not a viable option for those seeking religion. Unless Mennonites divorce culture from religion, he said, they will have a hard time growing and even surviving. He cautioned both Baptists and Mennonites against turning into a "bourgeois, middle class, nondescript Canadian Protestantism."

Inquiries about Mennonites

Over the years, I have kept a file of letters from a variety of sources asking for information about Mennonites. The inquiries came from university undergraduates, secondary school students, elementary school students, college professors and high school teachers. The letters, half from males and half from females, came from 33 Ontario communities, three provinces, and two states.

At the encouragement of the University of Waterloo sociology department, I offered, as an experiment, a summer school course on the sociology of Mennonites. I anticipated that possibly as many as eight or ten students would take the course, but to my surprise 33 students enroled. Moreover, not one of the students was a Mennonite, although two had a Mennonite family background. On the first day of class, I asked each student to tell in a paragraph why they enrolled for the course. Following are extracts from some of their statements:

> I am hopeful of examining the values found in the Mennonite com-
> munity as a possible value to cope with the impersonality of
> bureaucratic and urban life. S.A.

> I have drifted away from the Mennonites. Now that my boy friend
> is interested in the Mennonites I too have become more intrigued
> by the changes that have and are taking place. . . . I would like to
> find out why liberal and progressive Mennonites so often resent
> being called Mennonites. S.B.

> It is hoped that by taking this course a better understanding of the
> local Mennonite community will arise. I.C.

> I come from a little island in the Mediterranean [Malta] and the
> majority of people there are farmers. . . . When I moved to the K-W
> area, I started teaching in St. Clements, which is surrounded by a
> lot of Mennonites. I would daily see these people walking along the
> road or riding in buggies. I always tried to find out if they are sim-
> ilar to the people in Malta. When this course was offered I thought
> it was a good opportunity to satisfy my curiosity. V.C.

> As I have worked in Roman Catholic educational institutions I find
> it gratifying to be able to study and come to some understanding of
> another religious faith. J.D.

> I want to discover whether their strict behaviour and social inter-
> action creates more satisfied individuals than in our society. D.G.

> Having grown up in this community I was always interested in
> Mennonites. Intrigued by their distinctiveness and uniqueness as
> a group. I wish to know more about them. S.I.

> I hope this course will give me a better understanding of why the
> Mennonites live as they do and how they resist change to the
> extent of refusing any government help. P.L.

> Being brought up in this area I have always seen Old Order Men-
> nonites and have been curious to know more about them. I have
> wondered how the more modern groups are related to them. K.L.

> My main reason for taking this course is that it gives me a chance
> to study and observe a people who are not trapped in this [our]
> capitalistic society and where children are not educated to be 'con-
> sumer trainees.' . . . I strongly feel that urban living alienates the
> individual from all that is intended to be natural and basic in the

inner person. M.M.

I would like to know more of their culture. I am intrigued by a group that seems to resist change and yet get along so well with the majority groups around them. P.M.

Urbanized Mennonites are initiating and administering progressive community-betterment programs but I wish to know more about the range of philosophy found within the Mennonite culture and their unifying bonds. W.M.

As a child I had heard stories of Mennonites and their way of life. One instance in particular stood out. It was of a local farmer who had moved to a Mennonite community in the Elmira area. He claimed that he was 'forced out' in about two years. I felt this was an excellent way to get some facts about the Mennonite way of life. J.R.

I chose this course because I wanted to further my interest in community living and to find out more about my Mennonite neighbours. J.S.

I have been very interested in country life and communes. I have read material on communes, some of Thoreau's writing, and Walden Two by Skinner. I would like to study the Mennonites as an example of organized group living. Perhaps some of their thought or ways can be applied to modern experimental group living. H.S.

Concern to understand the Mennonites

The reasons university students give for wanting to study the Waterloo area Mennonites vary. Yet there is one overriding reason, namely, a desire to better understand this religio-ethnic minority group. Both those who have lived in the area all their lives and those who have come to the area recently seem to know little about the life, faith, and culture of the Mennonites.

For some, their study was motivated by a desire to discover values which could be put to use in the societies in which they were living. At the end of the course, after doing some systematic reading and study and after going to church services of Old Order, moderate, and progressive groups and visiting in their homes and schools, students expressed genuine respect for the Mennonites they had come to know. Some of the myths and mysteries with which they had begun the course had disappeared.

The following testimonial illustrates the power of an example of disciplined religious living by those with whom the student came into contact during the course in 1973. Neither the professor nor the class members were aware of the student's personal problems, nor were they aware of the life-changing experience he was having until after the course had ended.

> This is just a personal note of explanation for turning in a late paper on a topic not originally planned. My reasons for choosing this topic is outlined briefly in the paper, but there is much more to it.
>
> Six months ago I was separated from my wife of nine years and two children. We subsequently engaged lawyers and were in the middle of divorce proceedings, when I became involved with the Mennonite study. I had already read the prescribed texts and numerous others but had not really identified with the values until I encountered the three worship services and home visitations. My own family and many friends who shared my rural Christian upbringing were either unable to help me see clearly, or they did not try. It was during the visitations that a number of revealing events took place. I now began to feel what the Amish and Mennonites were all about. I felt it strongly in the progressive services and also in the house church.
>
> In all sincerity, I believe I was searching for more than a sociological experience, and I found it. I believe also that to try to study such a group as Mennonites without developing those experiences in the affective domain would be a disservice to the meaning and purpose of these people. As a religio-culture, the Amish and Mennonites have proven to me that they can be a vehicle to a life of meaning and purpose even in a contemporary society. Their method of demonstrating values is necessary for their survival but also to reflect upon us our worldly ways.
>
> To make a long story short, my wife and I have been reconciled. We have grown much in the past six months.

County school children study Mennonites

No non-Mennonites view of Mennonites comes with more authority than the 182-page workbook prepared by Waterloo elementary school teacher Carolyn Yandt and David P. Woodhall, senior consultant to the Waterloo County Board of Education. The student's workbook is called "The Old Order Mennonite Community."[3] It was produced in 1978 by the Integrated Studies Department of the Waterloo County Board of Education. The introduction gives the rationale for this curriculum piece.

"Present Day Cultures in Waterloo County" is a unit in the Environmental Studies program included in order to introduce the students to the groups of people who are from different cultural backgrounds within our own Waterloo Region. By studying groups who live lifestyles where a visible cultural distinction can be made the students should develop higher levels of understanding and tolerance for sociological differences of all kinds. The Old Order Mennonite Community seems to be an excellent culture to study due to the uniqueness of their lifestyle, their present day contribution to the Region as farmers, their contribution to the history of our Region, and the ideas that we can learn concerning their moral and religious motivations. Through this study the students will be exposed to one vital and extremely interesting community within our Region. Respect for alternate lifestyles and the Old Order lifestyle in particular should grow throughout this unit.

The book provides a historical background and a general overview of the Old Order Mennonites, a series of teaching strategies of the family, the home, the church, the school, social customs, the rural environment, and technology. Eleven appendices include maps, stories about Old Order children's life activities, selected readings from Mabel Dunham's popular novel *The Trail of the Conestoga* and Edna Staebler's *Sauerkraut and Enterprise*. A series of Etril Snyder's and Marlene Jofriet's pen sketches depicting Old Order subjects and twenty-three pages of photographs further enhance this resource.

The book is a model that could well be adapted to other racial, ethnic and religious groups in school systems and other settings to teach children understanding and respect for cultural minorities.

Government interests in Waterloo Mennonites

In 1976, the National Film Board of Canada sent a nine member film crew into Waterloo County to produce a thirty minute film depicting old and new methods of farming among Mennonites. The purpose of the film was to show the Canadian television audience traditional ways of farming still being used by Old Order Mennonites in contrast to the newest methods among progressive Mennonites.

The two farmers chosen were at the time both highly successful. The progressive farmer had huge, expensive, late-model machinery, and several hundred head of beef cattle in large automated feedlots. He was growing feed on large acreages in the county. A decade later, this farmer experienced serious financial reverses. In contrast, the Old Order farmer was shown in his traditional setting using horse-drawn wagons and farm machinery, manual work, and a smaller diversified livestock program requiring the services of all family members. The conservative farmer experienced no comparable economic reverses. The film attempted to show how the different methods of farming affected the religious, cultural, and environmental aspects of community life.

Mennonites and the Ontario Department of Highways

In the late sixties and early seventies, the Ontario Department of Highways began looking at plans for the building of a four-lane highway north from Waterloo to connect with the recently constructed bypass around the eastern end of the twin cities. From the beginning, the University of Waterloo Department of Planning and local county planning committees raised questions about the impact such a highway would have on the Mennonite farming community. A *Kitchener-Waterloo Record* headline in 1970, spread over five columns, read: "Planners Hope to Keep Mennonite Culture."[4]

The article began with two questions: 1) Should future development in Waterloo County be planned in a way that will encourage the continuance of the Old Order Mennonite community? 2) Should the Mennonites be permitted to withdraw from the region in deference to increased urbanization?

After grappling with the questions, the county area planning board favoured recognizing the Mennonite influence on the region's cultural and ethnic heritage. Members agreed that any plan for future development that would drive Mennonites away should not be considered. The planning board concluded that the best way to protect the agricultural influence of the Mennonite community was to concentrate growth of industry and housing along the existing Galt (now Cambridge) corridor to the south of the twin cities.

Since the proposed highway would have split the Old Order Mennonite community so that it would be difficult for horses and buggies to cross a high speed road, the question of overpass or underpass was raised in behalf of the Mennonites. The Provincial planning engineer said no special provisions for buggy traffic to cross the highway had been made nor did it seem warranted. The *Kitchener-Waterloo Record* headline following this announcement read, "Buggies Get Brush-off."[5] The interest of the public in this issue was reflected in the following newspaper headlines during 1970-71. "Mennonites still hope for underpass."[6] "Ruling reserved on road closing."[7] In this article the reporter said:

> Old Order Mennonites who use the east-west section of Waterloo Township Road 43 to get to their church, their school, and to St. Jacobs have wanted to know for a week or two if their soft-spoken, low-keyed objections to the closing of the road carried any weight with the Ontario Municipal Board. Two members of the board reserved judgment on the road's closing after a 2 1/2 hour hearing attended by about fifteen Old Order Mennonites.

Two days later another headline said, "Overpass for St. Jacobs favoured by three candidates."[8] Three weeks later the *Kitchener-Waterloo Record* carried this three-column headline: "Mennonites following tradition of non-resistance over parkway." The article contained the following statements supporting the headline:

> Ervin W. Shantz, minister and senior spokesman for the Old Order Church, said the thing that is important is that we in the Old Order didn't demand or even request anything at all. They came to us. It was they who proposed to make the Highway 85 overpass eight feet wider than a normal motor overpass just so we could use it for our horses. They just did it out of their own good will. And the feeling of our people as a whole is that we are very thankful and happy about the way we were used."[9]

The significance of the above information about the Waterloo Mennonites and the government officials is that county, provincial, and university officials were all sensitive to the problems created by the construction of a high speed, four-lane traffic way through the heart of the Old Order farming community. It is also significant that the Old Order Mennonites wanted to be on record as not having aggressively demanded privileges for their convenience, although they clearly stated how such a roadway would affect them. The construction of an over- or underpass was of course a safety concern for motorists as well as for horse-and-buggy traffic. The incident illustrates once more the respectful relations that exist between Mennonites, the government representatives, and the local press. There was nothing in the law books which required this special consideration for a tiny minority's social customs; however, there was a great deal of emotional weight attached to local sentiments and traditions existing between Mennonites, their neighbours and the larger public. By free and open discussion, by patience and concern for the objectives of all parties, a solution was worked out to the satisfaction of all concerned.

Mennonites as tourist attractions

An example of the Waterloo County press' sensitivity to the possibility of Old Order Amish and Old Order Mennonites being exploited by agencies promoting tourism is reflected in three newspaper headlines in the county: "Sect won't be used for tourists,"[10] "Elmira and Mennonites join in low-key tourism project,"[11] "There is much more to Mennonites than wearing black and driving buggies."[12] The articles state that while the various chambers of commerce want to promote tourism, they studiously avoid mentioning the name Mennonite in their promotional brochures. A group of members from the Elmira Chamber visited Lancaster County, Pennsylvania, in 1973 and resolved they would not want the kind of cheapening commercialization of Amish and Mennonites that they found there.

The Chamber of Commerce entered into a co-operative arrangement with the progressive Mennonite Church in Elmira which provided leadership for bus tours through the surrounding countryside. Women of the church served Pennsylvania German meals in the church basement to scheduled bus loads of visitors. Other efforts to control the nature of tourism in Waterloo County were discussed in Chapter 14.

In a four-column editorial, the Elmira *Citizen* criticized those promoters of tourism who advertise directly for people to come to "see the Mennonites."

> Tempting as it may be to exploit for personal profit, no entrepreneur has any right to exploit the Old Order Mennonites. However, that is what is happening, and it threatens to become as much a disgusting circus as Lancaster County in Pennsylvania, where there is a veritable Disneyland of tourist attractions based on exploitation of the presence of horse-and-buggy Mennonites.[13]

The editorial then describes the Meeting Place, established by a group of progressive Mennonites as an information centre for tourists. The editor points out that the centre offers an "educational experience that is impressive in both its graphic excellence and the power with which it tells the message of what Mennonites represent." The editorial concludes by saying, "No tourist who comes to Waterloo County to 'see the Mennonites' should fail to spend at least an hour in the Meeting Place in St. Jacobs. In fact, every resident in Waterloo County would find something worthwhile in a visit here. Many long-time residents who know little about Mennonites are unable to give visitors any accurate information about them."

The London *Free Press* carried almost a full page of pictures and print under the headline "In an age of conformity, a placid dissent."[14] J. K. Elliott, the *Free Press* editor emeritus, reports on his impressions and sobering reflections of his visit to Waterloo.

> In these days when there is so much concern over what man is doing in the world about him—and to himself—and so much disillusionment, it is a relief to find a haven of peace and apparent security.
>
> I was fortunate enough to be included in a group taken in a tour of the region around Elmira, where many of the people are Mennonites. It is a striking paradox that Waterloo County contains the bustling twin cities of Kitchener and Waterloo and the new experiment in regional government . . . and should also harbor people who have made a resolution to stop the world. Equally striking is the revelation that the county which gave to Ontario the institution known as Hydro . . . should have townships where concession after concession shows prospering farms with no hydro lines and even no telephones. Equally at variance with the hustle of highways elsewhere is the sight of horse-drawn buggies.
>
> One is driven to question the worship of 'progress' which has been so notable a feature of the life in North America. One is also likely to wonder about the type of symbolism chosen by people who stubbornly struggle to preserve the past. To a question about this the interesting reply was given—some of the things they do don't make much sense to the rest of us, but some of the things we do don't make much sense to them either.
>
> Thus it became an interesting question as to which is the more ridiculous, a soberly dressed farmer in a horse-drawn vehicle, or a gaudily attired tourist in a glimmering giant of an automobile. The one represents a way of life that maintains or improves the productiveness of the land, while the other typifies a reckless wastage of non-renewable resources.

Mennonites provide an example to other Christian denominations who are disturbed over the ecumenical movement by showing
that they can respect differences in belief on the part of their
brethren and still work together. Nor is their idea of brotherhood
confined to their co-religionists. A member of the Catholic Church
in the Elmira area had his barn burned and, after his Mennonite
neighbors rebuilt it, he told reporters: "Mennonite neighbors are
better than insurance."

During the late 1960s, when the conservative Mennonites and
Amish were struggling with the provincial government over the
centralization of schools and the introduction of compulsory health
insurance and with the federal government over the introduction
of compulsory social security, the newspapers devoted much space
to the controversies. Canada's largest newspaper, the Toronto
Star ran a provocative editorial. Because of its relevance to the
topic under discussion in this chapter, the editorial is quoted in its
entirety.

How Much Dissent Is Tolerable?

The centuries-old way of life of Ontario's 2,000 Old Order Amish
and Old Order Mennonites is not for most of us. They live with
admirable dedication to exacting precepts.

In the twentieth century, they shun modern conveniences:
cars, tractors, radios, television sets.

They won't vote, won't go to war—and haven't been forced
to—won't go to court, won't swear an oath, refuse to accept old age
pensions or family allowances, won't buy insurance. In times of
loss or need, they look after each other—and others.

These beliefs are now resulting, and not for the first time, in a
confrontation with public authority. Members of the sects disapprove of 'worldly' centralized schools; in the past they have refused
to pay workmen's compensation premiums, and balked at applying
for licenses to produce milk.

Now the federal government is seizing their milk checks to
recover payment for Canada Pension Plan premiums. Sect members have refused to pay the $180 a year premiums on the grounds
of religious belief. Their concern is deep and real.

We sympathize with their distress. But it is hard to see what
Ottawa can do. No taxpayer is exempted from paying pension plan
premiums. Nor should he be. If every citizen decided his conscience or beliefs should dictate whether he pay or withhold taxes
for this or that, the result would be anarchy.

An Amish spokesman has talked of possible immigration to South America because life here is no longer compatible with their religious beliefs. That would be regrettable.

These are good and gentle people, an asset to Canada. This may not be the most tolerant country in the world but we'd hate to think that Canada's atmosphere is so hostile toward religious dissenters that it would impel them to flee elsewhere.[15]

The editorial is an interesting commentary on conservative Ontario Mennonites. It reflects the honest struggle many non-Mennonites have with a conservative religious minority that steadfastly refuses to march to the drum beat of secular society. It happens that Waterloo Mennonites are among the oldest, most distinctive of religious minorities in Ontario, and therefore may be better known than many groups who came to this country more recently. Canada expects loyalty of its citizens but not uniformity of behaviour, thought, or language.

Mainline Protestants and Waterloo Mennonites

In twentieth century North America, what religious denominations or local congregations think of each other is generally not publicly expressed, but attitudes have been generally cordial. Of all denominations, Mennonites have been among the least guilty of "stealing sheep" or proselyting from other denominations. They have depended for membership increase largely on producing their own or by the process of births exceeding deaths. For this reason their numerical growth has not been a threat to other churches.

Out of this non-evangelistic background during the past half century, the progressive Mennonites have developed effective outreach programs of their own, largely in the form of religiously motivated social service programs in local communities and in about fifty countries of the world. The co-operative efforts of the Mennonite Central Committee are carried on under the simple slogan "In the name of Christ." More than half of MCC's so-called employees, presently numbering about 1,000, are serving voluntarily. They receive only a subsistence allowance and serve for terms ranging from one to three years and some longer. The other, paid half are engaged in administering the world-wide service programs. The Canadian MCC program began in Waterloo County and has always been the headquarters for the Ontario MCC program.

It is on the basis of the numerous service programs by the progressive Waterloo Mennonites on the one hand, and the successful farming enterprise and the distinctive lifestyles of the conservative Mennonites on the other, that other denominations tend to evaluate the Waterloo Mennonites. Two recent events illustrate this point.

The *Kitchener-Waterloo Record* interviewed A. C. Forrest, editor of the United Church *Observer*, on his return from a two week trip to Asia.[16] Forrest reported his visit to an MCC aid program in Bangladesh. Because of the efficient way funds were used by MCC in practical relief projects, he recommended that part of the United Church's Christmas collection be given to the MCC. The *Observer* editor said Canadian government officials serving in Bangladesh had unqualified praise for the work Mennonites were doing and for these reasons he strongly recommended that a special contribution, estimated at upwards of $500,000, be made to support their projects. Funds contributed by the United Church were matched by the federal government.

In an editorial in the same issue, under the heading "Joint effort is best,"[17] the *Kitchener-Waterloo Record* pointed out the practical value of joining efforts in foreign relief, rather than trying to operate unco-ordinated efforts without adequate long-term supervision. Furthermore, such joint efforts might encourage other relief agencies to do the same. The editor expressed the opinion that the reason for the high level of Mennonite aid projects of this kind was the use of volunteers. That kind of direct involvement, he said, often by people with exceptional qualifications, was part of the secret of MCC success.

A second evaluation of Waterloo Mennonites was made by Finlay G. Stewart, long-time pastor of St. Andrew's Presbyterian Church in Kitchener. Interestingly, Stewart was not speaking to a Mennonite audience. He was addressing the national conference of the English-Speaking Union at Kitchener's Valhalla Inn on the subject "The Power of a Great Tradition." The three-column headline in the *Kitchener-Waterloo Record* read: "Mennonites' thrift and integrity cited for making K-W unique."[18] Dr. Stewart's comments were reported as follows:

The penetration of the Mennonites into society has come from more than just the confessing members of the Old Order and new order.

Besides these people, the Twin Cities have been influenced by people of Mennonite origin living a life and rendering a service in the conviction and under the standards which are ingrained into their very personalities, training and respect for their forefathers. Every church, business, and profession has profited by this overflow of the Mennonite influence.

Dr. Stewart said the Mennonites have the independent thought producing strong civil leadership locally and in the broadest national sense. He also underlined the effect of the Mennonites' constant striving for excellence. They have always done well to the limit of their training and this influence rubbed off on the community just like their characteristics of thrift, industry, and integrity. He said he observed the Mennonite culture here for a third of a century. It has colored the whole area, not just the back concessions. It has shown that the exercising of moral judgment is the only thing that can give a community integrity. "You can't legislate integrity," said Dr. Stewart. It is not by chance that this is a unique community. I am proud to pay tribute to the Mennonite folk.

I lived in Waterloo County half as long as Dr. Stewart did and met him from time to time, but had no idea how seriously he valued Mennonite contributions to the Waterloo area. His reference to those former Mennonites who presently are serving with distinction in leadership roles was especially perceptive. He spoke with understanding of not only the conservative but also the progressive Mennonites; those of the past as well as those of the present. The words of Dr. Stewart are especially weighty because he spoke not as a freshly impressed tourist, but as a long-time neighbour and observer who had plenty of opportunity to reflect on the subject he was talking about: "The Power of a Great Tradition."

Comments of Mennonite critics

Readers may wonder if Waterloo Mennonites have no critics from outside: no negative assessments, no well-known weaknesses, no chronic antagonists. Mennonites do have critics, as do all religious, racial, ethnic, or cultural groups. However, such criticisms are generally private, low-key, and personal rather than organized and publicly expressed.

Conservative Mennonites are faulted by some for rejecting new technology; for denying their children education beyond the elementary level; for their separation from the rest of society; for restricting their members occupationally and for rejecting the assumptions of science while at the same time accepting the products of science in their farming. In time of war, Mennonites are criticized for failing to support their country by performing military service or purchasing war bonds. It is ironical that Mennonites are praised in time of peace for their independent spirit and courage to defy the government by rejecting the state's compulsory pension system, medical care, and centralized rural schools, but roundly criticized when refusing to obey the government when it comes to supporting wars.

Critical comments are heard from time to time about Mennonites driving non-Mennonites out of communities by outbidding all others at farm sales. Some complain that Mennonites occupy all the best land in the county. Such criticisms however are made by only a small percentage of the population and in some cases the statements are personal opinions not based on facts. Critics are not an organized opposition nor is criticism consistently focused on a single issue or any one group of Mennonites.

It is probably safe to assume that some of the reasons for the infrequent criticism of Mennonites are related to the fact that they have not actively sought to introduce radical social change or to drastically alter existing forms of government. Although a significant number of the Mennonite branches practise various forms of separation from the world as reflected in their restricted social behaviour, dress, transportation, and patterns of living, these distinctions are generally inoffensive, largely because they are a vestige of a lifestyle that was common to most of rural North America a century ago. Both conservative and progressive Mennonites have traditionally not been zealously evangelical, not seeking to proselyte others to their religious beliefs. Hence, they have not given cause for resentment as competitors for church members. Mennonite lifestyles, whatever their degree of nonconformity, are merely one more alternative in the Waterloo area. The present vogue of multiculturalism in Canada embraces all manner of lifestyles. Mennonites cannot properly be called a counterculture nor a left-wing religious radical group as they originally were.

Their most distinctive and visible contemporary earmarks are nonconformity and the separation by the conservatives and a pronounced commitment to material sharing with and service to the poor and powerless at home and abroad. This is seen by many as effective peacemaking and peacekeeping efforts in line with their longstanding adherence to living by the principle of nonviolence.

The sources quoted above reflect a cross section of non-Mennonite attitudes and opinions about Mennonites in Waterloo. It is not the result of a scientific opinion poll. Each reader must assess the information shared in the light of his or her experience and personal judgment.

A Waterloo gift to the Queen
This final illustration of the regard for Old Order Mennonites in the Waterloo community is provided by community civic leaders. In 1975, when the Queen of England and Prince Philip visited Kitchener-Waterloo, the community leaders in charge of hosting the royal couple decided that a suitable token gift for them would be a six-inch tall bronze casting of an Old Order Mennonite couple.

I am not certain what prompted its selection by the local leaders. Perhaps it was because the Old Order Mennonites had something in common with the royal couple. They both depended heavily on horse-drawn vehicles to get around; the Queen from palace to Parliament and the Mennonites from home to church. There is, of course, a significant difference between their buggies. The Queen's chariot has a fancy top and gilt-edged doors while the Mennonite buggies are topless and doorless and drawn by one or two horses rather than four. A final touch of similarity is that quite a few of the horses of the Mennonites seem to have the same regal bearing as the Queen's royal four.

Chapter 20

Tomorrow turns on choices made today

The Waterloo Mennonite community is composed of a number of separate groups with remarkably similar confessions of faith. Howard John Loewen, the compiler of these confessions, says that of the seven categories the one receiving the greatest attention concerns the church and its mission.

The goals of the Mennonite churches are based upon the New Testament, especially the four Gospels. Church discipline, based on Matthew 18:15-17, is assumed in all Mennonite confessions, and a redemptive attitude is stressed. Believers are urged not to take an oath and not to resort to legal proceedings. They are to pray for their government and to be obedient unless its demands are contrary to those of God. Moderates and conservatives stress enforcement of discipline more rigidly and consistently than do progressives.

Essence of the Mennonite faith

It is often said that the Mennonite church is short on theology and long on ethics and service. In 1943 the president of the American Society for Church History, Harold Bender, spoke of "The Anabaptist Vision." He described the essence of the Mennonite church: 1) Christianity as discipleship, 2) as brotherhood, and 3) governed by the ethics of love. The goal of the Mennonite church is to be a community of disciples following the teachings of Jesus in everyday life. Putting these teachings into practice is also expressed as "building the kingdom of God," as Jesus expressed it in his model prayer: "Thy kingdom come, thy will be done on earth as it is in heaven." Because of this, words and phrases like peace, nonresistance, love, mutual aid, humility, simplicity, hospitality, sacrifice, willingness to suffer, accepting the servant rather than the master role have become generally accepted Mennonite ideals. True,

these ideals are lofty and difficult to attain. Nevertheless, Mennonites believe these are God-given goals toward which to strive and
by which to live while on their earthly journey.

In the Waterloo Mennonite community, there is a wide spectrum of opinion, attitudes, interpretation, and behaviour regarding these goals and how they can and should be understood and
followed. Yet the community, however divergent its churches,
holds in common:

> A religious heritage based on New Testament teachings of Jesus.
>
> Adherence to the doctrines of evangelical Christianity.
>
> A congregational system of autonomous church government.
>
> Adherence to the principle of adult voluntary believers' baptism.
>
> The observance of communion and baptism as ordinances only.
>
> A long history of suffering for the faith which they hold.
>
> A common historical experience of migrations in search of religious
> freedom.
>
> A common objection to all military service, war, and violence as
> directly contrary to the teachings of Jesus and to the belief in a
> God of love. Allegiance to God must take precedence over alle-
> giance to the state.
>
> A belief in the scriptural teaching of separation of the church and
> the world as requiring alternative lifestyles.
>
> A common objection to the taking of an oath and to initiating litiga-
> tion against a fellow believer.

These beliefs are strengthened by attitudes of respect towards
differing conservative and progressive church organization, customs, and social practices—lifestyles; furnishings; transportation;
interaction with non-Mennonites; courtship and marriage practices; occupations; relation to the state; consumer items and lux-
uries; the mass media; membership in social, civic, or economic
organizations.

Another difference is the contrasting attitude toward freedom of choice. In the conservative sector, individual choice is subordinate to group will or consensus based on religious tradition. The progressive Mennonites, especially those with a Swiss background, have gradually moved away from church discipline and group control. This shift began in the Franconia Mennonite Conference in eastern Pennsylvania in the mid-nineteenth century. John Oberholtzer and his followers assumed that New Testament teachings such as nonresistance, simplicity, opposition to the oath, the courts, and participation in politics would be voluntarily observed, and that some of the emphasis on group conformity had no real biblical basis. Over the course of the next century, the demand for more individual freedom expanded and church discipline steadily declined. As a result, the social gap between the Waterloo conservatives and progressives increased.

Following World War I and World War II, arrival of Mennonites from Russia unintentionally widened the behavioural gap between the two groups. The Mennonites from Russia never had the strict regulations on dress and social customs so deeply entrenched among the Swiss, nor were they on principle opposed to inventions. On the contrary, they were innovators in the use and manufacture of farm machinery. They also favoured secondary and higher education, even though their economy in Russia had been agricultural. Their presence in Waterloo County had a strongly progressive influence on Mennonite life and culture.

Conservatives today look for church growth by way of Christian nurture of their young. They believe in witnessing to the outside world by their life and work. The progressives believe this, too, but support evangelism, mission, and service programs as well.

In welfare, the conservatives care for their own poor, aged, orphaned, and ill. The progressives take part in the social security, hospitalization, and welfare programs provided by the various levels of government, but in return provide a variety of institutional services locally, provincially, and nationally in areas not covered adequately by government.

The forty-year period following World War II witnessed a number of social trends which had profound impact on Waterloo Mennonites of all shades. There was a widespread decline in the use of High German, Pennsylvania German, and Low German. Among the progressives, ethnic foods and distinctive dress ceased to be prominent except at family anniversaries and group celebrations. Family sizes declined. Married women and mothers with small children, as well as single women, have entered the labour market in large numbers. Mennonite women have become more nearly egalitarian in family decision-making and as breadwinners. Divorce, which before World War II was practically unknown in Mennonite circles, has become more common.

Progressive Mennonites greatly increased their social interaction with individuals and groups outside their church. Few progressive Mennonites hold memberships in country clubs or service clubs, but almost all are active in their respective churches. Of the members of the Mennonite churches in the Waterloo area, 45 percent are male—a high percentage compared to the ratio in urban churches generally.

A new burst in service and witness

The past forty years' founding of service organizations has had a profound impact on Mennonite life as well as on the wider Waterloo society. I believe that underlying the founding of most of these organizations has been the vision, the gifts, and the commitment of time and money of the rising generation of men and women who have remained loyal and active in the church. In former generations, this leadership element tended to leave the church and, often, the community because the church was opposed to its members entering business and the professions. Over the past four decades, the progressive Waterloo Mennonite churches gave their members freedom to start new enterprises both within and outside the official structure of conferences and congregations. These new institutions have become avenues of expressing practical Christianity. They have given church members causes around which to rally and in which to use their professional training, personal gifts, and money.

In 1945 Rockway Collegiate was built by the Mennonite Conference of Ontario and later supported by the Western Ontario Conference and the Stirling Avenue Mennonite Church. The collegiate was in part a protest to the growing militarism in the Waterloo area public high schools and in part a desire for an alternative to public high school education. In 1963, Conrad Grebel College was founded under the sponsorship of three Mennonite conferences and Stirling Avenue Mennonite Church, at that time at independent congregation. It was the first four-year Mennonite college in Canada, and pointed the Ontario Mennonites in a new educational direction.

Rockway Collegiate and Conrad Grebel College may each, it its own way, illustrate the old adage, "As the school, so goes the church," a saying often identified with the Old Order's defence of their elementary parochial schools. The Mennonite high school and college indeed influence and provide leadership to the Ontario progressive Mennonite churches. Whether the churches will continue to follow the leadership of these two schools remains to be seen. There is an inherent conflict between a denomination and its schools. Education, by its nature, is always seeking new truth and new methods of doing things. It is in the forefront of change. Religion and the church, on the other hand, tend to resist change and are reluctant to experiment with the new and the unfamiliar. While denominations and their schools may share common long-range objectives, they tend to disagree on the necessary rate of change. Eternal vigilance is not only the price of freedom; it is also the price of co-operation between churches and their schools.

Also in 1963 the Mennonite Central Committee of Ontario, formerly a branch office of the international MCC organization with headquarters in the United States, was organized as an independent provincial organization. This change made a local group responsible for program, staffing, and support, and led to the creation of almost a dozen new service programs.

The Mennonite Credit Union was organized in 1964; by 1987 it had a main office and five branches, a membership of over 6,000 and assets of $62,000,000. This denominational co-operative banking venture capably operates a large and sophisticated business exclusively for the benefit of its members.

In 1971, the Mennonite Publishing Service was formed in Waterloo. Every other week it publishes an inter-Mennonite, 20-page tabloid, the *Mennonite Reporter*, supported by the Conference of Mennonites in Canada and the newly formed Mennonite Conference of Eastern Canada. The paper has a circulation of 12,000 reaching across Canada from British Columbia to Newfoundland.

The House of Friendship, organized in 1938, was revitalized and its services to homeless men professionalized in 1978. Its director Martin Buhr, a trained social work administrator, has significantly expanded its program of rehabilitative services. The House of Friendship offers its clientele the kind of respectful treatment and competent service not usually received by homeless men.

One of the newest Mennonite group innovations in the Waterloo area, Community Justice Initiatives (1981), is trying to introduce into the Ontario judicial system a program of mediation and face-to-face negotiation between criminal offenders and their victims. Mennonite volunteers hope, through this service, to persuade the courts and police to accept a new approach to solving minor criminal offences.

The progressive sector of Waterloo Mennonites, having founded and successfully operated these major and minor service agencies, has moved quietly but unmistakably into the mainstream of Waterloo society. The move was not by the usual process of social assimilation. Rather, doing useful and socially significant service in the Waterloo and wider world community has led to a special corporate identity. The service agencies are not the work of a few outstanding men or women, but of a few thousand people expressing their religious convictions through service to the entire community. They illustrate the maxim, "Work is love made visible."

Peace witness changes from passive to active

The Mennonite churches have long been known for their doctrine of nonresistance and peace. Since World War II there has been a major shift in philosophy and method, from a passive to a more active role. The conservative and moderate branches of Mennonites remain largely passive. The progressives have formed a separate Peace and Social Concerns section within the Mennonite Central Committee. Its agenda includes concerns for land and resource conservation, raising awareness of food production issues in developing countries, organizing more-with-less seminars, co-operating with other international peace agencies in protesting militarism and in supporting nuclear disarmament. Formal appeals and protests concerning vital social issues are directed to proper government agencies. These activities reflect the new face of Mennonite peace efforts.

The Mennonite Conference of Eastern Canada

A significant new organization, formed by Ontario Mennonites but with headquarters and the majority of its members in the Waterloo area, the Mennonite Conference of Eastern Canada (MCEC) unites three of the four largest progressive church conferences in Ontario and a few churches in Quebec. The newly formed union has a combined membership of 14,000.

Over the past forty years, the Mennonite Conference of Ontario, the Western Ontario Mennonite Conference, and the United Mennonites of Ontario co-operated extensively to create and/or support many service agencies. Today, in the Kitchener-Waterloo area, the MCEC means that instead of 36 congregations speaking and acting through three separate bodies, there will be only one body and one voice.

During the time the union was being consummated, the Mennonite Brethren Conference of Ontario (the fourth of the progressive Mennonite conferences in the Waterloo area) was debating whether to drop the name Mennonite from its official title. Those in favour of the proposal maintained that the name Mennonite was too ethnic in character and a hindrance to church growth. The name proposed as an alternative was Evangelical Anabaptist. At the time of this writing, the conference had not come to conclusion on the issue.

A final trend of the last four decades is the steady rise in both the standard and level of living. A constantly rising level of living can be expected to create a dilemma for Mennonites who presumably made a vow at the time of baptism to become disciples of Jesus throughout their lives. Economic affluence places a strain on the integrity of a community of believers committed to lifestyles marked by simplicity, humility, frugality, and compassion for those in need.

Whatever the individual religious conviction concerning lifestyle, from external evidence it is not possible to distinguish most progressive Mennonites from the general population of Waterloo. For progressive Mennonites wealth is no longer an embarrassment. Wealthy conservatives, however, tend to conceal their wealth in order not to reflect pride or to cause envy within the brotherhood. What the current high material level of life means for the future is not easy to predict; if history provides a clue, the present road may lead to cultural assimilation rather than a return to a more disciplined life. Yet economic prosperity presents possibilities for both individual and collective greatness as well as for individual and corporate spiritual and moral collapse.

The meaning of being a Mennonite

One hundred and thirty-six persons in leadership positions in 34 progressive congregations were asked what it means to be a Mennonite. The question elicited a wide variety of answers.

Table 20-1 What it means to be a Mennonite	%
Separation of church and state	43
Brotherhood	42
Spiritual separation from the world	27
Nonresistance	25
Discipleship	24
Faith in God, commitment to Christ	23
Would rather say what it means to be a Christian	16
Simple lifestyle	15
Being born a Mennonite, no special meaning	10
Having a rich heritage	10
Importance of Bible for interpreting problems	7
Mission and service-centered religion	6

While the responses vary, all items reflect a consciousness of the main ethical teachings of the church. In spite of many accommodations to contemporary culture, Waterloo Mennonite progressives identify strongly with their religious heritage.

Of special interest is the strong consciousness of separation reflected by 43 percent (separation of church and state) and 27 percent (separation of the church and the world) of the respondents. Seventy percent or better than two out of three respondents feel that the traditional gulf between the Christian and the world or the state is still important to them. In light of what has been said about Mennonite materialism, one must ask if the meaning of separation is theory or practice. Among the conservatives, it is both spiritual and spatial.

Asked what it meant to him to be a Mennonite, John Harder, a Mennonite university student who assisted me in this study, replied:

> Because it is a base, a guide for my life. I have come to appreciate the values, the lifestyle, the small. I like the way which Mennonites have discriminated values between themselves and the larger society. I have come to appreciate my Anabaptist heritage. It was a part of my environment before I was old enough to know what it meant. I grew up with it. More recently, it was enhanced through reading, drama, and my high regard for voluntary service and disaster service as well as the philosophy behind those practices.

This single illustration states clearly and intelligently the views of one young man about the church to which he belongs. If this statement is not typical, it may still be a model for others who have not reflected on an answer to the question.

Mennonite house churches

A significant, though small, segment of Kitchener-Waterloo Mennonites who collectively but quietly demonstrate what they think it means to be Mennonite are the five existing house churches. These small, close-knit apostolic-like groups, totaling about 100 members, are composed mostly of middle-aged and younger persons. They believe that the larger and older Mennonite congregations fail to embody the essentials of New Testament Christianity. They, like the Old Order Amish, meet in each other's homes, have no paid ministers, and elect leaders from their own ranks. Worship services consist of reading and studying the Bible, singing, praying, and discussions. John and Louise Miller, who were leaders in starting Reba Place Fellowship in Evanston, Illinois, have given consistent leadership to the Kitchener-Waterloo house church units.

Over the twenty years that the oldest of the units has been in existence, there has been little numerical growth. A strength of the house churches is their sensitivity to each other's spiritual, social, and economic needs. In many ways, these churches function as extended families do in older rural communities. This is especially meaningful for urban families who may be separated geographically and spiritually from their biological families. The house church units are not communal in the sense of having property in common or living in one or more large collective families.

There is no convincing evidence that the house churches had a measurable influence on church renewal in the traditional Waterloo progressive or conservative congregations.

Personal observations

One important cultural change since 1945 is the high proportion of Mennonites who have moved from rural to non-farm and urban areas. That change will alter the character of the Waterloo Mennonite churches in the twenty-first century. I realize it is an inevitable result of economic and social pressures, but it seems to me a great impoverishment of the Mennonite heritage. In this connection, I cannot resist quoting a few lines from Oliver Goldsmith's poem "The Deserted Village," written at the time of the great enclosure system in the eighteenth century when tenant farmers were driven from their acres by rich and powerful landowners who wanted the land for sheepwalks to produce wool.

> Ill fares the land to hastening ills of prey,
> Where wealth accumulates and men decay.
> Princes and lords may flourish or may fade,
> A breath can make them as a breath has made.
> But a bold peasantry, a country's pride,
> When once destroyed can never be supplied.

It seems to me the Mennonites who have resisted moving to the towns and cities and pooled all their earnings to buy land and secure their children on family farms, usually at great sacrifice, are pursuing ultimately the wisest vocational course.

In praise of mutual respect

A point I want to emphasize is the positive attitude of respect shown toward each other by the two Mennonite sectors at opposite ends of the spectrum. While the conservative Mennonites have little formal education as far as schooling is concerned, they have a great deal of education when it comes to basic Christian virtues. They have a quiet confidence that they are doing the will of God by organizing life as they do, but they express no envy or malice toward those who do not feel called to adopt the same life patterns. Throughout my more than twenty years of visiting with many church leaders and lay families, I have not sensed people being judgmental of each other's lifestyles. Nor did I notice attitudes of pride in achievements or praise of self. The two Mennonite sectors, so different in many ways, may well live peacefully side by side indefinitely as long as attitudes of mutual respect prevail. Both groups have lessons to teach each other and values to share.

No nationally famous Mennonites
In the course of two hundred years, the Mennonites have produced many good leaders, but so far as I was able to ascertain, not one Waterloo Mennonite ever became nationally or internationally famous. Several former Mennonites, or descendants of Mennonites, like E. W. B. Snider of St. Jacobs and D. B. Detweiler of Kitchener, were given major credit for bringing hydro-electric power to the area. J. Y. Shantz, a Kitchener businessman, was made honorary mayor for a day because of his popularity as a successful business entrepreneur. Isaiah Bowman, a Waterloo County Mennonite, became an internationally famous geographer, author of a popular geography text, and president of Johns Hopkins University in Baltimore, Maryland. However he retained no Mennonite connections after leaving Waterloo County.

For a Mennonite, fame reflects an incongruity or an inconsistency; it contradicts the profession of social equality and personal modesty. To exalt one person over others is to encourage pride rather than humility. Furthermore, the Mennonite restriction on vocation to that of farming or closely related occupations eliminated the likelihood of achieving a distinctive claim to fame. Mennonites were traditionally discouraged from entering the worlds of business, industry, the professions of law, medicine, and university teaching, areas in which fame might be claimed. When I asked an Old Order, highly intelligent and successful farmer why his church was opposed to Sunday school, he replied that some people would know more and speak up, thus embarrass others who could not express themselves well or were too uninformed to participate in discussions. This answer suggested how important was the concern for internal harmony and a sense of equality in that branch of the church. One must conclude that Waterloo Mennonites over the centuries specialized in producing good common people rather than a few heroes of the faith or one or two persons who by one means or another achieved worldly fame.

What if a severe depression strikes?

My studies indicate that there is practically no Mennonite unemployment except for seasonal or temporary interruptions, or through illness and physical handicaps. In other words, there are no wretchedly poor among Waterloo Mennonites. There are those who are relatively poor. There are undoubtedly those poor, as the philosopher Lucian said, "not because of the little they have but because of the much they want."

What would happen in the event of a great economic recession? The progressive Mennonites, who have no social security program of their own, would need to look to the government for subsistence. By contrast, the conservative Mennonites would have their own social security in place and would still have access to housing and food supply. It is not a pleasant thought to contemplate; nevertheless, history has taught us that all economic systems are like a wheel, always moving, one part upward and another downward. No economic conditions forever move only in a single direction.

How to confront and live to tell about it

Waterloo Mennonites, both conservative and progressive, have learned how to confront the government at the municipal, provincial, and national level and live to tell about it. In this sense, they have not been totally nonresistant although totally nonviolent. With the help of the MCC, the conservatives negotiated solutions to conflicts at the municipal level over the issue of centralized elementary schools and compulsory school attendance to the age of sixteen. They did the same at the provincial level over the question of compulsory health insurance, and at the national level on the issue of compulsory social security payments. In each instance both parties were satisfied with the ultimate solutions. God be praised that both the powerful government representatives and the powerless Mennonite farmers were willing to use the techniques of intelligent negotiation and reconciliation to work out acceptable solutions. Progressive Mennonites have freely consulted members of Parliament and interceded with government officials about controversial issues of spiritual concern to the church.

I conclude my observations and reflections with an overarching concern for the survival of the Mennonite church's vision of the church as a truly Christian community. If it no longer conceives of itself as a fellowship of believers, as a voluntarily disciplined body of followers of Christ, it will have lost its reason for existence. Then its members might as well join a Baptist, Lutheran, Calvinist, or Catholic church as disinterested Mennonites have done in the past. To be a genuine community, a church must have more than a confession of faith to verbalize its theology and a constitution to describe its structure and intended function. It must also have a means of keeping its members spiritually alive and open to new revelations from God.

My deep concern is that the secularizing influences of an urban-industrial environment, or what the apostle Paul might have called "the powers of darkness," will quench the light and drain the salt from the community. A secular culture has a way of gradually reducing a Christian community's social, moral, and spiritual norms to its own level and calling it good. If that happens to Waterloo Mennonites, it will make the church largely irrelevant so far as a healing and cleansing influence in a secular society is concerned.

As Waterloo area Mennonites head into the twenty-first century, it is urgent that they give serious attention to two important religious considerations. For the progressives, the consideration is the crucial component of church discipline. It implies concern for voluntary commitment to the church's ideals as defined by the church rather than as interpreted entirely by individual members, according to their own liking.

For the conservatives, the primary consideration is the factor of social and cultural change. When is it spiritually appropriate to accept and when to oppose social and technological change so as to assure spiritual vitality in the church community?

In both groups, if Mennonitism as a meaningful Christian faith is to survive, the central issue is a balance between individual freedom of choice, on the one hand, and social control of group behaviour on the other. Blessed be the church that finds a healthy balance between the two.

Appendix 1

Identification of Mennonite groups in the Waterloo study

CONSERVATIVES

The Old Order Amish are the oldest of the existing splits from the original Mennonite body in Switzerland. They separated in 1693 and have retained conservative customs ever since. Over the centuries many of their more progressively minded members, individually and as groups, again joined the main body of Mennonites. They have been the most persistent of all Mennonite bodies to resist social and technological change. Only twenty-five Amish families live in Waterloo County, but five congregations are located across the northwestern county line in Perth County. The original Amish migrated directly from Alsace and Bavaria in South Germany to their present location in 1824 and the following decades. Between 1953 and 1960, eight additional Amish congregations were established by immigrant family groups from the United States. These groups settled in scattered areas in southern Ontario but have no close family connections with the older Amish community around Milverton in Perth County. In 1974, the Milverton Amish had a total of 103 families with an estimated total population of 700 men, women, and children.

The Old Order Mennonites separated from the Mennonite Conference of Ontario in 1889 because of differences over proposed innovations in the church. Controversial issues included the introduction of Sunday schools, revival meetings, and the use of the English instead of the German language. A conservative minority felt the church was becoming too worldly. Twenty-eight years later (1917), another split occurred, this time led by a conservative deacon, David Martin, over minor quarrels between individual families. The David Martin group still maintains its separate identity with three meetinghouses and approximately 400 members. This minority is even more conservative than its mother church. It has no interaction with any other Mennonite body. A third church split in 1957 resulted from the excommunication of Elam Martin, a minister in the David Martin group. This group took the name Orthodox Mennonite Church. It always remained small, never having a hundred members. The group disbanded in 1979 when some members moved to Gorrie, Ontario, others returned to the David Martin group, and some families joined a more moderate Mennonite group.

The Reformed Mennonites had their origins in Pennsylvania in 1812. The first church in Canada was established in the Niagara region in 1825 and in Waterloo County in 1844. At one time there were eight meetinghouses, but as of 1986 only two congregations remain extant; one in Stevensville in Lincoln County and another in Wilmot Township with a combined membership of less than two hundred, 62 percent women, 38 percent men. The church adheres to traditional Mennonite theological beliefs and social practices. It holds to strict church discipline, nonresistance, uniform dress, and separation from the world, which includes other Mennonites. It emphasizes the new birth and administers excommunication and the ban in its exercise of church discipline.

Old Colony Mennonites derive their name from the fact that their forebears were the first Mennonite settlers to move from Prussia in the late eighteenth century and establish a large colony in Russia. These descendants moved to the prairie provinces in the late nineteenth century. Some of them in turn migrated in the 1920s to Mexico. In the 1960s and 1970s, some of these former Canadians began returning to Canada and specifically to southern Ontario to work in the fruit and vegetable harvests along the coast of Lake Erie. Eventually, some decided to remain in Ontario rather than return each winter to Mexico. In 1979, a congregation of the Old Colony Mennonites in Waterloo County was located in Elmira. It is composed of a group of about thirty families widely scattered throughout the county, the result of members having found more or less steady work in different areas. In Mexico, the church from which they came is extremely conservative and rigidly disciplined. Many of those who returned to Canada are poor and some have been excommunicated. Being scattered as individual families, with only a poor sixth-grade education, no skills other than as farmers or common labourers, no knowledge of the English language and desperately poor, their prognosis for the future as individuals and families as well as a cohesive church body appears dismal.

MODERATES

Beachy Amish are represented in this study by two congregations, the Nafziger church, founded in 1904, and the Lichti church, founded in 1912. They stand midway between the Old Order Amish and the Western Ontario Mennonite Conference. They were too progressive to have happily remained in the Old Order Amish fellowship and too conservative to join with the more progressive Western Ontario Conference. Their worship practices, meetinghouses, conservative dress, use of the dialect in the family and informal settings, and conservative lifestyles reflect a conservative heritage. However, their adoption of modern conveniences, cars, and modern technologies reflect their accommodation to ways of the world adopted by the progressive Mennonites. Both congregations are located in the open country in Wellesley Township. The combined membership in 1971 and in 1986 was 300.

Waterloo-Markham Conference is the result of a division in the Old Order Mennonite Church in 1939. The separation occurred as a result of a desire for freedom to adopt the automobile, electricity, and electrical appliances in the home and on the farm. Interestingly, the small Old Order church in Markham, Ontario, east and north of Toronto, did not prohibit the use of these modern conveniences to its members. As a consequence, members of the Waterloo Old Order churches began to observe communion at the Markham church since they were forbidden to do so in Waterloo if they wished to own cars and remain in good standing in the church. Those opting for the modern conveniences withdrew from the mother church and formed their own congregations. Those who were satisfied with the restrictions remained in the Old Order congregation. The W-M Conference had six congregations and 800 members in 1972, but by 1986 had eight churches and about 1,000 members. One new church was founded in a new settlement by eleven families near Beachburg in the Ottawa Valley in the early eighties. Three meetinghouses have been shared on alternate Sundays by both groups in the Waterloo area since 1939.

The Conservative Mennonite Church was established in 1960 by a group of dissatisfied members largely from the Ontario and Western Ontario Conferences who felt their mother churches were becoming too worldly. Originally, there were three small congregations established, one each in New Hamburg, Heidelburg, and Elmira. Later one was established at Milverton. The combined membership in 1972 was 224.

The Evangelical Mennonite Mission Church is a mission effort initiated by a mother church in Manitoba which focuses on winning over Old Colony Mennonites returning from Mexico. The group in Ontario became active in 1968. In 1979, it had a membership of less than fifty. The High German and the Low German dialect are used in worship services.

PROGRESSIVES

Mennonite Conference of Ontario (and Quebec) is the oldest and largest Mennonite group in Waterloo. Twenty-one congregations were included in this study. As indicated above, it formerly included also those who are today referred to as Old Order Mennonites. It has in times past been referred to as the (Old) Mennonite Church to distinguish it from new churches that split from it. One illustration is the Missionary Church which was formerly known as Mennonite Brethren in Christ. In the middle 1980s the official name of the conference added the word "Quebec" to acknowledge several new congregations joining the conference from that province. This conference was organized in 1820 at a time when it represented the only Mennonites in all of Canada. Its membership is composed almost totally of Swiss Mennonite stock that came to Upper Canada by way of Pennsylvania. It has been a source of members for numerous small and large groups which have separated from it over the past two centuries. In 1972, it had approximately 3,000 members in the Waterloo area. Its total membership in the conference in 1986 was about 5,000. This conference became extinct as a result of uniting with two other progressive Ontario conferences in 1987.

The Western Ontario Conference is the second largest of the Mennonite groups in the Waterloo area with an estimated 2,500 members. It separated from the Old Order Amish in 1886. It, like the MCO, has shed its distinctive vestiges of plain dress and separation from social interaction with the larger society and joined with the MCO in its mission and Christian service programs. Its congregations are still located in rural communities rather than in the larger cities. It joined in the merger of the Ontario and United Mennonite Conferences in 1987, thus no longer has a separate existence.

United Mennonites of Ontario is composed of Mennonites who immigrated from Russia in 1924 and organized a congregation in 1925. This conference has 24 churches in Ontario, but only two in Kitchener-Waterloo. The membership in 1972 was 750. As of 1987, this conference passed out of existence as a result of the union of three Ontario conferences.

Ontario Conference of Mennonite Brethren is composed of Mennonites who immigrated from Russia in 1924 and formed its first congregation in 1925. It is unique in that it is the only Waterloo Mennonite body that practices baptism by immersion and prohibits the use of tobacco as a basis of church membership. In 1972, the combined membership of three churches was 555 and in 1982 it was 670. This body did not unite with the other three progressive conferences in the formation of a single provincial conference.

The Mennonite Conference of Eastern Canada was formed in 1987 when the first three of the above four Mennonite progressive conferences officially joined together to form a single new conference. The combined membership is 14,000. The three conferences had been cooperating freely for more than a decade prior to the merger. This union is historically significant because it brings the three largest Ontario and Waterloo Mennonite bodies together. The union is important also because it brings three distinct ethnic background groups, the Swiss-German, Swiss-French-German Amish, and the Dutch-German-Russian groups, together into a single body. These conferences jointly sponsored the founding of Conrad Grebel College and continue to support it.

Appendix 2

Waterloo County becomes the Regional Municipality of Waterloo

1. Bridgeport was incorporated wholly within the city of Kitchener.
2. Hespeler, Preston, and Galt were amalgamated to become the city of Cambridge.
3. Elmira became incorporated into the township of Woolwich.
4. New Hamburg became incorporated into the township of Wilmot.
5. Wellesley became incorporated into the township of Wellesley.
6. Ayr became incorporated into the township of North Dumfries.
7. Cities of Kitchener and Waterloo retained identity as separate municipalities.
8. The former township of Waterloo was divided between the township of Woolwich and the city of Cambridge. (This means that the township of Waterloo no longer exists.)

The villages and towns absorbed into the new township municipalities did not retain any "internal structure." They are represented by the Township Council which is made up of elected representatives (either elected at large or by ward or a combination of the two). January 1, 1973

*Source of information: Mrs. E. Stettner, Regional Clerk, the Regional Municipality of Waterloo, Waterloo, Ontario.

Appendix 3

Occupational categories, gainfully employed Waterloo area Mennonites, 1972

	Occupational Category	Number	Percent
1.	Farm owner	1188	28.3
2.	Domestic service	349	8.3
3.	Farm worker	311	7.4
4.	Kindergarten and elementary teacher	160	3.8
5.	Truck driver	154	3.6
6.	Carpenter	141	3.3
7.	Secretary, stenographer	123	2.9
8.	Horticulture, animal husbandry	85	2.0
9.	Graduate nurse	83	1.9
10.	Janitor, charworker, cleaning	72	1.7
11.	Secondary school teacher	66	1.5
12.	Motor mechanic	63	1.5
13.	Sewing machine operator	60	1.2
14.	Construction labourer	58	1.1
15.	Packing company, canner, packer, butcher	56	1.1
16.	Accountant, bookkeeper, clerk	51	1.0
17.	Office equipment and machine repairs	51	1.0
18.	Commodities sales clerk	50	1.0
19.	Nursing assistant	50	1.0
20.	Wood furniture maker	48	0.9
21.	Salesman	47	0.9
22.	Clergyman	47	0.9
23.	Electrical equipment assembly and repair	41	0.8
24.	Metal products assembly	40	0.8

	Occupational Category	Number	Percent
25.	Flour miller	37	0.7
26.	Chef, cook	37	0.7
27.	Labourer in service industry	35	0.7
28.	Nursing aide, orderly	35	0.7
29.	Sales supervisor	34	0.7
30.	Unspecified construction	33	0.6
31.	Electrician, construction, repairman	32	0.6
32.	Tailor, dressmaker	31	0.6
33.	Excavating and paving foreman	30	0.6
34.	Machine tool setter	29	0.6
35.	Nurse-in-training	27	0.5
36.	Metal processing	26	0.5
37.	Shipping, receiving clerk	26	0.5
38.	Senior official in industry	26	0.5
39.	Farm manager	25	0.5
40.	Milk processor	24	0.5
41.	Farm tenant	23	0.5
42.	Excavator, grader	22	0.4
43.	Clay, glass, stone processor	22	0.4
44.	General office clerk	22	0.4
45.	Mission worker	21	0.4
46.	Teller, cashier	20	0.4
47.	Unspecified medicine and health service	20	0.4
48.	Welder, flame cutter	20	0.4
49.	Typist	19	0.4
50.	Receptionist, information clerk	17	0.3
51.	Milk and breadtruck delivery man	17	0.3
52.	Buyer in wholesale, retail merchandising	17	0.3
53.	Other farm occupation	17	0.3
54.	Industrial machine assembly	16	0.3
55.	Chemical, petroleum, rubber, plastic processing	16	0.3
56.	Social worker	16	0.3
Total		4186	

Comments: The above Waterloo area Mennonites represent 83 percent of the total gainfully employed. The remaining 17 percent have less than sixteen Mennonites.

Farm owners represent almost one-fourth of all Mennonites gainfully employed. If related farm occupations in the table such as those in numbers 2, 3, 8, and 39 were added, it would represent 38.6 percent of all gainfully employed Mennonites. Items 2 and 3 represent largely Old Order young men and women who work as hired men and housemaids for other church members between the time they leave school and the time they marry.

The list of occupations reveals a low number of professions with the exception of teachers. Were an occupational census taken twenty years later it would include doctors, lawyers, accountants, engineers, and the newer scientific and technological specialities that have emerged as a result of the computer.

Appendix 4

Size of congregations in ten conferences

According to progressive (4); moderate (4); conservative (2).

	Progressive MCO, WCO, UMO, MB	Moderate EMMC, CC, W-M, BA	Conservative OOM, RM	Totals
0 to 49	1	3	0	4
50 to 99	11	3	2	16
100 to 199	13	7	9	29
200 to 299	4	0	0	4
300 to 399	4	0	0	4
400 to 499	3	0	0	3
500 to 599	1	0	0	1
Totals	37	13	11	61

Comments: One-third of the Waterloo Mennonite congregations have fewer than 100 members each. Almost one-half (47.5%) have memberships between 100 and 199. This means that 81 percent or four out of five Waterloo County Mennonite churches have memberships of less than 200. Only four churches, all urban, have memberships over 400. This data is based on a church census by the author in 1972.

Appendix 5

House of Friendship program, 1987-1988

The program of the House of Friendship reflects both a number of innovative services and a progressive philosophy of Christian social work. The philosophy combines intelligent and profound Christian motivation and the latest and best knowledge and methods of helping to rehabilitate a segment of society that society generally considers lost and largely hopeless. It ministers to physical needs, providing 700 meals per day and over 100 beds in its various shelter and housing facilities. But beyond the bare day-to-day physical needs of food, clothing, and shelter are the even more significant ministries to the social and spiritual needs of the House's many clients. These are costly ministries because they require long periods of time, great patience, and profound insights into human nature. Many if not most of the men and women who come for help come with lives that have been wrecked and personalities that have been badly damaged. The House of Friendship's philosophy and purpose is dedicated to helping poor and severely disorganized individuals and families rebuild their lives; to help them discover human resources they may have and need encouragement to express.

Martin Buhr and his dedicated and well-trained staff of 40 full-time and 35 part-time persons are demonstrating new ways of helping disorganized persons. A significant innovation by the House at its 1987 annual business meeting was to build its program around story-telling by clients. The annual budget for 1986 and 1987 hovers around $1,500,000. This amount is raised from the following sources: governments (50%), donations (33%), clients (16%), other (1%).

Residential Programs

	Purpose	No. Beds	Comments
1.	Emergency shelter for homeless men	64	New facility in 1982
2.	Community based residence for male parolees from Federal penitentiaries	51	New program in 1982
3.	Home for socially disadvantaged and former psychiatric patients	12	New program in 1985
4.	Home for permanently unemployable males	5	Program established in 1968
5.	Recovery Home for male alcoholics	15	In operation since 1975
6.	House for graduates of the Recovery Home	9	In operation since 1976
7.	Home for socially disadvantaged males 16-21	6	New program in 1986
8.	Permanent housing for socially disadvantaged single women and men	56 (Apts)	$3.5 million project to be begun in 1988 and completed in 1989

Community Programs

		Persons	
1.	Emergency year-round food hampers for needy families	12,500	Majority are women with children and single males
2.	Christmas hampers	4,750	For needy families and individuals, served by staff and volunteers
3.	Live and Learn	30	Low income women attend weekly meetings and are visited in homes
4.	Family Support Worker	unknown	Assistance to women with children
5.	Camp Sponsorship	100-115	Children and youth; week long experience
6.	Interest-Free Loans	50	Majority women with children; 93% of loans repaid; $135,000 goods and services purchased

7.	Repair appliances, etc.	850	New in 1980; mostly women
8.	County Support Worker	300-500	Resolve crises, housing, finances counselling, program since 1986
9.	Chaplaincy		Sharing of faith, calling people to faith, healing and making whole
10.	Recreation		Healthy lifestyles encouraged

Appendix 6

Explanatory comments on Mennonite census taken by J. Winfield Fretz

Mennonite Church Census Data for all Mennonite Congregations in Waterloo County (now the Regional Municipality of Waterloo) and Immediately Surrounding Counties, 1971.

1. *Total church membership*: by military service, alternative service, university, Mennonite college, inactive status, and place of residence (farm, town, and rural nonfarm); members received since 1960; members of non-Mennonite parentage; marital status of members; age and sex of members; age and sex of unbaptized children.

2. *Education and occupation of members*: type of professions listed; total ex-members, 1950-1970, by type of membership termination and year of termination; non-conference transfers by denomination of transfer.

3. *Age and sex of ex-members*: education of ex-members; occupation of ex-members; type of profession of ex-members.

4. *Total ex-members*: by military service, alternative service, university, Mennonite college, inactive status, and place of residence (farm, town, and rural nonfarm); members received since 1950; marital status, age and sex of members and of unbaptized children of ex-members; ex-members of non-Mennonite parentage.

5. *Ex-members*: Education; occupation, type of membership, and type of membership termination.

Comment: The census takers gathered the data from the ministers, deacons, or other authorized church spokesmen who worked from an official church membership list. In the case of the Waterloo-Markham and Old Order Mennonite congregations, two young women school-teachers were engaged to gather the data for those Mennonite bodies. The census did not include small independent Mennonite or ex-Mennonite congregations nor the Old Order house churches in Perth County. The Amish membership was secured from David Luthy, the archivist and historian for Ontario Amish.

Endnotes

Chapter 1

1. P. C. Rump, "A History of Water Pollution in the Grand River Watershed, Ontario," *The Waterloo County Area Selected Geographical Essays*, A. G. McLellan, ed., Department of Geography, University of Waterloo, 1971 (hereafter *WCASGE*), p. 184ff., quoting Charles M. Johnston, ed., *The Valley of the Six Nations* (Toronto: University of Toronto Press, 1964).
2. Rump, p. 185.
3. Rump. The most notable of these settlers was the Nelles family, who were granted 4,254 acres in 1788.
4. Rump.
5. E. Roy Officer, "Waterloo County—Some Aspects of Settlement and Economy Before 1900," *WCASGE*, p. 12.
6. John English and Kenneth McLaughlin, *Kitchener* (Waterloo: Wilfrid Laurier University Press, 1983), p. 2. Based on E. A. Cruickshank, "The Reserve of the Six Nations Indians on the Grand River and the Mennonite Purchase of Block No. 2," in *Waterloo Historical Society Annual Report 19*, (1927): p. 303ff, and Johnston, op. cit.
7. E. Roy Officer. Information based on Mabel B. Dunham, *Grand River* (Toronto: McClelland and Stewart, 1945), pp. 67-71.
8. Charles M. Johnston, ed. *The Valley of the Six Nations* (Toronto: University of Toronto Press, 1964), pp. 34-39.

Chapter 2

1. Franklin Hamlin Littell, *The Anabaptist View of the Church* (American Society of Church History, 1952), p. 20.
2. Followers of Caspar Schwenckfeld (1489-1561), a German nobleman from the province of Silesia and founder of the sixteenth-century Anabaptist pietists known as Schwenckfelders who settled in Pennsylvania among the Mennonites in the eighteenth century.
3. Leland Harder, *The Sources of Swiss Anabaptism* (Scottdale, Pa.:

Herald Press, 1985), pp. 341-342.

4. George Huntston Williams, *The Radical Reformation* (Philadelphia: Westminster Press, 1962), p. 119.

5. Paul Peachey, "Social Background and Social Philosophy of the Swiss Anabaptists 1525-1540," *Mennonite Quarterly Review* 28 (April 1954): 102-127.

6. Peachey, op. cit., p. 106.

7. Harold S. Bender, "Mennonites," *Mennonite Encyclopedia*, Vol. 3, p. 586.

8. C. Henry Smith, *Story of the Mennonites* (Newton, Kan.: Faith and Life Press, 1981), pp. 172ff.

9. C. Henry Smith, *The Coming of the Russian Mennonites* (Berne, Ind.: Mennonite Book Concern, 1927), pp. 18ff.

10. Cornelius Krahn, "Russia," *Mennonite Encyclopedia*, Vol. 4, pp. 381-393.

11. Littell, op. cit., p. 91ff.

12. Walter Rauschenbusch, *A Theology for the Social Gospel* (New York: Abingdon Press, 1917), pp. 195-196.

Chapter 3

1. Between 1874 and about 1890 approximately eight thousand Mennonites immigrated to Canada from Russia, settling first in Manitoba, then later in Saskatchewan and Alberta. See C. Henry Smith, *Coming of the Russian Mennonites* (Berne, Ind.: Mennonite Book Concern, 1927).

2. Wilbur J. Bender, "Pacifism Among the Mennonites, Amish Mennonites and Schwenkfelders of Pennsylvania to 1783," *The Mennonite Quarterly Review*. Vol. II, No. 4: p. 21. The article was based on a thesis written at Harvard University in 1927.

3. Richard MacMaster, unpublished paper, Dec. 17, 1976, Historians and Sociologists Seminar, Goshen College.

4. Quoted from extant letters of Benjamin Hershey in a pamphlet, "A Mennonite Response 1776-1976." Published by the Franconia Mennonite Conference, November 1975.

5. Hershey, op. cit.

6. Written on the margin of the Samuel Pannebecker family Bible.

7. From family tradition cited in *The History of the Mennonites* by Daniel Cassel, 1888 and quoted in "A Mennonite Response 1776-1976." Published by the Franconia Mennonite Conference, 1975.

8. From family tradition in the *Moyer Family History*. Quoted in "A Mennonite Response." Published by the Franconia Mennonite Conference, 1975.

9. A. J. Fretz, *A Brief History of John and Christian Fretz* (Elkhart, Ind.: Mennonite Publishing Co., 1890), p. 22.
10. C. Henry Smith. *The Mennonite Immigration to Pennsylvania* (Norristown, Pa.: Norristown Press, 1927), p. 287. An entire chapter is devoted to "The Oath and War" in which he provides in detail the Mennonite responses to wartime treatment.
11. John L. Ruth, *Maintaining the Right Fellowship* (Scottdale, Pa.: Herald Press, 1984), pp. 159 ff.
12. Ruth, p. 160.
13. Ruth, p. 161.
14. Ruth has a footnote explaining his source of new historical information about the first Mennonite group to settle in Upper Canada. He refers to Joel Alderfer, Harleysville, Pa., Gary Kulp, Niagara Falls, Ont., and John L. Overholt, Kilmarnock, Va. who examined deeds, wills and archival records in local areas and found evidence to substantiate some extant information and correct other erroneous historical data.
15. Ruth, p. 162.
16. Ruth. See also Frank H. Epp, *Mennonites in Canada, 1786-1920* (Toronto: Macmillan of Canada, 1974), p. 70.
17. A. J. Fretz, *A Brief History*, p. 22
18. L. J. Burkholder, *A Brief History of the Mennonites of Ontario* (Markham, Ont.: Mennonite Conference of Ontario, 1935), p. 14 quotes from Simcoe's Papers, Vol. III, p. 17. Burkholder reports that between 1783 and 1785 an estimated 50,000 Loyalists came to Canada, mostly to Upper Canada.
19. C. Henry Smith, *The Story of the Mennonites*, 5th ed. (Newton, Kan.: Faith and Life Press, 1981), p. 377, states that reasons for Mennonites leaving Pennsylvania for Canada were cheap and more easily accessible land than in western Pennsylvania and Ohio. This conclusion is in contradiction to the evidence presented in his earlier volume, *The Mennonite Immigration to Pennsylvania* (p. 271) and to the evidence in this chapter.
20. Don Yoder, *Pennsylvania Folklife*. Spring 1976, Vol. XXV, No. 3, p. 12. See also letter by Benjamin Rush to his mother-in-law for his evaluation of Germans in general and Mennonites in particular. Conrad Grebel College archives.
21. Frank H. Epp, *Mennonites in Canada, 1786-1920* (Toronto: Macmillan of Canada, 1974), p. 54.
22. Epp, p. 55.
23. Smith, *Story of the Mennonites*, p. 379.
24. Burkholder, p. 25.

25. Orlando Gingrich, *The Amish of Canada* (Waterloo, Ont.: Conrad Press, 1972), p. 28.
26. Gingrich, p. 31.
27. John Hostetler, *Amish Society*, 3rd ed., p. 66ff., points out that the Amish in Europe pretty well died out as a distinct group by the end of the nineteenth century. Those who did not migrate joined the Mennonites or possibly other denominations.
28. The Mennonites in Waterloo who came from Russia were citizens of Russia, but in spite of having lived in that country for over a century they never adopted the Russian language and culture. The High German language was used formally and the Low German dialect informally. Hence the use of the phrase "Mennonites from Russia" rather than "Russian Mennonites" when discussing this group of Waterloo Mennonites throughout this book.
29. Famine in Russia after World War I, plus the social upheaval caused by the Bolshevik Revolution, prompted the organization of the Mennonite Central Committee in the United States in 1920.
30. Frank H. Epp, *Mennonites in Canada, 1920-1940* (Toronto: Macmillan of Canada, 1982), p. 149.
31. See Frank Epp's "Immigration from Russia" in *Mennonites in Canada, 1920-1940* (Toronto: Macmillan, 1982), pp. 139-179, for an excellent discussion. See especially pp. 175-176. Epp provides a full account of the heroic leadership, the many frustrating delays and the difficulties encountered in raising the necessary money to bring 20,000 impoverished immigrants to Canada.
32. William Janzen, "The Old Colony Mennonites of Mexico Moving to Ontario and Adjusting," *MCC News Service*, November 1, 1977. Janzen estimated that 8,000 Mennonites came to Ontario from Mexico between 1950 and 1970. This seems an exceedingly high estimate. In the same article, he says there were about 750 church members in four congregations scattered over a 200-mile area along Lake Erie from Leamington on the west to Port Rowan on the east. It would appear that from 2,000 to 4,000 would be more nearly the number of Old Colony Mennonites returning from Mexico in Ontario, with less than 100 in Waterloo County.
33. Burkholder, pp. 185-186. Jacob H. Janzen, the elder and organizer of the 1923-1929 migration of Mennonites from Russia to Ontario, provides authentic, firsthand information about the Mennonites now known as the United Mennonite Church of Ontario. Locations in three different geographical areas of Ontario are mentioned as places of settlement: first Waterloo, New Hamburg, Port Rowan, Vineland, Dunnville, and Toronto. A second group located in Essex County,

along Lake Erie about thirty miles southeast of Windsor, at Leamington, Kingsville, Harrow, Windsor, and Pelee Island. The third group located in Barker, Eilber, and McGowan townships in northern Ontario in the district of Cochrane. The Reesor Church in the latter area is now extinct. All except one bachelor schoolteacher, John Enns, left this settlement after means of earning a living from cutting pulp wood had come to an end.

Chapter 4

1. Blaine Mercer, *The American Community* (New York: Random House, 1956), p. 26.
2. Norman Goodman, Gary T. Marx, Karl Erikson, *Society Today* (New York: Random House, 1977), p. 557. See also Mercer, pp. 24-27.
3. Goodman, Marx, and Erikson.
4. Baker Brownell, *The Human Community* (New York: Harper and Brothers, 1950), p. 201.
5. Mircea Eliade, *The Sacred and Profane* (New York: Harcourt, Brace & World, 1957, 1959), passim.
6. Robert Redfield, "The Folk Society," *The American Journal of Society* (January 1947):293-298.
7. Charles Horton Cooley, *Human Nature and the Social Order* (New York: Charles Scribner & Sons, 1902), p. 152-153.
8. Cooley.
9. Charles Loomis and Allen Beegle, *Rural Sociology* (Englewood Cliffs, N. J.: Prentice-Hall, 1957). The entire text is devoted to the theory of social systems.
10. Jessie Bernard, *The Sociology of Community* (Glenview, Ill: Scott Foresman, 1973), p. 4. Quoting Melvin M. Webber, "The Post City Age," *Daedalus* (Fall 1968): 1099.
11. Rosabeth Kanter, *Commitment and Community: Communes and Utopias in Sociological Perspective*, 5th printing (Cambridge, Mass.: Harvard University Press, 1972), p. 75ff.
12. Kanter.

Chapter 5

1. E. Roy Officer, "Waterloo County—Some Aspects of Settlement and Economy Before 1900," *WCASGE*, p. 13-14.
2. Officer.
3. L.J. Burkholder, *Mennonites in Ontario*, p. 34ff. C. Henry Smith, *The Story of the Mennonites*, p. 379. Ezra E. Eby, *A Biographical History of Waterloo Township: A History of Early Settlers and Their Descendants* (Berlin, Ontario: Published by the author, 1895). (Copy

in the Conrad Grebel College Archives) *The Mennonite Encyclopedia* (Scottdale, Pa.: Mennonite Publishing House, 1955-1959), "Waterloo County," by J. Boyd Cressman, p. 897ff.

4. Ivan Groh, "Disabilities of the Dissenters." (Typewritten copy in Conrad Grebel College Archives.)
5. William Warren Sweet, *The Story of Religion in America* (New York: Harper and Brothers, 1930), p. 7.
6. The Canadian Government 1971 Census report is based on answers to the very general question: What is your religion? The answers thus provide data on Canadians' religious preference rather than actual church membership. Religious preference has no significant relationship to tither membership or participation.
7. Table I. Population by Religion (3) For Waterloo Census Subdivision, 1981 (August 30, 1985) Statistics Canada (1981).
8. Officer, "Waterloo County," *WCASGE*, p. 13-14.
9. Census of Canada: 1861-1971. See also R. A. Murdie, "The Mennonite Communities of Waterloo," *WCASGE*, pp. 22-30.
10. Census of Canada Data, 1971, and Waterloo Mennonite Research Study Data, 1971.

Chapter 6

1. Orland Gingerich, *The Amish of Canada* (Waterloo: Conrad Press, 1972), pp. 41.
2. Boundary maintenance means a group's use of socio-psychological and control devices to limit social interaction with outsiders, or separation from the world.
3. Government of Canada, Federal Census Data (1881-1971) Dominion Bureau of Statistics, Birthplace and Ethnic Group.
4. Frank H. Epp, *Mennonites in Canada, 1786-1920*, p. 52-62.
5. C. Nicholson, Jr., "A Geographic Study of the Ethnic Composition of Waterloo County" (B.A. thesis, University of Waterloo, 1964) quoted in *WCASGE*, p. 57.
6. A. J. Fretz, *A Brief History of John and Christian Fretz* (Elkhart IN: Mennonite Publishing House, 1890).
7. L.J. Burkholder, *Mennonites in Ontario*, p. 103-106.
8. W. Bausenhart, "The Waterloo Pennsylvania German Dialect Community," *WCASGE*, p. 34.
9. Bausenhart, p. 35.
10. Melvin Gingerich, *Mennonite Attire Through Four Centuries* (Breiningsville, Pa.: The Pennsylvania German Society, 1970), pp. 7-8. Advocates of plain dress did not at first defend distinctive dress on grounds of nonconformity but rather as a defence against pride.

11. John A. Hostetler, *Amish Society*. 3rd ed. (Baltimore: Johns Hopkins University Press, 1980), p. 39.

Chapter 7

1. Robert E. Park and Ernest W. Burgess, *Introduction to the Science of Sociology* (Chicago: University of Chicago Press, 1924), p. 796.
2. J. Milton Yinger, *Religion, Society and the Individual* (New York: Macmillan & Company, 1957), p. 144. See also Ernst Troeltsch, *Social Teachings of the Christian Churches* (New York: Macmillan & Co., 1931), passim.
3. Norman Goodman and Gary Marx, *Society Today*. 3rd ed. (New York: Random House, 1976), p. 379.
4. Howard John Loewen, *One Lord, One Church, One Hope and One God* (Mennonite Confessions of Faith) (Elkhart, Ind.: Institute of Mennonite Studies, 1985), p. 37ff.
5. Loewen, p. 41.
6. Loewen.
7. Loewen.
8. Loewen.
9. Loewen, p. 42.
10. Loewen, p. 43.
11. Loewen, p. 47.
12. Loewen, p. 45.
13. Loewen, p. 46.
14. John A. Hostetler, *Amish Society*. 3rd ed. (Baltimore: Johns Hopkins University Press, 1980), p. 22.
15. Yinger, p. 144ff. Quoting Troeltsch, p. 336.
16. Yinger, p. 145.
17. Troeltsch, p. 336.
18. Alan F. Kreider, "The Anabaptists and the Suffering Church," *Mennonite Quarterly Review* 58 (January 1984): p. 6.
19. Franklin H. Littell, *The Anabaptist View of the Church* (The American Society of Church History, 1952), p. 50.

Chapter 8

1. A good indication of the number of congregations in each of the largest denominations in the Waterloo area is reflected in the number of congregations listed in the 1986 Regional Municipality of Waterloo, Guelph (1986) telephone directory, pp. 49-50: United Church of Canada, 39; Lutheran, 34; Roman Catholic, 26; Anglican, 22; Baptist, 22; Presbyterian, 19; Missionary, 10; Pentecostal, 7. There were 29 Mennonite congregations listed in the directory and an additional 37

congregations known but unlisted for a total of 66 Mennonite churches in the area.

2. The format for the private census was one worked out by Leland Harder and used in the *General Conference Fact Book of Congregational Membership*, 1971. Census data was gathered by student research assistants and Old Order Mennonite schoolteachers through personal interviews with leaders in each congregation.

3. *Society Today*. 2nd ed. (Del Mar, Calif.: CRM Books), p. 527.

4. Franklin H. Littell, *The Origin of Sectarian Protestantism* (New York: Macmillan Co., 1964), p. 94. Littell says that church historians find in Anabaptism one of the first lay church governments in Christian history.

Chapter 9

1. This individual from the Beachy Amish joined the Old Order Amish. It is a safe assumption that this person married an Old Order Amish spouse or returned to the group which he or she had earlier left.

2. H. P. Krehbiel, *Mennonite Churches in North America: A Statistical Compilation Collected and Arranged Under the Auspices of the Mennonite General Conference of North America* (Berne, Ind.: Mennonite Book Concern, 1911), pp. 83-90, Mennonite Archives, Conrad Grebel College. This compilation includes the following information about each congregation: name, county, location of church building in or near a town, the name of pastor, assistant pastors, deacons, conference identification, number of church and Sunday school members.

3. John English and Kenneth McLaughlin. *Kitchener: An Illustrated History* (Waterloo: Wilfrid Laurier University Press, 1983), p. 107ff.

4. Emily Schmitt (Burgetz), "Members of the First United Church of Waterloo Who Are of Mennonite Background," term paper, 1969, Sociology 230, University of Waterloo.

5. L. J. Burkholder, *Mennonites in Ontario*, p. 188-196.

Chapter 10

1. Peter Francese, "There's No Typical Household Anymore." Cowles Syndicate, *The Wichita Eagle-Beacon*, July 4, 1985.

Chapter 11

1. *The Toronto Globe and Mail*, July 12, 1968.

2. Robert Bornhold, *Kitchener-Waterloo Record*, Nov. 4, 1967.

3. *The Milverton Sun*, April 18, 1966 (date uncertain).

4. Clarence Fretz, "A History of Mennonite Bible Schools in the Menno-

nite Church," *Mennonite Quarterly Review* Vol. 26, No. 2 (April 1942).

Chapter 12

1. J. B. Mohr, review of Ernst Correll's *Das Schweizerische Täufertum* (Tübingen, 1925).
2. John A. Hostetler, *Amish Society.* 3rd ed. (Baltimore: Johns Hopkins University Press, 1980), p. 89.
3. Hugh Getty Laurence, "Change in Religion, Economics, and Boundary Conditions among Amish Mennonites in Southwestern Ontario" (Ph.D. dissertation, McGill University, 1980).
4. Muriel Maybee, "The Agricultural Systems of Three Mennonite Orders" (senior honours essay, Department of Geography, Faculty of Environmental Studies, University of Waterloo, 1979). This study is excellent in quality but is not suitable as a basis for statistical generalizations because of the limited number and distribution of cases examined.
5. R. A. Murdie, "The Mennonite Communities of Waterloo County," *WCASGE*, pp. 24-25.
6. Murdie, pp. 24-25.
7. Maybee, p. 48.
8. J. A. Mage, "Selected Aspects of the Agricultural Economy of Waterloo County," *WCASGE*, p. 85.
9. Mage, p. 85.
10. Mage, p. 90.
11. Mage, p. 91.
12. Mage, p. 90.
13. Mage, p. 94.
14. Maybee, p. 5.
15. Maybee, p. 46.
16. Maybee, pp. 54-55.
17. The Bearinger farm was equipped with electricity when it was bought, as were most other homes purchased in the Mount Forest area by Waterloo Old Order Mennonites. They use this convenience without censure from the church. This illustrates the way technological change is quietly accepted because it is practical and is not destroying other religious values.
18. Lynn McKinda, "Kitchen Economy of the Mennonite Women in Waterloo County," unpublished term paper, Conrad Grebel College, Waterloo.

Chapter 13

1. Ivan Groh, "History or Fiction," *Waterloo Historical Society*, Vol. 51, 1963, pp. 54-58.
2. W. V. Uttley, *A History of Kitchener* (Waterloo, Ontario: Wilfrid Laurier University Press, 1975), pp. 152 and 197-198. (Originally printed in Waterloo in 1937 by the Chronicle Press.)
3. Uttley.
4. Resolution of the Mennonite Conference of Ontario, 1921, said that "in view of the call for investigation of certain business organizations by Conference, it is the sense of this Conference that our brethren keep in mind the dangers of association with business organizations and conscientiously consider the principles and practices of such organizations before entering into union with them."
5. E. A. Haldine, "The Historical Geography of Waterloo Township, 1800-1855," unpublished M. A. thesis, McMaster University, 1963, pp. 90-92.
6. E. Roy Officer, "Waterloo County—Some Aspects of Settlement and Economy Before 1900," *WCASGE*, pp. 17-18.
7. J. Winfield Fretz, "Agricultural Survey in Waterloo County, 1969-1970," Conrad Grebel College, Waterloo, Ont. (Unpublished.)
8. Emil Durkheim, *The Division of Labor in Society*, trans. George Simpson (Glencoe, Ill.: Free Press, 1964). (Originally published in 1893.)
9. The church becomes an association rather than a body of disciplined or committed believers. An association is merely a specialized interest group within a community. Robert MacIver, *Society* (New York: Farrar and Rinehart, 1937).
10. Calvin Redekop, *The Promise of Work* (Waterloo, Ontario: Conrad Grebel College, 1983).
11. Douglas Snyder, "Waterloo County Mennonite Work and Leisure Study" (honours paper under the writer's supervision, Conrad Grebel College, 1976).
12. Snyder.

Chapter 14

1. Joffre Dumazedier, *Sociology of Leisure*. (New York: Elsevier, 1974), p. 68f.
2. *The Mennonite Reporter*, June 9, 1986.
3. Susan Seredynsky, class notes, July 1976.
4. Muriel Hall, notes from class assignment, July 1979.
5. Hall.
6. J. E. Lewis, "Recreation and Tourism in Waterloo County,"

WCASGE, pp. 70-71.

7. Anthony Bender, "Work and Leisure Attitudes of Waterloo Mennonites" (senior honours paper in the Department of Recreation, University of Waterloo , 1977.) Douglas Snyder, op. cit. Both studies are based on church members of progressive churches.

8. Wilmer Martin, former pastor of the Tavistock, Ontario, Mennonite Church, course term paper for the writer, 1977.

Chapter 15

1. "Life without Welfare," *U.S. News and World Report,* July 24, 1961, pp. 50-53.

2. *Kitchener-Waterloo Record,* June 6, 1969.

3. *Kitchener-Waterloo Record,* November 4, 1974. The article carried the following interesting comments relevant to the struggle for exemption:

> A ray of hope in a two-year battle for exemption from the Canadian Pension Plan for the Old Order and Amish Mennonites came from Ottawa Thursday.
>
> Health Minister John Munro, replying to a question from Max Saltsman (NDP-Waterloo), told the Commons the cabinet is considering exempting the Old Order people.
>
> Mr. Munro added that there is a danger in setting a precedent by exempting any group from the plan's compulsory provisions but he felt that the case raised by the Old Order and Amish Mennonites is special and could not be considered a precedent that would be cited by other groups opposing the scheme. . . .
>
> The request for exemption had evoked "verbal explosions" in the House of Commons when being debated a year earlier. In the end Parliament, on a day when Mr. Horner (its vigorous opponent) was not in the House, the bill was sent through second reading, apparently with all-party agreement.

4. I am personally indebted to Mark Yantzi for factual data and insightful comments pertaining to this aspect of Mennonite deviance in the Waterloo area.

5. "The Accommodation and Integration of Rural Mennonites to Urban Life," 1978 research project by Susan Boes, Tim Lies, Ruth Martin, and Lynn Pychel, under the direction of J. Winfield Fretz.

Chapter 16

1. M. V. Uttley, *A History of Kitchener* (Waterloo, Ontario: Wilfrid Laurier University Press, 1975, reprint of 1937 edition), p. 31: quoting the consolidated by-laws of Waterloo Township.
2. Ivan Groh, "Disabilities of Dissenters," unpublished paper in possession of the writer (undated).
3. Groh.
4. Donald Sommer, "Peter Rideman and Menno Simons on Economics," *Mennonite Quarterly Review*, Vol. 28, July 1954, pp. 205-223.
5. Edgar Metzler, "Why another look at church-state relations?" *Report: A New Look at Church & State Issues* (Akron, Pa.: MCC, 1966.) Other conferences were held at Winona Lake, Indiana, in 1950; in 1956 a conference at Laurelville, Pa., on "Nonresistance and Political Responsibility;" in 1959 a major conference in Winnipeg on "The Church and its Witness to Society," and in 1961 a major conference on the "Church and Society" sponsored by the General Conference Mennonite Church and held in Chicago.
6. In connection with organizing, building, and operating senior citizens' retirement homes and Conrad Grebel College, Ontario Mennonites have been helped directly and indirectly with government financial assistance, either with direct long-time, low-interest loans, or with guarantees of loans made by private financial institutions. In at least one Mennonite institution, Wintario funds generated by the Ontario lottery were considered acceptable as government grants.
7. Metzler, p. 2.
8. The Mennonite Central Committee Ottawa office sources: *History of Federal Electoral Ridings, 1867-1980; The Canadian Parliamentary Guide, 1867-1983,* and the Library of Parliament, Ottawa.
9. John Dueck, "Forsake a 400-year tradition: Mennonites enter politics by the dozen," *Mennonite Reporter*, 12 January 1976.
10. *Mennonite Weekly Review*, 6 March 1980.
11. *Mennonite Reporter*, 12 January 1976, pp. 10-11.
12. Frank H. Epp, "Mennonites in Civil Service," *Mennonite Life*, Vol. 23 (October 1968). See also T. D. Regehr, in the same issue.
13. Frank H. Epp, "Reflections on an Evolving Christian Vocation," *Mennonite Reporter*, April 29, 1980, Vol. 10, No. 9, p. 9.

Chapter 17

1. Claus Peter Clasen, *Anabaptism, A Social History (1525-1618)* (Ithaca, New York: Cornell University Press, 1972), p. 466, note 93.
2. J. Winfield Fretz, "Mennonite Mutual Aid a Contribution to a Christian Community" (Ph.D. dissertation, University of Chicago, 1941), pp. 92-97.
3. Douglas Snyder, "Waterloo Mennonite Work and Leisure Patterns" (honours paper, Conrad Grebel College, 1976)
4. Dominion of Canada Bureau of Statistics, 1971.
5. Snyder.
6. Urie Bender, ed., *Working Together: Twenty-fifth Anniversary Booklet* (Mennonite Credit Union [Ontario] Limited, 1985), pp. 46-48.
7. Bender.
8. Bender.

Chapter 18

1. Ian Robertson, *Sociology* (New York: Worth Publishers), p. 562.
2. Robertson. See also p. 551.
3. Robertson.
4. Robert Temple and Joseph Needham, *The Genius of China* (New York: Simon and Schuster), inside front and back covers: charts of inventions and discoveries and dates compared with contemporary inventions.
5. Robertson, pp. 547-553.
6. Robert Friedmann, "Ausbund," *Mennonite Encyclopedia* Vol. 1, pp. 191-192. See also John H. Hostetler, *Amish Society*. 3rd ed. (Baltimore: Johns Hopkins University Press, 1980), pp. 225-230.
7. Minutes of the Mennonite Conference of Ontario, 1926.
8. A committee of three persons, Oscar Burkholder, S. F. Kaufman, and Gilbert Bergey, in 1929 reported a list of changes the Conference had adopted over an 82-year period (1857-1929). The 1957 resolution seems more antiquated than those of a generation earlier. It appeared as an addition to the earlier list.
9. Ibid.
10. Edward Byron Reuter, *Handbook of Sociology* (New York: Dryden Press, 1950), pp. 79-90.

Chapter 19

1. Gregory Baum, *Religion and Alienation* (Toronto: Paulist Press, 1975).
2. "Theologians re-examine Anabaptists' 1525 revolt." *Kitchener-Waterloo Record*, 14 November 1975.

3. David Woodhall and Carolyn Yandt, *The Old Order Mennonite Community* (The Waterloo County Board of Education).
4. *Kitchener-Waterloo Record*, 14 August 1970.
5. *Kitchener-Waterloo Record*, 6 and 26 June 1970.
6. *Kitchener-Waterloo Record*, 9 October 1971.
7. *Kitchener-Waterloo Record*, 12 October 1971.
8. *Kitchener-Waterloo Record*, 14 October 1971.
9. *Kitchener-Waterloo Record*, 3 November 1971.
10. *Kitchener-Waterloo Record*, 12 October 1973.
11. *Kitchener-Waterloo Record*, 19 July 1974.
12. Elmira *Citizen*, 14 May 1980.
13. Elmira *Citizen*, 14 May 1980.
14. *London Free Press*, L. K. Elliott, London, Ontario, 2 July 1973.
15. *Toronto Star,* editorial, "How Much Dissent Is Tolerable?" 8 January 1968.
16. *Kitchener-Waterloo Record,* 21 December 1974.
17. *Kitchener-Waterloo Record,* 21 December 1974.
18. *Kitchener-Waterloo Record,* 10 June 1972.

Bibliography

Books

Armour, Rollin Stely. *Anabaptist Baptism: A Representative Study*. Studies in Anabaptist and Mennonite History, No. 11. Scottdale, Pa.: Herald Press, 1966.

Baum, Gregory. *Religion and Alienation: A Theological Reading of Sociology*. Toronto: Paulist Press, 1975.

Brownell, Baker. *The Human Community*. New York: Harper & Brothers, 1950.

Burkholder, L. J. *A Brief History of the Mennonites in Ontario*. Toronto: Livingstone Press, Ltd., 1935.

Clasen, Peter Claus. *Anabaptism: A Social History, 1525-1618*. Ithaca, New York: Cornell University Press, 1972.

Cober, George. *A Historical Sketch of the Brethren in Christ Church, Known as Tunkers in Canada*. Gormley, Ontario: published by author, 1953.

Coffman, Barbara F. *Samuel Fry the Weaver and Mennonites of the Twenty*. Canadian German Folklore, V.8. n.p.: Pennsylvania German Folklore Society of Ontario, 1982.

Confessions of Faith of the Mennonites, Also, A Translation of Church Regulations Published by Benjamin Eby, Berlin, Ontario, 1841. n.p.: The Committee (Old Order) Mennonites, 1935, 1940 (revised), 1948.

Correll, Ernst. *Das Schweitzerische Täufertum*. Tübingen: Mohr, 1925.

Driver, John. *Community and Commitment*. Scottdale, Pa.: Herald Press, 1976.

Dumazedier, Joffre. *Sociology of Leisure*. Amsterdam: Elsevier Scientific Publishing Company, 1974.

Dunham, Mabel. *Grand River*. Toronto: McClelland and Stewart, 1945.

Durkheim, Emil. *The Division of Labor in Society*. Translated by George Simpson. Glencoe, Ill.: Free Press, 1964.

Eby, Ezra E. *A Biographical History of Waterloo Township, A History of the Early Settlers and Their Descendants*. 2 vols. Berlin, Ont.:

Published by the author, 1895.

English, John, and Kenneth McLaughlin. *Kitchener.* Waterloo: Wilfrid Laurier University Press, 1983.

Epp, Frank H. *Mennonites in Canada, 1786-1920: The History of a Separate People.* Toronto: Macmillan of Canada, 1974.

——. *Mennonites in Canada, 1920-1940: A People's Struggle for Survival.* Toronto: Macmillan of Canada, 1982.

——. *Mennonite Peoplehood: A Plea for New Initiatives.* Waterloo, Ont.: Conrad Press, 1977.

Fretz, A. J. *A Brief History of John and Christian Fretz.* Elkhart, Ind.: Mennonite Publishing Co., 1890.

Fretz, J. Winfield. *Mennonite Colonization: Lessons From the Past For the Future.* Akron, Pa.: Mennonite Central Committee, 1944.

——. *The Mennonites in Ontario.* Waterloo, Ont.: Mennonite Historical Society of Ontario, 1974.

Gingerich, Melvin. *Mennonite Attire Through Four Centuries.* Breinigsville, Pa.: Pennsylvania German Society, 1970.

Gingerich, Orland. *The Amish of Canada.* Waterloo, Ont.: Conrad Press, 1972.

Glock, Charles V., and Rodney Stark. *Religion and Society in Tension.* Chicago: Rand McNally & Co., 1965.

Goodman, Norman, and Gary Marx. *Society Today.* 3rd ed. New York: Random House, 1976.

Gratz, Delbert L. *Bernese Anabaptists and Their American Descendants.* Scottdale, Pa.: Herald Press, 1953.

Groh, Ivan. *Pennsylvania German Pioneers of Waterloo, 1799-1889.* Canadian-German Folklore, V. 4. n.p.: Pennsylvania German Folklore Society of Ontario, 1971.

Hershberger, Guy F., ed. *The Recovery of the Anabaptist Vision.* Scottdale, Pa.: Herald Press, 1957.

Horst, Mary Ann. *My Old Order Mennonite Heritage.* Kitchener, Ont.: Pennsylvania Dutch Craft Shop, n.d.

Hostetler, John A. *Amish Society.* 3rd ed. Baltimore: Johns Hopkins University Press, 1980.

Johnston, Charles M. *The Valley of the Six Nations.* Toronto: University of Toronto Press, 1964.

Jones, R. L. *The History of Agriculture in Ontario, 1613-1880.* Toronto: University of Toronto Press, 1946.

Kauffman, J. Howard, and Leland Harder. *Anabaptists Four Centuries Later.* Scottdale, Pa.: Herald Press, 1975.

Klaassen, Walter. *Anabaptism: Neither Catholic nor Protestant.* Waterloo, Ont.: Conrad Press, 1973.

Krehbiel, H. P. *Mennonite Churches in North America: A Statistical Compilation Collected and Arranged Under the Auspices of the General Conference of North America.* Berne, Ind.: Mennonite Book Concern, 1911.

Landon, Fred. *Western Ontario and the American Frontier.* Toronto: McClelland and Stewart, 1967.

Littell, Franklin. *The Anabaptist View of the Church.* 2nd ed. Boston: Starr King Press, 1958.

Loewen, Howard John. *One Lord, One Church, One Hope and One God: Mennonite Confessions of Faith.* Elkhart, Ind.: Institute of Mennonite Studies, 1985.

McLellan, A. G., ed. *The Waterloo County Area Selected Geographical Essays.* Waterloo, Ont.: A. G. McLellan, Dept. of Geography, University of Waterloo, 1971.

MacMaster, Richard K., with Samuel Horst and Robert F. Ulle. *Conscience in Crisis: Mennonites and Other Peace Churches in America, 1739-1789: Interpretation and Documents.* Scottdale, Pa.: Herald Press, 1979.

A Manual of Conference Resolutions of the Mennonite Church of the Canada Conference District. Berlin, Ont.: E. S. Hallman, 1904.

Mercer, Blaine E. *The American Community.* New York: Random House, 1956.

Nyce, James M., ed. *The Gordon C. Eby Diaries, 1911-1913: Chronicle of a Mennonite Farmer.* n.p.: Multicultural History Society of Ontario, 1982.

Park, Robert A., and Ernest W. Burgess. *Introduction to the Science of Society.* Chicago: University of Chicago Press, 1924.

Patterson, Nancy-Lou Gellerman. *Swiss-German and Dutch-German Mennonite Traditional Art in the Waterloo Region, Ontario.* Canadian Centre for Folk Culture Studies, No. 27. The Mercury Series. Ottawa: National Museums of Canada, 1979.

Rauschenbusch, Walter. *A Theology for the Social Gospel.* New York: Macmillan, 1917.

Reaman, G. Elmore. *The Trail of the Black Walnut.* Toronto: McClelland and Stewart, 1957; reprint ed., 1974.

Redekop, Calvin. *The Old Colony Mennonites: Dilemmas of Ethnic Minority Life.* Baltimore: Johns Hopkins University Press, 1969.

——. *The Promise of Work.* Waterloo, Ont.: Conrad Grebel College, 1983.

Robertson, Jan. *Sociology.* New York: Worth Publishers, 1977.

Rosenberger, S. M. *The German Elements in Bucks County.* Bucks County Historical Society, V. 3. Riegelsville, Pa.: B. F. Fackenthal, 1909.

Ruth, John L. *Conrad Grebel, Son of Zurich*. Kitchener, Ont.: Herald Press, 1975.

——. *Maintaining the Right Fellowship*. Scottdale, Pa.: Herald Press, 1984.

——. *'Twas Seeding Time*. Scottdale, Pa.: Herald Press, 1976.

Sauder, Dorothy, ed. *Sesquicentennial of the Amish Mennonites of Ontario*. Waterloo, Ont.: Mennonite Historical Society, 1972.

Scott, James. *Of Mud and Dreams*. Waterloo, Ont.: Ryerson Press, University of Waterloo, 1967.

Smith, C. Henry. *The Coming of the Russian Mennonites*. Berne, Ind.: Mennonite Book Concern, 1927.

——. *The Mennonite Immigration to Pennsylvania*. Norristown, Pa.: Norristown Press, 1929.

——. *The Story of the Mennonites*. Newton, Kans.: Mennonite Publication Office, 1957.

Smucker, Donovan E., ed. *The Sociology of Canadian Mennonites, Hutterites and Amish: A Bibliography with Annotations*. Waterloo, Ont.: Wilfrid Laurier University Press, 1977.

Spetz, Theobold. *The Catholic Church in Waterloo County: Book I*. n.p.: Catholic Register and Extension, 1916.

Stein, Maurice R. *The Eclipse of Community*. New York: Harper & Row, 1964.

Sumner, William G. *Folkways*. New York: Ginn and Co., 1906.

Troeltsch, Ernst. *The Social Teaching of the Christian Churches*. London: George Allen & Unwin, 1931.

Uttley, W. V. *A History of Kitchener, Ontario*. Waterloo, Ont.: Wilfrid Laurier University Press, 1975.

Weber, Max. *The Protestant Ethic and the Spirit of Capitalism*. Translated by Talcott Parsons. New York: Scribner's, 1930.

Wenger, John C. *History of the Mennonites of the Franconia Conference*. Telford, Pa.: Franconia Mennonite Historical Society, 1937.

Williams, George Huntston. *The Radical Reformation*. Philadelphia: Westminster Press, 1962.

Wood, Ralph, ed. *The Pennsylvania Germans*. Princeton, N.J.: Princeton University Press, 1942.

Woodhall, David, and Carolyn Yandt. *The Old Order Mennonite Community*. Waterloo: Waterloo County Board of Education Program Division, Integrated Studies Department, 1978.

Yinger, J. Milton. *Religion, Society and the Individual*. New York: Macmillan Co., 1957.

Zeman, Jarold K., Walter Klaassen, and John D. Rempel, eds. *The Believers' Church: Papers from the Study Conference in Winnipeg,*

May 15-18, 1978. Published by the Baptist Federation of Canada and the Mennonite Central Committee (Canada), 1979.

Articles

Bausenhart, W. "The Waterloo Pennsylvania German Dialect Community." In *The Waterloo County Area Selected Geographical Essays,* pp. 31-40. Edited by A. G. McLellan. Waterloo, Ont.: Department of Geography, University of Waterloo, 1971.

Bender, Harold S. "New Source Material for the History of the Mennonites in Ontario." *Mennonite Quarterly Review* 3 (January 1929): 42-53.

———. "The Anabaptist Vision." *Church History* 13 (March 1944): 3-24; also in *Mennonite Quarterly Review* 18 (April 1944): 67-88.

Bender, Wilbur J. "Pacifism Among the Mennonites, Amish Mennonites and Schwenkfelders of Pennsylvania to 1783." *Mennonite Quarterly Review* 1 (July 1927): 23-40 and (Oct. 1927): 21-48.

Burkholder, L. J. "The Early Mennonite Settlements in Ontario." *Mennonite Quarterly Review* 8 (July 1934): 103-122.

Coffman, Barbara F. "Extracts from J. S. Coffman's Diaries." *Mennonite Quarterly Review* 23 (July 1949): 147-160. This article discusses the influence of the nineteenth-century Mennonite leader, J. S. Coffman, on groups in Canada and the U.S.

Correll, Ernst. "The Sociological and Economic Significance of the Mennonites as a Culture Group in History." *Mennonite Quarterly Review* 16 (July 1942): 161-166. On pages 165-166 the author discusses the attention given Mennonite agricultural achievements by federal and provincial bodies in Canada (and the U.S.).

Cressman, J. Boyd. "History of the First Mennonite Church, Ontario." *Mennonite Quarterly Review* 13 (July 1939): 159-186 and (Oct. 1939): 251-283.

Epp, Frank H. "Mennonites in Civil Service." *Mennonite Life* 23 (December 1968): 179.

Fretz, Clarence. "A History of Winter Bible Schools in the Mennonite Church." *Mennonite Quarterly Review* 16 (April 1942): 51-81 and (July 1942): 178-195.

Fretz, J. C. "The Early History of the Mennonites in Ontario." *Mennonite Quarterly Review* 27 (Jan. 1953): 55-75.

Fretz, J. Winfield. "Mutual Aid Among the Mennonites." *Mennonite Quarterly Review* 13 (Jan. 1939): 28-58 and (July 1939): 187-209.

Gingrich, Freeman, and Mary Gingrich. "A Thousand Evenings—Well Spent." *Mennonite Life* 1 (Jan. 1946): 12-13.

Gingerich, Melvin. "Jacob Y. Shantz, 1822-1909, Promoter of the

Mennonite Settlement in Manitoba." *Mennonite Quarterly Review* 24 (July 1950): 230-247.

Graeff, Arthur D. "The Pennsylvania Germans in Ontario, Canada." *The Pennsylvania German Folklore Society* 11 (1948).

Klaassen, Walter. "The Church's Involvement in Higher Education—A New Venture." *Mennonite Life* 20 (April 1965): 83-85. This is about Conrad Grebel College.

Kreider, Alan F. "The Servant Is Not Greater Than His Master: The Anabaptists and the Suffering Church." *Mennonite Quarterly Review* 58 (January 1984): 5-29.

Kreider, Robert. "Anabaptism and Humanism: An Inquiry into the Relationship of Humanism to the Evangelical Anabaptists." *Mennonite Quarterly Review* 26 (April 1952): 123-141.

Kreider, Robert. "The Anabaptist Conception of the Church in the Russian Mennonite Environment, 1789-1870." *Mennonite Quarterly Review* 25 (January 1951): 17-33.

Lehman, James O. "The Mennonites of Maryland During the Revolutionary War." *Mennonite Quarterly Review* 50 (July 1976): 200-229.

Lemon, James T. "The Agricultural Practices of National Groups in Eighteenth-Century Southeastern Pennsylvania." *Geographical Review* 56 (October 1966).

Lewis, J. E. "Recreation and Tourism in Waterloo County." In *Waterloo County Area Selected Geographical Essays*, pp. 63-74. Edited by A. G. McLellan. Waterloo, Ont.: Dept. of Geography, University of Waterloo, 1971.

Luthy, David. "Old Order Amish Settlements in 1974." *Family Life*, December 1974, pp. 13-16.

Mage, J. A. "Selected Aspects of the Agricultural Economy of Waterloo County." In *Waterloo County Area Selected Geographical Essays*, pp. 84-95. Edited by A. G. McLellan. Waterloo, Ont.: Dept. of Geography, University of Waterloo, 1971.

Murdie, R. A. "The Mennonite Communities of Waterloo County." In *Waterloo County Area Selected Geographical Essays*, pp. 22-30. Edited by A. G. McLellan. Waterloo, Ont.: Dept. of Geography, University of Waterloo, 1971.

Officer, Roy. "Waterloo County: Some Aspects of Settlement and Economy Before 1900." In *Waterloo County Area Selected Geographical Essays*, pp. 11-20. Edited by A. G. McLellan. Waterloo, Ont.: Dept. of Geography, University of Waterloo, 1971.

Peachey, Paul. "Social Background and Social Philosophy of the Swiss Anabaptists, 1525-1540." *Mennonite Quarterly Review* 28 (April 1954): 102-127.

Schroeder, Widick. "The Emergence of the Voluntary Church." *The Chicago Theological Seminary Register*, Spring 1976.

Smucker, Donovan E. "The Theological Triumph of the Early Anabaptist-Mennonites." *Mennonite Quarterly Review* 19 (January 1945): 5-26.

Sommer, Donald. "Peter Rideman and Menno Simons on Economics." *Mennonite Quarterly Review* 28 (July 1954): 205-223.

Unruh, Benjamin H. "The Mennonites of Russia." *Mennonite Quarterly Review* 11 (January 1937): 61-67.

Miscellaneous

Butterfield, L. H., ed. *A Letter by Dr. Benjamin Rush.* Copy Number 303. Princeton, N.J.: Princeton University Press, 1945. Conrad Grebel College Archives.

Correspondence: bound copy of 157 letters written between 1872 and 1899 by friends in St. Jacobs to relatives and friends in Lancaster County, Pennsylvania, and in other states. (The letters were found in the 1970s in a box behind a chimney in the attic of the *Grossdädi Haus* now occupied by Erwin Shantz, a senior minister in the Old Order Church.)

Cronk, Sandra Lee. "Gelassenheit: The Rites of the Redemptive Process in Old Order Amish and Old Order Mennonite Communities." Ph.D. dissertation, University of Chicago, 1977.

Fretz, J. Winfield. "Mennonite Religious Institutions in Chicago." B.Div. thesis, Chicago Theological Seminary, 1940.

——. "Mennonite Mutual Aid: A Contribution to Christian Community." Ph.D. dissertation, University of Chicago, 1941.

Groh, Ivan. "Disabilities of Dissenters." Unpublished paper in possession of author.

Haldine, E. A. "The Historical Geography of Waterloo Township, 1800 to 1855." M.A. thesis, McMaster University, 1963.

Harder, Leland. "The Quest for Equilibrium in an Established Sect: A Study of Social Change in the General Conference Mennonite Church." Ph.D. dissertation, Garret Biblical Institute, 1962.

Henkel, Peter. "Impact of the Conestoga Parkway Extension (Highway 85 extension) Upon the Mennonites." English essay, University of Waterloo, 1978.

Horst, Isaac. *Lieder Sammlung.* An English commentary on the hymns used by the Old Order Mennonites since 1836. Copy in Conrad Grebel Archives.

Laurence, Hugh Getty. "Change in Religion, Economics, and Boundary Conditions Among Amish Mennonites in Southwestern Ontario."

Ph.D. dissertation, McGill University, 1980.

MacMaster, Richard. "The Mennonites in Pennsylvania During the American Revolution, 1775-1783: A Glimpse at Five Mennonite Communities." Paper presented at a meeting of Goshen College Mennonite Historians and Sociologists, Goshen, Ind., 17 December 1976.

Martin, Isaac G. "The Story of Waterloo-Markham Mennonite Conference." Unpublished paper, 1953, Conrad Grebel College Archives.

Martin, Wilmer. "The Recovery of Mutual Aid in the Urban Mennonite Church." Term paper, University of Waterloo, 1979.

Maybee, Muriel. The Agricultural System of Three Mennonite Orders." Honours essay, University of Waterloo, 1979.

Moyer, Bill. This Unique Heritage. Kitchener, Ont.: CHYM Radio, 1971.

Von Baeyer, Cornelius. "The Sociolinguistics of Worldliness." Paper prepared for the World Congress of Sociology, 1974.

——. "A Linguist's View of Pennsylvania German." Address delivered to the 23rd annual meeting of the Pennsylvania German Folklore Society of Ontario, New Dundee, Ontario, 2 November 1974.

Articles in the Annual Reports of the Waterloo Historical Society

The following list of references is extracted from the annual reports of the Waterloo Historical Society (WHS) between 1913 and 1969. The articles are generally not written by professional historians; nevertheless, many contain interesting, and sometimes valuable, factual data. Some information is based on family records, old diaries and letters, and some is in the nature of personal reminiscences.

Allan, A. S. "Reminiscences of Early Waterloo." WHS 13 (1925): 139-143.

Bauman, Salome. "First Mennonite Church, 1813-1963." WHS 51 (1963): 19-26.

Bergey, Mrs. David D. "Hagey Mennonite Church, 1842-1953." WHS 58 (1970): 33-34.

——. "The Mennonites and Their Faith." WHS 47 (1959): 8-17.

Bergey, Lorna L. "History of Pinehill S. S. No. 7, Wilmot." WHS 52 (1964): 16-21. This essay mentions some of the patterns of settlement of the Wilmot area by Pennsylvania German people.

——. "A History of Wilmot Township." WHS 50 (1962):48-61.

——. "The Huron Road." WHS 57 (1969): 11-15.

——. "Wilmot Family Farms." WHS 51 (1963): 70-73. This article offers an historical sketch of the settling of farms in Wilmot.

Boshart, Ruth Anne. "The Hamlet of St. Jacobs, Ontario." WHS 52 (1964): 73-78. This essay, written by an 8th grade student, documents the history of settlement of the community of St. Jacobs.

Bowman, H. M. "Jacob Y. Shantz—Pioneer of Russian Mennonite Immigration to Manitoba." *WHS* 12 (1924): 85-100.

——. "The Mennonite Settlements in Pennsylvania and Waterloo with Special Reference to the Bowman Family." *WHS* 10 (1922): 225-244.

Breithaupt, W. H. "Address Delivered at the Dedication of the Memorial Tower, August 28, 1926." *WHS* 14 (1926): 220-225. Breithaupt was the Honorary President of the Waterloo County Pioneers' Memorial Association.

——. "Early Settlement in Upper Canada." *WHS* 11 (1923): 11-17. This paper was presented by the president of the Waterloo Historical Society as part of the "President's Address."

——. "Historical Notes on the Grand River." *WHS* 18 (1930): 219-229. This paper was first read at Chicopee on 2 August 1930.

——. "President's Address." *WHS* 1 (1913): 11-15. Breithaupt delivered his address as president on the subject, "Some German Settlers of Waterloo County."

——. "The Settlement of Waterloo County." *WHS* 36 (1948): 27-31.

Bricker, I. C. "Century-Old Pottery at Conestoga." *WHS* 55 (1967): 33. This article notes the unearthing of pottery made at the William Eby pottery.

——. "The Trek of the Pennsylvanians to Canada in the Year 1805." *WHS* 22 (1934): 123-131.

Coffman, S. F. "The Adventure of Faith." *WHS* 14 (1926): 228-233. This was one of the addresses delivered at the dedication of the Memorial Tower on 28 August 1926.

Cowan, Jennie F. "Principal Immigration Groups of Waterloo County." *WHS* 62 (1954): 26-27. The information in this article was obtained from a display card in the History Tent at the International Plowing Match, 1954.

Cressman, Ella M. "History of Village of Breslau." *WHS* 57 (1969): 32-43.

Cressman, J. Boyd. "Bishop Benjamin Eby." *WHS* 29 (1941): 152-158. This is a life sketch of Ben Eby who was a Mennonite bishop.

Cruickshank, E. A. "D. B. Detweiler." *WHS* 7 (1919): 93-94. This is a biography of D. B. Detweiler, who came from a family of Mennonite ministers.

——. "The Reserve of the Six Nations on the Grand River and the Mennonite Purchase of Block No. 2." *WHS* 15 (1927): 303-350.

Detweiler, John D. "The Detweiler Meetinghouse—the Old Stone Church." *WHS* 53 (1965): 36-40.

Dickson, F. W. R. "Bridgeport." *WHS* 53 (1965): 12-18. This article gives an account of the settling of the community of Bridgeport.

Dunham, B. M. "Benjamin Eby." *WHS* 48 (1960): 16-18.

——. "A Mennonite's Legacy for Educational Purposes in Waterloo." *WHS* 58 (1970): 74. Abraham Erb donated some money in 1829 to assist in providing education for poor and needy children.

——. "The Story of Conestoga." *WHS* 33 (1945): 16-23.

——. "Mid-European Backgrounds of Waterloo County." *WHS*, 36 (1948), pp. 7-20.

——. "A Short History of the New City of Waterloo." *WHS* 35 (1947): 34-38.

Eichler, Idessa. "Blacksmith for 59 Years." *WHS* 54 (1966): 10. This article notes the blacksmith William Fritz and his years of work in Erbsville.

——. "Bridgeport, A History." *WHS* 38 (1950): 30-37.

Featherston, C. "Floradale." *WHS* 49 (1961): 47-48. This is a history of Floradale. The district was first settled by Mennonites. There are Mennonite churches in Floradale.

——. "A History of Bridgeport." *WHS* 27 (1939): 80-83. Bridgeport was first settled by Mennonites.

Fretz, A. J. "The Exodus to Canada." *WHS* 17 (1929): 133-135. This is an excerpt from Moyer Family History by A. J. Fretz. It was contributed by Mr. W. T. Stauffer of Newport News, Virginia. "German Peace Festival 1871." *WHS* 54 (1966): 78-80.

Groh, Ivan. "Ephraim Weber." *WHS* 50 (1962): 98, 101. E. Weber was the great-grandson of Bishop Benjamin Eby.

——. "The First Community Cemetery and Church in the Preston Area." *WHS* 52 (1964): 31-33.

——. "History or Fiction." *WHS* 51 (1963): 54-58. This essay discusses the popular conceptions about the Pennsylvania German pioneers of Waterloo County, and the accuracy or inaccuracy of these conceptions.

Hamilton, O. "The Amish Settlement in the Township of Wilmot in the County of Waterloo." *WHS* 32 (1944): 15-21.

Hamilton, O. A. F. "New Hamburg Historical Notes." *WHS* 24 (1936): 229-234.

Hess, Albert. "From Baden to Baden." *WHS* 58 (1970): 35-42. This article is concerned with the origins of the early people in Waterloo County.

——. "Origin of Names in Waterloo County." *WHS* 57 (1969): 70-71.

High, Norman. "A Point of View of History." *WHS* 48 (1960): 24-33. This article gives some interesting information on the Pennsylvania Germans.

Johannes, J. "History of Blair." *WHS* 29 (1941): 162-164. The first settlers in the area of Blair were Mennonites from Pennsylvania.

Johnston, M. A. "A Brief History of Elementary Education in the City of Waterloo." *WHS* 53 (1965): 56-68.

Kaiser, T. E. "Origins and Early Pennsylvania Dutch Settlements in Upper Canada." *WHS,* 20 (1932): 309-314.

Kinzie, Harry S. "History of Blair." *WHS* 42 (1954): 7-10.

Klinck, George. "The Early Days of Elmira." *WHS* 15 (1927): 285-296.

Klotz, Otto. "Sketch of the History of the Village of Preston." *WHS* 5 (1917): 24-40. "Sketch of the History of the Village of Preston" was first published in 1886 in the *Preston Progress,* which in 1917 was long out of print and unavailable. The above article was given from the original manuscript, edited by J. E. Klotz and D. Forsyth.

Koch, Mrs. Lester. "Biehn Mennonite Church." *WHS* 52 (1964): 61-62.

Martin, John S. "Characteristics of the Pennsylvania German in Canada." *WHS* 14 (1926): 217-219.

Panabaker, D. N. "Extending Our Frontiers in Canada West—An Example of Self-reliance and Enterprise 80 Years Ago." *WHS* 22 (1934): 132-135.

——. "Organization and Early Political History of What Is Now Waterloo County." *WHS* 18 (1930): 213-218. This paper was presented at the Rotary Club Luncheon in Preston.

——. "Pastimes among the Pennsylvania Dutch in Waterloo." *WHS* 19 (1931): 245-249.

——. "Pioneer Woollen Mills in Preston, Hespeler and Vicinity." *WHS* 21 (1933): 45-52.

——. "President's Address." *WHS* 22 (1934): 75-80.

Pearce, Thomas. "School History, Waterloo County and Berlin." *WHS* 2 (1914): 33-48.

Pitcher, Rosemary. "Founder of Preston Commemorated." *WHS* 48 (1960): 22-23. This is a brief biography of John Erb, the founder of Preston.

——. "Waterloo County Centennial." *WHS* 40 (1952): 11-12.

Richmond, Elliott. "E. W. B. Snider." *WHS* 9 (1921): 183-188. This is a biography of E. W. B. Snider, contributed by Mr. Elliott Richmond of St. Jacobs.

Schweitzer, Vera. "The Trail Blazer." *WHS* 57 (1969): 44-47. This is about Jacob Schneider.

Sherk, A. B. "Recollections of Early Waterloo." *WHS* 3 (1915): 13-19.

Sherk, M. G. "The Pennsylvania-German in History." *WHS* 14 (1926): 237-246.

Smith, Marvin C. "St. Jacobs—Its Early History." *WHS* 56 (1968): 33-48.

Snyder, Mrs. O. A. "The First Mennonite Sunday School." *WHS* 51

(1963): 27-28.

Stroh, Jacob. "Reminiscences of Berlin (Now Kitchener)." *WHS* 18 (1930): 175-207.

———. "Reminiscences of Berlin (Now Kitchener): Part II.—Churches, Roads, Miscellaneous." *WHS* 19 (1931): 274-284.

———. "Suddaby School—formerly Central School, Kitchener." *WHS* 30 (1942): 228-239. This articles mentions one of the early schools in Berlin named Eby's School after Bishop Benjamin Eby who first used the building as a Mennonite meetinghouse.

Taylor, A. W. "John Steekle Recollects." *WHS* 53 (1965): 47-52. This is a recollection of the history of the German settlement in this area.

Uttley, W. V. "Joseph Schneider: Founder of the City." *WHS* 17 (1929): 111-119.

———. "Waterloo County Before 1852." *WHS* 51 (1963): 44-50.

———. "Woolwich Township—Its Early Settlement." *WHS* 21 (1933): 10-32.

———. "Waterloo County: Census by Religion—1861." *WHS* 15 (1927): 263.

———: "Township of Waterloo—The First Far-Inland Settlement in Upper Canada." *WHS* 47 (1959): 29-41.

Weber, Eldon D. "Waterloo Township, German Company Tract Lot Number 16." *WHS* 58 (1970): 8-16.

Weber, Lorne B. "The Trek of the Conestoga, 1952." *WHS* 40 (1952): 13-16. One of the Waterloo County Centennial projects was the re-enactment of the arrival of the pioneers. An original covered wagon retraced the 1801 trek of the pioneers from Lancaster, Pennsylvania, to the county.

Weber, M. "The Part Played By Immigrants from Waterloo County to the Didsbury, Alberta, Settlement in 1894." *WHS* 38 (1950):13-21.

Wells, Clayton W. "Apprenticeship of Edward Davis . . . to Christian Schwartzentruber, a Farmer of Wilmot Township, 1 June 1839." *WHS* 57 (1969): 80-81.

———. "A Historical Sketch of the Town of Waterloo, Ontario." *WHS* 16 (1928): 22-67.

Index

progressive growth, 110; refugee source, 111, 112; sources, 109; stability, 126; statistics, 89, 110, 115, 119, 331; types, 120; unbaptized children, 118, 119; urban church growth, 115; winning and losing, 109

Church of England, 250. *See also* Anglican Church

Churches, conservative, 44, 45, 96, 329, 330, 331; moderate, 44, 45, 96, 331, 332; progressive, 45, 46, 96, 332, 333

Civil rights, 284

Clear View school, 153

Clemens family, 70, 249; George, 249

Clergy, 101

Clothing industry, 205

Communion, 8, 78, 82

Communism, 265

Community, 35; Amish view, 83; as social system, 40, 41; Christian ideals, 47; contractual vs folk, 38; defined, 35; Gemeinschaft vs Gesellschaft, 36; in congregation, 17; mass society, 37; shaped by faith, 77; social system elements, 41; social control, 327; sociological type, 43; technology's impact on, 44; threatened by highway, 304. *See also* Groups, Gemeinschaft, Gesellschaft

Community Justice Initiatives, 245, 320

Community Services Committee, 245

Conestoga, 249; church, 116; Creek, 224, 249; wagons, 29

Conference of Mennonites in Canada, 319

Confessions of faith, 78, 80, 81,

315, 327

Conflict theory, 288

Conformity, 83; voluntary nature of, 280

Confrontation, 326

Congregation, as community, 17; family name used for, 70;

Congregational church, 123

Conrad Grebel College, 159, 161, 162, 163, *171*, 262, 294, 298, 318, 319; advantages of affiliation, 162; resource to constituency, 162; supplements university, 162

Conservative Mennonite Conference, 45, 60, 91, 93, 99, 110, 111, 125, 152, 332

Cornelsen family, 256

Correll, Ernst, 182

Courtship, 316; casual dating, 143; engagement symbols, 144; group dating, 141, 142; patterns of, 141; premarital sex, 142, 143, 144; progressive practices, 143, 144

Credit defined, 182

Credit union, 270, 271, 273; arbitration, 276; as cooperative, 275; as democracy in business, 275; as lay organization, 273; as modified capitalism, 275; banking services, 276; business and service, 273; cancellation of debt, 276; church partner, 279; church relatedness committee, 275, 279; committees, 275; credit committee, 275; farm loan categories, 277; farming, 183; Fellowship Fund, 276, 277; impact on future, 280; interest forgiveness, 276; leadership, 274, 275; loan capital low, 279; loan services, 277; mediation, 276; member

148, 151, 152; moral values, 147;
Ontario school laws, 149, 150;
parochial school, 106, 149, 151,
152, 154, 155; philosophy of, 149;
Private Schools Act of Ontario,
151; public schools, 153; public
schools for Mennonites, 156;
Pupil's Creed, 155; rural schools,
147; teachers, 148, 152, 153, 154;
teachers' salaries, 148; univer-
sity, values, 159, 161; vocational,
149, 152. *See also* Conrad Grebel
College; Rockway Collegiate
Elam Martin Old Order, 45, 60, 91,
93
Electronics, 205
Eliade, Mircea, 38
Elliott, J. K., 307
Elmira, 52, 53, 55, 56, 125, 183,
222, 223, 235, 256, 273, 301, 306,
307, 308; church, 223, 308; City
Council, 259; Missionary
Church, 127, 128
English Speaking Union, 310
Epp, Frank H., 64, 256, 259, 261,
262; Herbert, 255, 256; Jake, 258
Erb, Abraham, 31, 249; Albert,
259; Dilman K., 255; family, 249;
Jacob, 31; James, 259; John, 249,
250; Peter, 204; Samuel, 31, 249
Erb Street Church, 32, 33, 116, *173*
Ethnicity, 59, 60, 66; conservatives
of, 71; dress, 12, 73, 74, 75, 318;
Dutch, 59; family names, 66;
food, 71, 73, 74, 247, 318; German population ratio, 64; intermarriage, 66; language, 75; language role, 75; loss of, 75; nicknames, 68, 69; nonconformity,
74, 75; Palatinate Germans, 203;
Pennsylvania German community, 71; Swiss, 59; Waterloo

County composition, 65. *See also*
Nonconformity
Europe, 20, 59; Alsace, 5, 20, 31,
59, 60, 61; Danzig, 11, 12; Elb-
ing, 11, 12; France, 11, 20; Mora-
via, 7, 9, 12; Lorraine, 59; Neth-
erlands, 6, 11; Palatinate, 5, 11,
29; Prussia, 11, 12, 31; Rhine
River valley, 5, 11; Silesia, 7;
Switzerland, 5, 6, 11. *See also*
Germany, Russia
Evangelical Mennonite Mission
Church, 34, 45, 60, 61, 91, 93,
332
Evangelism, 243, 252, 290
Evolution, 284
Excommunication, 79, 80

Fairview, 239
Faith, common values, 316;
essence of, 315; shaping community, 77. *See also* Confessions of
faith
Fame, barriers to, 325
Family, adolescent rebellion, 241;
affected by cultural changes,
133; age segregation, 131; alternate arrangements, 131, 132;
authority respected, 241; birth
control, 293; Canadian social situation, 131, 132; caring for
elderly, 236; changes, 293; childless, 132; decision making, 140;
decline of influence, 39; deviance
low, 241; equalitarian, 139, 140;
family households, 131, 132;
farm children, 191; farm factor,
134; fragmented, 138, 207; functions, 136; grandparents, 239;
home ownership, 211, 212;
homes like motels, 138; household size, 135; incomes, 266, 267,